Bradt

Slow
Sussex
& South Downs National Park

Local, characterful guides to Britain's special places

Tim Locke

Edition 1

Travel Guides Ltd, UK
Pequot Press Inc, USA

M4

Basingstoke

Farnborough

Aldershot

Farnham

Wey

Guildford

Dorking

Godalming

Alton

New Alresford

1

A31

Haslemere

Kingsfold

Horsham

Winchester

M3

Itchen

Meon Valley

2

A3

Rother

Petworth

A272

Arun

Eastleigh

Petersfield

4

Midhurst

Rother Valley

Meon

A24

Storrington

A283

M27

A27

S   O   U   T   H

outhampton

Fareham

Havant

Arundel

5

Lower Arun Valley

Arun

Worthing

Gosport

3

Chichester

Littlehampton

Cowes

Spithead

Portsmouth

Bognor Regis

Ryde

Selsey

Selsey Bill

E N G L I S H
C H A N N E L

Newport

Medina

Yar

Isle of Wight

Shanklin

N

0 ——— 10 miles

0 ——— 15km

t Catherine's Point

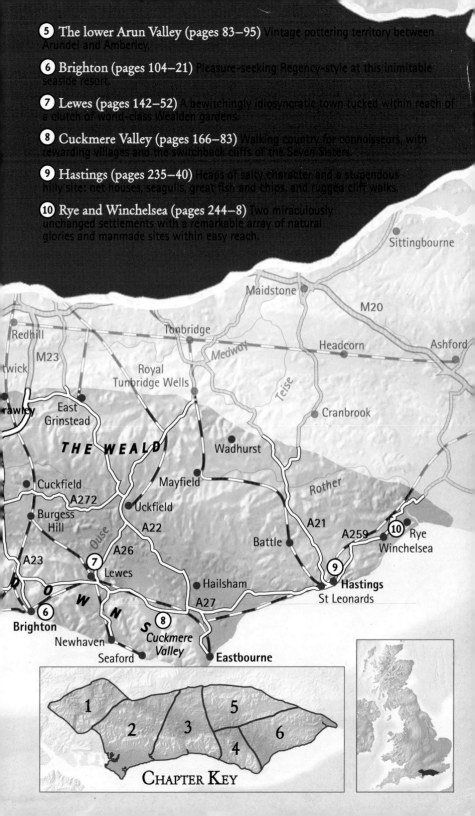

Sittingbourne

Maidstone

M20

Redhill

M23

Tonbridge

Headcorn

Ashford

Medway

twick

Royal Tunbridge Wells

Teise

rawley

East Grinstead

Cranbrook

THE WEALD

Wadhurst

Cuckfield

Mayfield

Rother

A272

Burgess Hill

Uckfield

Ouse

A22

A21

A259

10 Rye Winchelsea

Battle

A23

A26

7 Lewes

Hailsham

9 **Hastings**

A27

St Leonards

6

Brighton

8

Cuckmere Valley

Newhaven

Seaford

Eastbourne

1

2

3

5

4

6

CHAPTER KEY

A Sussex & South Downs National Park Gallery

The Bluebell Railway makes the ultimate Slow arrival into deepest Sussex: the stations and trains are a marvellous journey backwards in time. (TL)

Cycling or walking up on the South Downs escarpment gives an exhilarating sense of escape and of being on top of the world. (ES/A)

The secretive woodlands and acid heaths of the Weald deserve time for a close-up look, with some seasonal shows of fungus such as this fly agaric toadstool. (DBP)

HORSTED KEYNES

Amberley Museum presents a wonderfully authentic collection of historic workshops, where you can meet working craftspeople such as this besom-maker. (AM)

Taking a Slow approach

Going Slow means taking time to find out about those little nuances that make one place distinct from its neighbour.

The Weald and Downland Open Air Museum is a supreme evocation of rustic life, and offers a range of courses on countryside and building skills. (W&DOAM)

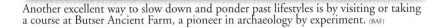

Another excellent way to slow down and ponder past lifestyles is by visiting or taking a course at Butser Ancient Farm, a pioneer in archaeology by experiment. (BAF)

The South Downs end in dizzying style at the Seven Sisters and Beachy Head (where the coast turns a corner); the clifftop walk ranks as one of Britain's very finest. (TL)

Sussex by the Sea

Handily linked by good rail services, coastal Sussex mixes historic forts, ports and seaside pleasure grounds with scope for rugged outdoor adventure.

Bexhill's startlingly original De La Warr Pavilion is a sleek modernist masterpiece that looks much younger than its 70-odd years. (SS)

The seafront promenade from Brighton westwards has a changing series of cameos such as these beach huts and Victorian houses at Hove. (TL)

The notable range of wildlife in Chichester Harbour features a resident population of seals, who are fitted with GPS devices so their movements can be tracked. (CHC/MS)

Pleasingly untidied-up, with boats, nets and assorted fishing paraphernalia, Hastings beach exudes a real sense of place. (TL)

For years this magnificent bandstand at Brighton stood derelict and neglected, but enthusiastic locals campaigned for its restoration, and it is once again used for concerts. (T/S)

Eastbourne's enchantingly ornate pier, one of the grandest on the English coast, is full of period details picked out in trademark blue and white. (SS)

Hollows and bulges in the chalk landscape give the Downs a sculptural quality; the corduroy texture of some steep grass slopes, like miniature terraces, is the result of soil creep after the last ice age. (TL)

The Downs were once dotted with windmills; these two – known as Jack and Jill – are in prime walking country not far from Ditchling Beacon, north of Brighton. (TL)

Southdown sheep, developed at Glynde and a common sight in the 19th century, are still seen here and there. However Welsh 'mules' are much more prevalent, and in places Herdwicks from Cumbria are grazed to keep the scrub at bay. (DM/FLPA)

Up on the South Downs

Spreading eastwards from Hampshire to Beachy Head in East Sussex, the South Downs are classic chalk country, dominating much of the region.

Much of the Downs have thin, chalky soil, where dwarf woodlands cloak the slopes, and lonely hawthorn trees like this are shaped by the prevailing winds. (J/FLPA)

The South Downs Way crosses the Cuckmere valley, where the Cuckmere River meanders towards the sea. (DBP)

Towns and villages

Some of the older towns abut very special countryside, making for excellent walks – notably Arundel, Midhurst, Lewes, Hastings, Petworth and New Alresford – while many Wealden and Downland villages also have superb settings.

Amberley, gorgeously thatched and ranged around a grid of streets, is seemingly made for Slow travel, with its own railway station and a number of outstanding attractions and walks within car-free reach. (TL)

Village signs vary splendidly in style. Loxwood is a starting point for boat trips on the partly defunct Wey and Arun Junction Canal, happily now being restored by an army of volunteers. (TL)

You can walk across Rye in minutes, but it deserves savouring slowly and having every street and back alley explored; known as the 'wipers', the Ypres Castle Inn is an idyllically positioned but easily missed pub. (TL)

Keeping its Georgian architecture admirably intact, 'New' Alresford, in Hampshire's watercress country, has a contented, prosperous look and an array of admirably individual shops. (SS)

Bohemian Sussex: the parade of houseboats in Shoreham always offers something new to look at – including this one with bits of a brown Reliant Robin incorporated into its walls. (TL)

Lewes looks good from all sorts of angles; this view is from the Paddock and looks across the author's allotment to the Norman castle. (TL)

The Sussex Weald has world-class gardens such as High Beeches, worth seeing at any time of year but at their most exuberantly colourful in late spring and early summer. (SB/HBG)

These servants' bells at Stansted Park on the Sussex–Hampshire border evoke life 'below stairs' for the domestic staff, whose quarters are meticulously preserved. (SPF)

Charleston was the much-loved country retreat of Bloomsbury artists Vanessa Bell (Virginia Woolf's sister) and Duncan Grant. (TL)

The interior of the Royal Pavilion in Brighton lives up to the Oriental promise of its astonishingly unconventional exterior. (EH/P)

Around Parham House – a stately Elizabethan mansion – the deer park and woodland are carefully managed for biodiversity, and harbour cormorants, nightjars, greylag geese and rare field crickets. (PH&G)

Houses and gardens

West Sussex has a particular wealth of huge mansions in their own estates, while further into the Weald is an extraordinary concentration of truly great gardens.

Tucked away behind Midhurst, Cowdray was a Tudor house outsized only by Hampton Court. It has been an eye-catching ruin since a fire devastated the building more than 200 years ago. (BP/S)

A delectable feature of Borde Hill Garden is its series of vistas across the deep Wealden countryside, including to the railway-age marvel of the Ouse Valley Viaduct. (BHG)

Pallant of Arundel prides itself on selling quality food and drink products, many from Sussex. (PoA)

Overlooking the sea at Littlehampton, the highly unconventional-looking East Beach Café has won much praise for its imaginative seafood. (SS)

Lewes's extremely successful farmers' market is a place to sample Sussex cheese, organic fruit and veg, and local meats, and even to purchase Lewes pounds – the town's very own currency. (SS)

Nutbourne Vineyard, near Pulborough, is quite an adventure to reach, along twisty, tiny lanes; once there, you can sample the wines within a sail-less tower windmill and enjoy views across to the South Downs. (TL)

The fish couldn't be fresher at various points along the Sussex coast: here at Hastings you can browse the day's catch at a series of booths. (TL)

Food and drink

Delights of a Slow kind include tucking into local shellfish, chatting to stallholders at a farmers' market or chancing across a farm shop selling locally shot game or home-grown produce.

By the Ouse Bridge on the Cliffe side of Lewes, Harveys brewery produces a terrific selection of seasonal brews in addition to its excellent Sussex Bitter. (TL)

Much of the pleasure of visiting churches hereabouts is for the churchyards, with fine examples of stone-carvers' calligraphy on tombstones, abundant wildlife and even remnants of earlier pagan sites. In Wilmington churchyard, vast props hold up a yew tree purported to be 1,600 years old. (TL)

The otherwise simple village church at Berwick was uniquely adorned by artists living at nearby Charleston Farmhouse. (TL)

Churches

Ecclesiastical treasures range from humble country churches with 1,000-year-old wall paintings to lavish Anglo-Catholic 19th-century interiors in Brighton and Hove.

Among several centuries' worth of memorials to the local Gage family is John Piper's striking 1985 stained-glass window depicting William Blake's concept of the Tree of Life. (E&EIL/P)

Chichester Cathedral, the only medieval cathedral in England to be in view from the sea, has delectable surroundings, including the Bishop's Palace Gardens. (CC)

Author

Tim Locke lives in Lewes in East Sussex. He began his work in freelance travel writing in the 1980s when he was commissioned to write guidebooks to walking and various national parks in Britain. He continues to specialise in travel writing about Britain but has since branched out into other areas, including consultancy work on sustainable tourism, children's history books and guidebooks covering variously Europe by rail, New England and Thailand, as well as editorial work for a number of publishers, including Rough Guides and the Good Pub Guide. He is also the project manager of the Bradt's Slow series. A member of the British Guild of Travel Writers, he has a website at www.timlocke.co.uk.

Author's story

As a child living in London, Sussex and the South Downs seemed to me a far-flung, exotic destination, less accessible than Kent or Surrey for our car-free family. Occasionally we ventured by train or bus and picnicked on Beachy Head, steamed along on the Bluebell Railway to Sheffield Park or got extremely but happily lost in the wilds of the Ashdown Forest. At the age of 14 I decided to devise my own Michelin Green Guide to our own house, with star ratings for everything including the cat; such measurements of quality evidently must have gripped my imagination, as I urged my parents to take us on the train to Lewes, for the simple reason that it got a star in the *Shell Guide to Britain*. The book didn't let us down in that respect, and some years down the line I joined the ranks of the DFLs ('Down From London') in that very town. I do think living in a place from where you can see straight into the hills is very special, and the relationship between Lewes and the South Downs that surround it is very much cherished by both residents and visitors.

The area covered by this book is simply made for seeing with a Slow attitude. I'm still nosing out new places within a cycle ride of my house, and as far as walking goes the landscape has such variety and perfect sense of scale that there's a freakishly wide range of really special walks. I've even cross-country skied from my front door up on to the Downs and on those rare winter days when it's possible that's very special too – while checking the proofs for this book, a huge dump of snow arrived, so I skied up towards Black Cap and met a jogger in shorts braving the Arctic conditions, an artist who had set up his easel to capture the winter landscape and an unseen bagpiper tweedling away in the background; this was Slow bordering on the Surreal.

I have been delighted to have the opportunity to work with Bradt in shaping the Slow series. The authors who wrote the first three books all told me they really had fun writing them, and it's been quite a journey designing the brief and creating a product which I feel is very much what 21st-century travel should be about.

First published April 2011
Bradt Travel Guides Ltd
IDC House, The Vale, Chalfont St Peter, Bucks SL9 9RZ, England
www.bradtguides.com
Published in the USA by The Globe Pequot Press Inc,
PO Box 480, Guilford, Connecticut 06437-0480

ISBN: 978 1 84162 343 6

British Library Cataloguing in Publication Data
A catalogue record for this book is available from the British Library

Photographs
Amberley Museum (AM); Andrzej Gibasiewicz/Shutterstock (AG/S); Ashdown Forest
Llama Park (AFLP); BasPhoto/Shutterstock (BP/S); Borde Hill Garden (BHG);
Butser Ancient Farm, www.butserancientfarm.co.uk (BAF); Chichester Cathedral (CC);
Chichester Harbour Conservancy/Matt Simmons (CHC/MS); Dave Brooker Photography,
www.mappingideas.co.uk (DBP); Derek Middleton/FLPA (DM/FLPA); E&E Image
Library/Photolibrary (E&EIL/P); Edward Simons/Alamy (ES/A); English Heritage/
Photolibrary (EH/P); ImageBroker/FLPA (I/FLPA); Mary Lewis/Sustainability Centre
(ML/SC); Pallant of Arundel (PoA); Parham House & Gardens, West Sussex (PH&G);
Paul Ransome/Dreamstime.com (PR/D); Rob Allchin, shutterclutter.co.uk (RA); Roger
Wilmshurst/FLPA (RW/FLPA); Sarah Bray/High Beeches Gardens (SB/HBG); Stansted
Park Foundation (SPF); SuperStock (SS); Tim Locke (TL); tlorna/Shutterstock (t/S); Weald
& Downland Open Air Museum, Singleton, Nr Chichester (W&DOAM); Wowo (W)

Front cover artwork Neil Gower (*www.neilgower.com*)
Illustrations Peter Gates (*www.petergates.co.uk*)
Maps Chris Lane (*www.artinfusion.co.uk*)
Colour map contains Ordnance Survey data © Crown copyright and database 2011

Typeset from the author's disc by Artinfusion Ltd
Production managed by Jellyfish Print Solutions; printed in Europe

Contents

Featured walks

GOING SLOW IN SUSSEX AND THE SOUTH DOWNS NATIONAL PARK

The Slow Mindset

Hilary Bradt, Founder, Bradt Travel Guides

We shall not cease from exploration, and the end of all our exploring will be to arrive where we started and know the place for the first time.
T S Eliot

This series evolved, slowly, from a Bradt editorial meeting when we started to explore ideas for guides to our favourite country – Great Britain. We wanted to get away from the usual 'top sights' formula and encourage our authors to bring out the nuances and local differences that make up a sense of place – such things as food, building styles, nature, geology, or local people and what makes them tick. Our aim was to create a series that celebrates the present, focusing on sustainable tourism, rather than taking a nostalgic wallow in the past.

So without our realising it at the time, we had defined 'Slow Travel', or at least our concept of it. For the beauty of the Slow movement is that there is no fixed definition; we adapt the philosophy to fit our individual needs and aspirations. Thus Carl Honoré, author of *In Praise of Slow*, writes: 'The Slow Movement is a cultural revolution against the notion that faster is always better. It's not about doing everything at a snail's pace, it's about seeking to do everything at the right speed. Savouring the hours and minutes rather than just counting them. Doing everything as well as possible, instead of as fast as possible. It's about quality over quantity in everything from work to food to parenting.' And travel.

So take time to explore. Don't rush it, get to know an area – and the people who live there – and you'll be as delighted as the authors by what you find.

A couple of things about the title of this guide need explaining at the outset. First, this book covers my favourite parts of Sussex, and the South Downs National Park – which is mostly within Sussex but also spills into eastern Hampshire. Then there's that word 'Slow'. This is one of a series of Slow guides written by local authors. It's more than Slow food or Slow cities – it's more an attitude, taking time to ponder, savour, explore and reflect. Slow tourism is about changing down a gear and enjoying the essence of a place, rather than a headlong, high-carbon, non-sustainable, superficial dash around. Ultimately it's a realisation that one can often get a fuller picture by immersing oneself in a small area.

In this book I have attempted a Slow, sideways look at the familiar as well as the little known, celebrating the present as much as the past. I hope it goes beyond the obvious and will appeal to seasoned residents as well as newcomers. It is very much a selection of aspects that make the region special and I apologise to those places that haven't made it into these pages. I have lingered in a scattering of locales that struck me for their sense of place.

The Slow concept tunes in with a reaction against 'clone town' Britain in an age of increasing standardisation, with the realisation that it makes no sense to travel without an awareness of one's surroundings. I feel that personal contact is one of the most rewarding aspects of travel, so I've chatted to local people including garden owners, craftsmen, curators of rural museums, shopkeepers and wildlife experts – among many others.

I do hope this book inspires you to encounter some of those special qualities of Sussex and the South Downs National Park. Perhaps to mingle among locals at a farmers' market and nibble a few samples of Sussex cheese, to become a volunteer at the likes of the Weald and Downland Open Air Museum or the Bluebell Railway, to take a guided walk with a naturalist to find wildflowers or butterflies on the grasslands of the Downs, to drink a pint of Harveys bitter after a walk on the heathy heights of the Ashdown Forest, to munch a fresh crab sandwich on the beach amid Brighton's wonderful seaside paraphernalia, or to forage for mushrooms in the woodlands of the Weald. There are endless ways to make the most of pottering around in the Slow lane.

I have lived in Lewes for over 15 years, and while researching this book realised that this wonderfully diverse corner of southeast England seems to expand as you get to know it. For all its centuries of civilisation this mere smudge at the bottom of the map of Britain is quite extraordinarily hard to know in its entirety. For me Sussex and the South Downs have no equal among lowland landscapes in their abundance of delights and idiosyncracies – seemingly made for savouring slowly and returning to again and again.

Sussex and the South Downs National Park

The idea of Slow may have connotations of exploring rural places, but it also embraces the built-up environment. This is a long-settled area with distinctive historic towns and cities such as Chichester, Winchester, New Alresford, Lewes, Rye, Petworth, Hastings, Midhurst, Brighton, Eastbourne and Arundel. Some of it feels hundreds of miles from London, yet the capital's proximity drew many here, and still does: it is dotted with country retreats ranging from diminutive beach houses to great rural estates. In the railway age, new money was tastefully deployed into creating some of the finest gardens in the country, with a notable concentration on the acid soils of the High Weald. Literary and artistic figures such as Henry James, Rudyard Kipling, Duncan Grant, Virginia Woolf, Eric Ravilious, Hilaire Belloc and Alfred Lord Tennyson revelled in the beauty of the countryside and attracted others to visit or join them.

This book includes the new **South Downs National Park** – which extends from the brink of Winchester in eastern Hampshire to Beachy Head, just above Eastbourne, and covers a good deal of the Weald in West Sussex, not geologically part of the South Downs but of very high landscape quality. At last this hugely cherished area has been given the status that campaigners have been pushing for over many decades. It hasn't been an easy ride, and designation of the national park was held up by the legal intricacies of whether an area so shaped by human hands would qualify as a natural landscape. Despite the massive pressures from the modern world and towns and cities that lie in close range, it's an area of extraordinary rural charm. The unifying feature of the South Downs themselves is chalk: they rise to no great height but have the knack of looking much larger than they are, and have a huge significance for the entire region. You can hardly fail to notice them – a long, remarkably unpopulous range running west to east, with a steep escarpment along much of their northern sides, and shelving gently to the sea to the south. World War II propaganda posters exclaiming 'Britain: fight for it now' harnessed the emotional impact of the South Downs, the most English of landscapes – variously depicting the old village of Alfriston and a shepherd guarding the cliffs towards Belle Tout lighthouse in East Sussex.

The South Downs are the southernmost segment of the area's symmetrical geology: north to south it's basically an end-on sandwich of chalk, clay, sandstone, clay, and chalk again, with a few intervening complexities too: the northern layer of chalk is the North Downs, across Surrey and Kent, and the area between – known as the **Weald** – includes sandstone hills, huge country estates and an endless patchwork of hedge-lined fields and woodlands. The effect of this is that the area can show great unity if you travel west to east, but go north to south and it changes astonishingly fast. The coastal strip, hugely built up and suburban for the most part, has its great landmarks. Up on the South Downs, it is a land of dry valleys, rolling cornfields flecked with poppies, windblown hawthorn trees beside lone dewponds and with skylarks and blue butterflies for company. Further into the Low Weald and High Weald it's a different world: convoluted heathlands, tile-hung cottages around triangular greens in woodland clearings, patchworks of hedge-lined fields, grand country houses set in sweeping parkland behind estate walls, and some of the lushest and most luscious gardens you will find anywhere on this planet.

Sussex's best-known feature, its **coast**, is mostly built up, but is hugely rewarding if you pick your way around it carefully. Facing France and a potential invasion site for centuries, it has impressive and abundant relics from the Roman period to World War II that indicate its former defensive importance. Brighton, Eastbourne and Hastings each have their own personality, and less fêted spots like Shoreham and Bexhill deserve seeking out too. The shores reveal great beauty in the marshy expanses of Chichester Harbour and Rye Harbour, the sandy beaches at either end of Sussex (West Wittering and Camber Sands), the dizzying chalk cliffs between Seaford and Eastbourne and the rugged sandstone heights east of Hastings.

How this book is arranged

Each of the six chapters begins with a map, with places numbered as they appear in numbered headings in the text. I've listed some **accommodation** – a mixture of bed and breakfast, camping and self-catering – in places that struck me for location, or friendliness, or vast character, or a mixture of the three. Please note the **accommodation prices** are just a guide; they were correct at the time of going to print, but inevitably some will change. I've picked out some useful ways of **exploring areas without a car** – this can work very well in some parts, less so in others. If you wish to explore local bus routes, two handy source of references come in the form of the website www.traveline.org.uk (though it can be tricky to navigate if you don't know where to start from) and free maps of public transport routes for Hampshire, West Sussex and East Sussex available from Tourist Information Centres, which themselves are listed at the beginning of each chapter. I've also highlighted some of the joys and logistics of **cycling** onroad and offroad in each chapter.

Under **places** mentioned in the text, I've given website links and phone numbers where they seem useful, and opening times if they're not standard (though it's always worth checking websites as things can change from one year to the next). I have also added selections of cafés and favourite pubs, plus anything else involving food or drink that has struck me; I haven't included restaurants as I feel they would deserve a separate book.

Here and there I have described and mapped out ten of my favourite **walks** in the region. I have also pointed towards some others that are well publicised through websites or are ready-made trails. Sussex and the South Downs are extraordinarily rich in good walks – I've written numerous walking guides in the past, and this area really stands out for walks worth travelling across the country to do. Somehow the excellent rights-of-way network and diversity of the scenery, and a good smattering of viewpoints and manmade and natural places to discover, all combine to make this high-quality walking terrain. The clearly marked South Downs Way is a source of many more outstanding strolls and longer hikes from Winchester to Beachy Head, and you can cycle or ride a horse along the entire route except the section down the Cuckmere valley and along the Seven Sisters.

No charge has been made for the inclusion of any business in this guide.

A Slow miscellany

As an illustration of some of the area's many facets, here are some unrelated Slow-style cameos.

Skylarks and dragonflies

I ventured to Woods Hole, the headquarters of the Sussex Wildlife Trust, and spoke to Mike Russell. 'What in a nutshell is special about wildlife in this area?'

'The great thing Sussex has is its variety. It has the largest coverage of deciduous woodland in England, while the chalk grasslands harbour a range of blue butterflies. If there's one species that is the essence of the Downs, it's the skylark. Its population nationally has declined by 50% in the last 25 years because of agricultural change, but many spots along the downs are the best place to hear it. Then the heathlands have many scarce specialities like black darter dragonflies, keeled skimmer dragonflies or small red damselflies, and attract special birds like nightjars and Dartford warblers. On the other hand, Rye Harbour, Pagham Harbour and Chichester Harbour are internationally important for migrating birds.'

Cheesy highlights

A Slow journey hereabouts may well include an encounter with local cheeses. Jonathan Brantigan – who together with Mark Robinson runs one of Sussex's best-known food stores, Pallant of Arundel (see page 94) – picks out a trio of favourites: 'Flower Marie and Golden Cross are both made by Kevin and Alison Blunt at Greenacres Farm near Golden Cross in East Sussex. Flower Marie is a sheep's milk cheese – square and soft; the sheep's milk gives it a sweetish flavour, while Golden Cross is a goats' cheese, not so different from some of the best you'd find in France. These two I'd rate as the finest of their type in the UK. I'm also very impressed with Lord of the Hundreds, from the Traditional Cheese Dairy in Stonegate, near Wadhurst in East Sussex. It's a hard ewe's milk cheese that pairs very well with quince jelly.'

Saddling up

I asked Alison Wyatt of Castle Cottage B&B near Fittleworth about the logistics of doing the South Downs Way on horseback. You can carry your stuff on the horse, but it's best to dump the horse's food for each night at B&Bs with horse accommodation along the route. 'The horses love it – it's going back to their roots and following migration routes. When you're with them all day you get very close to them.' Typically you could cover 30 miles a day at normal walking pace.

John Ruler, Bradt author and specialist writer on equestrian tourism, told me 'Sussex and the Hampshire Downs are a horse rider's heaven. The Bed & Breakfast system run by the British Horse Society for horses and riders offers a handy guide to West Sussex rides and driving routes. Not that you need your own horse: the whole South Downs Way from Winchester to Eastbourne is peppered with local riding stables. Look out for those approved by the BHS or Association of British Riding Schools (*www.abrs-info.org*). Then saddle up for the likes of Firle Beacon and Friston Forest behind Newhaven (with Firle Place home to horse trials) in East Sussex. For seasonal **beach rides** head for Normans Bay, Pevensey or West Wittering beach. Inland, the **Ashdown Forest**, with some 80 miles of sandy riding tracks, offers riding from the East Sussex village of Danehill or from Crowborough.

You'll need a permit from the Ashdown Forest Centre, however, if you take your own horse. **Carriage driving**, that seemingly most genteel of equestrian activities – save for challenging carriage trials – is well suited to Sussex, especially around the lanes of Arlington or Friston Forest; you can also see it in action at various Sussex shows. The All England Jumping Course at Hickstead is home of the country's two leading outdoor horse shows, the British Jumping Derby Meeting in June and the Longines Royal International Horse Show in July. It is also the UK's only permanent dressage show ground. **Horse-racing**, with family or introductory events, is also big-time, with courses at Glorious Goodwood, Brighton, Plumpton, and Fontwell Park between Arundel and Chichester.'

Owning a woodland

At the massive and hugely fascinating Wealden Wood Fair held each September at Bentley Wildfowl, I met small woodland owner and writer Julian Evans, who told me how more and more people are buying small woods for reasons other than making money from the sale of timber or firewood. 'In the past decade, buying small patches of woodland has been a big upward trend – previously only the very wealthy were in on this, buying huge chunks of woodland as tax breaks, but the law has changed. You could for example buy say just seven or eight acres. Although you wouldn't be allowed to build a house on it or anything like that, the freedom is pretty much unlimited. There are all sorts of reasons why people buy a woodland. They might see it as a corner of England to themselves, or they might want to revive rural crafts. Or there's the sheer pleasure of owning it, or it's so they have a place where their children can camp and play in safety, or it's because of the wildlife interest.'

Learning the Slow way

The variety of courses with a Slow theme really struck me while researching this book. Rural crafts and countryside skills can be learnt at the Weald and Downland Open Air Museum at Singleton or the Sustainability Centre on the Hampshire Downs near the Meon Valley. Plumpton College's Flimwell outpost in far east East Sussex gives opportunities to learn woodland skills, green woodwork and how to make hazel hurdles, trugs, chestnut gates or charcoal. The Hampshire Wildlife Trust and Sussex Wildlife Trust have lively calendars of events including courses on nature and wildlife such as bushcraft, plant and tree identification and fungus forays. Another leading centre for nature is WWT Arundel, which also runs courses on wildlife photography as well as art workshops. A number of businesses teach woodland and survival skills, including Wilderness Wood (Hadlow Down), Bison Bushcraft (near Heathfield) and So Sussex (various locations near Brighton and Lewes), or you can camp at Wowo at Sheffield Park and join an expedition foraging or tracking animals. Tilton Farmhouse, near Lewes, offers food-centred courses and yoga-type retreats.

Digging up the past

I've spent many hours with a trowel in hand exploring Sussex's archaeological secrets. The first time I went out was exactly as I'd hoped it would be – scraping and brushing away soft sand to reveal a huge Romano-British storage pot almost exactly as it had been left in the ground. It isn't always like that though: a whole week up on Mount Caburn near Lewes yielded only a single pottery sherd a little smaller than my thumbnail. The great thing about this area is that any interested novice can join in, through one of its very active archaeological societies such as the Brighton and Hove, Worthing and Mid-Sussex groups. Along with the chalklands of Wessex, the South Downs were the birthplace of British archaeology in the late 19th century, and the tradition has continued. Modern excavations have shown that prehistoric people weren't in fact concentrated on the Downs – it's just easier to see the remains in the thin-soiled, grassy landscape – but you can't help imagining them striding along enjoying the same views, and if you know what to look for (see page 125) you can easily find their flint tools just lying on the surface. The website of the Council for British Archaeology gives hints on joining a dig: www.britarch.ac.uk.

Telling tales

Writers' imaginations have long been fired by the landscapes and atmospheres of this supremely varied area: the novels written in or about it, or both, are equally varied. In *Pride and Prejudice*, completed at her village home in Chawton, Hampshire, Jane Austen depicts the young Lydia longing to go to Brighton, where the soldiers are encamped – and her downfall when she does so. Brighton's disreputable side is shown again in Graham Greene's *Brighton Rock* (1938), though the racecourse slashing is said to be based on an incident at Lewes. H G Wells went to school in Midhurst and set the opening scene of *The Invisible Man* (1897) in the village of Iping; Kipling made his final home at Batemans, in the Weald, which inspired the historical fantasy stories of *Puck of Pook's Hill* (1906). Back in Lewes the precocious Daisy Ashford, aged nine, had produced the unconsciously comic *The Young Visiters* [sic] in 1892, beginning with the words 'Mr Salteena was an elderly man of forty-two'. Over to the east, a cluster of novelists settled in Rye in the early 20th century: among them master stylist Henry James, his friend E F Benson, who wrote the delicate social comedies of the *Mapp and Lucia* series, and Radclyffe Hall, pioneering lesbian author of *The Well of Loneliness*. Meanwhile in Hastings socialist Robert Tressell was enduring the life of desperate working poverty he portrayed in *The Ragged Trousered Philanthropists* – this became hugely influential in the Labour movement, although he did not live to see it. Between the wars, the proceeds of *Mrs Dalloway* paid for indoor plumbing at Virginia Woolf's country home at Rodmell, while from the safety of Hampstead, Stella Gibbons satirised the rural gothic genre by setting *Cold Comfort Farm*, ludicrously, in the Sussex Downs. A A Milne immortalised his son Christopher Robin and some of his toys' adventures in the Ashdown Forest in the *Winnie-the-Pooh* stories. More mobile novelist lifestyles were probably the reason why such a concentration of creativity did not re-form after World War II, but Lewes does make an unexpected late appearance in John Fowles' *The Collector* (1963), as the town where the novel's chilling central character does his shopping.

Acknowledgements

Huge thanks to all those who chatted to me and showed me around their museums, vineyards, B&Bs, campsites, cottages, farm attractions, nature reserves or generally helped me during the researches for this book. These people include (in no particular order) the staff at Sussex Past, Eleni Clarke from Borde Hill, Rachel Gander and Ellen Simpson from Winchester City Council, Paul Hashfield from Amberley Museum, Cathy Clark and Julie Aalen from the Weald and Downland Open Air Museum, Anne Locke for lots of things (including archaeological insights), Emma Robertson from the Pallant House Gallery, Chris Lane at Artinfusion for his patience, Peter Gates for the line drawings that punctuate the book so well, Neil Gower for his brilliant cover and a pleasant pint of Harveys at the Lewes Arms, Robin Thorpe from the Seven Sisters Country Park and another pint of Harveys at the Lewes Arms, Jonathan Brantigan from Pallant of Arundel, Nick Heasman from the South Downs National Park for showing me round his corner of Hampshire, Sandra Barnes-Keywood of Old Chapel Forge, Ali Beckett of the Chichester Harbour Conservancy, the staff at the Towner in Eastbourne, Sue Berry, Ami Bouhassane at Farley Farm House, Janet Sinclair from Stansted Park, Sarah Bray from High Beeches, Linda Johnson from Ashdown Forest Llama Park, Jenny Passmore from Church Farm, James Piell of Goodwood House, Robert Stent of Park Farm Cottages, John Ruler, Hilary Bradt, Janice Booth for her careful editing, Elspeth Beidas and Anna Moores at Bradt, Huw Prendergast of the Ashdown Forest Conservators, Katharine Hale from Collabor8, Pat Warren of the Arundel Wetland Centre, Bridget Gladwyn of Nutbourne Vineyard, Marilyn Creese from the Brighton Greeters, Pete Smith of Sussex Voyages, Mike Russell from the Sussex Wildlife Trust and many others who helped out on the way. Apologies to any I've missed out, and sorry I wasn't able to squeeze in every bit of information gleaned from my travels.

Request for feedback

Sussex and the South Downs National Park are stuffed with people who have specialist knowledge on their part of the region, and although we've done our best to check our facts there are bound to be errors as well as the inevitable omissions of really special places. You can post your comments and recommendations, and read the latest feedback from other readers, online at http://updates.bradtguides. com/sussex&southdowns.

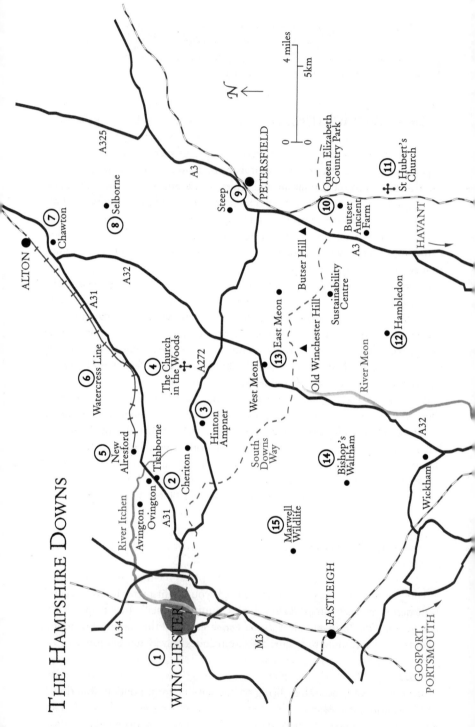

THE HAMPSHIRE DOWNS

4 miles

5km

N

A325

A3

PETERSFIELD

Queen Elizabeth
Country Park

(11)

St Hubert's
Church

Selborne

(8)

Steep

(9)

(10)

Butser
Ancient
Farm

HAVANT

(7)

Chawton

A32

A3

Butser Hill ▲

ALTON

A31

East Meon (13)

Sustainability
Centre

Hambledon

(12)

Watercress Line

(6)

(4)

The Church
in the Woods

A272

Old Winchester Hill ▲

River Meon

(3)

West Meon

Hinton
Ampner

New
Alresford

(5)

Tichborne

(2)

Cheriton

South
Downs
Way

A32

(14)

Bishop's
Waltham

Wickham

River Itchen

Avington

Ovington

A31

A34

WINCHESTER

(1)

M3

Marwell
Wildlife

(15)

EASTLEIGH

GOSPORT,
PORTSMOUTH

1. WINCHESTER AND THE HAMPSHIRE DOWNS

I t says Sussex on the cover of this book, but the South Downs, on a west-to-east journey, start in Hampshire. My abiding image of this part of the South Downs National Park is a close-up: gazing down from a tiny bridge over the River Itchen on a still autumnal day, as a kingfisher made a momentary appearance over the shallow and improbably clear waters, the current combing the riverbed weeds, a habitat around which otters and water voles are almost commonplace. The rivers here are as clear as air; the meadows around them have a lush, watery quality that belongs uniquely to this area. These most delicate of landscapes make their way almost to the centres of Winchester and New Alresford, which aren't in the national park but are of such quality and physical beauty that I have included them.

Indeed surface water plays a much bigger role – in providing clear streams for some of the most renowned trout fishing in the country, and which account for the centre of Britain's watercress industry. The Downs here are not that much like the Sussex Downs and not all of the area is worth exploring mile by mile – there's no appreciable northern escarpment and not as many abrupt slopes and dry valleys. East of the Meon, things change, though, with Old Winchester Hill and Butser Hill providing notes of sudden drama.

It's not an area stuffed with formal sightseeing, but I like it for that, and what there is very much represents the area. The Watercress Line, from Alton to Alresford, is the quintessentially Slow way to travel, while amid the 'hangers' – referring to the beech woods that cling to the slopes north of Petersfield – the naturalist Gilbert White is remembered at his house in Selborne. Jane Austen's house at Chawton is similarly evocative, and Butser Ancient Farm gets you closer than any conventional museum to rural life some 2,000 or so years ago.

Getting around

There's scope for car-free travel to many of the places mentioned in this chapter. Driving around is mostly a pleasure, though you might prefer to avoid central Winchester at busy times. Hampshire County Council's free map entitled *Hampshire: Bus, Train and Ferry Travel Guide* shows all the country bus routes, colour-coded according to frequency, and includes railway stations too.

Train
Winchester is easily accessible, being on the rail line from London Waterloo to Southampton. New Alresford has steam and diesel services on the Mid Hants Railway (usually known as the Watercress Line), which runs from there to Alton,

for mainline services to London Waterloo – a rare instance where a heritage railway joins the national network and gets you somewhere useful. Petersfield station is handy for the east side of the area: I've used it as a starting point for a very rural, hilly cycle ride into the Meon Valley and past Old Winchester Hill.

Bus

Winchester, (New) Alresford, Alton and Petersfield are the main hubs, with several useful hourly services on weekdays at least. From Winchester, frequent services take in the upper Itchen Valley, passing through Alresford and carrying on to Alton. Another useful service from New Alresford to Petersfield takes in Cheriton, Hinton Ampner, Bramdean, West Meon and East Meon, while the service from Alton to Petersfield takes in Selborne, and the Petersfield–Havant bus passes by the Queen Elizabeth Country Park. For Chawton and Jane Austen's House, an hourly bus service runs from Alton (which is very close by) to Winchester via Chawton.

Cycling

So long as you keep off the main roads, this is perfect country for exploring on two wheels, and some of the more gently rolling terrain is rather better for cycling than walking. The South Downs Way and a multitude of bridleways are ideal for off-roading, although eastwards from the Meon Valley to the Sussex border it gets appreciably hilly. Hampshire County Council have good choice of downloadable routes on their website (*www3.hants.gov.uk/cycling*), though quite a few are outside the South Downs. The Sustrans NCN route 3 runs 23 miles from Basingstoke to New Alresford via Alton, from where you can proceed along the Itchen Valley (the proposed route of NCN route 23) on quiet lanes to the very centre of Winchester. In Winchester itself the Bikeabout scheme (from the Tourist Information Centre and Shopmobility in the Brooks Shopping Centre) allows unlimited cycle loan for up to 24 hours at a time once you have paid the £20 registration fee; cycle helmet and reflective jacket are provided.

Accommodation

Giffard House Hotel 50 Christchurch Rd, Winchester SO23 9SU ☎ 01962 852628 ⌨ www.giffardhotel.co.uk. B&B in an imposing Victorian house in a quiet residential street; 13 very well appointed rooms and five-star comfort. As well as the resident boxer, parrot and cat, look out for the magnificent stained-glass windows on the staircase, by pre-Raphaelite artist Henry Holiday, a follower of William Morris, and for the possibly unique 'weeping beech' tree in the garden – a beech grafted on to a weeping willow. £89–£125 twin or double, £69 single.

Meon Springs Coombe Rd, West Meon, GU32 1HW ☎01730 823870
⌂ www.meonsprings.com. Five luxury yurts (beyond a piggery, and a couple of hundred yards from the South Downs Way), each sleeping six, with a 'yurtery' – a communal sitting room and kitchens, and a patio overlooking the Downs. Just down the road is the trout fishing area (with a small campsite where walkers can pitch a tent for a night; £5 per person). There are some outstanding walks nearby in the Meon Valley and on Old Winchester Hill. Bookable for three, four or seven nights (or two nights off-season); a three-night weekend or four-night midweek stay costs £265–£395.

Park Farm Cottages Avington SO21 1BZ ☎01962 779955
⌂ www.avingtonholidays.co.uk. Two superbly done new self-catering cottages close to the River Itchen and a few steps away from Avington Trout Fishery. Clad in oak outside, they are thoughtfully laid out, spacious, peaceful, tastefully decorated in a modern idiom and very well equipped. One sleeps four, the other six, and an adjoining door can be unlocked so that it is all in one unit. Reduced rates for the adjacent golf course (which they also own).

Pink House 25 Broad St, Alresford ☎01962 733468
⌂ www.thepinkhousealresford.com. Immaculate pink Georgian B&B house with antiques in the rooms, and a good, central location. Breakfast is cooked on the range, and the back garden is pleasantly restful. Double £70, single occupancy £40.

St Margaret's 3 St Michael's Rd, Winchester SO23 9JE ☎01962 861450
⌂ www.stmargaretsbandb.com. Ten minutes' walk from the centre, and charmingly homely with antiques and cats, and a piano in the breakfast room. Two shared bathrooms between four rooms, with one double, one twin and two singles. B&B £62 for two sharing; single £40.

Stubbs Farm South Hay, Kingsley, Hampshire GU35 9NR ☎01420 474906
⌂ www.stubbsfarm.co.uk. Virtually at the northernmost point of the national park, this secluded farm east of Alton offers high-quality self-catering, with three en-suite rooms in a converted granary for six people (£550–£875) or for two in a converted 19th-century coach house (£275–£390).

Sustainability Centre Droxford Rd, East Meon GU32 1HR ☎01730 823166
⌂ www.sustainability-centre.org. Not pretty at first sight, being in a revamped naval building high up on the Downs, but the sustainable ethos is very wholesome once you get close to it. This is right on the South Downs Way some 20 miles from Winchester – so it's often used by walkers as their first stop on the route as well as by those attending all manner of courses on sustainability. Wetherdown Lodge hostel accommodation (B&B £22.50 in a dormitory with three beds; own room £25) and a very attractive campsite below, beneath the trees, with tent pitches, a yurt (£15 per person) and a tipi (£12 per person); bring your own bedding for the yurt or tipi. Hostellers can self-cater, and there is some food for sale; takeaway vans will deliver.

Two Hoots Sutton Wood Lane, Bighton SO24 9SG ☎01962 772242
⌂ www.twohootscampsite.co.uk. A small campsite near Alresford, off a winding country lane in former farmland with views towards the Downs and woods on

either side. The two hoots you might hear are from the owls and from the steam trains on the Watercress Line which passes nearby. As well as five pitches for vans and ten for tents, in the copse there are a couple of newly erected and rather cosy pods – which look like upturned boats but are effectively heated wooden tents, insulated with wool, with wooden shingles on the roof and proper beds – commodious enough for a family of four. £35–£55 for a pod; tents £7; caravans £7 or £10.50.

Upper Parsonage Farm Harvesting Lane, East Meon GU32 1QR ✆01730 823490 ⌨ www.upperparsonagefarm.co.uk. In a flint farmhouse draped with roses, this has comfy bedrooms with private facilities, for B&B in a super, remote position on the lane up Butser Hill – the farm land extends up towards the top of the hill; they also plan to offer accommodation in a former shepherd's hut. £85 double. Camping just outside the house is £7.50; shower facilities.

Tourist information centres

General information ⌨ www.visitwinchester.co.uk.
Alton 7 Cross and Pillory Lane ✆01420 88448.
Petersfield County Library, 27 The Square ✆01730 268829.
Winchester Guildhall, High St ✆01962 840500.

① Winchester

Now with a population of 41,500, Winchester is very pleasantly manageable with some memorable views from hilltops and the rooftops of the Westgate and cathedral. 'Wintonians', as they call themselves, are passionate about their city, and it looks exceedingly prosperous and cared for. The area around the cathedral and River Itchen is inviting to explore with its captivating sense of the past and swathes of greenery; not many cathedral cities co-exist quite so successfully with otters and water voles. Walkers, cyclists and horseriders take advantage of the fact that the Pilgrims' Way begins here, as does the modern South Downs Way.

Each summer, city-based arts festivals take the streets by storm. The Hat Fair, the UK's longest-running celebration of street entertainment, attracts huge crowds on the first weekend of July. And there are also the more highbrow Winchester Writers' Conference, the multi-arts Winchester Festival and the Festival of Art and Mind. See www.festivalsinwinchester.co.uk or watch the films showcasing various festivals at www.youtube.com/visitwinchester.

Winchester's origins are distinctly heady. Founded as Venta Belgarum, Latin for 'market place of the Belgae tribe', it was the fifth largest Roman town in England. The city became an important centre of learning during Anglo-Saxon times when the original cathedral was built. In the 9th century, King Alfred the

Great refounded the city, establishing the grid-plan street system we use today, and made it the administrative centre of his kingdom, Wessex. He is very much the local hero, venerated on www.twitter.com/king_alf – his huge bronze statue looming over the Broadway was faithfully replicated as a snow sculpture in the big freeze of 2010 by the local twitterati.

Orientation in Winchester is straightforward, with the compact historic centre extending southeast from the rail station. **Westgate**, on the High Street, is one of two surviving gates (originally there were five), with gun ports, portcullis slot and opening for dropping various nasties on unwelcome visitors. From the 16th to 18th centuries it became the debtors' prison – graffiti etched into the walls bear witness to those times. Today it lives on as a small (free) museum. Visit to see the definitive set of weights and measures that became the ultimate reference point from the 10th century when Edgar decreed the Winchester bushel to be standard throughout his kingdom. Steep steps lead up to the rooftop for a magnificent view along the High Street to St Giles Hill.

A few steps away stands the **Great Hall**, a notable remnant of the 13th-century castle built for Henry III and largely destroyed by Cromwell's men in the Civil War. A medieval hall as splendid as Westminster Hall in London, it was restored in the 19th century as a law court. The huge oak Round Table, painted in segments and hung on one wall like a giant darts board, bears the names of the 24 Knights of the Round Table; inscribed 'This is the rownde table of kyng Arthur w(ith) xxiiii of his namyde knyattes', it was for some time reckoned to be the real thing, around which King Arthur sat his knights, but is now known to have been created in the 13th century for Edward I, keen to promote his supposed Arthurian antecedents (he also sponsored excavations of 'Arthur's tomb' at Glastonbury). It was repainted in its present form during the time of that other great self-publicist, Henry VIII. The imposing seated statue of Queen Victoria, looking suitably unamused, is by Alfred Gilbert of Eros (Piccadilly) fame. All the flowers in the adjacent Queen Eleanor's Garden are chosen because they have religious connotations. Close by, the **military museums**, mostly on the site of the vanished, never-finished palace of Charles II, continue the city's long soldierly associations, although the regiments have moved out of the surrounding barracks, which have been turned into desirable flats. It's an inspired bit of recycling – grouped around fountains and lawns, the neoclassical buildings constituting Peninsula Square have a graciously collegiate look. Four of the museums are free: Horsepower, the King's Royal Hussars Museum (chronicling the story of mounted soldiers through the ages), the Guardroom Museum, the Royal Hampshire Regiment Museum and the Rifles' Information Display, while the Gurkha Museum and the Rifles Museum charge small entrance fees.

Returning to Westgate, a wander further down the sloping **High Street** takes you past a miscellany of historic landmarks. There's the half-timbered **Godbegot House** which originated as a group of 15th-century tenements, plus the ornately gothic **City Cross** or **Butter Cross** of the same era. Where the thoroughfare tapers out into Broadway with its huge statue of King Alfred there's the

Guildhall, all very high Victorian gothic and with a municipal swagger more commonly found in the town halls of Yorkshire and Lancashire. You can usually peek inside to see the recently restored banqueting hall or items on display from the City Museum and art collection if you ask nicely.

Keep walking till you cross City Bridge to reach the **City Mill** of 1744 – a National Trust property spanning the River Itchen. A CCTV camera has been installed here to record the nocturnal activities of local otters. The interior has in recent years been revamped with a new waterwheel of European oak and new millstones from Holland; an informative video explains it all, and below is access to the mill race. The mill is at a point where a riverside walk leads off past **The Weirs** and gets views of some very choice back gardens. It passes **Wolvesey Palace** (emphatically private, as it's the bishop's residence) built in 1715 and arguably the city's finest example of architecture of this period. Adjacent are the substantial ruins of its predecessor, **Wolvesey Castle**. During April to September you can roam freely around this moated site, where the Tudor Queen Mary stayed at the time of her marriage to Philip of Spain.

Kingfishers and warblers frequent **Winnall Moors Nature Reserve**, a surprisingly wild triangle of land just north of the city centre and fringed by the Itchen. With good disabled access it is an excellent birding spot; an observation board records sightings, and chatty volunteers will tell you what's current. Water voles can sometimes be seen feeding on floating weed by the river banks.

The cathedral and precincts

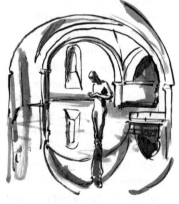

A place of worship for over 1,400 years, the cathedral marks the start of the Pilgrims' Way, on its cross-country route to Canterbury. Look on the lawn immediately outside and you can see the outline of the original minster founded in the 7th century when it was part of a community of Benedictine monks.

The cathedral owes its present form to a rebuilding begun in 1079 by William I who wished to create the biggest and best cathedral in the world. Using stone mostly brought in from the Isle of Wight, he certainly succeeded in terms of length, creating the longest medieval nave anywhere. Although much of the building dates from later – with a preponderance of Perpendicular Gothic in particular – you can see the original Norman work in the crypt and transepts. Here the building quite noticeably lists downwards, its well documented past problems of subsidence much in evidence.

There's a huge amount of detail to admire, including a magnificent Norman **font** of Tournai marble (strikingly similar to that at East Meon), a 12th-century wall painting in the Holy Sepulchre chapel, and a range of superb monuments,

A diver to the rescue

Winchester Cathedral owes a tribute to the heroics of the deep-sea diver William Walker (1869–1918), a statuette of whom is in the cathedral. From 1906 to 1911 he singlehandedly shored up the foundations with concrete at a time when the building was close to collapse because of the high groundwater level. He dived into the opaque waters and worked for five years in complete darkness, from 09.00 to 16.00 with a lunch break, installing nearly a million bricks and 115,000 concrete blocks, and using 25,000 bags of concrete. Then at weekends he somehow mustered the energy to cycle home to Croydon to see his family.

including the **chantry chapels**, where masses were said to bishops buried within; William of Wykeham's Chantry, on the right side of the nave, is the outstanding example. Near the font is a ledger stone to Jane Austen, who died in 1817 at the age of 42 in nearby College Street (the house is still extant, and marked by a plaque). Although she's recorded on the stone merely as the daughter of a clergyman rather than as a novelist, this was later redressed by the intallation of a brass wall plaque which is constantly, and rather touchingly, adorned with fresh flowers by the volunteers who staff the cathedral today. A three-day Austen Trail is available to download at www.winchesteraustentrail.co.uk.

Izaak Walton, of *Compleat Angler* fame, is also commemorated in the cathedral. The **choir stalls** display an entertaining variety of carved misericords with green men, beasts and the like – one depicts a pair of beggars holding out hats, one smiling with money in his hat and the other pulling his beard because he has nothing. And there are secret fold-down seats for flagging choristers. The 12th-century **Winchester Bible** in the gallery is a masterpiece of medieval illuminated calligraphy, all of it written out by the same scribe and the initial drop capital at the beginning of each book drawn and coloured by a team of artists. The colours are remarkably fresh. Before you turn into the gallery look left into the exquisitely preserved, parchment-scented library.

The **tower** can be climbed for a phenomenal view over the entire city, while the **crypt** is one of only four remaining Norman ones anywhere in Britain. It was built not for burial but to raise the chancel, and as a hiding place. The water table is only three feet below the ground, and the cathedral was built during a dry cycle of weather; flooding ensued within decades, and rubble was brought in to counteract the flooding – you can see the depth of the rubble, as well as the modern brick that has been used to replace the original wood and peat foundations, and the place where the tower was shored up in 1107. The crypt still floods periodically. Generally the atmosphere is of stark, ancient emptiness apart from pieces of excavated stonework, worn statues and, very wonderfully, Anthony Gormley's lead sculpture *Sound II*, with a figure studying the depth of his soul through the water cupped in his hands: it looks quite other-worldly when reflected in flood water.

If you can make it for evensong at 17.30 each evening, you will be treated to the world-class cathedral choir; the cathedral music shop sells CDs of their music, and there is a regular programme of other cathedral music. The Christmas carol services still use the King James Bible and are among the finest in the country; outside in winter you'll find a strikingly atmospheric Christmas market and skating rink. You can get a good taster of the city's seasonal offerings at www.christmasinwinchester.co.uk.

In front of the cathedral, the **City Museum** (free entry) was Britain's first purpose-built museum outside London when it opened in 1903. Displays survey Winchester's history through archaeology from prehistoric times onwards, lucidly laid out on three floors. There are historical costumes for children to dress up in and Roman ceramics to handle plus ever-changing spotter trails (with token rewards). Downstairs meticulously recreated Victorian and Edwardian shops – Foster's tobacconists and Hunt's chemists give an idea of the High Street in decades past, while Bosley's Shop operated from a front room of a terraced house in Western Road. Upstairs, models illustrate the development of the city, its shape immediately recognisable from early times, and there are examples of coins from Winchester's own mint, which existed from the time of Alfred to Henry III. On the top floor are bits of the old Saxon minster, including a chunk of vividly coloured wall painting, and a near-intact mosaic from Sparsholt Roman Villa – the building is replicated in its entirety at Butser Ancient Farm (see page 26).

The spacious **precincts** deserve wandering round for the views of the cathedral from all angles. The **Deanery** is within the former Prior's lodging, and houses a remarkably well stocked and keenly priced secondhand bookshop of donated items beneath a trio of pointed arches: look on the right as you go in for one of the strangest shop floors anywhere, made out of bits of Roman mosaic from nearby and from Rome, as well as some chunks of medieval tiles. Just south of the cathedral an archway leads into Dean Garnier Garden, a secretive space giving superb views of the cathedral – and all its subsidence. Close by, the ancient **Priory Gate** adjoins half-timbered **Cheyney Court**, built into the city wall and formerly the courthouse of the Bishop of Winchester.

In summer, outdoor theatre (*01962 857275; www.winchester-cathedral.org.uk*) takes place in the cathedral precincts – Shakespeare features frequently, alongside the likes of Oscar Wilde and dramatisations of Jane Austen's novels; bring a picnic, blanket and something to sit on.

Beyond the precincts, Kingsgate is the other of the two medieval gateways, and has the Church of St Swithun upon Kingsgate on top of it, accessed by a steep stairway. The streets accessed from here – College Street, Canon Street and Kingsgate Street among them – are extraordinarily tranquil and unchanged, with a handful of charmingly traditional shops. It's not difficult to imagine the invalid Jane Austen venturing out from her final home at 8 College Street, with her sister Cassandra, for fresh air during her last weeks.

Winchester College

As well as serving as Bishop of Winchester and enlarging the cathedral, William of Wykeham (1366–1404) founded this, one of the foremost public schools of Britain (American readers note: this is not public school in the American sense at all, but fee-paying and very exclusive). His purpose was to prepare pupils, still known as Wykehamists, for New College, Oxford – which he also founded. To this day Old Wykehamists have a reputation rivalling Etonians for being clever, argumentative and influential.

The tour round puts you in the company of such alumni as Anthony Trollope, Geoffrey Howe, Reginald Bosanquet, Douglas Jardine and Tim Brooke-Taylor. You are led into the collegiate dining hall, to the chapel, with its carved misericords, and through the cloisters where lessons are held in the summer term, or Cloister Term. It's all very Oxbridge, both in its look and in terms of its stock of anecdotes, and the sense of history permeates throughout; several centuries-worth of graffiti can be seen on the stonework. By the Buttery look out for a curious painting depicting The Trusty Servant, a composite creature with stag's feet for swiftness, a pig's head (so would eat anything) and a padlocked mouth for discretion. In Victorian times this was much-reproduced on crockery and other items.

Life here can't have been that comfortable for much of the school's history; until 1904 the water supply was so bad that the school had to brew its own ale to drink instead. The 70 scholars, who wear special gowns to distinguish them, reside in a lodge in Chamber Court, which until 1987 had no heating and just a single tap. One scholar is said to have built a snowman and taken it inside to his room, where it lasted three days.

In term time, evensong is sung at 17.30 in the chapel by the College Quiristers, and members of the public are welcome to attend.

The Hospital of St Cross

This extraordinarily unchanged institution – thought to be the oldest almshouse in Britain – is a hospital in the old sense of a place giving hospitality. An agreeably bucolic mile's walk leads along the water meadows from the city centre: start from the bridge in Bridge Street and take the riverside walk opposite the City Mill, passing Wolvesey Palace and Castle, after which turn left into College Walk, from which it is signposted off to the right – or drive south to the nearby car park by a pub called The Bell.

The Hospital has provided food and shelter for over 850 years, and is still very much a living community, where elderly gentlemen live in rooms off staircases like an Oxford or Cambridge College. The brothers, as they are called, wear collegiate gowns, either black to signify the original foundation for paupers, red or 'marry', a kind of maroon which once denoted 'noble poverty', for gentry

Two hilltop viewpoints

St Giles Hill rises abruptly on the east side of Winchester, and is easily walked up from the city centre. Just walk along the High Street, past King Alfred's statue, over the river by the City Mill and continue on the road up the hill ahead. Zig-zag streets in the more built-up areas to your left were created to assist horse- and human-drawn carts on their way to the old market place on the hill as the ascent was so steep the heavy loads would start to drag backwards down the hill. Where the main hill bends left, a path on the right leads up to the summit, with the city spreading beneath you. In autumn the foliage up there can be a magnificent wall of colour.

Across the valley from St Cross Hospital you see **St Catherine's Hill**, worth walking up for the great views of the city and watermeadows. On the top are the ramparts of an Iron-Age hill fort, the remnants of a chapel and a turf mizmaze, a curving pattern cut into the grass. Supposedly knights unable to go to the Crusades did penance by crawling around it. That would have given them plenty of time to contemplate the rich chalkland flora and numerous chalkhill blue butterflies that still characterise the site today. A poem written in Latin in 1647 described a cricket match played up here by Winchester College boys, one of the very earliest written records of the game anywhere. Ask in the Tourist Information Centre or see www.cricketingwinchester.co.uk for a three-day trail that links in with the Austen trail above.

To reach St Catherine's Hill from the entrance to St Cross Hospital, walk to the end of the access road, go into the watermeadows by the white gate and walk towards the hill, with a wall on your right. At the wall corner turn left, through another gate, and continue forward until you reach a road. Turn right on the road and just before it goes under a railway arch turn right through a car park, under a smaller arch, and take the path uphill forking right after the next gate to the top of the hill. Return the same way.

fallen on hard times. There's no distinction these days as brothers are taken in on their merits. Some act as guides for visitors.

You come in by the porter's lodge where under an ancient trust any traveller can request Wayfarer's Dole. If you do you'll get a small mug of beer and piece of bread. There's no charge for this modest refreshment; in summer the Hundred Men's Hall offers more conventional fare (they are famed for their cakes). To the left is the Master's Lodge, and to the right the almshouses, with their distinctive tall chimneys. Here you may look into the Brethren's Hall, which retains its original medieval layout with a central fireplace – with no chimney, the smoke simply going up through the ceiling – and a musicians' gallery. Behind is the former kitchen which was used for 500 years and is as it was in Georgian times; today all the establishment is self-catering.

The church, where brethren attend services every day, is the only surviving part of the Norman foundation, begun 1135, almost cathedral-like and unexpectedly grand inside and with a crossing soaring to a jazzy-looking ceiling with red and blue zig zags. The organ is rated among the 50 best in the country, and the church sometimes hosts choral concerts.

Look out for a small door in the wall on the left, leading into the gardens, a secret paradise with walled lawns and a long lily pond with fountains.

Food and drink

No problem finding somewhere for a bite. Near the cathedral and City Museum, **Cadogan and James** at 31a The Square is a fine deli with a notable cheese selection. The **farmers' market** in Middlebrook Street on the second and last Sunday of the month is Britain's largest, with over 100 stalls. **Bendicks chocolates** are made in Winchester, and local Wickham wines are sold at the **Wine Shak** in the Broadway, opposite the Guildhall.

Black Boy Wharf Hill ☎ 01962 861754 ⌨ www.theblackboypub.com. Just away from the river, this splendidly idiosyncratic pub is full of intimate corners and it's worth just coming in for a drink to see the décor. There are collections of objects grouped together: keys, spectacles and watches hanging from the ceiling, model planes, a wall of fire buckets and various stuffed animals. Bar food at lunch time, with more ambitious evening fare (no food Sun evening, Mon or Tue lunchtime) and a very good range of mostly local real ales. I came here with a seasoned fellow travel writer once, and he rated it as the most enjoyable pub he'd ever visited. Open all day.

Cathedral Refectory Winchester Cathedral. Airy and modern glass-and-steel structure with a vaulted roof, making an excellent daytime stop for lunch, cream tea, home-made cakes or a snack.

Wykeham Arms 75 Kingsgate St ☎ 01962 854411. Full of animated chatter, this historic pub is very much a hub of Winchester life (note that children are not allowed inside). Old college desks from Winchester College make up part of the décor, which has candlelit wooden tables, panelling and a collection of walking sticks hanging from a ceiling. There are Ronald Searle cartoons among the huge collection of pictures, tankards hanging from the ceiling, Winchester College caps, and a bishop's mitre in a glass case. The menu is imaginative, with reasonably priced lunchtime food available in the bar, and more elaborate evening fare served in the restaurant only; a good choice of real ales on handpump and plenty of wines by the glass. Open all day.

Walking tours

Registered **city tourist guides** (*www.winchestertouristguides.com*) give tours on a range of themes, such as literary trails in the footsteps of Jane Austen and John Keats and family tours; tickets are available from the Tourist Information Centre. At the time of publication Winchester had also just embraced the excellent **Greeter scheme**, where local volunteers take you round for free (similar to the scheme in Brighton; see page 120) – book via the website www.visitwinchester.co.uk.

Into the Hampshire Downs

The South Downs National Park starts on Winchester's eastern fringes. The Downs are more diffuse in character than their Sussex counterparts. It's lovely cycling country with some very pleasantly rolling and peaceful back roads, but really outstanding walks tend to be limited to a few pockets – notably around the Meon Valley and the oak hangers around Selborne and Steep. The clear rivers and streams make this prime fishing country, as well as a watercress-growing area (in the Arle valley). Petersfield, the main town, is a useful base for car-free visitors. Further east, the terrain becomes sandy; Woolmer Forest near Liss is an area of heathland that is home to every type of reptile and amphibian found in Britain.

② The upper Itchen valley

Just east of Winchester, the Itchen wends through some delectably watery landscapes and timelessly unaltered villages such as Easton, Avington, Ovington, Tichborne and Cheriton, built of a mixture of brick, flint, timber and clay tile. On its south side, the wriggling, little-frequented lane connecting these settlements makes ideal cycling terrain and is part of National Cycle Network route 23, with the numerous bridges giving windows over the Itchen. There's a refreshing feeling that nature still has the upper hand here: egrets and herons are in evidence, there are deer on the fields and trout, grayling and perch in the cleanest imaginable river. Otters and water voles put in frequent appearances, and can even be seen not far from central Winchester.

The unspoilt village of **Avington** has the handsome unrestored red-brick Georgian church of St Mary, lit by clear glass and with high boxed pews and triple-decker pulpit typical of the period. Nearby stands a grand classical mansion, **Avington Park**, now a wedding and conference venue and worth catching on its open afternoons on Sundays and bank holidays in summer. At **Ovington**, a path leads off from near the Bush pub across the river – a fine spot for gazing at the passing grayling and trout. In the churchyard stands a detached arch of the former church beside its Victorian successor.

Tichborne has an abundance of thatch. Its church, up a side lane and on a rise on the edge of the village, is one of only three in the country that is used jointly by Protestants and Catholics, and has kept a lot of its old character, with ornately carved box pews and some tiny arched Saxon windows; the modern Millennium windows, depicting the local setting, are nicely understated. The local bigwigs, the Tichbornes, are a Catholic family that has been here since the 12th century, and their forebears are remembered in some imposing memorials the north aisle.

The Tichborne name is known to many through the 1998 film *The Tichborne Claimant*, a true story about a scuppered claim to a family's estate. The saga began in 1854 when Roger Tichborne, the nephew of Sir Henry Tichborne and heir to a massive fortune, disappeared in 1854 in a shipwreck in South America – and was thought lost until someone claiming to be him was found in Australia. The mother recognised him as her son, although the rest of the family believed this man, hugely more portly than the youthful, slim Roger they had seen years before, an impostor. He attempted to claim the family fortune but lost his case and was subsequently tried for perjury – a case that lasted ten months. He lost and was sentenced to 14 years penal servitude.

On 25 March (Lady's Day) the bizarre ceremony of Tichborne Dole takes place in the village. The story goes that in the 13th century Lady Tichborne lay dying and wasting away and asked her miserly husband to donate food to the local poor each year. He agreed he would do so, but limited it to the amount of corn contained in the land around which the wretched woman was capable of crawling while bearing a blazing torch. The tradition duly took place over many centuries, for fear of a curse that dictated that failure to give out the Dole would result in the collapse of the family home and the demise of the family name. Finally, the ceremony was dropped in 1796 when it started to bring in all sorts of undesirable freeloaders to the area, but seven years later the house started to fall down, and perhaps for superstitious reasons the Dole was reinstated. Today families in Tichborne, Cheriton and Lane End duly receive a gallon of flour for each adult and half a gallon for each child.

Ducks waddle on to the road at **Cheriton**, around the green from the infant Itchen which runs under a series of little bridges. Tiles and bricks were once made in Cheriton, hence the name of the Flower Pots pub – at one stage a super-size brick was made there, with the idea that it would speed up bricklaying – but proved far too bulky and heavy to handle. The village name is remembered for a particularly gory Civil War battle in 1644 in which the opposing sides surprised each other in a misty wood a mile or so to the east of the village.

Food and drink

Flower Pots Cheriton SO24 0QQ ☎01962 771318. Long-standing family-owned village local, a mile northwest of Hinton Ampner, that will appeal to those who like unfussy, unpretentious pubs. They brew their own beer, and you can have a tour round the brewery by arrangement.

Tichborne Arms Tichborne SO24 0NA ☎01962 733760. Thatched village pub with local ales and food daily, and a pleasant garden; children welcome; closed Sun evening.

West Lea Farm Shop near Itchen Abbas SO24 0QP ☎01962 732476. A shack by the B3047 between Itchen Abbas and Alresford, this has its own watercress beds, and sells locally produced honey and cakes, watercress soup from Alresford and bargain-priced trout.

Fishing, Hampshire-style

Izaak Walton and Charles Cotton famously celebrated the joys of fly fishing on Hampshire and Peak District rivers in *The Compleat Angler, or Contemplative Man's Recreation*, first published in 1653 but later expanded. The clear waters of rivers such as the Meon and Itchen are still celebrated spots for anglers – several still-water trout fisheries in the area cater for experts as well as beginners, and the trout ponds are replenished each day; the fish are sterile, so keep their condition year round.

If you have never held a rod before, you should book in for an hour's tuition: all the gear is supplied, and you keep what you catch. Keith Poulton at Meon Springs Trout Fishery explained to me 'the art of a fly rod is very slow. If you bash it down on the water, like many novices do, every trout in the district will have disappeared.' He showed me the difference between an overhead cast – which gives more distance – and a roll cast, where the line never goes behind you as you cast, and gives more precision. The fly itself is always artificial, and varies in size and colour; you use a brightly coloured fly to get a more aggressive response, for instance, but in the afternoon tend to use smaller green or brown flies when the trout are not feeding as much.

Avington Trout Fishery has held records for cultivated rainbow trout: their biggest weighed in at 24 pounds 10 ounces, and their reception area has some fine stuffed specimens in glass cases. A happy and evidently very well exercised fisherman told me there at the end of the day as he was gutting his catch 'The lakes here are so clear that people come here and stalk a particular big fish. At Avington the atmosphere, picturesque setting and friendly staff help make it special. But I just love the fish – the trout are the hardest biting I've found – they're reasonably easy to catch but while you're trying to land them they put up a stern test – hence a beer is always needed at the end of the day.'

Avington Trout Fishery Avington SO21 1BZ ☎01962 779312 ✆ www.avingtontrout.com. One of the leading fisheries of its kind in the country, beautifully set near the Itchen and famed for the size of its trout.
Meon Springs Trout Fishery West Meon GU32 1HW ☎01730 823134 ✆ www.meonsprings.com. Very well geared to beginners (as well as experts), with tuition available to novices – including children, if they're strong and tall enough. This is also a top venue for clay pigeon shooting – for £165 you can have half a day learning shooting and half a day fishing, with a three-course lunch in between.
Moorhen Trout Fishery Warnford SO32 3LB ☎01730 829460 ✆ www.moorhentroutfishery.co.uk. In the Meon Valley, near West Meon.

③ Hinton Ampner

'We are both fully aware that a garden can never remain stationary: if it does not go forward, it goes back.'
Ralph Dutton in *A Hampshire Manor.*

The house (*01962 771305; www.nationaltrust.org.uk*), placed on a rise, is the first thing you notice as you approach up the curving driveway past undisciplined grazing sheep, but as you wander around, the scope and diversity of the grounds become apparent. From the top there are wonderful downland views, across to the Isle of Wight in clear weather.

Although on an older estate, this is essentially a 20th-century creation by Ralph Dutton (1898–1985), the eighth and last Lord Sherborne. In 1936 he rebuilt the Victorian Gothic mansion which he considered 'of exceptional hideousness' and which his grandfather had created in the comprehensive remodelling of the original 18th-century house. The new brick mansion was in neo-classical style, though he kept the older house's cornices, mouldings and fireplaces in the Drawing Room.

A massive fire caused comprehensive damage one day in 1960, when Dutton was out walking in the grounds and noticed smoke rising from the roof. 'I rushed across the garden and found firemen already at work... It seemed inconceivable that the house which I had left serene and tranquil so short a time before should now be engulfed in such terrible convulsions.'

Many contents perished in the conflagration; books were so vitrified they had to be hacked out with a pickaxe. But he built it once again, only minus the top floor so that it would sit more happily in the landscape. Its sumptuous contents reflect his devotion to all things classical, with Georgian and Regency furniture, a reconstructed Robert Adam ceiling and a wealth of paintings, porcelain, clocks and other objets d'art. In the hall, Dutton's Italian predilictions hit you immediately, with classical busts and a painting by Pellegrini. For some years during World War II the house served as a school evacuated from Portsmouth.

The great gardens at Sissinghurst in Kent and Hidcote in Gloucestershire struck a chord with Dutton, who – an expert in horticultural history – was inspired to create a series of outdoor rooms in his grounds, with low hedges serving as walls. The main terrace and lawn have downland views; beyond them drops a series of rather secretive spaces, each subtly characterised and leading the visitor through a sequence of visual experiences – a Long Walk with clipped yews and views into the Sunken Garden with its shapely topiary and leading to a pair of benches within a contemplative Temple, a Yew Garden, an arcing Philadelphus Walk that leads into the shady Dell, with its cascades of foliage, and a Walled Garden in the process of restoration.

Guided walks take place round the garden from time to time, and there's a restaurant on the premises. The Flower Pots at Cheriton (see page 13) is recommended.

The Wayfarers' Walk

This waymarked long-distance path clips the corner of the Hinton Ampner estate: look for the signpost by the gate over the road near the estate church. Marked with WW markers and extending 71 miles (114 kilometres) from Emsworth in Hampshire to Inkpen Beacon in Berkshire, this is a good route striding across some bewitching chalkland countryside. On the way it passes through Hambledon and Droxford in the Meon Valley, Cheriton, New Alresford and over Watership Down.

④ The Church in the Woods

You need to time it carefully to get to evensong at this remarkably out-of-the-way 'tin' church in the middle of the woods in Bramdean Common: the sign by the road indicates services are on the second and fourth Sunday at 15.00 between July and September, and at other times you will probably have to be content with peering through its windows. As a simple place of worship, it must rank among the quaintest: access is by a woodland track, and it is all green and white corrugated iron and twirly gables. It dates from 1883, when the rector of Bramdean decided to provide a place of worship for itinerant gypsies, charcoal burners and commoners.

⑤ New Alresford

Just outside the South Downs National Park, this conspicuously handsome town – which topped a poll by *Country Life* magazine of favourite market towns in the Southeast – could count itself unlucky to be excluded from the national park. Usually known as plain 'Alresford' (pronounced 'awlsford') this settlement was originally Novum Forum when laid out along a T-shape of streets in medieval times as one of six new towns built for the Bishop of Winchester. It replaced Old Alresford, still extant, on the far side of a large pond – part of an ambitious canalisation project by Bishop Godfrey de Lucy, whose palace was nearby. The town suffered massive fires in 1689 and 1736, and was thoroughly redeveloped in the 18th century. Thankfully much of that comprehensive rebuild survives intact and today Broad Street in particular is often cited as the finest Georgian ensemble in all Hampshire. Previously in its early wool-rich days the town had a market hall in the middle of this street, though nowadays the Thursday market is in the street itself. East Street, just off from here, has a cheerful array of colour-washed frontages.

A tiny 1881 fire station at the bottom of Broad Street is a reminder of the town's propensity to burn down; nearby are several venerable buildings that survived the conflagrations: the succinctly named Old Timbers, a few steps further on from the fire station, dates from the 14th century and is quite probably the oldest house in town. You can continue down Ladywell Lane and then along a footpath to join a lusciously verdant stretch of the River Arle. Really the town should logically be called Arlesford, but a spelling blip in the Domesday Book made it the cross-eyed Alresford instead. The Arle originally had 11 mills and the very clear waters of gravelly chalk streams are full of trout. Spanning the shallow, clear water a couple of hundred yards on is the thatched, timber-framed Fulling Mill; a more perfectly composed picture of a rural idyll would be hard to imagine. The waters and surroundings provide a rich habitat for otters, water voles, water rail and kingfishers.

Alresford's dodgiest historic memento is marked by the unglamorous red-brick public loos just outside the rail station. During the Cold War days, the Portland spy ring members used to leave messages for each other here to assist the Soviet cause: a plaque recalls Harry Houghton's part which cost him a 15-year sentence.

Watercress growing

It's hard not to be reminded that you're in watercress country in Alresford, having arrived by the Watercress Line and had a watercress-based scone or pâté at one of the town's eateries. Come here on the third Sunday of May and the hugely successful Watercress Festival (*www.watercressfestival.org*) features cookery demonstrations, local produce stalls, tours of local watercress farms, live jazz, face-painting and maybe a 'world watercress-eating championship'.

The Arle valley has ideal conditions for watercress growing and it has been harvested for many centuries here, with Vitacress at Old Alresford being by far the biggest grower. Things really got going with the arrival of the railway in 1865 so that watercress could be taken to Covent Garden Market in London, and it is now the biggest watercress-producing area in Britain, with the mineral-rich, alkaline spring water feeding purpose-built rectangular trays. From seeding to hand-picking the process takes six weeks, allowing six crops to be harvested each year from September to June. This crop, rich in vitamin C, iron and calcium, fell out of favour a few decades back but has had an impressive renaissance in recent years, and is used in a variety of products such as the particularly wonderful watercress pesto.

Food and drink

For **shopping**, the prevalence of prosperous-looking, independent shops such as **Mange2Deli** at 144–6 High St makes the compact town centre prime browsing territory, with several good cafés too, among them the **Tiffin Tearooms** at 50 West St and **Caracoli** (also incorporates a very classy food shop) at 15 Broad St. There's a small **Thursday market** in Broad Street. Alresford no longer has 32 **pubs** as it did in its ale-swigging heyday; for food, the **Bell** (corner of The Dean and West St ☏01962 732429) is a smart, neatly kept Georgian coaching inn warmed by a log fire.

Itchen Valley Brewery Shop New Farm Rd, Alresford SO24 9QF ☏01962 735111. Brown signs point the way to the brewery in the industrial estate on the west side of town, where the shop sells the full range of bottled beers and casks of real ales, which are available in several pubs in this part of Hampshire.

Opera

Grange Park Opera ☏01962 737360 ⌂ www.grangeparkopera.co.uk. In high summer opera-lovers may like to fit in a visit to Grange Park Opera (⌂ *www.grangeparkopera.co.uk*), north of Alresford, where a theatre in the neoclassical magnificence of Northington Grange provides a memorable country-house setting for high-class opera performances, and like Glyndebourne in Sussex the long interval allows plenty of time for leisurely picnics in the grounds.

⑥ Watercress Line (Mid-Hants Railway)

They pride themselves on getting all the details right here at this museum-piece railway (*01962 733810; www.watercressline.co.uk; note days of operation as posted on the website; disabled access on trains; tickets give unlimited rides all day*), which closed in 1969 after just over a century in service, and reopened four years later thanks to the efforts of a band of volunteers. Now it certainly looks the part, with staff dressed in period uniform who clip tickets at the beautifully cared-for stations, where stacks of old leather trunks await a porter's trolley, and ancient advertising signs try to tempt you to stock up on Rinso, Lyon's Tea and Nosegay. The green-painted carriages are mostly post-1951 British Rail rolling stock

This voyage into the land of the watercress gives enough of a ride on this heritage railway to evoke the feeling of a proper long-distance trip, along a steeply graded 10-mile stretch of line through the pastoral Hampshire countryside between Alton and Alresford, climbing to the highest station in southern England at Medstead & Four Marks, passing through Ropley (notice the proud displays of topiary on the platform), where you can look at the engine yard and make use of a picnic site. The locos are a mixture of steam and diesel-hauled, and it's a feasible, amiably gentle car-free day trip from London Waterloo direct to Alton; then step across to platform 3 and carry on by this route to Alresford, with plenty of time to browse the railwayana at the Old Goods Shed shop and stroll into town.

The railway runs numerous special events, like murder mysteries, the Watercress Belle Saturday evening dining train, World War II days, a Real Ale Train with a couple of regional brews on offer and the ever-popular Thomas the

Tank Engine Days. Serious steam-cravers who just have to get even closer to the full whiff and clatter of the loco can splash out on a footplate ride (not cheap, but gets booked up for literally months ahead) or take a seven-hour course to work a steam engine as a driver and as a fireman.

⑦ Jane Austen's House at Chawton

In 1809 Jane Austen's brother Edward arranged for his widowed mother and her daughters Jane and Cassandra to live at this late 17th-century house (*01420 83262; www.jane-austens-house-museum.org.uk*). Jane's career as a writer was already well on course, but her time at Chawton represents the flowering of her literary output. It was here that she revised *Pride and Prejudice, Sense and Sensibility* and *Northanger Abbey*, and wrote *Mansfield Park, Emma* and *Persuasion*. It was Jane's last permanent home; in 1817 she spent only a brief period in Winchester seeking treatment for the illness that soon killed her. Cassandra continued to live here until 1845.

The house was then on an important road junction between Portsmouth, Winchester and Guildford. It's now bypassed by all but local traffic, and the position is still rural; you can picture Jane Austen wandering out to see neighbours or pottering around in the family's donkey cart.

As a building, the Chawton house itself is far from grand; in the pre-Austen era it had a history of being a 'low ale house' before becoming the accommodation for the bailiffs of the Chawton estate. The Austens installed the pretty Gothick sash windows in 1809 to get a better view of the garden. There was lots of work to be done even though it was not a big establishment – they kept a pig and a donkey (for carriage), and water was pumped up from the well and heated in the wood-fired bakehouse. The family had a live-in manservant, while village girls would come in to help with the rough work.

A lot of family possessions had remained in the area and many were donated to the museum after a trust was set up for the house in 1949. Within the daintily wallpapered rooms is a good deal of Austen memorabilia. These include the modest 12-sided table where Jane did all her writing (her manuscripts on display show neat, sloping handwriting); she asked for her door to be kept unoiled, so that its creaking could alert her to the arrival of any visitors. There are portraits, family letters, the Austens' donkey carriage, the family teapot, the Austens' kitchen and a patchwork quilt containing scraps of the sisters' dresses. Look out too for the topaz crosses given to Jane and Cassandra from their sailor brother Charles; they inspired the scene in *Mansfield Park* where the heroine Fanny Price's sailor brother gives her an amber cross – she then faces an awkward social dilemma about which gold chain she should wear with it. Visitors are welcome to try the Austen-era square piano, which produces a hauntingly tinny sound and conjures up Jane sitting here for her early-morning practice.

Also in Chawton, Jane's brother Edward's house is now the Chawton House Library, housing a collection of women's writing from 1600 to 1830 and accessible by appointment. From Winchester bus station and Alton station, there is an hourly bus service (X64) – get off at Alton Butts and then walk (12 minutes) into Chawton. A taxi from Alton would not be expensive.

Food and drink
Just a step across the road from Jane Austen's house and with colourful flower boxes outside **Cassandra's Cup** (✆ *01420 83144*) is a pretty tearoom. Also here is the **Greyfriar** pub (✆ *01420 83841*), open all day and serving food.

⑧ Selborne

At the foot of this hill, one stage or step from the uplands, lies the village, which consists of one single straggling street, three-quarters of a mile in length, in a sheltered vale, and running parallel with The Hanger. The houses are divided from the hill by a vein of stiff clay (good wheat land), yet stand on a rock of white stone, little in appearance removed from chalk; but seems so far from being calcareous, that it endures extreme heat. Yet that the freestone still preserves somewhat that is analogous to chalk, is plain from the beeches which descend as low as those rocks extend, and no farther, and thrive as well on them, where the ground is steep, as on the chalks.
Gilbert White, *The Natural History and Antiquities of Selborne*

Selborne village, stretching beneath the densely wooded slopes known as 'hangers', will be forever associated with the pioneer naturalist Gilbert White (1720–93). His house here in the High Street, known as The Wakes, a long, many-gabled range of buildings in stone and brick, is open to visitors as **Gilbert White's House and the Oates Museum** (*01420 511275; www.gilbertwhiteshouse.org.uk. Closed Mon*). His seminal work *The Natural History and Antiquities of Selborne* observed the natural world through a series of letters. Still highly readable today and never out of print since the day of its publication, it has both literary and scientific merit, spawning the romantic traditions of writing about nature as well as inspiring the great Darwin himself. White broke new ground, for instance, in realising that birds migrate rather than spend winter in holes in the ground, and that earthworms play a crucial role as part of an ecosystem (as we now call it).

As was still possible in the 18th century, White managed to be in the forefront of knowledge in more than one field. He was an antiquarian, an active clergyman and an innovative gardener, doing the best he could on a modest income to follow the horticultural and landscaping advances of his day. His lifetime encompassed Carl Linnaeus, the father of plant classification, and the start of the industrial revolution.

He was a keen recorder of the weather, and kept a seed catalogue along with books of sermons – these are on display along with the manuscript of his book, displayed in a glass case, which was bought in 1980 as first acquisition of the National Heritage Memorial Fund (from unclaimed war bonds). His bedroom is kept dimly lit to conserve his bed hangings, which were appropriately embroidered with plant themes by his four aunts. He kept his wine warm in a cupboard above the fire, and rehabilitated persecuted creatures like the fern owl (also known as the short-eared owl) that was thought to kill calves.

Richard Jeffries said of White in the preface to one edition of the book:

His mind was free and his eye open... He gathered his facts very slowly; they were like experience, which takes a lifetime to grow.

Also within the house, the Oates Gallery celebrates naturalist Laurence Oates (1880–1912), who perished in Captain Scott's doomed Antarctic Expedition, his last words famously being, as he left his tent: 'I am just going outside and may be some time.' There's also material about his naturalist uncle Frank Oates; a descendant from the family, Robert Washington Oates, helped to purchase the house in 1954.

Restored over many years and sloping up to the Hanger, the **gardens** are little changed since White's time, when he put into practice the landscaping ideas of the likes of Kent and Capability Brown within his own modest budget. He created planned vistas and architectural features, and the result is full of engaging Midsummer Night's Dream moments, with paths meandering past apple trees, stone seats, a Giverny-like bridge, areas of wild flowers, a laburnum arch, a 'plant theatre' for displaying pot plants, exotic-looking globe artichokes, a ha-ha and a shelter painted to look like a classical folly; there is also an area for plant sales. The busy calendar of events includes talks, workshops, exhibitions and (both in June) an unusual plants fair and a jazz day.

In the **churchyard** a plaque placed by the British Tree Council honours the honeysuckle-covered remains of a colossally old yew as one of the 50 great British trees; it lived for about 1,400 years until its final demise in 1990. A section of the largest branch has been lovingly polished up and is displayed in the church porch. Gilbert White was parson at this church for 11 years; his grave is a simple affair on the northeast side of church marked only with date and initials 'GW 26th June 1793', sunk into the ground between lichen-covered stones.

Just by the green, or Pleystow, near the church, the **Selborne Gallery** (closed Monday) has art for sale by the Mouth and Foot Painting Artists and the Hampshire Artists Co-operative. Close by, the thatched houses along **Gracious Street** make up a particularly photogenic group.

Food and drink

Gilbert White's Tea Parlour Inside Gilbert White's House and the Oates Museum is a civilised tearoom hung with oil paintings and looking out on to the village street.

Lavender Fields Hartley Park Farm GU34 3HP (on B3006 north of Selborne) ☎ 01420 511146 ⌨ www.thelavenderfields.co.uk. In late June and July the fields around here are a glorious blaze of purple. Tim and Anne Butler run the business on this former hop farm – an acre or two of hops are still cultivated but the hops are sold only for decorative purposes. Lavender is remarkably versatile – as the produce in the shop indicates: as well as the usual fragrances, there are jams, marmalades, jellies, lavender-and-honey ice cream and lavender-and-lemon biscuits. The shop is open seven days a week (five days in the depths of winter), and in July the Butlers have four open days with farm tours and cream teas – on Friday and Saturday on the first week, and Saturday and Sunday the week following.

Two walks around Gilbert White's Selborne

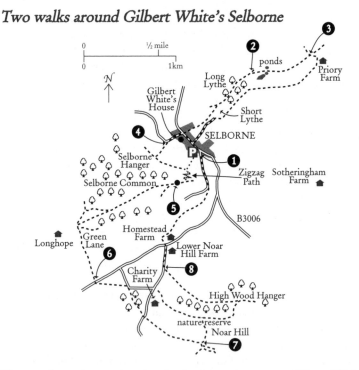

The two loops here epitomise the landscape known to Gilbert White. **Short Lythe** and **Long Lythe** are very beautiful, unimproved fields owned by the National Trust – they were a favourite strolling ground of White and inspired his poem *Summer Evening Walk*. The second loop follows the base of **Selborne Hanger**, where some beech trees are up to 300 years old, climbs up to **Selborne Common** by the **Zigzag Path** cut by White and his brother, and continues to **Noar Hill Nature Reserve**, an important grassland habitat.

If you prefer a short stroll around the village and beneath Selborne Hanger, start at point **❹**, then turn left at the foot of the Zigzag Path by the National Trust sign for Selborne Common to return to the car park. This takes you along Gracious Street and gives views of the garden of The Wakes – a much better way of appreciating the village's setting than from the main street.

Selborne has a shop and two pubs, and there is a loo at the starting point.

Start (both walks): Free car park in Selborne, signposted off village street. A signposted path leads from here to Selborne Common and the zigzag path.

First loop: the Lythes

❶ Go out of the entrance to the car park and turn left along the village street, past the Selborne Arms on your left, then Gilbert White's House and the Oates Museum also on your left. Turn right on Hangers Way in front of the Selborne Gallery, through the churchyard. **Gilbert White's grave** is marked by a simple stone marker on the far side of the church. Exit the far end of the churchyard by a National Trust (NT) sign for Church Meadow, drop down to the bottom, over a footbridge, past a NT sign for **Short Lythe**, just inside the woods and avoiding the path on the right down steps, then just after kissing gate avoid another path rising to the left. The main path then goes through a kissing gate by a sign for **Long Lythe**.

❷ Emerge into a field (at a NT sign for Long Lythe, facing the other way), and keep right, past the lily pond, and then between two further ponds, and over a stile into woodland, which the path soon leaves by another stile into a field. Carry on towards Priory Farm.

❸ Turn right on a gravel track (red waymarkers) past **Priory Farm**, which stands on the site of **Selborne Priory**, an Augustinian house founded in 1232; after Dissolution, its stone was carted off by locals and some of it ended up in buildings in Selborne.

By the last building in the farm the track turns right. About 50 yards later, avoid the tarmacked lane bending to the left, but keep forward past a house on your left on a grassy path between hedges: this soon enters a field – carry on along the left edge. Eventually this enters a woodland and becomes a clear track: this is part of the **Via Canonorum** – or Monks' Way – that linked the priory with Selborne. Past a cottage it becomes a tarmacked lane, which leads to Selborne's main street by the Queen's Inn.

Second loop: Selborne Common and Noar Hill

❶ Turn left out of the car park, past the Selborne Arms pub and the museum, both on your left. Carry on past the Selborne Gallery, then turn left into Gracious Street, with its thatched cottages.

❹ Where the road bends right at the end of the village, keep forward through a gate into a field, and follow the left edge to reach a stile into woodlands. Turn left along the base of **Selborne Hanger** for ¼ mile, with views of the rear of **The Wakes** to your left. At a National Trust sign for Selborne Common (where you can return left to the car park) turn right up the **Zigzag Path**, cut by Gilbert White and his brother. Keep to the main path (near the top, fork left) to reach the very top, marked by a boulder and a bench. Take the path behind the bench and turn right along it, with the hedge and house on the left.

5 Go through a gate into **Selborne Common**, an area beloved of White, and used as a grazing ground by commoners up to the 1950s, after which habitats have been lost to the invasion by scrub; it is owned by the National Trust and work is under way to restore glades and grassland ecosystems.

Keep to the main (very well defined) path all the way, ignoring minor side turns: after ¹/₂ mile reach a semi-open area of bracken and gorse to your right at a fork of grassy tracks and fork left. This leads down to a signpost inside the woodland edge and just before a gate ahead: turn left (signposted bridleway), immediately past a second signpost and keep forward downhill.

6 Cross a road and take the path opposite, bearing diagonally left across a field. In the far corner, turn right on a lane, then immediately keep forward on a woodland path where the lane bends left. Follow this to a lane, cross over and take the path opposite, up the left side of a field along a hedgerow, with intermittent views of Noar Hill to the left. Where the hedgerow bends left, turn left alongside it and 200 yards later take a path waymarked with a yellow arrow on the left into the woodland.

7 This reaches a junction of woodland tracks: turn left, on the bridleway that falls and then rises in a woodland strip between fields. Go through a gate into Noar Hill Nature Reserve and 50 yards later turn right at a signpost. After you leave the nature reserve by another gate, the view opens out to the right, towards Hawkley Hanger and the hills near Petersfield. At the next signposted junction of tracks, turn left on a bridleway that leads downhill for ¹/₂ mile (ignore side turns).

8 Turn right on the road, and at the T-junction take the path opposite and follow Hangers Way waymarks back to the start: you follow the left edge of the first field, turning right in the corner, still along the field edge; the route is obvious as it leads first between hedges and then along the right side of fields. Finally emerge on a driveway by a house called Lavenham, and keep forward. This becomes a tarmacked lane, which leads down to the car park.

⑨ Steep and Petersfield

Edward Thomas, eco-critic and poet, rented houses around Steep from 1906 so that his children could attend the progressive and co-educational Bedales school. He was delighted to find Steep was so close to Gilbert White's Selborne, and often walked there – there's still a commemorative walk each year around the time of his birthday (3 March). Like White, the founder of English nature writing, Thomas was inspired by his feeling for landscapes and the natural world: his 1909 book *The South Country* evoked the character of the South Downs. His wife Helen remembered him enjoying drinking and smoking in the village inns – the Harrow can scarcely have changed since his time – much to the disapproval of the high-minded teetotallers who ran Bedales. His best-known poem is probably *Adlestrop*; although his poetry flowered after 1914 he rarely wrote directly about the War. He was killed at the Battle of Arras in 1917.

Thomas is commemorated in a window in **Steep church**, where one of his poems is etched into glass (look out here too for the prayer hassocks embroidered with natural history themes by local women). The **Shoulder of Mutton** hill just outside the village has a sarsen stone memorial to him.

The market town of **Petersfield** is the largest settlement in the Hampshire part of the South Downs National Park. Although not particularly a tourist destination in itself, it has a decent supply of accommodation and good transport links, and the farmers' market on the first Sunday of the month is one of the best in the region. Beside its heath is a boating lake, while the Petersfield Museum (open Tuesday to Saturday) is within the former magistrates' courthouse in St Peter's Road and also runs the Flora Twort Gallery in Church Path, within the former cottage and studio of the Petersfield artist Flora Twort (1893–1985); numerous local scenes by her are on display. Tucked away in a walled medieval burgage plot off the north side of the High Street is the Physic Garden, created in the late 1980s in tribute to the local 17th-century botanist John Goodyer, with features typical of his day, such as a knot garden, rose bower and topiary walk.

Food and drink

Harrow Steep GU32 2DA ☎01730 262685 ⬦ www.harrow-inn.co.uk. Miraculously unchanged and unspoilt, this delightfully chatty village pub has been in the same family for over 80 years. Three real ales tapped from the cask, and they have local wine; food is simple and pubby and includes their trademark ham-and-split-pea soup. Children are not allowed inside, but there is a spacious garden.

Trooper Steep GU32 1BD ☎01730 827293 ⬦ www.trooperinn.com. A more foody option than the Harrow, and a bit further up the hill; good views from the restaurant and garden, a decent choice of local ales. Closed Sun evening and Mon lunchtime.

⑩ Butser Hill and the Queen Elizabeth Country Park

This is the high spot of the South Downs, literally. Butser Hill rises to 886 feet, and even the road up from the Meon Valley has something of an exhilarating upland feel to it. At the top, a car park gives easy access to the wind-battered plateau summit – designated a Site of Special Scientific Interest for its grassland species. To get an excellent idea of the setting, take the stile just above the loo block (to the left as you face uphill) and follow the obvious path that keeps to the high ground. Very soon a stupendously steep-sided dry valley appears below to the left: after you pass above its head, bear right up the slope to see the view on the other side, and head back past the mast to the car park. Views extend east to the Hog's Back, Black Down and Beacon Hill near Harting, and south over the Solent to the Isle of Wight.

Butser Hill lies within the **Queen Elizabeth Country Park**, which straddles the A3 (fortunately well out of earshot and sight from the summit). On the east side, the Forestry Commission manages an area of beech and conifer plantation laced with sheltered forest trails for walkers, horse riders and mountain bikers: this gets hugely busy at peak times, but it is remarkably easy to lose the crowds completely. Strangely, Butser Hill – infinitely more spectacular in my view – doesn't get the visitor numbers to the same extent. Buriton to the north and Chalton to the south are two very attractive villages to tie into an extended tour on foot or by cycle.

The Sustainability Centre

I am full of admiration for what has been achieved here in the ugly former medical centre for HMS Mercury, a naval establishment that closed in 2000 and formed a nasty blot on the landscape, high up on the Downs not far from Butser Hill. The brutalist buildings have been recycled into something much greener – with solar panels, a biomass boiler running on wood chips from their own and nearby woodlands, insulation from sheep's wool and pitched roofs placed over the former ratings block accommodation that now functions as a hostel; they get 60% of their total energy usage from renewables.

The Sustainability Centre is run by a charitable foundation as a place to take courses on all types of subjects connected to sustainability, such as willow craft, wild food exploration, permaculture, hurdle or yurt making, practical coppicing, green wood working or clay oven building. All their funding for the day-to-day running comes from course fees, hostel and camping accommodation and natural burials. Courses last a day or longer, and if staying here you will be very much in the company of like-minded people. The organic veggie café (open Thursday to Sunday) is terrific too.

Butser Ancient Farm

On the downland slopes between Chalton and Butser Hill is this celebrated recreation of the past (*Chalton Lane, Chalton PO8 0BG; 02392 598838; www.butserancientfarm.co.uk; open daily Jun–Aug; Mon–Fri rest of year*), set up by the archaeologist Peter Reynolds in 1972 as a place where archaeological theories could be put to the test, showing how our ancestors lived during the Iron Age and Roman period. Effectively an open-air laboratory and much used as an educational resource, it particularly comes into its own if you take a course here – which might include flint knapping, cave painting, practical archaeology, Roman cooking or pottery making – but the general public are welcome to come in and look round whenever it is open. The reconstructed buildings feature a group of Iron-Age houses of varying types, and a Roman villa. The buildings are all meticulous recreations of how real sites that have been excavated elsewhere might have looked: archaeologists might uncover post holes filled with soil a different colour from the surrounding natural soil, and from this the shape and size of a building can be deduced.

When I visited, school children were finding out what life was like a couple of millennia or so ago, getting covered with woad and making tools. Maureen Page, one of the staff here, told me 'Children are often surprised by the Tardis-like size of the Iron-Age houses, and how warm and waterpoof they are. The smoke rises and trickles out through the straw thatch: we don't have any holes in

the roof, because we've found that the smoke is a very important, usable commodity, used to smoke meat and fish, and keeps bugs out of the roof so that the birds don't peck at it – which is why modern thatched houses have wire netting over them. The smoke also preserves the timbers.' And as this is a farming community, there are livestock as well as crops – pigs and Soay, Manx Loaghtan and Shetland sheep breeds – that would have been found in a farming community some 2,000 years ago. Characteristic wattle fencing, made from hazel coppice, pens them in.

Over the years they have conducted numerous experiments here. In the hut known as Little Woodbury, based on an excavation near Salisbury, they found the first carpentry joints they made were wrong and the building became unstable, so they revised the building technique. The wall colours include iron oxide paint, using natural pigments – this based on contemporary accounts written by Romans who observed that the British natives lived in brightly coloured houses. They have also carried out metal smelting and bronze sword making, constructing a clay oven, creating speculative structures that attempt to solve riddles such as single post holes (possibly a central post for a haystack), and sealing storage pits with clay capping to see how grain could be preserved.

The Roman villa reconstruction, based on one excavated at Sparsholt, west of Winchester, was the first such building to be erected using authentic techniques and materials since Roman times. It was built mostly by volunteers under the eye of a TV series and lots of lessons were learnt – for example the sheer length of time it would take for the plaster to dry out in the British climate. They were also somewhat hampered in certain details by planning restrictions and building regulations, which is why it lacks an upper storey. However the end result vividly evokes the villa set-up better than any museum I have seen, with its painted interior walls and working hypocaust.

Above the site, Windmill Hill is so called for Chalton Windmill, an early 19th-century tower mill (now a private house) on its summit.

⑪ St Hubert's Church, Idsworth

The remote parish church serving the minute dot on the map that is Idsworth is an extraordinary survival, at the top of a field off a little-frequented lane. Dating from the 11th century and little altered since medieval times, it is one of the most striking country churches in Hampshire. In 1864 limewash was removed to reveal impressively intact wall paintings dating from around 1300, depicting scenes from the life of St Hubert. Later additions are all charming: a set of box pews, a 17th-century pulpit and the modern Millennium Fresco above the chancel arch, the colours of which give a vivid idea of the original impact the older wall paintings must have had before their colours faded.

⑫ Hambledon

Going south from the Sustainability Centre towards Hambledon, you reach a crossroads by the tile-hung Bat and Ball pub; here is the famous Broad

Halfpenny Down, a gently rounded platform of downland where the first recorded cricket match in something approaching its modern form took place around 1750. This was at a time when the game was played at every stratum of society, on village greens and in grand country estates. Until then there was no governing body for the game, and no set of defined rules: playing away matches can't have been easy. Wealthy patrons set up the Hambledon Cricket Club, which played here from 1750 to 1780 with teams made up mostly of farmers and tradesmen. In 1777 they beat England by an innings and 168 runs, which makes them sound fairly handy.

Regarded as the cradle of cricket (rather than its birthplace; see box), it is as romantic as a cricket enthusiast might hope it to be, and a bucolic spot for watching the village version of the summer game. A chunky memorial in one corner celebrates the ground's longevity, but from the 1790s to 1920s Hambledon saw no cricket, until Winchester College bought it. Its present club, the Broad Halfpenny Brigands, have played there since the 1950s.

Here the various manners of batting and bowling were refined into something recognisable to the sport today. The pub itself originally doubled as the pavilion. Its landlord for part of the 18th century was Richard Nyren (c.1734–97), said to be the finest all-rounder of his day – at a time when bowling was done underarm – and the first successful left-hander, both as a batsman and a bowler; he also played for Hampshire. In September 1771, Nyren captained Hambledon against Chertsey, and took issue alongside one of his players with the excessive width of the bat of one of the opposition; he effected a change in the laws of the game which subsequently limited the width of a cricket bat to 4¼ inches. Another important landmark for the game's evolution occurred in 1775 when a single-wicket five-a-side match was played against Kent; the Kent bowler 'Lumpy' Stevens – thought to have been a pioneer in the flighted delivery, rather than one in which the bowl was skimmed along the ground – beat one of Hambledon's batsmen three times, only for the ball to go between the two stumps that were the norm at that time, leaving them undisturbed. The laws were duly altered, and a third stump was made a requirement. In 1787, with the opening of Thomas Lord's cricket ground in London and the formation of the MCC, Hambledon lost its status as the effective headquarters of the game.

Cricket's prehistory

The origins of cricket are murky and decidedly rustic. It certainly stretches a long way before its first recorded reference in 1598, perhaps to Norman or even Saxon times, and until the 17th century is thought to have been played mainly by children rather than adults. In 1611, Sussex men were punished for skipping church and playing cricket instead. The South Downs may well have been the game's birthplace – quite possibly with a ball made of wool or rags, with short, sheep-nibbled downland turf as the playing area and the batsman defending a wicket gate with a stick or shepherds' crook. In fact the crook – or a similar word for stick or staff in Middle Dutch or Old English – might have given us the word *cricket*.

⑬ Meon Valley

West of the Meon Valley, the Downs are more gently rolling and have more of a Wessex look than they do further east. Beacon Hill is the first dramatic slope on the South Downs Way after it leaves Winchester: the area of grassland is reached by an obscure, unsignposted car park under the trees. The old railway track along the valley floor is now a bridleway, running from West Meon to Wickham – perfect for off-road cycling or uncomplicated strolls.

Wickham, towards the southern end of the valley, has Georgian and earlier houses lining a huge central square, while close by are eight acres of watermeadows that have been restored by voluntary effort. The handsome early 19th-century Chesapeake Mill (closed Monday) has imaginatively been converted into retail use, with antiques, home and furnishing dealers, while the Hampshire Deli in the Co-op is worth a look for its local food products.

West Meon looks a treat, like so many other villages hereabouts, only this one has had some enlightened developments of late. Its failing village shop was taken over by the community, with villagers buying shares in the West Meon Community Shop Association, and now flourishes as a grocery, internet point and very pleasant café with a seating area outside at the back. It also became the subject of a radical experiment to do away with all the white lines and signage, while kerbstones were lowered and the road surface was changed, with the result that motorists passing through felt less confident at speed and slowed down appreciably: the villagers love the result. Nick Heasman from the South Downs National Park explained it to me. 'Take away the comfort and motorists will respond. Everyone is citing this as a fantastic project.' Thanks to this farsighted removal of road-engineering clutter the village certainly feels even more inviting than it did a few years back.

East Meon could stake a claim as the most photogenic village in the area, with the shallow Meon running down the centre of a street crossed by little bridges and lined with half-timbered, brick and thatch-roofed houses. The church is on a rise, slightly aside from the village, and has bold Norman arches at the crossing of the chancel and the nave and an astonishing Tournai font, a gift from the Bishop of Winchester and very similar to one in Winchester Cathedral. It dates from 1150, each of its four sides richly carved with various beasts, including the dove of peace pursued by dogs of war, and Adam and Eve. Near the church, the steeply roofed Court House originated as a hunting lodge for the lords of the manor.

A walk from East Meon

The downland around East Meon works just about better for circular walks than anywhere else in the Hampshire Downs. This 5½-mile route gets utterly lovely views for much of the way, with a sheltered section in woods, full of pheasants when I last walked there.

Start: signposted car park in East Meon, near village hall.

❶ Turn right out of the car park into the village, keeping forward at the next junction, past the village shop, then at the main village street with the Meon running beneath its little bridges, turn left past the Olde George Inn, and past the almshouses.

❷ Go up through the churchyard, passing to the left of the church; the path bends left and leaves the top corner of the churchyard (ignore steps up on right), and goes through two fields and drops down to Chalk Dell Barn.

❸ Cross the road and take the path opposite and slightly to the right, along the right edge of two fields and straight across a third (larger) field to a stile visible in a break in the hedgerow, then down to Drayton Farm.

❹ Turn left on the road towards East Meon. After 200 yards you pass a house on the right, then just after (where the road bends left) turn right into Halnaker Lane, signposted 'right of way'. Where after a few houses this lane bends right after a house called Highcroft, keep forward on the signposted, unmade track (with a sign prohibiting motor vehicles), through woodland and on the level (avoid any side turns). After nearly a mile, keep forward at a signpost and four-way junction, now along the South Downs Way. Views intermittently open out on the left.

5 Half a mile later, cross a road by houses at Coombe Cross and continue ahead, on the South Downs Way, which soon rises steadily for about ½ mile.

6 As soon as the path stops rising and the view opens out near power lines, turn left over a stile (all the rest of the walk is signed with yellow waymarkers) and cross the grass, keeping just to the right of trees in the dip, going down into the valley and up the other side (where a glorious view opens up over the dry valley below the trees), joining a fence on the left. At the top, turn left through a gate, along the ridge, with views either side.

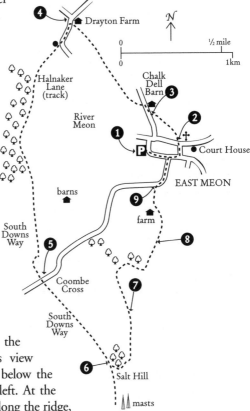

7 Carry on through the next gate, still keeping along the top of the ridge. As this begins to drop, you are joined by a fence on the left, which you follow down through another gate and to a woodland fence – turn right, along the field edge, and right again (avoiding a gate to the left) at the next field corner, then take the next left (with waymarker arrows on the gate) to walk through the woodland and along a field edge.

8 Carry on as waymarked – across a field to a corner of a hedgerow and then along the hedgerow towards East Meon village. When level with Duncoombe Farm away to your left, go through a kissing gate and head down the next field to the next kissing gate to the right of the houses.

9 Emerge on a road the edge of East Meon and turn right to the village centre (the car park is reached by the next turning on the left).

Old Winchester Hill

A signposted road from Warnford leads up to this magnificent National Nature Reserve, high above the east side of the Meon Valley. Just before you reach the main car park, views briefly open up eastwards from the road to indicate how much of a ridge this runs along. In summer a visitor to Old Winchester Hill might encounter clouds of chalkhill blue, speckled wood and silver spotted among its 30 butterfly species, and fragrant orchids are similarly plentiful. A waymarked circular walk goes along the mid contour of the steep grass downland slope – a crescent shape leading up to the Iron-Age ramparts. A V-shaped ditch encompasses the inner wall and palisade, enclosing hut circles, grain storage pits and barrows – the latter excavated in the 19th century.

Food and drink

Bakers Arms Droxford SO32 3PA ☎01489 877533
⌂ www.thebakersarmsdroxford.com. Very well run and free house, with interesting food the main attraction, though you're welcome if you just want to pop in for a drink. Rather cosy, with a log fire; children welcome.

The Shoe Exton SO32 3NT ☎01489 877526 ⌂ www.theshoeexton.co.uk. Usefully placed on the South Downs Way, with a garden overlooking the river. Children welcome.

Thomas Lord West Meon GU32 1LN ☎01730 829244
⌂ www.thethomaslord.co.uk. A firm emphasis on local produce in the well thought-out food, and a good choice of ciders and Hampshire ales; the back room is lined with a huge selection of secondhand books, sold for 50p in aid of the church and school. Thomas Lord was the chap who founded Lord's cricket ground in London, hence the splendid array of cricketing paraphernalia. Closed Mon; children welcome.

⑭ Bishop's Waltham

The glory of this pleasantly unassuming little town lies on its edge in the form of the building that gives Bishop's Waltham its name. In 1135 the Bishop of Winchester, Henry de Blois, established a palace at the Saxon settlement of Waltham, where he could stay while he travelled around the richest diocese in the country. In 1182 Henry II met his barons at the palace, and 12 years later Richard the Lionheart stayed here.

Now maintained by English Heritage, and with free entry, the substantial, partly moated and wholly roofless ruin poignantly evokes past splendours. As you enter, you will see the guesthouse lodgings, built in red brick and stone 1438–43; to the left are the bakehouse and brewhouse, parts added to the complex in 1378–81 by Bishop Wykeham, who died here in 1404. His immediate successor Bishop Beaufort further modified and enlarged the building. The main group is across the lawn, with the kitchen, massive west tower and great hall – the last of these hinting at its past magnificence with its tracery and huge windows,

Note that parking is rather obscurely located in a dedicated space opposite the Crown pub. Or you can easily park in the town centre, which has some pretty

Georgian corners, from where it is only a few minutes' stroll.

Bishop's Waltham Museum, in the Farmhouse at the palace ruins, is a free local collection, open on summer afternoons at weekends.

Food and drink

Baker's Wine Merchants 6 High St ☏ 01489 895773. The oldest wine merchant in the country, this dates back to 1617, and once served the Bishop's Palace. Its original cellars downstairs are now a separate wine bar. They also own Titchfield Vineyard, and run tours in summer; you can buy the wine in the shop.

Rising Sun Swanmore SO32 2PS ☏ 01489 896663. In the next village east of Bishop's Waltham this is a relaxed old coaching inn that is very good all round for food, beer and wine, though it does get busy at Sunday lunchtime. Children welcome.

Wickham Vineyard Botley Rd, Shedfield ☏ 01329 834042

⁂ www.wickhamvineyard.co.uk. Audio tours and tastings, and open daily; restaurant.

⑮ Marwell Wildlife

When set up in 1972 this became one of the first zoos in the country to function as a conservation zoo (*Thompsons Lane, Colden Common SO21 1JH; 01962 777407; www.marwell.org.uk*). The breeding programme here includes numerous exotic species, among them the scimitar-horned oryx from Tunisia and rhinos in Zimbabwe. Animals released in Britain from here have included natterjack toads in Cumbria and sand lizards in the New Forest.

Run as a charity and considered one of the best zoo collections in the country, this is in beautifully rolling parkland, where animals look very happy in semi-naturalistic enclosures. There's a huge amount to take in and walking around it can take quite a time, with more than two miles of paths, but a road train provides an easier option. The animals tend to be more lively when it is not too hot; a very rewarding option is to book a sunset safari, when you get to see round the site after the crowds have gone home.

Some 250 species live in the 140-acre park. The former kitchen garden is now home to lemurs, while a rocky enclosure recreates the habitat for snow leopards from the Himalayas, and ostriches and zebra roam freely in an 'African valley'. Humboldt penguins inhabit an area with a rock outcrop, stony beach, pool and nesting tunnels. The ups and downs of the park allow privileged views of the animals from different angles. A high-level platform virtually gets you nose to nose with giraffes, and the penguin enclosure features a special window through which the penguins can be seen swimming underwater.

Good-value annual season tickets give admission to nine other zoos. A free hourly bus runs from Eastleigh station on Sundays and bank holidays (*02380 902400*).

CHICHESTER HARBOUR
TO THE ARUN

2. CHICHESTER HARBOUR TO THE ARUN

I have a soft spot for Kingley Vale, the mysterious yew forest on the Downs. No one knows why it's there, and it's enough of a trek to mean that only the most dedicated get to it. From the top, the view is utterly sublime, far over Chichester Harbour, Sussex's answer to East Anglia – a lowland of great water channels and saltmarshes. This waterscape could hardly be more different from the South Downs, and makes best sense explored by boat; I particularly like the solar-powered craft that glides silently and slowly around the harbour – the perfect way of slowing down. At its northern end, Chichester is one of a quartet of sharply contrasting historic centres in this corner of Sussex, which along with Midhurst, Petworth and Arundel all have their special places to savour – the Bishop's Palace Gardens forming an unexpected haven in the heart of Chichester, Midhurst with its melodramatic Cowdray Ruins, Petworth for its juxtaposition with a huge park and house, and Arundel, where you can swim in a lido with a view of the castle or encounter the wildlife at the Wetlands Trust.

Art is particularly strong here, with Pallant House at Chichester being one of the country's top modern art collections, and the Cass Foundation's contemporary sculpture park in the heart of the Goodwood Estate being one of the most magical. Petworth House has the foremost art collection of any National Trust house – though for me the Grinling Gibbons carvings steal the show. Stansted Park and Uppark are fascinating houses to visit and compare, each destroyed by fire and rebuilt at either end of the 20th century. And more ancient offerings are there in the form of exceptional mosaics at Bignor Roman Villa and Fishbourne Roman Palace and little-known 900-year-old wall paintings at Hardham that are understandably faded but miraculously still in their complete form.

At Loxwood and Chichester you can travel slowly by canal boat on a short cruise along canals being rescued by volunteers. The same spirit of voluntary dedication has gone wholeheartedly into two of the finest rural museums in this book – the Weald and Downland Open Air Museum at Singleton, and the Amberley Museum; both are in choice settings in the South Downs, with plenty else to justify staying and exploring the area. Amberley village is a picture of perfection with its thatched houses and views across the Wild Brooks, part of a watermeadows wetland that merges into Pulborough Brooks RSPB reserve.

Walking on the Downs escarpment is boosted by some glorious greensand countryside immediately north – as at Bignor for instance. But if there's a favourite view here, for me it is further north, in the High Weald, from the heights of Black Down or from the obscurity of Woolbeding Common, where you look to the Downs across a foreground of heather – a scene that almost appears too wild to be in Sussex.

Getting around

The A27 and the more leisurely A272 form the main west–east routes; generally things are a lot pleasanter for leisurely pottering around on roads if you keep north of the A27.

Trains

The **Portsmouth to Brighton** line stops at Fishbourne (for the Roman Palace) and Chichester, with a branch line to Littlehampton (handy for getting to the beach at Climping). Trains from **London to Bognor Regis** go through Horsham and then three places in the Arun valley – Pulborough, Amberley and Arundel – where it's very rewarding to walk between them and get the train back.

Buses

The free map *Getting Around West Sussex by Public Transport* shows how the bus routes fit together. Chichester has decent services to Pagham Harbour, West Wittering, Singleton, Midhurst, West Dean and Uppark. From Midhurst, a useful regular service runs to Worthing via Petworth, Pulbrough, Cootham (near the entrance to Parham House) and Findon (useful for Cissbury).

Cycling

Around Chichester By using Chichester as a base and cycling out, you can see quite a lot of the area along designated cycle routes. The busy A27 bypassing the city to the south is a no-go for cyclists, but there are neat routes avoiding it. See www.chichester.gov.uk for downloadable cycle maps, which feature the Salterns Way (Chichester to East Head), the Centurion Way (Chichester to West Dean), Itchenor to Bosham and Chichester to Pagham Harbour. The leisure routes converge on the city cross at the heart of Chichester.

Westwards, you can cycle via West Street, Westgate, through an underpass beneath the A27 to Fishbourne Road (west). From there you can visit Fishbourne Roman Palace and carry on along to Bosham (partly via a dedicated cycle path by the A259), and over the seasonal ferry through West Itchenor and round the east side of Chichester Harbour to East Head; this uses sections of upgraded public footpaths and quiet lanes and is highly recommended. The 12-mile **Salterns Way** provides another route (around the east side of Chichester Harbour) via Bircham and West Itchenor to West Wittering and ending near the landward end of East Head – handy for beating the traffic queues at summer weekends. There's also the **Chichester Canal towpath** which heads south from Chichester canal basin (near the station), then west at Hunston to reach the marina at Birdham Pool.

Southwards the route through North Mundham to **Sidlesham** has less going for it scenically but makes a handy way of taking in Pagham Harbour, from where you can explore Selsey Bill and end up on the beach by Bracklesham Bay. Eastwards, the A259 between Chichester and Bognor Regis has a dedicated cycle path – no fun at all, but useful if you need to come that way.

Northwards, the **Centurion Way**, a route for cyclists and walkers, runs five miles from Chichester to West Dean with wacky and entertaining artworks along the route. Some reflect the area's Roman heritage like the 'amphitheatre', while others are just plain quirky – such as a bridge hung with bits of dangling metal. Local schoolchildren helped in the making of a triumphal Roman Archway, topped by a prancing bull, a ship and various other devices. The level route follows the track bed of a long-defunct railway that ran between Chichester and Midhurst, and starts in a suburban road in Chichester; out of town it passes through Mid Lavant, and continues alongside a stretch of road to end at West Dean – you can easily tie in a visit to West Dean Gardens or the Weald and Downland Open Air Museum, and take a more energetic return route up to the Trundle and downhill for a glorious if bumpy mile to East Lavant.

Into the South Downs Cycling is particularly lovely west of the busy A283, where you're on to lush, forgotten country lanes that are too crooked and narrow for much traffic to bother with – I particularly enjoy the ride out past Bignor to Sutton, then north to Burton Mill and past an unexpected tract of heathland known as Lord's Piece. It's very sandy hereabouts, so the off-road cycling is completely useless – the only time I tried it, my bike sank into the sand after about thirty seconds, and I got off and pushed the rest. Up on the Downs, as usual, off-road is much better, with long lonely bridleways in all directions; as well as the South Downs Way, the Monarch's Way up from Houghton through Houghton Forest and along The Denture is a nice, steady way up, and Stane Street (see page 67) is a Roman road cutting dead straight through the trees.

Bike hire

Bike Master Clay Lane, Chichester PO18 8AH ☎07944 302 974
🖰 www.bike-master.co.uk. Mobile bicycle hire service, Tue–Sat; helmets supplied free of charge. Adults' bikes. Delivered in Chichester area (£5 delivery charge).
M's Cycle Hire ☎07852 986165 🖰 www.m-cyclehire.co.uk. A mobile cycle hire service; they'll deliver and pick up bikes free of charge anywhere between Chichester and Lewes; helmet, lock, lights and tool kit are provided.

Tourist information centres

General information: 🖰 www.visitchichester.org.
Arundel 61 High St ☎01903 882268.
Bognor Regis Belmont St ☎01243 823140.
Chichester 29a South St ☎01243 775888.
Littlehampton The Look & Sea Centre, 63–65 Surrey St ☎01903 721866.
Midhurst North St ☎01730 817322.
Petworth The Old Bakery ☎01798 343523.

Accommodation

During the Goodwood events (the Revival, Festival of Speed and Glorious Goodwood) accommodation gets booked up far in advance, and prices are often increased.

Adsdean Farm Funtington PO18 9DN ☎01243 575464 ⌨ www.adsdean.co.uk. Two self-catering units on a farm a few miles northwest of Chichester, very well placed for walks and cycle rides, with Kingley Vale and the Downs in walking distance, and good cycling to Chichester Harbour. The Courtyard sleeps four in a recently converted stable, with an open-plan living area and a utility room (£380–£500 per week); the smaller Annexe sleeps two (£240–£340 per week). No pets. The farm shop on site sells own-cured bacon and ham, and nearby Funtingdon, with its shop and pick-your-own fruit farm, is within a mile.

Billycan Camping Manor Farm, Tortington, Arundel BN18 0BG ☎01903 882103 ⌨ www.billycancamping.co.uk. Spiritually refreshing back-to-nature tents-only camping: lanterns, tea lights, no electricity, camp fires, communal Friday night stews and eco shower room. Equipment (including tent) is provided, and you get a breakfast hamper for Saturday morning. From £195 for two-night weekend in tent sleeping two to three (bring your own duvet/sleeping bag); also two yurts sleeping four to five and a large tipi sleeping 4: around £350 for a three-night weekend.

Canute Cottages Cobnor House Chidham PO18 8TE ☎01243 572123 ⌨ www.canutecottages.co.uk. Four self-catering cottages (the largest sleeping six) on the Chidham peninsula imbued with a great sense of peace and space, with own private water frontage on Chichester Harbour. Excellent disabled access. Gold Award from the national Green Tourism Business Scheme.

Castle Cottage Coates Castle, Fittleworth RH20 1EU ☎01798 865001 ⌨ www.castlecottage.info. In a super-tranquil setting in the trees close to the Strawberry Hill Gothic mansion of Coates Castle, this B&B is a highly distinctive place to stay. The three imaginatively done rooms are all in separate buildings and comprise a room upstairs in the weatherboarded cottage, a high-ceilinged converted barn with spiral steps ascending to the bedroom and – the latest addition – a treehouse with the trunks of the chestnut tree on which it perches going straight up through the room either side of the bed, and with hammock chairs on a veranda; owners Alison and Ron have lived in Africa, and took the African game lodges as an inspiration. Breakfast is in a conservatory – the former stable and pens – and two very friendly cats welcome guests. £115–£145 double.

Colliers Farm Fernhurst GU27 3EX ☎01428 652265 ⌨ www.colliersfarm.co.uk. Peaceful farmhouse offering five-star B&B accommodation with eight acres of grounds and woodland, in lovely partly wooded country north of Midhurst near the Surrey border. Three sympathetically arranged rooms (two doubles, one twin) with calming colours and antique-style beds; exposed beams, and southerly views from the double rooms. The tennis court is all-weather, and has its own clubhouse with fridge and loo. Marina and Will Shellard have their own very free-range chickens, ducks and guinea fowl, and their own eggs are served for breakfast;

Marina also bakes a cake every day for afternoon tea. No dogs or under 12s. £60 per person sharing; single £80.

George Bell House 4 Canon Lane, Chichester PO19 1PX ☎01243 813586 ⌂ www.chichestercathedral.org.uk. Eight-bedroom guesthouse in a fine location in the Cathedral Close, owned by the cathedral and refurbished to a high standard. All ensuite; doubles and twins £99 and £120 per room, single with facilities for the disabled £70; breakfast £8.90.

Gumber Bothy near Slindon BN18 0RN, grid reference SU 961119 ☎01243 814730. A traditional flint-built barn adapted for camping, this is owned by the National Trust, and is on a wonderfully remote site close to Stane Street Roman road and the South Downs Way. It has a kitchen, drying room, barbecue and camping field. Open late Mar–Oct. £10 adult; £5 under 16s.

Martins Cottages Martins Lane, Birdham, near Chichester PO20 7AU ☎01243 512222 ⌂ www.martinscottages.co.uk. Two very well equipped five-star self-catering cottages in a building set away from the owners' house, sleeping four each, which can be joined together by opening up a soundproofed locked door for a party of up to eight. Croquet and badminton are available. It is as quiet as could be, on a back lane in a bypassed village overlooking a three-acre meadow (which you are welcome to use), near the eastern side of Chichester Harbour. A stroll up the lane takes you over Birdham Pool; the Salterns Way passes by, and boat trips from West Itchenor are not far away. £400–£850 per week per unit.

Old Chapel Forge Lagness, near Chichester PO20 1LR ☎01243 264380 ⌂ www.oldchapelforge.co.uk. Green Business Gold Award winner: spacious, spotless rooms in a neatly converted 1611 chapel, across the garden from the main house, and two in a separate cottage (which can be taken as a family suite) adjoining the main house, where Sandra and Charles, adherents of the Slow food movement, give an excellent breakfast made from carefully chosen, locally sourced ingredients. Plenty of thoughtful touches in the rooms, such as DVDs and sun cream, and the simple oak and iron décor suits well. At the back a view extends over unspoilt flat fields. Just north of Pagham and Bognor, though it feels quite rural; Pagham Harbour's bird life, Goodwood and Chichester are within easy reach. Cold supper trays are available on request (not weekends), and the Royal Oak a mile up the road at Lagness serves hearty pub food. Around £50–£95 per room.

Old Railway Station Petworth GU28 0JF ☎01798 342346 ⌂ www.old-station.co.uk. Just over a mile south of Petworth and tucked away from the A285, this surprisingly grand country station has a colonial feeling with its internal shutters and high ceilings, and has been sympathetically adapted into a very comfortable, high-class B&B, with two bedrooms in the main building and eight in the two historic Pullman carriages alongside the old platform. Erected in 1892, this was where the future Edward VII arrived when he went to the races at Goodwood – hence the opulence of the building. The line closed to freight in 1966; a model of the last steam engine to come through stands on the mantelpiece in the former waiting room – now a spacious breakfast room and sitting room with leather armchairs and sofas. If it's sunny, you might like to take breakfast out on the platform. Morning coffee and afternoon tea served to non-residents.

Rose Cottage Singleton PO18 0HP ☏ 01243 811607 ✆ www.1rosecottage.com. Roses figure everywhere at this neatly kept B&B in a flint 18th-century cottage: real roses around the front door and in a vase on the window sill, and pictorial ones in the décor. It has just one well-appointed double, with its own bathroom, nicely separate from the rest of the cottage, so there's plenty of privacy. The sheltered garden is tempting for breakfasting out if it's fine, or eat in the breakfast room by the antique dresser. Very usefully located in a downland valley on the edge of Singleton village, and just a stroll from the Partridge pub, which has a walled garden and log fires. West Dean Gardens and the Weald and Downland Open Air Museum are within walking distance too.

Rubens Barn Droke Lane, East Dean PO18 0JJ ☏ 01243 818187 ✆ www.rubensbarn.co.uk. On a lane east of East Dean and the Weald and Downland Open Air Museum. Luxurious contemporary conversion of a 17th-century flint barn for B&B or self-catering, very well positioned on a little-frequented lane in the Goodwood Estate right in the midst of the Downs, with walks through the deer-populated woods from the door and use of a tennis court; the spacious back garden has a barbecue. Minimum stay two nights at weekends. Double room, with extra twin if required; open-plan kitchen and living room area, garden. £150–£200 per night for the whole barn; discounts for longer stays.

Thatched House Hog Lane, Amberley ☏ 01798 831329 ✆ www.thatchedhouseamberley.co.uk. Not actually thatched, but in the much-thatched village, this former alehouse has choice views from the tranquil garden and from the back of the house over the Wild Brooks. Bedrooms are cottagey and beamed: a twin room or double with private bathroom, and second bedroom possibly available for a family group. B&B twin £80, single £60.

Chichester Harbour and Chichester

Forming the smallest Area of Outstanding Natural Beauty in the southeast, Chichester Harbour has a watery beauty that is unlike anywhere else in Sussex. Footpaths skirt parts of its shores, but it all makes best sense from the water – most easily done by taking a harbour boat tour from West Itchenor. Boating has been the thing here for many centuries, with four broad water channels providing safe haven and trading routes. Fourteen villages dot the coast on the peninsulas that jut into the harbour. Nowadays leisure boating is the big thing here: of 10,000 boats registered in the harbour, only 30 or 40 are working boats.

The water, intertidal mudflats and 53 miles of coastline with its hinterland form a cherished site for wildlife. It encompasses the seventh largest area of saltmarsh in Britain, and the waters are home to 43 species of fish in addition to limpets, sponges, anemones, crabs and worms. The local seal population is particularly visible at low tide: their movements are tracked as they are fitted with GPS devices, and at the last count they numbered 13 harbour seals and one grey seal.

The boating routes are along four channels, running a total of 17 miles; around them are 53 miles of coastline, 33 of which are defended from coastal erosion by stone walls.

The **Chichester Harbour Conservancy** (*www.conservancy.co.uk*) undertakes the work of conservancy, maintenance and improvement of the harbour. Its website is full of information about boat trips, nature and water sports; scroll down to the walks link for downloadable 'suggested walks' with maps and public transport information. Devising satisfying circular walks around Chichester Harbour isn't easy; it's utterly beautiful by the waterside, utterly flat and arable inland. Then there's the risk that paths may be submerged at very high tides; phone the Harbour Office (*01243 512301*) for information.

Activities and tours

The sheltered waters are superb boating territory. For instruction there are two sail training centres at Cobnor, near Chidham, that have benefited from grants from the Sustainable Development Fund, allowing the purchase of boats and equipment and to fund training for children: Cobnor Activities Centre (✈ *www.cobnor.com*) has a fleet of RS Feva dinghies, much loved by youngsters because of their speed and design; the Christian Youth Sailing Centre (✈ *www.cye.org.uk*) also does powerboat training and has accommodation on a former navy minesweeper. The Thursday Club (✈ *www.hisc.co.uk*) on Hayling Island is for children aged 11 to 16 who want to try their hand at sailing.

Chichester Harbour Water Tours ☎ 01243 670504
✈ www.chichesterharbourwatertours.co.uk. Up to five trips around the harbour a day, leaving from Itchenor.
Chichester Watersports Coach Rd, Chichester ☎ 01243 776439
✈ www.chichesterwatersports.co.uk. Kayaking, canoeing, dinghy sailing hire, waterskiing and windsurfing hire and tuition. Based at Westhampnett on the A27 by a lake. The main watersports centre for the area.
Solar Heritage Boat Tours Itchenor ☎ 01243 513275 ✈ www.conservancy.co.uk. 90-minute general, birdwatching, history and nature tours of Chichester Harbour on a solar-powered catamaran. This ultimate form of Slow travel is very good value: you ride on on a totally silent and fume-free, environmentally friendly craft that glides across the water. It's very stable, and you're unlikely to feel any movement. A guided commentary points out the sights, and binoculars are passed around as you travel. Powered by means of solar panels attached to the roof, this was one of three craft used to ferry people to an exhibition of alternative energy

sources held on a lake in Switzerland. 'She's quiet, doesn't scare wildlife, uses no oil or lubricants and doesn't cause wake', said my guide. One of the other craft was sailed (if that's the word) across the Atlantic to the US, where it faces retirement in a museum; I think this one's fared better. The craft is available for charter. See the website for sailing dates.

① Thorney Island, Chidham and Bosham

The harbour comprises four peninsulas, which are quite a hike if you approach them by road. The T-shaped Hampshire island of **Hayling Island**, a centre of yachting and windsurfing, bounds the west side and is linked to the mainland by Langstone Bridge and by ferry to Portsea. It lies in Hampshire, with a three-mile beach along its southern end; the Hayling Island Sailing Club (HISC) is the largest such club in the harbour. At the western end of Sussex's coastline, **Thorney Island**, joined to the mainland by a land reclamation project, was taken over by the RAF as an airfield in the 1930s. Then the village of West Thorney was closed, including its 13th-century church. The RAF moved out in 1976 and for a while it became a haven for the Vietnamese 'boat people' fleeing turmoil in their country at the end of the Vietnam War. It remains MOD property, with the Royal Artillery now in possession of a peninsula, and is largely Ministry of Defence land and out of bounds because of its Royal Artillery base. Happily, its shores are accessible by the Sussex Border Path which runs the entire way round the 8½-mile perimeter, giving an outstandingly scenic and very easily followed coastal walk which you can start from just south of Emsworth (which has a rail station), and you can look in on West Thorney church. The military establishment gives it an intriguingly sinister ambience: you press a buzzer to gain permission to enter, a camera zooms in to identify you and a voice asks you for your name, address and purpose of visit. The southerly extremity, Longmere Point, gives an exhilarating sense of being alone with the elements right in the middle of the huge natural harbour. This walk (downloadable from the Conservancy website) offers some wonderful birdwatching and seal-spotting opportunities.

Further east, the village of **Chidham** has its own peninsula ending at Cobnor Point (which occasionally gets submerged at high tide), with views across the water to Bosham, and just offshore a lone stretch of dyke that marks a failed 19th-century land reclamation project. The shoreline walk gives a consistently interesting circuit of five miles, of which a mile and a half are inland link sections along quiet lanes and across fields; there's a car park on the south side of Chidham. The 17th-century pub on the west side of Chidham, the Old House at Home (*01243 572477; www.theoldhouseathome.co.uk*), is useful. You can also start from Nutbourne station to the north, which adds an extra mile. Again, the whole route is on the Conservancy website.

On the next peninsula to the east, **Bosham** (pronounced 'Bozzum') has a very pretty waterfront with cottages and the yard of the Anchor Bleu pub looking out over waddling ducks and the yacht-filled Chichester Channel. Car-bobbing is big here: avoid parking on the waterfront, unless you really know what the tides are doing, as oblivious visitors are repeatedly foiled by high tides and find their vehicles semi-submerged. You only have to look at the barriers in front of the garden gates here to realise that those signs saying 'this road floods each tide' are serious. King Canute, who had a palace here in the 11th century, famously failed to turn the tide back here when he wanted to demonstrate to his fawning courtiers that even he couldn't command at will. His daughter is thought to have been buried in Holy Trinity Church, in one of two stone-slabbed coffins at the east end of the nave. This is the oldest Christian community in Sussex, one that has certainly existed here since the 7th century. The 11th-century horseshoe-shaped chancel arch is said to be just post Norman Conquest, although part of the chancel layout and the tower are Saxon. You'll find a reproduction of part of the Bayeux Tapestry depicting Bosham church (the only church depicted on the tapestry), from where Harold II sailed to Normandy in 1064 to get William's assent to support his claim to the English throne – an overturned promise if there ever was one, as William conquered England three years later. In the churchyard, several sad epitaphs on tombstones act as reminders of man's uneasy alliance with the water.

South of Bosham a **ferry** (*07970 378350; www.itchenorferry.co.uk; roughly every 15 mins, Apr–Oct; 09.00–18.00*) takes foot passengers and bicycles across to West Itchenor at summer weekends and bank holidays, itself useful for the boat trips that start from West Itchenor.

② The Manhood peninsula: West Wittering to Pagham Harbour

Sussex's southern extremity between the Chichester Channel and Bognor Regis is termed the Manhood peninsula – a name probably derived from 'men's wood' or common land. The flat, fertile farmlands are interrupted by water channels and on the eastern side by Pagham Harbour, making it extremely fiddly to travel west to east around the coast. The villages are mostly modern and suburban looking, though some parts, such as the western side of Bognor and West Wittering, have quite a show of rather lovely mock-Tudor thatched residences.

West Wittering has by far the best beach in West Sussex, a long, glorious expanse of sand, flanked by that great rarity for Sussex – sand dunes – and a multicoloured row of beach huts. The beach attracts nose-to-tail jams along its approach roads at summer weekends; the signposted **Salterns Way** bike path from Chichester makes a useful way of avoiding the queues and meanders for an agreeable 11 miles around quiet farmland, passing close to **Dell Quay**, the former port for Chichester, and two boating marinas at Birdham. From there it is a short stroll to National Trust-owned **East Head**, a sandy peninsula that has rotated some 90 degrees over a couple of centuries; it gives views over nearby Hayling Island and towards the Isle of Wight. The long beach extends along **Bracklesham Bay**, which has shallow, sandy waters, ideal for families. Famously this is fossil-hunting territory, where it is possible to find fossilised sharks' teeth, shells (including turritella shells, typically an inch or two in length, and oyster shells), ray fish and bits of turtle shell – dating back 45 million years to when this was a tropical sea. The best place to look is immediately east from Bracklesham car park, towards Selsey, towards the end of the shingle. Specimens often wash up on the sand, so you don't need to dig down. The sandy, shallow bay makes for very gentle, family-style bathing, and there's miles of it.

Selsey Bill is the most southerly point in Sussex. No one could claim it as one of nature's great glories, but the beach westwards is extremely inviting on a summer's day. Poke around the amorphous, mostly modern village of Selsey that spreads around the Bill and you'll find the lifeboat station, the early 19th-century tower mill and a few houses adapted with much ingenuity from railway carriages. These inter-wars plotlands are becoming something of a rarity nationally, as the more temporary structures have been replaced, but at **Pagham Beach** there's an even richer concentration of splendidly individualistic adapted single-storey dwellings and railway carriages with names like Pagham Halt and Sea Sidings along a grid of unmade roads. Between here and Selsey, 50 Mulberry Harbours were assembled during World War II in preparation for the invasion of Normandy; one of these failed to be raised, and its remains are visible at low tide.

Pagham Harbour, a beautiful, almost landlocked water, is the most easterly and smallest harbour of the Solent and forms part of the eponymous local nature reserve that includes shingle, saltmarsh, mudflats, farmland and copses. Of international importance for wildlife, it attracts numerous wildlfowl and waders in autumn and winter, and summer migrants such as wheatears, sandwich terns, brent geese and curlews. Rare plants such as the childling pink flourish in the shingle ridges along the coast. You can walk virtually the whole way around Pagham Harbour by means of waterside footpaths, and some stretches are suitable for wheelchairs; note that some parts can be wet at any time of year, even at low tide. A self-guided nature trail starts from near the visitor centre south of Sidlesham, on the west side of the water, and a hide nearby looks on to Ferry Field, a part of the reserve to which there is otherwise no public access. From the Bognor Regis side to the east you can start either from a car park at the far end of the shore near the harbour mouth, or from the 13th-century church at the old part of Pagham village, and walk along the inland side of the water along a raised dyke.

Food and drink

Anchor Bleu Bosham PO18 8LS ☎01243 573956. With a terrific position by the water's edge, this pub is open all day. Not surprisingly, fish is a strong theme in the menu. There's a cosy bar (can get very full) and a small back terrace that has the views. Children welcome.

Crab and Lobster Mill Lane, Sidlesham PO20 7NB ☎01243 641233
🖰 www.crab-lobster.co.uk. Tranquilly placed rural dining pub on the northern side

of Pagham Harbour, between the visitor centre and Pagham church. The emphasis is on the very good, though expensive, food (particularly fish and shellfish), and the bedrooms are stylishly arranged. If you're wandering in from a walk and just want a pint or one of their well-chosen wines by the glass, that's OK too – there's a pubby little bar and an idyllic back terrace overlooking the reserve.

③ Fishbourne Roman Palace

Most Roman villas in Britain were fairly modest country houses, but Fishbourne (*Salthill Rd, Fishbourne PO19 3QR; 01243 789829; www.fishbourne romanpalace.com; café; good access for cyclists, with Sustrans NCN route 2 running past; Fishbourne rail station is 5 minutes' walk*) is something else: unique in Britain (as far as anyone knows) and built on the scale of an imperial palace. What you see are the excavated floor-level remains of one side of a complex which enclosed a great quadrangle of formal gardens – the other sides extended right across to the present village main street. A waterside landing stage was probably the main way of arriving in Roman times, when Chichester Harbour was navigable further inland. You can get an idea of the palace's **original harbour setting** by taking Mill Lane, past the duck pond (a former spring in Roman times) – but reeds make it hard to see much.

At the entrance, the **model** of the palace helps you get your orientation: what you see as you look along the 1960s cover building corresponds to the left-hand side of the model. The **film show** cleverly recreates how the palace is thought to have looked. It's also worth seeing what is on – there are daily guided tours, and often demonstrations of Roman crafts, as well as special events and re-enactments some weekends. The **Collections Centre** has handling tours of artefacts (from Chichester and from the palace) on some days; otherwise you can go in and have a look through the windows and perhaps see highly skilled conservators at work or browse through a cabinet of sample artefacts.

Fishbourne is absolutely huge. There were more than 100 rooms, making it the largest Roman building yet found north of the Alps: a standard-size British villa would fit into half the garden. In Italy however there were similarly palatial villas, often, like Fishbourne, visible from the sea. As many as a hundred people may have lived here, enjoying the luxuries of underfloor heating, baths, fine wines and tableware – it would have positively bustled. Fishbourne is even grander than anything that would normally have been provided for an imported Roman governor, and was started very early in the Roman period. This has prompted theories that the conquerors had it built as a very public reward for a British ruling family who cooperated with the invasion.

The key figure here – though he did not live to see Fishbourne at its grandest – was probably Togidubnus, the enigmatic local king referred to on the Togidubnus stone found in Chichester and now in front of the Council House (see page 49). He may have lived in Rome in his youth and may have been brought to power by the Romans: some believe he used his influence to make Fishbourne an early safe haven for the Roman army. But so far there is little

Fishbourne's rediscovery

There were a few clues before: a 'Roman urn' mentioned on old maps, a 19th-century bill of sale for a house mentioning 'a curious Roman pavement in the back garden' and the story of a schoolgirl learning about the Romans who went out to dig in the nearby field and (as she had expected) found a mosaic straight away. However it was workmen laying a water main in 1960 who reported the site. There was huge excitement, along with fear that the farmland could be lost to housing development or roadbuilding. A £50,000 donation bought the field for the Sussex Archaeological Society in 1963, and volunteers excavated the site over nine summers. Many eminent archaeologists started their professional careers here, including Barry Cunliffe, a Cambridge undergraduate when he started directing the work. 'The most amazing time was the last day of the first season', he said. 'What they found just below the ploughsoil was the Dolphin mosaic. We just stood there on the grass looking down on this mosaic, and saying "it can't be true, this is absolutely amazing!"'.

direct evidence about him. Christine Medlock, the Director of Fishbourne, told me 'What we'd really love to find is his tomb – it is strange that we haven't found one to someone so important. But the most remarkable thing is that it's a mystery – everyone loves a mystery.'

Fishbourne's **mosaics** are surprisingly varied. The black and white geometric ones date from the time the palace was built and are some of the earliest in Britain; the ones with mythological creatures are later. Some of the designs are mysterious: the so-called shell mosaic appears to be two scallop shells, but Italian workers restoring it in the 1990s referred to it as a peacock. Cupid on a Dolphin, the best preserved and most famous, has a pronounced dip in it, because it was laid over an older rubbish pit which then subsided. Excavations in 1979 found that there had been another mosaic underneath. The borders of the Medusa mosaic were bungled – probably by an inexperienced craftsman (the label assumes he was therefore local, but I don't see why they couldn't have duff craftsfolk from anywhere in the Roman Empire).

The **museum**, near the entrance desk, has a choice collection of finds. There are fragments of delicately painted wall plaster, a sculpture fragment of a boy's head, possibly Nero, and a life-size reconstruction of part of a room with furniture and painted walls. Some of the tiles bear footprints and pawprints from when they were being made. The **shop** has plenty of replica Roman souvenirs – siege machines, miniature caligulae (Roman soldiers' sandals), coins and so on.

Remarkably the bedding trenches for the Roman **garden**, cut into the local clay, survived in the archaeology. The intricate wiggly hedging patterns of what was probably the first formal garden to be laid out in Britain have been re-planted, and on the far side you can see an engaging reconstruction of a Roman potting shed, complete with the voice of a grumpy gardener.

The palace was eventually destroyed by fire around AD270–280 – this may have been an accident, or an attack by raiders from the sea. You can see where stone from the ruined building was taken away – some of this may well have ended up in Chichester's city walls – and where later burials were cut through the floor. In one room the mosaic has collapsed back into pre-existing post holes of a storage building or granary dating to the time of the Roman invasion. Within a few hundred years the remains of Fishbourne were hidden beneath fields, and faded from local memory until its dramatic rediscovery in 1960.

④ Chichester

Very different in feel from anywhere else in Sussex, Chichester is remarkably orderly and uncomplicated, with its hot-cross-bun layout of circular walls enclosing a simple crisscross of streets – named simply North Street, East Street, South Street and West Street, the whole presided over by the massive presence of the medieval cathedral. The settlement originated in Roman times as Noviomagus Reginorum ('new market of proud people'), when the city walls were erected; their medieval successors follow the same line, and much of it can be followed on foot.

There are bits and pieces of Roman reminders here and there – a corner of Little London car park harbours some fragments of Roman columns from public buildings that stood nearby, and beneath the Council House in North Street is a stone inscription to a temple dedication.

With its impressive legacy of medieval buildings and handsome Georgian houses, Chichester is a hugely satisfying place to walk around, but walking out of it isn't at all appealing except along the canal towpath. Just about all the interesting features are contained within the town walls; the busy road that rings it is daunting and uninviting, but within that it is very pedestrian-friendly. It's usually pretty buzzy with shoppers, students and tourists, though the pace is leisurely rather than hectic.

Practicalities

If you're arriving by **train**, you simply walk up the station approach and turn left up South Street. **Parking** is free on Sundays; otherwise you need to opt for one of the five long-stay car parks as on-street voucher parking is for one hour maximum. There's a helpful leaflet about all the car parks which gets quite enthusiastic about the functional places to rest your vehicle – the Cattle Market (a good option if you're arriving from the east; the actual cattle market is on Wednesdays and Saturdays) is an 'attractive car park' while Avenue de Chartres goes one step better: 'an award-winning modern car park... a light airy building which provides some of the best views of the cathedral'.

Guided walks leave from the tourist information centre on Tuesday at 11.00 in summer and Saturday at 14.30 all year (and possibly Sunday), subject to demand; best to pre-book on 01243 775888. There are additional guided walks during the Chichester Festivities. The substantial **town walls** still stand mostly intact, and are rewarding to walk around. Particularly fine sections are reached just beyond the Bishop's Palace Gardens, and around Priory Park.

At the meeting of the four main streets the **Market Cross** bristles with pinnacles, is capped by a weathervane and has a central column supported by eight flying buttresses. Erected by Bishop Edward Storey in 1501 and built of Caen stone from France, it served as a shelter for traders who could not afford their own market stall and was in use until the early 19th century, when the market house was erected in North Street in 1807.

Just west of the cross, **Chichester Cathedral** (*free entry; free and informative tours Mon–Sat at 11.15 and 14.30*) has the distinction of being the only medieval cathedral in England within sight of the sea, which means that sailors who just happened to be looking the right way at the right time one day in winter 1861 would have witnessed its spire collapsing entirely, after months of shoring-up operations to rectify the alarming cracks that had appeared over the preceding months. After its completion under Bishop Luffa in 1108 it caught fire twice during the 12th century; stone vaulting then replaced the wooden roof, and an elegant extension was added behind the choir. It had to undergo a massive restoration project after its foundations proved wobbly in the extreme in the mid-1950s. More happily in 2002 peregrine falcons took up occupancy on the spire, nesting there from April to June and swooping from great heights to get their prey; a webcam in the Cloisters Café charts their comings and goings during the nesting months. The medieval builders might have seen what was coming and removed the bells to a separate, detached belfry built of Isle of Wight sandstone that has stood the test of time less well than the Caen stone of the cathedral; it serves as the box office for the Chichester Festivities.

Particularly fascinating are the range of monuments and art, ancient and modern. Touring the building anti-clockwise from the entrance, you encounter an exceptionally lifelike stone carving depicting Lazarus at Bethany, dating from 1125 but rediscovered in 1829, close to Graham Sutherland's painting *Noli Me Tangere* (1961), showing Christ ascending a staircase on his way to the Father (shown as an eye-like aperture in the wall). Next comes John Piper's notable tapestry woven in France in 1966 and depicting the Trinity and the Evangelists, the latter symbolised by beasts; then the vibrantly coloured window by Marc Chagall. Further round is the Arundel Tomb – which inspired a poem by Philip Larkin ('and that faint hint of the absurd – the little dogs under their feet') – to the 13th Earl of Arundel (died 1376) holding hands with his lady, who is turned towards him in a gesture of unmistakable tenderness. Much less celebrated (partly tucked behind display boards), to the left as you enter, in the northwest corner, is the memorial to Matthew Heather Quantock, drowned in a skating accident in 1812 aged 30 – surely the only memorial of its kind in an English cathedral, with its intricately carved skates: 'Gay pastime oft, in man's mysterious doom, has prov'd a prelude to an early tomb…' In the nave, a glass panel gives a view of a now-subterranean section of Roman mosaic.

The **cathedral precincts** make up one of my favourite urban spaces of any place in this book. Beyond the cloisters – built as passageways around the burial ground rather than for any monastic purposes, as the cathedral was never a monastery – and shop and café is **Vicars Close**, built in the 15th century for the Vicars Choral, who officiated at services, and with lavishly flower-filled front gardens. This leads into Canon Lane (also reached through the archway of 16th-century Canon Gate from South Street), which ends by the entrance to the private Bishop's Palace. Here is one of the glories of Chichester that many visitors miss, the tucked-away, surprisingly spacious and blissfully free-access **Bishop's Palace Gardens**, which date in part back to the 12th century and provide the finest picnic spot in the city, with the cathedral peeping up above a pergola walk and Tudor wall. An arboretum spreads across much of the garden, containing many rarities.

Along pedestrianised North Street is the Palladian red-brick **Council House**, where embedded into the wall behind glass beyond the arches is the Neptune and Minerva Stone, discovered in a neighbouring cellar – recording dedication of a Roman temple to the gods of the sea and mentioning Togidubnus, or Cogidubnus, who may have been associated with Fishbourne Roman Palace. The Assembly Room in the building dates from 1783; the great violinist Paganini and pianist Liszt played recitals in it.

Much of the pleasure in strolling around is venturing beyond the main four streets. In St Martin's Street blue doors signify properties belonging to **St Mary's Hospital**, an almshouse founded nearby in 1158 and moved here in 1252 – the gothic arched doors still in evidence of the main hospital building. The chapel is not open except by appointment (*01243 783377*) but if you peer from the car park behind you can see the chapel's vast medieval roof. From there you can continue into Little London and to **Priory Park**, with its beautifully placed cricket ground, with the remains of a motte in the northeast corner – a prominent lump by the cricket pitch. A coadstone statue of Neptune, formerly positioned over the public water conduit in South Street, lurks by the bowling green. Nearby is the late 13th-century medieval **Guildhall** (*very limited opening times; guided tours through Chichester District Museum, 01243 784683*), originally the chancel of a Franciscan friary and given to the city after Dissolution; it has also served as town hall and courthouse – William Blake was put on trial here for sedition, but acquitted. The **Chichester District Museum** is a local collection, being moved to Tower Street from Little London at the time of writing. It is hoped it will be fully open during 2011 and will incorporate on-site remains of a Roman bath unearthed here in the 1970s; there are family activities, research facilities, talks and free guided tours of the Guildhall (*01243 784683*).

In the southeast quadrant of the city, North Pallant, East Pallant, South Pallant and West Pallant constitute the **Pallants**, at the hub of Georgian Chichester, a name from 'palatinate' – the prince concerned being the Archbishop of Canterbury, who owned this area. The houses (including Pallant House Gallery; see below) are full of period details – including imposing entrances and fine brickwork, as well as boot scrapers installed in the days when sheep and cattle were a common sight on the streets and there was generally more muck around than now. Tucked round in St John's Street and now redundant, the octagonal **Chapel of St John the Evangelist** is a Grade I listed Georgian proprietary chapel of 1813, one of the few of its period in southern England to survive untouched – built at the time of chronic overcrowding in Church of England churches in the city. It was financed by renting and selling pew space, and apart from the insertion of Victorian pews its layout remains intact, with box pews in the gallery; most unusually the triple-decker pulpit is in its original position.

Arty Chichester

Justifying a special visit to Chichester in itself, **Pallant House Gallery** (*www.pallant.org.uk*) occupies a Queen Anne house of 1712 – nicknamed Dodo House because of the un-ostrich-like ostriches (the crests of the Peckham family for whom it was built) flanking the main entrance – in the middle of the area known as the Pallants. In 1982 it opened its doors as one of the finest modern art galleries in the south, and since then has gone from  strength to strength thanks to a major extension that since 2006 has allowed most of the collection to be displayed. The room attendants are all volunteers, and passionate about art, so it's well worth asking them about their favourite pictures. There are spaces at ground level where the public has free access – including the print room and the garden designed by Christopher Bradley-Hole, Chelsea gold winner, with its Paolozzi sculptures and London plane trees.

Highlights include *Swingeing London 67* by Richard Hamilton, taken from a photo of the charge at Chichester Magistrates Court of Mick Jagger and art dealer Robert Fraser after a drugs raid in West Sussex; *The Beatles 1962* by Peter Blake (of the Fab Four before they became famous; pity they never signed their names into the spaces allocated to them on the painting); and the *Trajectory Field III* by Antony Gormley – the arrangement of steel rods reveals a deconstructed humanoid as you walk around it. Much of the gallery space is devoted to changing exhibitions; this is a place to return to again and again.

Essentially this is a collection of collections assembled by various art lovers with modern British art at its core but also featuring other areas such as the Geoffrey

Freeman collection of 18th-century porcelain from the Bow factory in London. One who contributed to it was Professor Colin St John ('Sandy') Wilson, who contributed some of the British pop art as well as the likes of Lucian Freud and Eduardo Paolozzi. He was an adviser to the setting up of the gallery – his wife M J Long and Rolfe Kentish (who had designed the much-admired National Maritime Museum in Falmouth) were the architects of the daring new extension, which was a challenging project being in a conservation area and adjoining a Grade I listed building, but it admirably fits into a Georgian streetscape without attempting pastiche. The new rooms in the gallery are elegantly simple, with natural, reflected lighting. Wilson's collecting began in 1947 when he picked up a collage by Paolozzi for a princely 37s 6d (£1.87^1/$_2$p).

Two absorbing free art galleries are the **Otter Gallery** at the University of Chichester, College Lane (*www.chi.ac.uk/ottergallery*), with the university's

Chichester Festival Theatre

Janice Booth, Bradt author and editor

There was huge theatrical excitement when it opened in July 1962: the first modern theatre to be built with an apron stage, in which Sir Laurence Olivier was both directing and performing. However, I had loved the ornate proscenium arch and heavily swishing curtains of traditional theatres, and approached this newcomer warily. The building squatted on the grass of Oaklands Park like some futuristic hexagonal mushroom – but once inside the auditorium, I was completely seduced. The steel 'spider's web' roof soared above its famous apron, thrusting the action out into the heart of the audience and giving a warm sense of immediacy. None of its almost 1,400 seats was more than 20 yards from the stage, and the massive overhead battery of lights could switch the atmosphere from epic to intimate in the bat of an eyelid.

The casts during those early seasons were the stuff of dreams: who could forget seeing Olivier, Michael Redgrave, Sybil Thorndike, Lewis Casson, Joan Plowright, Fay Compton and Rosemary Harris all together in *Uncle Vanya*? Or Plowright in Shaw's *St Joan*, with Jeremy Brett as Dunois and Derek Jacobi as Brother Martin? I still remember the chilling excitement of *The Royal Hunt of the Sun* in 1964, so spectacularly staged, with its golden Inca masks, dramatic use of sound and colour – and Robert Stephens hypnotic as the exotic, sinuous Atahuallpa. Apparently the lavish costumes seriously depleted Britain's stock of Chinese pheasant feathers! Other great productions and great names followed (Maggie Smith, Peter Ustinov, Eileen Atkins, Alastair Sim, Alec Guinness...), and from 1963 to 1965 Chichester was the home of the National Theatre. The innovative newcomer had become a national institution.

The productions there today are still top-class: if you like theatre, don't miss it. And spare a thought for its history, and the ghosts from those early shows who probably still pop in from time to time to enjoy the odd performance.

collection of modern British art as well as changing exhibitions, and the **Oxmarket Gallery** (*www.oxmarket.com*), with frequently changing exhibitions of paintings, decorative art, sculpture and photography in four galleries in a converted church in Little London car park.

Entertainment is top-drawer in Chichester. During June and July, the extremely popular **Chichester Festivities** (*www.chifest.org.uk; the box office is in the cathedral belfry*) feature 17 days of music (mostly classical), art, drama, talks and other events in one of the major arts festivals on the south coast. In Oaklands Park, **Chichester Festival Theatre** (*www.cft.org.uk*) with the smaller Minerva Theatre is a leading regional venue for new drama, comedy and musicals, while **Chichester Cinema** in New Park Road (*www.chichestercinema.org*) is an excellent arthouse cinema with an international film festival during August and September. There are screenings of the celestial kind at the volunteer-run **South Downs Planetarium** (*www.southdowns.org.uk*) on the south edge of the city near the A27. Near the railway station in Via Ravenna, **Westgate Leisure** (*01243 785651; www.chichester.gov.uk/leisurecentres*) has comprehensive exercise facilities, with three pools, water slide, sports hall, squash courts, crèche, a health suite, fitness room and skate park.

Food and drink

The city centre offers plenty of opportunities for eating, drinking and assembling picnics (particularly idyllic picnic spots are the Bishop's Palace Gardens and Priory Park). The **Farmers' Market** takes place 09.00–14.00 in North Street and East Street in the very centre on the first and third Friday of the month.

Cathedral Cloisters Café ☎01243 782595. Fine cathedral café in modern style, with conservatory-like area, lunches and snacks using fair-trade suppliers and (best of all) a spacious, secluded garden. In spring a screen here monitors the nest of the cathedral's celebrated resident peregrine falcons.

Field and Fork Pallant House Gallery ☎01243 784701. Super daytime venue attracting rave reviews (also open for dinner Wed–Sat), seasonal menu; stylish, bright, glass-walled interior and tree-shaded courtyard with Paolozzi sculptures.

Little London 35 Little London ☎01243 774900. Bright and contemporary café in a slim Georgian house in the city centre, with modern prints on the wall, very good light meals and sandwiches.

St Martin's Tearooms 3 St Martin's St ☎01243 786715 www.organictearooms.co.uk. Full of cosy corners and with a miscellany of wooden antique furniture this is a pleasantly intimate place, with a rack of newspapers encouraging a leisurely stop. Choose from a range of organic wholefood produce and great open sandwiches, accompanied by fruit smoothies, and organic teas and coffee. It's central but quiet, just off the main shopping area and there's a gorgeous garden at the back. A notice encourages 'Please feel free to play the piano. Any form of self expression would be appreciated – even Chopsticks.'

Sussex's purple patch

For a week in July you can get a privileged look at the only lavender fields in Sussex at Lordington Farm. Andrew Elms gave up his dairy farm and in 2002 plumped for lavender instead because it was a crop that could be grown without pesticides or fertilisers, and would encourage wildlife species to proliferate alongside – such as the endangered bumblebee. His land also harbours barn owls, skylarks and ten other red-listed birds (the highest conservation category for endangered species, in which there's been a severe drop in numbers over the past 25 years or more).

As well as being wildlife-friendly lavender is extraordinary stuff in that it can be put to so many uses. As well as soaps and bath oil, he makes a pillow spray to assist a sound sleep, a dog shampoo that repels ticks and fleas, an application for burns and bruises and an air freshener. And the lavender essence is used for making cakes, cones, shortbread and icecream. 'The hand cream is as good as the best quality Jo Malone' said one woman shopper to me as I browsed his stall at a farmers' market.

Lordington Farm, Lordington PO18 9DX ☎ 01243 378312 🖰 www.lordingtonlavender.co.uk. Shop open Wed afternoons only; Andrew sells his products at farmers' markets (including Arundel, Chichester and Lewes), Chichester tourist information centre and cathedral shop – see website for outlets.

⑤ Chichester Canal

It is easy to miss Chichester's very own canal (*01243 771363; www.chichestercanal.org.uk*), just south of the railway station, which runs four miles from here to a large yacht marina near Birdham, on the Chichester Channel of Chichester Harbour. Opened in 1822 to carry coal to the local gasworks and last used commercially in 1906, this was part of the Portsmouth and Arundel Canal – itself a link in a waterway system forming a route from London and Portsmouth, that was used as a through route up to 1855, serving as a ship canal from the harbour to Chichester and capable of taking vessels up to 85 feet long. After it carried its last cargo, it was left to rack and ruin before a band of volunteers formed a society and took it over in 1984.

Wendy Baker, one of the volunteers, acts as lady skipper and has been here for several years. 'It was chocker with weeds, and the basin was cleared first. It all took a huge effort by a dedicated group of people. We now have over 60 active volunteers, including marine engineers, crew members, skippers, carpenters, people to mind the shop.' They welcome people who'd like to spend, say, a week volunteering, though Wendy stressed it's not glamorous – clearing weeds, gardening, litter clearance; they're also widening the towpath for electric buggies.

West Sussex County Council matches them penny for penny. They're aiming to make the whole stretch navigable to the harbour by 2015, at the cost of £1 million. 'We had to stop restoration work during 2009 because we spotted a vole. We've also nesting pairs of kingfishers, a pair of swans that nest each year, and carp, gudgeon, perch and pike.' It's a popular stretch of water for fishing (day licences available).

Part of their income comes from running very enjoyable scheduled **narrowboat trips** on the 12-seater *Egremont* four times daily, taking 75 minutes for the round trip (*worth booking, particularly at weekends: you can just leave your name and pay on the day; 01243 771363*); also rowing boat hire, and themed cruises including Father Christmas and Easter Bunny trips. They also have the Richmond for hire, and have themed events like jazz cruises and cream tea trips.

Whether going by boat, cycling, pushing a wheelchair or walking, you'll pass Poyntz Bridge (1820), the only swing bridge left and now kept as a curio; it was moved to its present site near the basin from Hunston, further down, where the canal makes an abrupt west turn (it originally ran east from here). Turner painted two pictures of the view from Hunston looking back to Chichester – one hangs in the Tate, the other at Petworth House; he used plenty of artistic licence, showing the sun apparently setting in the north, and the cathedral bell tower moved to create a better composition.

Sussex's westernmost Downs

From the Goodwood Estate to the Hampshire border, this is the South Downs at their most enticingly rural, with some very quiet back lanes meandering past remarkably unspoilt villages.

⑥ Uppark

Acquired by the National Trust in 1954, this remote country house (*near South Harting GU31 5QR; 01730 825857; www.nationaltrust.org.uk; open Sun–Thu, late Mar–end Oct*) suffered a devastating fire in 1989 which has resulted in an unexpectedly happy twist of events, and caused a bonanza of positive publicity and extra visitors.

Built in Dutch style to a design of William Talman around 1690, its exterior was little changed in 300 years until workmen used a blow torch on the roof to weld lead on what was the penultimate day of a year of roof repairs. It wasn't the ideal house for a fire to be extinguished: alone on a hilltop and far from any water source, meaning water had to be pumped in from a mile away. An immense effort was made to rescue the contents, which were passed from hand to hand, and 27 fire engines were in attendance at the height of the fire, but devastation was comprehensive and a charcoal gunge covered virtually everything. One fortuitous survival was the 300-year-old Flemish tapestries in the Prince Regent's bedroom, which had been sold by the family to raise death duties and were donated back in a generous gesture after the fire.

Fortunately the fire was covered by Sun Alliance under a policy first taken out in 1753, which paid for complete reconstruction. The National Trust decided not to replace the house as new but as it was the day before the fire, with its patina of age. Craftsmen were employed for all manner of tasks – creating great opportunities for craftspeople and builders (many of whom revived rare old skills) to work here at time of recession – as Uppark embarked on one of the most ambitious and meticulous restoration tasks of recent years. Marquees were erected to dry textiles and carpets, and the tradition of marking significant events on chimney pots was revived – one announces Margaret Thatcher's resignation ('MT resigned as I was making this pot'). The restoration was expected to take ten years but was completed in six.

Thus Uppark has regained its interior as it was for many years. Much of this is attributable to a marriage in 1825 between 71-year-old Sir Harry Fetherstonhaugh, whose parents furnished it lavishly, and his 20-year-old dairymaid Mary Ann. He lived another 21 years but she hugely outlived him, carrying on residing here with her sister in a Regency timewarp through the Victorian age, which largely passed them by. H G Wells, whose mother was housekeeper for a dozen years and whose room is cosy with brown panelling, remembered them as two old ladies archaically dressed in velvet.

One area to have survived virtually unscathed was the basement, including a line of antique fire buckets which presumably weren't much use in the house's hour of need. The basement includes the kitchens, abandoned in the 1900s in favour of a smaller kitchen, and a butler's room where the butler could check a gauge to see if the rooftop water tanks needed a top-up. Also down here is a very grand Uppark Doll's House, splendidly furnished with Georgian contents right down to the silverware.

The dairy, where Sir Harry's dairymaid worked, is an elegant room with ivy-leaf-pattern tiles. There was then a Marie Antoinette-ish fashion for the gentry to take part in the butter and cream-making, and do a few turns of the churn. Dairymaids were known for being comely, clean and appetising.

Harting Downs and a pre-semaphore system

Just to the east of Uppark, Harting Downs are grazed by sheep and retain the ancient appearance the Downs once had: this is a marvellous place for contemplating the view and browsing the carpet of chalk flora. Beacon Hill, the high point, about a mile's walk along the South Downs Way from a car park on the B2141, has vestiges of an 18th-century telegraph station, one of a series set up to enable a warning of French invasion to be given by means of opening and closing shutters on the roof. This way it was possible to relay a message from Portsmouth to London in a quarter of an hour.

As at Petworth, the landscaping creates the impression of being on the edge of a plateau, with lawns spreading right up to the house – a walk round the front of Uppark before entering helps to appreciate its situation.

Food and drink

Three Horseshoes Elsted GU29 0JY ℅ 01730 825746. East of Uppark and in a great position for walks in the Downs. Nicely rustic inside, with beams and log fires.

⑦ Stansted Park

The longest beech avenue on private land in England approaches this country house (*near Rowlands Castle PO9 6DX; 02392 412265; www.stanstedpark.co.uk; Sun and bank holidays 13.00–16.00 Easter–Sep, plus Mon–Wed Jun–Aug*). The goose-foot arrangement of three grand vistas cut through the forest gives views southwest to the Isle of Wight and east to Hampshire. It is a quite superlative setting, begun by Capability Brown and completed by James Wyatt; although you can see such a long way, no other buildings are in view, and the cricket pitch in front of the house has hosted matches ever since 1740. To get the full picture, walk from Rowlands Castle station, and along the mile-long grand central avenue. Fallow and roe deer can be seen in the estate's woodlands, which are largely accessible to the public.

The classical red-brick and Portland stone house is not what it first seems. The original but much remodelled Georgian house was devastated by fire in 1900 when the owners were at the races at Goodwood one day in September, and numerous paintings and Grinling Gibbons carvings perished in the blaze. It was a similar fate that befell nearby Uppark (see page 54) 89 years later, but in this instance the ruins were demolished and it was built afresh: the new house was created in the appearance of the original mansion, but with all the trappings of modern life too. Thus, although it has very much the feel of an 18th-century house in the proportions and styling of its rooms, this is Edwardian life at its most opulently comfortable, with the latest contrivances – among them electric lighting, garages for motor cars, an electric bell system for calling servants and an electric lift which still works and retains its panelling and bevelled mirrors.

In 1924 the 9th Earl of Bessborough purchased the house after the family seat in Kilkenny, Ireland, was itself burned down during the Troubles. His son, Eric Bessborough, was a minister in the Conservative government under MacMillan and a founder member of the Chichester Festival Theatre; he also set up a foundation so that the public could enjoy the forest, grounds and house in perpetuity. He died in 1993 and his successors live elsewhere on the estate. Today the state rooms on the ground floor are set up as they were in the 10th Earl's day. His favourite room, the study, has scarcely been touched, with the very magazines he was last reading still on his desk and the red government despatch boxes in one corner. His love of exotic birds is evident in the feathers kept on his desk and in the fantasy paintings in the stairway hall. The drawing room has a very 18th-century look with its paintings and applied art; look out for two pictures of the house, one in 1720 with two wings that were never built, although service tunnels still exist that lead off in the direction of where the wings would have been.

The evocation of life below stairs in the servants' quarters is one of the most fascinating aspects of Stansted Park. Last used in the 1950s and full of all the paraphernalia that would have been there, it vividly evokes the running of a great house, with its Acme mangles for laundry, servants' bells and speaking tubes, the housekeeper's cupboards stacked high with all the linen that would have been in use, a tin bath that all the footmen shared, high-ceilinged kitchen, cheery servants' hall and the butler's accounts books recording expenditure of every item. A former footman came here as a visitor many years later and found his uniform, last worn in the 1930s, still hanging with his name inside.

The Christmas fair in late November and early December is a great way to see the house, and there is a summer garden show, usually in June. The grounds contain a garden centre and a newly planted yew tree maze (2011).

✕✕✕✕

Food and drink
The Pavilion Stansted Park ✆ 023 9241 3432. Just across the lawn from the house in the restored fig house in a walled garden, this is a super spot for light lunches, cream teas and cake, full of happy chatter. Open daily 09.00–17.00.

⑧ Kingley Vale
Not exactly on the beaten track, Kingley Vale is for me one of the great Sussex sights. This, western Europe's largest yew forest, spreads across 200 acres over both sides of a downland ridge. It is thought to be 2,000 years old; no one knows why it's there, though interestingly pollen analysis on Mount Caburn, near Lewes (see page 157), indicates that the Downs there were covered with yew forest in prehistoric times. The 30,000 yews here are of all shapes and sizes, but the oldest are in a magical grove on the southeast side: here, massive trees create a dark, tangled canopy – some huge branches have fallen to the ground over the centuries and re-rooted into all sorts of bizarre, serpentine forms. It's a scene reminiscent of some Tolkien or Harry Potter fantasy. So not surprisingly various folklore has sprung up – tales of druids and marauding Viking warrior spirits abound, and it's supposedly a meeting point for witches too. Even on a bright summer's day, the forest exerts its spooky charms.

Long-living yews

Yews have a strangely immortal nature, as seen in the yew tree grove in Kingley Vale. When they fall, they do not necessarily die, but send out new shoots that often live to an immense age. Yew wood was for centuries used for making longbows – archaeologists have found them dating back 10,000 years. Yew forests were once widespread in western Europe, but this use contributed to their demise. However, English yew is not ideal for bows and arrows – and although it was probably employed for this purpose in prehistoric times, by the medieval period the yew used was more likely to be imported from Europe.

The wood, leaves and berries are poisonous to humans (though birds eat the berries), but yew has medicinal applications as an anti-cancer treatment. It is not clear why so many churchyards contain yew trees. It may be because of the trees' evergreen nature, or perhaps to ward off evil spirits, or because their toxic qualities deter wandering cattle from entering the churchyard.

At the top of the ridge the view opens out gloriously over Chichester Harbour, Chichester itself (with the cathedral spire) and the Isle of Wight (Culver Cliff, on the island's east coast, is prominent). Rising from the turf are the Devil's Humps: two Bronze Age bell barrows standing on flat platforms, believed to be burial mounds for ancient kings. There are 12 other scheduled ancient monuments in the reserve.

The site is maintained by Natural England as a National Nature Reserve, and includes other types of woodland as well as unimproved chalk grassland that harbours 39 of the 58 English species of butterfly (among them chalkhill blue, marbled white and brown argus) and a rich tapestry of flora, with numerous orchids such as twayblade, bee, fragrant and frog. You might also encounter roe or fallow deer, green woodpeckers, marsh tits, blackcaps, buzzards, sparrowhawks and tawny owls.

The one logistical snag about this wonderful place is that to do it justice you really need to climb up from both sides to see all the forest. If you have time and energy, start from Stoughton, walk up and over to join the nature trail and climb up through the yew grove. I much prefer this direction as the glories of Kingley Vale remain hidden until the later stages. If you just want to skip to the highlights (or want to reach the pub at Stoughton in the middle of the walk), start at West Stoke car park (turn off B2178 at East Ashling, northwest of Chichester, signposted West Stoke, then first left into Downs Road by a grass triangle, and the car park is very soon on the right). Note that it is signposted as 'National Nature Reserve' rather than as Kingley Vale. From there, a track leads to the foot of the downs and the entrance to the reserve, from where a clearly marked nature trail makes a circuit of the most spectacular part of the forest and reaches the top of the Downs by the Devil's Humps.

Food and drink

Hare and Hounds Stoughton PO18 9JQ ☎ 02392 631433. A mixture of traditional and contemporary at this village dining pub; pleasant seating areas outside – in front and in the garden; Harveys real ale and real farm cider. Children welcome if eating.

⑨ The Goodwood estate

One of the great estates of West Sussex, Goodwood has a tremendous presence. Occupying a great wedge of downland running almost into Chichester, the views from the heights range far and wide – but you can feel quite enclosed on its straight, narrow roads between high flint walls. Although Goodwood's business ventures are run on decidedly modern lines, much of the landscape seems little changed since the 17th century.

A visit to the house provides the explanation. In 1697 the 25-year-old Charles Lennox, 1st Duke of Richmond, one of Charles II's illegitimate sons, acquired the house and park as a base for country sports. The nearby village of Charlton was home to one of the earliest and most fashionable hunts, the subject of a Stubbs painting on view in the pillared entrance hall showing an almost unaltered scene: for centuries the estate has been dedicated to sport, along with farming, ensuring the conservation of open country and woodland cover.

Also carefully conserved has been the background of royal lineage. Charles II was quite unabashed about celebrating the continuation of his bloodline, albeit outside his marriage, and loaded the young Charles with titles. Goodwood's collection of portraits focus on the royal connections; the dark good looks shared by the king and his French mistress, Louise de Keroualle, seem to have survived through many generations, and the Dukedom of Richmond has passed from father to first-born son (always called Charles) in an almost unbroken chain.

Goodwood House (*01243 755000; www.goodwood.co.uk; open 60 days a year, by tours (first 13.20, last 16.00) most Suns and Mons mid Mar–early Oct, Sun–Thu in Aug*) owes its present appearance to the 3rd Duke of Richmond, a scientist, soldier, politician and art-lover, who among his other achievements founded the Ordnance Survey. His London house burned down in 1791, but the family art collection – including two Canaletto scenes of old Whitehall and the Thames – was rescued. To provide a suitable new setting for it he added two angled wings at Goodwood, lavishly furnished in Regency style, leaving himself heavily in debt. His successors added little during the Victorian period; Edward VII, a regular visitor, did not much care for the striking black and gold Egyptian room, and it was dismantled and painted over. Death duties and dry rot threatened through most of the 20th century, but since the mid-1990s an ambitious restoration project has brought the rooms back to their original splendour. The Egyptian room presented a particular challenge as no pictures of it had survived. Fortuitously, some door furniture had been left forgotten on the back of a locked door, and other items have been imaginatively reconstructed from architectural illustrations of the time. The guided tours (note the restricted opening times) are well worth seeking out.

Goodwood racecourse, the venue of the July race meeting that has been dubbed 'Glorious Goodwood' and was a favourite place of Edward VII, is high up on the Downs. Above it, masts mark the hilltop known as **the Trundle**, an impressive Iron Age hillfort with massive ramparts and a view the length of the Sussex Downs, all the way to Beachy Head, with the Isle of Wight also in sight. If you prefer to walk up from the bottom, the village of East Lavant makes a useful starting point. Lord March, the future 11th Duke of Richmond, recalls that when he was a child the public used to watch the racing from The Trundle. The police stopped traffic to allow the race to cross the road, which was spread with sand for the purpose, and it was said that one horse in the 19th century ran right on to Chichester without stopping.

The Goodwood estate is run as a self-sustaining organic farm: all the food for its animals is organically grown on site, and it exercises considerable clout in requiring vendors at its events to use local produce. The annual Festival of Speed sees Formula One racing on the park driveways, while the Goodwood Revival has historic racing cars, with their owners and fans dressed up in period costume, on the original racetrack, a former airfield on the Chichester side of the estate. However cars take second place in a new annual event launched in 2010, Vintage at Goodwood, celebrating and reenacting 'five decades of cool' from the 1940s to the 1980s, complete with music, fashion, film and hairstyles. Enthusiasts are encouraged to spend several days on site, with camping and 'glamping' available.

The Cass Sculpture Foundation

The road around the east side of Goodwood Park leads past the entrance to this modern sculpture collection, an outdoor art gallery where all the items are for sale, with the proceeds split between the artist and the foundation (*01243 538449; www.sculpture.org.uk; open Tue–Sun and bank holiday Mon, Apr–Oct; bus 99 from Chichester to Petworth can be prebooked on 01903 264776, minimum 30 minutes before travel, to go here any day except Sun*). Set up in 1992 as a charity by philanthropists Wilfred and Jeanette Cass, it occupies a woodland site that perfectly complements some 80 large-scale works by emerging and established sculptors, and is likely to appeal to children as much as to art lovers. Trails lace through the woods past eye-poppingly striking creations formed of a range of materials – wood, bronze, aluminium, granite, acrylic, polyester resin and marble perhaps. The stock changes as items are sold or lent out: the foundation commissions around 20 new works each year, and you might encounter human forms, abstract spirals and sleek geometric shapes, by turns thought-provoking, comical, monumental or simply beautiful in their own right. Prices tend to be in the five- and six-figure range, with the most expensive items on sale for over half a million pounds.

Food and drink

Goodwood Farm Shop Home Farm, Goodwood PO18 0QF ☎ 01243 755154. Signposted on the east side of Goodwood Park. All organic meat from the estate, with cheese and cream on sale. Hops and barley grown on the estate are brewed by Hepworth of Horsham – whose beers are on sale here.

⑩ Boxgrove and Tangmere

Either side of the A27, these two places have virtually nothing in common apart from their geographical proximity. In **Boxgrove** village are the substantial ruins of the guest house and other remnants of a **priory** founded in 1105 (free access) by monks from Lessay Abbey in Normandy. Beside it stands the capacious priory church, which survived the Dissolution. Its interior is a majestic blend of Norman and Early English styles with soaring arches and vaulted roof painted with flowers and berries. The 16th-century chantry chapel to Lord De La Warr is unique for its completeness in Sussex.

In the churchyard is a grave to Bill Fiske, the Chicago-born pilot who became the first US serviceman to die in World War II. He was stationed at **Tangmere**, a major military airfield that was in use until 1970 and was home to Nos. 1 and 43 squadrons; it's now the site of **Tangmere Military Aviation Museum**, one of the leading attractions of its kind. I visited expecting displays of impressive military hardware and, while there is plenty of that in the form of fighter planes outside and in the hangars, it has a huge number of human-interest stories from both world wars (and later) too. It is run by enthusiastic, chatty and extremely helpful volunteer staff (mostly ex-RAF); one visitor remarked 'I only came for a couple of hours but have now been here for seven!'. One of the most striking of many wartime relics is the reassembled wreckage of a Hurricane, shot down in Hove and recovered in 1998 with the body of the pilot Dennis Noble still inside. The more intimate museum displays are packed within the former radio maintenance area, where a model shows the airfield as it was in 1939; little is left outside nowadays, apart from the former control tower, and exhibits and photos tell of such events as Operation Manna, when 6,000 tons of food were dropped by British planes over starving war-ravaged Holland and the Germans had orders not to fire. There are displays about great agents such as Violette Szabo (executed January 1945) who received the George Cross, and the poem she had to learn is on display too – it reads innocently enough, and no one today knows what the coded message was. The range of flight simulators are a hit with children as well as adults, and the scenery below on some of them depicts wartime Tangmere; the most advanced simulator, where the scenery is projected on to a large screen, is suitable for experienced pilots, and is the sort of thing used for training.

Boxgrove Man: putting the clock back

This part of Sussex doesn't look at all exotic nowadays, but in the 1990s one of the most remarkable archaeological excavations of its time, in a nearby gravel quarry, uncovered an extraordinary snapshot of a long-lost world dating back some half a million years. The setting: a warm period between ice ages, when the land here would have looked more like Africa, and there were early humans roaming alongside lions and hyenas, hunting or scavenging extinct species of elephant, rhinoceros and deer. At the time the fossilised shinbone and two teeth from 'Boxgrove Man' were the earliest known human remains in Britain – their discovery in Sussex prompted a few cynical jibes in the press regarding Sussex's earlier associations with the Piltdown Man hoax (see page 201).

In this case they were from *homo heidelbergensis*, an ancestor both of our own species, *homo sapiens*, and of the neanderthals. The owner of the shinbone was clearly a tall, well built individual, more than capable of causing damage with the flint hand axes which were the universal throwing, cutting and scraping tools of the time. The sandy land surface preserved in the depths of the quarry was so little disturbed that archaeologists were able to reconstruct how half a million years ago a flint-knapper had sat cross-legged to work on one, leaving a V-shaped pattern of discarded flint flakes. English Heritage has now bought the site to save it for posterity, but unfortunately it's hidden away in country lanes, with nothing to see – the finds are still being worked on in London.

⑪ West Dean

Just below the Trundle, Singleton lies in a downland valley that encompasses the unspoilt flint-built villages of Charlton and East Dean, each with an excellent pub. Just north of Singleton and Charlton, **Levin Down**, a nature reserve owned by the Sussex Wildlife Trust, is a prominent hill, where the steep slopes have defied the plough, leaving it in its pristine state. Chalkland flowers and butterflies proliferate; the last time I walked up, a red kite rose abruptly just yards away – a quite startling sight. In the 18th century **Charlton** was renowned for its hunt: in 1738 the longest ever hunt ran for ten hours, and one of their number, Tom Johnson, has a memorial in Singleton church.

Weald and Downland Open Air Museum

Back in 1970 this opened as among the very first museums of its kind in Britain, and has been going from strength to strength ever since (*Singleton PO18 0EU; 01243 811348; www.wealddown.co.uk; open daily but open only weekends and Wed Jan –Feb (except half term) and 26 Dec–1 Jan*). The idea had been five years in the making: the vision of Roy Armstrong who after the end of World War II was surveying pre-19th-century buildings in Crawley prior to demolition, and came across a farmhouse built around a rare 14th-century medieval hall structure. He managed to get a preservation order slapped on it, only to find that the order was later reversed and the building pulled down. After witnessing the depressing spectacle of the historic timbers being burnt on a site bonfire, Armstrong recorded 'I have watched funeral pyres of at least two buildings which would have justified preservation had there been anywhere to store the frames.' This sowed the seeds for the concept of an open-air museum on the lines of what already existed in Scandinavia and elsewhere, and in 1965 Armstrong and some other enthusiasts met to discuss how this could be done in the Weald at a time when much of our fragile vernacular building heritage – dwellings, associated farm buildings and places of work – was being destroyed, and the conservation movement was still very young.

The museum was fortunate to be able to lease land from the West Dean estate, giving the museum a superb rural site in a scenic part of the South Downs. The setting really helps: it feels like a real village, with buildings grouped around, and feels very much part of the landscape. There are now over 40 buildings, among them such fragile evocations of yesteryear as a plumber's workshop, a brick-drying shed, a mid-19th-century village school, a windpump, a medieval shop and a toll cottage.

In displaying the buildings, the museum has often stripped away later features to get back to the original structure. One example is a medieval house from North Cray in the London borough of Bexley. It was dismantled during road-widening in 1968, and brought here; the 16th- and 17th-century modifications were removed, leaving the original hallhouse structure – with a central hall where a fire would be lit, and smoke would rise up through the roof. The museum also discovered that the external beams were originally painted red, as they are again today. The semi-detached pair known as Whittaker's Cottages, from Ashtead in Surrey, have been fascinatingly presented inside with the bare bones of the building construction revealed in one cottage and the other furnished as it might have looked in the 19th century. Sometimes unexpected twists in the tale appeared when the buildings were dismantled. For instance, a house from Walderton in Sussex that appeared to be 17th-century turned out to be much older: only when it was taken down did they discover the original wattle and found it was of medieval origins.

Deeper into the site, the woods are home to a variety of forest activities, including a very spartan-looking charcoal-burner's camp and a timber crane thought to be the only working one in the country; the trees are coppiced for a variety of uses: fencing, besom-making, thatching, charcoal and firewood, as well as for the health of the woodland itself.

A keynote to the museum's character is the presence of the sort of animals you might have expected to see in a rural community some centuries back. The heavy horses perform seasonal tasks such as harrowing, ploughing and cutting crops, and there are Tamworth pigs – chosen as being the closest-looking animals to an old breed that would have been here – chocolate-brown (officially 'red') Sussex cattle and chunky-looking Southdown sheep. When I visited they were training cows in ploughing – this process takes years rather than months and is done first in pairs, then later in two pairs; within each pair one cow has a name of one syllable, the other of two syllables so that the cows can know they're being addressed – Rose and Ruby, or Gwynne and Graceful.

They make a point of not going down the audio-tour route here; instead, chatty volunteers are on hand to explain the buildings to you, and the guidebook has full descriptions of every building on site. During the summer season some buildings host ten-minute talks at set times throughout the day. The pod-like modern building known as the Gridshell houses in its basement the artefact store: daily tours at 13.30 reveal a vast array of bits of buildings and items related to crafts and trades that have been accumulated, including the contents of a trugmaker's workshop.

Should you like to learn new skills or find out about rural life in the past, or own a historic building and want to know about conserving it, there is no better place to learn. A wide range of **courses** held here typically include those on traditional rural trades and crafts, early technology workshops like making prehistoric jewellery or tools, countryside skills such as coppice management or learning blacksmith's skills, and historic home life events such as singing Sussex songs or learning about historic clothing. They also run courses in historic building conservation, in which you could learn about timber repairs, Victorian carpentry or historic lime plasters and renders.

The **events** calendar is lively. For example on the Sunday and Monday bank holiday at the beginning of May is the Food and Farming Fair, showcasing foods from the southeast. And on the first weekend of June the Heavy Horse and Working Animal Show features various working animals from the museum and ones brought in by a loyal band of enthusiasts, while the third Sunday of July sees a Rare Breeds Day, followed by a Steam Festival in mid August and a Countryside Show in October. Anyone looking for somewhere to visit during the quiet days after Christmas should come to the museum for its Sussex Christmas, when many of the houses are presented to reflect how Christmas would have been celebrated at various times through the ages.

The **shop** has locally made crafts including trugs and wellie-boot racks, plus Montezuma's chocolate (made nearby in West Stoke). An impressive book selection features a host of books on vernacular architecture and practical building techniques.

Volunteers are essential to keeping the museum functioning. Charlie Thwaites is the volunteers coordinator, organising a force of nearly 600 people, who are trained up for a variety of tasks – learning about historical aspects,

Tudor brewing and baking, costumes, woodland management, blacksmith skills or helping in the shop or car park. It would be possible to come for just a week or so, although most attend on a regular basis, and they have students for a couple of months.

Food and drink

The Fox Goes Free Charlton PO18 0HU ✆ 01243 811461
⌂ www.thefoxgoesfree.com. In a delightful village and with a huge back garden, and a cosy and ancient-feeling interior. Welcoming staff, and children are allowed inside; open all day.

Star and Garter East Dean PO18 0JG ✆ 01243 811318
⌂ www.thestarandgarter.co.uk. Open all day at weekends, this welcoming gastro pub has very good seafood (among other dishes), local ales and a pleasant area for sitting outside. Children welcome. Open all day at weekends.

West Dean Gardens

The West Dean estate, which leases land to the Weald and Downland Open Air Museum, has a grand flint mansion that now houses West Dean College (*01243 818210/811301; www.westdean.org.uk; open Mar–Oct*), an inspiring setting for day and residential courses on arts and crafts (see box). The college opened in 1971 and resulted from a charitable trust set up seven years earlier by Edward James, the former owner of the house, who was variously a painter, poet and patron of surrealism. He supported Magritte and Dalí and constructed a series of sculptural creations in the heart of the Mexican jungle.

Restored after devastation in the 1987 storm, the 90-acre gardens that adjoin the house and flank the sweeping lawns are a visual treat: the formal part of the gardens is narrow and linear, with sudden changes in mood, and spreads along an intermittently flowing 'winterbourne' tributary of the River Lavant. The gardens include climbing roses, hydrangeas, an Edwardian vine-clad pergola, a totem pole, clematis, ferns, a lily pond, an arboretum and a spring garden with subtropical species, tree ferns and rustic flint bridges and a thatched shelter. In the walled fruit garden are beds edged with low box hedges, fruit trees trained against the walls and a splendid circular potting shed with a thatched roof. The kitchen garden, also walled, perpetuates the grand Victorian tradition of rearing tender plants in hot houses. A pavilion houses a good tearoom.

West Dean also hosts literary festivals, talks, exhibitions and garden courses. In August the ever-popular Chilli Fiesta features salsa dancing, fiendishly spicy food, Mexican minstrels and puppetry.

Going arty at West Dean College

Hilary Bradt, founder of Bradt Guides and author of Slow Devon and Exmoor

As West Dean junkies go, I'm only in the early stages of addiction. This year I will have attended three sculpture classes in this stimulating and beautiful place, but I have met students who attend six or more short courses a year on a regular basis. With over 700 courses to choose from anyone with an artistic bent can become addicted – and spoiled since in my experience the facilities and tutors are exceptional. And if you're not into making something, there's music, writing and gardening.

West Dean is arguably the leading centre in the country for the study of arts and crafts, which would have pleased Edward James, the original owner of this splendid house and a friend and patron of Salvador Dalí. The Edward James Foundation is a charitable trust which supports both the house and the gardens. Indeed, the gardens are what West Dean is best known for. With more than 6,000 acres of grassland grazed by pampered sheep and woods flaming with rhododendrons and azaleas, the estate is somewhere you can spend half a day exploring the trails, but my favourite is the walled garden, because I never knew you could persuade apple trees to hug a wall quite so self-effacingly and I love the mixture of flowering plants and vegetables.

Residential students have the best of all worlds. They can stride through the grounds, wander around the formal gardens, marvel at living, even briefly, in a stately home, or devote every waking hour to pursuing creativity. And there's no television. West Dean is definitely Slow.

⑫ Slindon

The beechwoods of Slindon Common flank this ambling downland village, owned in part by the National Trust, which has a policy of ensuring that local families and workers are given tenancies to keep the village community alive and thriving. Not far from the village pond are St Mary's Church and what is surely the only NT-owned thatched railway carriage, within the grounds of Church House and visible from the road. Slindon's cricket team continues a venerable tradition stretching back to the 18th century; the first known scorecard of any game dates to a match in 1744 between London and Slindon at the Artillery Ground in Finsbury – one of Slindon's men was Richard Newland (1713–78), the 'father of cricket', and one of the game's great all-rounders; the game has been played here since the 18th century.

To the north of the village, a folly known as the **Nore** stands on a partly wooded hill and makes a good objective for walks. Built as a sham ruin in the 18th century it serves no purpose whatsoever except to embellish the landscape.

Just to the south, across the A27, **Denmans Garden** (*01243 542808; www.denmans-garden.co.uk*) packs a lot into four acres, with a wild, romantic look to its gravel beds, walled garden and moorhen-populated pond. Formerly the garden to a country house, it is open all year, and has plant sales and a café.

⑬ Bignor Roman Villa and around

Bignor Roman Villa (*RH20 1PH; 01798 869259; www.bignorromanvilla.co.uk; closed Nov–Feb, and Mon except bank holidays; basic refreshments available*) makes an excellent excursion from Amberley. It's an eight-mile round trip on narrow and quiet country lanes, ideal to do by bicycle. Bignor village itself has gorgeously preserved old houses including the thatched, 15th-century Yeoman's House (or Old Shop), with its overhanging upper storey.

People have been coming to admire the Roman remains for quite some time. In 1811 a ploughman named Joseph Tupper chanced upon some of the finest mosaics yet discovered in this country while ploughing, and a local man named John Hawkins and the antiquary Samuel Lysons spent eight years excavating them. Hawkins put up thatched stone huts to protect the mosaics – these have a charm of their own, and are now listed buildings themselves, even if it's not quite the way archaeologists do things nowadays. People pottered out in horse-driven carriage trips from all over the south-east to see this 'new' wonder. The site is still family-run, by Tupper's descendants.

Although the first building dates from around AD190, most of what's in evidence is 4th century. It underwent a lot of extensions, probably to house separate parts of an extended family, who would have shared the bath suite. This featured a heated changing room (the one with the Medusa mosaic), and cold, warm and hot baths; the slaves would have kept the furnace going.

The mosaics depict scenes from the lives of gladiators and mythical subjects, and in places you can even walk on the still-durable surface of a Roman floor. Bignor's mosaics, underfloor heating and bath suite were the first real evidence of Roman-style living in the British countryside: previously scholars had thought of Britain as a backward frontier zone, with 'civilised' amenities only in the cities.

Since Tupper's fortuitous ploughing exploits, a great number of Roman villas have been discovered all across Sussex. One striking feature many have in common is their view of the Downs – it seems that along with their hot baths the villa owners appreciated a good view. But they were unlikely to have been Romans from Italy. They were probably the descendants of Iron-Age landowners who grew rich supplying such markets as the Roman palace at Fishbourne and the new city of Chichester: the villa would have been at the heart of their farming estates.

The villa was strategically positioned close to the London–Chichester Roman road, known as **Stane Street**, which you can still walk nearby on top of the South Downs. From Bignor village, take a lane which climbs for a mile south up the ridge (very steep at the start, but it gets easier). The car park at the top has a modern signpost with Roman names, and you can see the very clear raised bank (*agger*) of the road and sometimes the original flint surface where the local rabbits have nibbled away the turf. Return on the lanes the same way, or cycle the chalk track of the South Downs Way, following the top of the ridge then down a steep descent back to Amberley.

Bignor's **Church of Holy Cross** is a local hub of events, and its spacious proportions make it a venue for numerous concerts (classical, folk and jazz) and a weed and wildflower festival in July (odd-numbered years) that features the likes of fire dancing and country crafts. North of Bignor, **Burton and Chingford Ponds** is a Sussex Wildlife Trust nature reserve (actually called Burton Mill Pond on OS maps), with easy access from a car park by Burton Mill. Created in the 16th century as a hammer pond, the water and its surroundings form a rich habitat for birds, including kingfishers, woodpeckers and great crested grebes, and 23 species of dragonfly. The acidic peat and wet woodlands create conditions for southern marsh orchids, tussock sedge and bogbean. Access is via a nature trail which leads along paths and sections of boardwalk.

Follow the road southeast from Burton Mill towards the A29, and in a mile you come to **Lord's Piece**, a patch of lowland heath with beautiful views towards the Downs. There are two car parks on the western side; it's not a big area, but feels larger once you stroll around in it. Listen for the rare field crickets – it's one of the very few sites in the country where they're found. When I last visited there was local concern about plans to initiate sand extraction very close by, which some fear would threaten the tranquillity and character of this distinctive place.

Food and drink

White Horse Sutton RH20 1PS ☎ 01798 869221 🖰 www.whitehorse-sutton.co.uk. In the next village west from Bignor, from which it's a pleasant walk along the lane or through fields, this attractively placed village inn is furnished in contemporary style, with interesting bar food, beers and wines, and comfortable accommodation. Closed evenings Sun and Mon.

The Rother Valley and the north

Confusingly Sussex has two rivers named Rother. The western Rother rises in Hampshire and flows through Midhurst, joining the Arun near Stopham's historic bridge. Further north the land rises into heathy, wooded and enticingly secretive sandstone hills that aren't at all part of the South Downs but are of such high landscape quality that they were included the South Downs National Park. The huge estates of Cowdray near Midhurst and Leconfield at Petworth are very much a feature of country life here.

⑭ Midhurst

This is at the hub of the aristocratic Cowdray estate – centred at Cowdray House just outside the town – whose lands stretch far across this part of Sussex. The trademark mustard-yellow paint on doors and windows of estate buildings can be seen locally, particularly in Easebourne, the old village that lies just to the north. Midhurst's best moments are easily missed. Making for an enjoyable potter around, its villagey old centre, with its Market Square and market house of 1551, and Church Hill, is tucked behind the main street with overhanging jettied houses, tile-hung timber-framed buildings and Georgian facades often hiding older Tudor and Stuart structures. Listen out for the curfew bell that rings from the church tower every evening at 20.00 as ordered by William the Conqueror, and look out for the preserved shopfront of Boots – with its bow windows and black and gold lettering – and the original site of 'Midhurst Grammar School, founded in 1672, where H G Wells attended evening classes at the age of 15 while apprenticed at a chemist's shop in town, and taught there a couple of years later; at that time his mother was a housekeeper at Uppark (see page 55). There's also the very pretty South Pond, formed in medieval times as a fish breeding ground and later serving as a mill pond for fulling cloth. In recent years, parts of the town have been periodically transported back to 1945 as locations for the TV series *Foyle's War*.

Midhurst's grandest building, **Cowdray** is actually a Grade I listed ruin of astonishing proportions. The original lords of the manor here, the Bohun family, had a motte and bailey on St Ann's Hill close to the ruins. They erected a larger house in the 13th century, named 'Coudreye', after the Norman-French word for hazel woods. This was in turn replaced in the 16th century by William Fitzwilliam, a friend of Henry VIII who rather unusually stayed friends with the monarch all his life. Fitzwilliam's Tudor mansion, known as Cowdray, was second only in scale among Tudor mansions to Hampton Court, on which it was modelled.

In the 1770s Capability Brown was engaged to remodel the gardens. But in 1793 a fire devastated Cowdray, and despite locals helping themselves to free building supplies over the ensuing years its shell continued to stand and was much admired by tourists and antiquarians, and painted and sketched by many, including Turner and Constable. It was closed in the late 1980s as it became unsafe, but at the end of the 20th century the people of Midhurst asked Lord Cowdray to do something about restoring it as a tourist attraction before it crumbled away completely.

Operations manager Heather Ongley told me 'There's more here than first meets the eye. There are lots of rooms, including a chapel and a great hall.

We are very fortunate to have pictures by the Swiss artist Samuel Grimm showing what it was like in the 1780s.' Heather also pointed out to me a chunk of wooden staircase preserved in the visitor centre, with the Tudor rose and fleur-de-lis denoting Fitzwilliam's eternal devotion to the king. The more intact areas of the mansion include a wine cellar (where a 15-minute introductory film is shown) and a working, polygonal Tudor kitchen. A miraculous survival of 200 years of neglect is the unique porch with fan vaulting, made in 1538 for the visit of Henry VIII by an unknown Italian renaissance sculptor who reputedly practised first on the ceiling of the cottage in Midhurst where he was staying.

It's well worth trying to catch one of the **special events** here, which include 'picnic theatre' performances, ghost walks and historic re-enactments.

Adjacent to the ruins, the once-neglected kitchen garden has been given a joyous new lease of life. **The Walled Garden at Cowdray** (*01730 816881; www.walledgardencowdray.com; open Mon–Thu in summer, but best to check in case it is closed for a wedding*), as it is now known, is variously a garden open to visitors, a showroom and a wedding venue. When it was discovered by Jan Howard it was being used for allotments and the remainder consisted of rough grass with some mature conifers. Jan redesigned it as a hybrid of the Elizabethan style, compartmentalised into various areas – herbs, aromatics and a cottage garden for instance, with avenues of lavender and roses behind boxed parterres. The garden showcases her company Room in the Garden (*01730 816881; www.roominthegarden.com*), which produces elegantly crafted garden structures and furniture such as pavilions, gazebos and arches as well as plant supports and the like, and has exhibited to great acclaim at the Chelsea Flower Show.

Food and drink

By the entrance to the **Walled Garden**, there's a café. In the town centre, the **Coffee Pot** in Knockhundred Market (☎ *01730 814412*) has all-day breakfasts, lunches and afternoon teas. A **farmers' market** takes place on the fourth Saturday of each month. The 16th-century **Wheatsheaf** in Wool Lane (☎ *01730 813450*) is a characterful pub for a meal or a drink.

> **Cowdray Farm Shop and Priory Café** Cowdray Park GU29 0AJ ☎ 01730 812799.
> The shop has a selection of local food, including vegetables and meat from the Cowdray Estate, Sussex cheeses, bread baked on the premises and free-range poultry. The café offers breakfasts, cream teas and steak and chips – with the steak from the organically reared Cowdray herd.
>
> **Harveys Bottle and Jug** Red Lion St ☎ 01730 810709 🐧 www.harveys.org.uk.
> Harveys beers (brewed in Lewes) available in bottles and on draught, alongside a worldwide selection of wines, sold from a 15th-century property in the centre of Midhurst.

Polo at Cowdray

Famously, Cowdray Park Polo Club (*www.cowdraypolo.co.uk*) in Midhurst is the centre of the horseback sport of polo in Britain, although its origins in this country are Aldershot, where the Royal Hussars first played it in 1869. At Cowdray the lawns spread either side of Cowdray Ruins and Cowdray House, and the public are welcome to come and watch all matches (smart casual dress code); you pay as you enter. Matches are of various durations, played on a 'lawn' measuring 300 by 160 yards over seven-minute periods known as chukkas, and can be from four to six chukkas long – an hour to 90 minutes including intervals; every time a goal is scored the play changes end. The polo ponies, as they are known, are put through their paces and move at tremendous speed, necessitating the frequent intervals and changeovers of ponies. Although it's basically a game of scoring goals using sticks to hit the ball for a goal, the rules aren't that easy to grasp – for instance there is a notional 'line of ball' along which a player establishes right of way that an opponent is not allowed to cross if there is any risk of collision, and a player may hook an opponent's stick if he is on the same side of his opponent as the ball – but even if you have little idea what's going on, it does make a thoroughly engrossing spectacle.

The sport was first played here in 1910, when Harold Pearson got things going. He had played polo at Oxford and after his father purchased the estate in 1909 quickly set to having a polo ground laid out at Cowdray House and by the Cowdray Ruins. The sport enjoyed a renaissance of public interest after World War II when crowds flocked to see Prince Philip play – his uncle Lord Mountbatten was a polo enthusiast who encouraged his nephew. A Coronation Cup of six nations drew 15,000 spectators in 1953, and Prince Philip established his own polo club at Windsor. Prince Charles then became an aficionado of the sport and played at Cowdray many times until back problems forced him to retire from polo in 2003. Today some 450 matches are played each season, the highlight being the Veuve Cliquot Gold Cup for the British Open in summer, when some of the world's top players are in action.

⑮ Lodsworth to Black Down

This is a supremely rewarding, quiet and verdant corner of West Sussex, extraordinarily remote and unspoilt, with no great visitor attractions and woodlands to lose yourself in (often literally – this is a complex and confusing landscape), much of it on lands owned by the neighbouring Cowdray and Leconfield estates of Midhurst and Petworth respectively. **Lodsworth** and **Lickfold** sit comfortably in a rural scene. **Fernhurst**, further north, is larger, with a large village green that makes one of several good starting points for walks up to **Black Down**, at 919 feet the highest point in West or East Sussex, though it's only just south of the Surrey border; reputedly Black Down has the juiciest, tastiest wild bilberries hereabouts because of its altitude. The slopes of the hill are densely wooded or covered with scrub, but at the top the views open up in a few places; most notable is the Temple of the Winds, a viewpoint at the southern end, where the trees frame the distant prospect of the South Downs. The National Trust own Black Down and Marley Common to its west. Plans are under way to restore the pine and birch scrub to heathland in the interests of wildlife. The landscapes struck a chord with Alfred Lord Tennyson who in 1867 purchased 60 acres of land and built Aldworth House on the slopes of the hill. His study looked straight across the Weald, prompting him to record in a letter to a friend:

You came, and looked and loved the view
Long-known and loved by me,
Green Sussex fading into blue
With one gray glimpse of sea.

A mile west of Fernhurst, a large pond (*grid reference SU 879283; no road access, but public rights of way lead to the spot*) marks the site of **Fernhurst Furnace** (also known as North Park Furnace), said to be the best surviving example of an ironworking site in the Weald. It dates from the 17th and 18th centuries, when it used water power from the pond, and local ore and charcoal.

Hollycombe – Steam in the Country

On a hill just south of Liphook, this terrific collection of steam-powered engines was assembled by Commander John Baldock of Hollycombe House on his estate. He acquired the first engine in the early 1950s, and Hollycombe opened to the public in 1971; it is now run as an educational charity, all lovingly maintained by volunteers (*01428 724900; www.hollycombe.co.uk; open certain days May–Oct*). It has the largest traditional steam-powered fairground in Britain, where, thanks to the engineering prowess of the inventors, the numerous rides are virtually all robust enough to try out – you can swing on the steam swing boats, sample the spooky charms of the Haunted House or ride the Chair-o-Planes. The Bioscope is a replica of a very early form of cinema, with a steam engine powering an organ to get the punters into the rear tent, where early films of the Buster Keaton genre are screened. The oldest exhibit is Mr Field's Steam Circus, a simple, non-galloping merry-go-round dating from the 1870s and the world's oldest surviving mechanical fairground ride: it is somewhat fragile so is for admiring rather than riding. Additionally there are fairground organs, steam tractors, traction engines, diesel and steam locos, a steam sawmill, and a narrow-gauge railway giving a 1½-mile ride through the woodland. Note that opening dates are quite limited; they have some fairground evenings at night.

A walk: Woolbeding Common and the River Rother

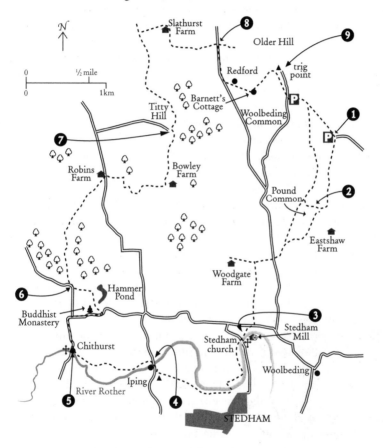

I have included this walk as it sums up all that is good in this area, with delectable views, heathland, woods and a section along the River Rother; the only thing it lacks is a pub. At 10 miles, it needs most of a day to complete, and there is a steep climb near the end. The crowning glory is the National Trust-owned area of Woolbeding Common, which has some of the choicest views in all Sussex from the spine of its ridge as at the end of the walk it opens into heathland. The paths are almighty complicated, so I have picked out a route that's comparatively easy to follow, having walked it with a local friend from Lickfold and discarded many variants until we found something that worked perfectly. On the way you see some remarkable trees – an extraordinarily old hollow yew tree in Iping churchyard and a noble oak north of Titty Hill. The forests contain evidence of coppicing and of hammer ponds left by the long-defunct Wealden iron industry.

If you want just a short stroll to take in the highlights, use the car park passed near the end of the walk and take in the view from Woolbeding Common, or explore the river between Stedham Mill and Iping.

Start: car park just beyond Woolbeding Common National Trust sign (300 yards south of Scotland Farmhouse as marked on OS map), at the end of a lane. From Midhurst go north and follow the A286 through Easebourne, just over a mile after which turn left (west) by a bus stop into King's Drive, then first right (Scotland Lane) near a hospital entrance. Park on the left just before 'no cars' sign. Grid reference SU875256.

❶ Find the three-way signpost at the bottom end of the car park: with the lane behind you take the left-hand path, which leads slightly downhill through woods. After ¹/₂ mile this emerges into the open by a signpost, and 50 yards later by another signpost fork right (leaving the signposted path which forks left). Follow this right-hand path down through the heath, with views of the South Downs ahead, to a triangular T-junction (it looks at first sight like a fork, but is a triangle of tracks). Turn right.

❷ You soon pass a woodland gate on the right marked 'no riding': veer left here, around the bottom edge of the open land. This eventually drops down near a house to the left, then keeps forward to rise to a double power line: follow the track downhill to the left here, to reach a road (a sign facing the other way says 'Dene House' just before you emerge on the road). Cross it and take the path opposite and slightly to the right, through woodland and along the left side of a large field. At the end of the first field away to your left, enter it via a stile and follow the right edge of this and the next field.

❸ When you reach the road, turn right on to it then after 40 yards turn left on a descending woodland path, keeping right at the next track junction. At the river opposite **Stedham Mill**, do not cross the bridge (except to have a look at the remnants of the watermill sluice), but turn right on the riverside path. You will see Tudorbethan-style Stedham Hall on the opposite bank – the path leaves the river and reaches a road at Stedham. Turn left, over the bridge; turn right immediately after, on a track (before doing this you might like to detour ahead to **Stedham church**, turning left at the first junction; in the churchyard, the hollow yew is thought to be 2,500 years old, while against the church are Saxon or pre-Saxon stone tombs, and remnants of Saxon crosses are embedded into the wall near the porch). The track follows the river for a section, then continues between fences, finally keeping left along a driveway as signposted. Keep straight on just past the cottage on the right where the driveway bends left, down a short cobbled path.

❹ Emerge on the lane at **Iping**, turn right over the river then left through the churchyard, finding an entrance into a field at the far side of the churchyard. Make for a signposted gate in the far left corner, near the river, then continue in this direction in the next field, at the end of which go over a footbridge slightly to the right and carry on just to the left of a triangular red-tiled roof (you may need to unhitch an electric fence – perfectly safe if you use the handle around the wire), carry on through the next field and then on round the left side of a farm and to the road, emerging opposite **Chithurst church**. This medieval building stands on an ancient mound; it has changed little since the 11th century, apart from some windows installed two centuries later; there's no electricity inside.

5 Turn right up the lane where you emerged opposite the church; this goes up between steeply incised sandstone banks, then bends right. Keep right at the next junction, soon passing the grounds of **Chithurst Buddhist Monastery**, a Theravada Buddhist residence for monks and nuns, who practise living in harmony 'through ethical guidelines, meditation and community work'. Drop into woods, then just before the bridge, turn left on the signposted path; the woods are owned by the monastery, and there are meditation huts in them, although you are more likely to see prayer flags attached to trees; to the right you shortly glimpse a **hammer pond**, beautifully set to the right.

6 Reach a road, turn right and immediately right again on a descending track (red arrow waymarker). Ignore side turns, and keep to the main track, eventually passing a house and reaching a road by Robins Farm. Turn right on the road and immediately left on a track marked with red arrows, soon rising through woodland, keeping right by a cattle grid, still ascending. Through a gate into a field, keep right along the edge (red arrow marker), then at the corner near a house turn left inside the field, then right 100 yards later by a signpost, along the right edge: views of the South Downs extend westwards to Chanctonbury Ring and beyond. Drop through an area of bracken, over two stiles close together near a cottage, keep left as signposted, then at the end of the field turn left on a track past Bowley Farm, dropping gently. Keep left at an oblique T-junction (where another track joins sharp right).

7 Reach a fork of tracks in front of a house with shutters at Titty Hill, and bear right (red waymarker). Keep to the main track, through woods (look out on the right for a spectacular oak tree, evidently coppiced a very long time ago) and after ¹/₂ mile into the open. Turn right at a track junction, through a field to Slathurst Farm, where the track bends right by the last building, then soon left across another field.

8 At a road, turn right along it, soon passing the Redford village sign. Take the first left, a metalled driveway leading up past the village hall. Follow the fence on the left a few yards further until forking as signposted half right uphill, over a plank bridge – the path crosses a driveway and continues ahead to reach a red tile-hung house called Barnett's Cottage. Turn left here, not on any of the signposted paths but up the steepest path leading up to the ridge, and to the highest ground. This eventually emerges into open bracken, and past a well-sited bench.

9 You soon pass the **trig point pillar** on the left, by another bench, as the **views** open out spectacularly across to the South Downs. The path is very clear here as it runs round the contour of the hill just below the trees to another signpost. Turn left, then immediately right on the small road. At a National Trust sign for Woolbeding Common, turn left through a **car park**, and follow signposts. 300 yards later, turn right near the edge of the woods at a T-junction with a broad track, and follow this back to the car park at the end of the lane where you started.

⑯ Petworth

The grand house backs straight on to this handsome small town, rather ignoring it – as do, sadly, many house visitors who are unaware of the treats in store. The traffic is really offputting and challenging, but you can escape into some very attractive and blissfully quiet back streets and paths. This is an estate town on a grand scale, and those who worked on the Petworth House estate (known as the Leconfield Estate) lived either in the servants' quarters by the house or in estate cottages in the town, where the ubiquitous brown paint appears on front doors in some 400 houses built in the 19th century; note the numbering system, allocated not according to geography but according to when they first appeared on the rent records.

The **Market Square** is at the centre of things and has hosted markets since 1541 and an annual fair in November since 1189. On it stands Leconfield Hall, the town hall, which sports a replica of a bust of William III by Dutch sculptor Honore Pelle; the extremely precious original is now found in Petworth House. Leading off from there is cobbled **Lombard Street**, the hub of the town's upmarket antiques trade.

Lombard Street re-emerges into the traffic opposite the **church of St Mary**. Much altered inside and out, it was restored by Charles Barry (of Houses of Parliament fame), and comprises an odd mixture of brick and stone, with a blue barrel-vaulted ceiling. A marble statue commemorates George O'Brien, 3rd Earl of Egremont, one of the great artists' patrons, who was instrumental in bringing JMW Turner to Petworth in the 1820s. Rather more architectural fun than the church is Barry's proposterously twiddly iron '**obelisk**' – opposite the church and near the entrance to Lombard Street – of 1851, topped by a street lamp, erected as a thanksgiving to Lord Leconfield who brought the town its gas lighting.

From near the obelisk, Bartons Lane leads down to the edge of town, where you can continue to the right along a scenic tarmacked path known as **Round-the-Hills** that contours round above the top of the Shimmings valley – a delicious rural outlook. Where it rejoins the town near the Roman Catholic Church, cross over the main road and explore some of the streets built for Petworth's huge servant force. **Egremont Row** in Angel Street was built to a higher specification than was the norm, and the builder was sacked for being so extravagant. Close by in blissfully tranquil Grove Street is **Percy Terrace**, with its strikingly tall chimneys. Further along at 346 High Street, in **Petworth Cottage Museum** (*01798 342100; open Apr–Oct, daily except Mon unless a bank holiday, afternoon only*) you can get a good idea how the servants lived. It is the former home of Mrs Mary Cummings who worked at the house and lived here from 1901 to 1930. The cottage has been furnished as it might have looked in her time, with gas lighting, a cooking range and a little cottage garden. Mrs Cummings ended her days in the striking Dutch-gabled building in North Street, an almshouse provided by the Leconfield Estate for elderly tenants.

Food and drink

Badgers ✆01798 342651. Gastropub outside Petworth on the A285, with a decent choice of food; adjacent to the Old Railway Station.

Lombards Lombard St ✆01798 344264. Cheery town-centre café offering light meals, coffee and tea; sit inside or out in the yard at the back.

Old Railway Station Petworth GU28 0JF ✆01798 342346
✆🛏 www.old-station.co.uk. See page 39. As well being as a memorable place to stay, this period gem of 1892, with its Pullman carriages and opulent waiting room, is open for morning coffee and afternoon tea to non-residents – inside or out on the platform. It is just off the A285 a mile or so south of Petworth, immediately south of the River Rother – turn off by the Badgers pub.

A grim reminder

Next to the Court House by Grove Street, a seemingly unexceptional wall encloses a small car parking bay. The bricks in the wall have been reused from the Petworth House of Correction. You can see re-used bricks carved with the names of prisoners from this locally notorious prison, built in the late 18th century at a time when offences such as theft could lead to transportation to the colonies or hanging. It was a very nasty place to be incarcerated. If you were a vagrant or petty felon, you might have had a term of hard labour and solitary confinement here to deliver 'short sharp shocks'.

Petworth Park

There's free access to this vast space in daylight hours, and there are several ways in. From the town side, you can walk down North Street (just below the church until the estate offices around the Cowyard (so-called because it used to house the park's celebrated cattle): on the far side of this, a tunnel leads through ornamental gates and into the park itself.

This is landscaping on a hugely ample scale: 700 acres landscaped by Capability Brown in the naturalistic English tradition that improved on nature itself. Dotted with specimen trees, the grass gives the illusion of being on a plateau that runs into the distant Downs. The largest herd of fallow deer in

Britain roams freely. Then the quite understated classical frontage of the house gives straight on to the parkland – with no formal gardens on that side.

Petworth House

The interior of Petworth House (*01798 343929; www.nationaltrust.org.uk; open Sat–Wed; closed most of Nov–early Mar*) is much grander and less restrained than its exterior suggests and contains the finest art collection in any National Trust property. Turner was a guest here, painting and fishing in the lake, and Petworth has many of his works, along with those of others including Van Dyck, Titian, Gainsborough, Bosch and Blake. The **Marble Hall** has genuine Roman statuary, with the Grand Staircase rising past murals of Prometheus and Pandora in trompe l'oeil style like stage scenery. The **Carved Room** is so named for the virtuoso wood carving by the incomparable Grinling Gibbons – such is its courageous delicacy and three-dimensionality that it almost looks as if it were wrought in metal, the details dripping with musical instruments, cherubs, lace, birds, beads and flowers. Turner's view of the park hangs opposite the point from which it was painted, and rather incongruously below Earl Seymour with his gold pompom shoes.

The hub of the art collection is in the **North Wing Art Gallery**, begun in 1754 and extended in the 1820s. The style of top lighting and paintings hung

The Mens and Ebernoe Common

Two very special Sussex Wildlife Trust woodland nature reserves are found close to Petworth. By the A272 northeast of town, **The Mens**, named after an Anglo Saxon word for common land, comprises a wild, often muddy and decidedly disorienting area of ancient woodland: this is the best survival in Sussex of an area of unmanaged woodland, and is a superb place for looking for fungi, while the Badlands Meadows in the southeast part of the reserve are speckled with wildflowers in summer, including dyer's greenweed and lady's mantle. The Trust occasionally hold some fungus-spotting events here in autumn; see www.sussexwt.org.uk.

North of Petworth, **Ebernoe Common** is another place to lose yourself in (literally). A prized area of low Weald woodland, it has 14 out of 16 of the native species of bats, including the rare barbastelle and Bechstein's varieties, and is prized for its lichens and mosses as well as purple emperor butterflies. The area was used for centuries as a wood pasturing ground by locals, where cattle and pigs would graze, and was also a hive of rural industry, with a pond used in the 16th century to power an iron furnace and a preserved moulding shed and kiln of a small brick work, dating to at least 1678 and now a scheduled ancient monument. A heritage trail threads through the reserve.

one above the other against dark-red walls is similar to that of London's Dulwich Picture Gallery, designed by Sir John Soane in 1811 as England's first public art gallery. As a lifelong friend of Turner, Soane may well have been involved in designing the Petworth extension. The north bay of the gallery was designed around John Flaxman's *St Michael overcoming Satan*, where the saint is about to spear the serpentine tail (completed in 1826, the year of Flaxman's death). Look out for the depiction of a fête held at Petworth for the poor in 1835, when 6,000 were fed at tables laid in three semi-circles on the lawn.

Wander across a back yard to the block containing the fascinating **kitchen and servants' quarters**. That isn't the way the domestic staff would have gone, though: they used steep steps to take a tunnel across to the house, thus keeping them discreetly out of sight as well as necessitating a lot of carting stuff up and down the stairs. Light and airy, the kitchens were cutting-edge in the late Victorian period, and were in use until World War II; the huge gas cookers date from the 1920s. In all they contain about 2,000 brass and copper vessels, now cleaned once a year by volunteers – a gargantuan task that takes two months.

A country walk into the Leconfield Estate from Petworth

Within three miles, this short route takes you out from central Petworth into the working estate for Petworth House: it's an aspect of the town and its hinterland that many visitors never see, but the views over the estate, and the estate village of Byworth (with its pub), are special qualities, and at the end you pass the estate houses in Petworth and the Petworth Cottage Museum.

1 From the main car park in the centre of Petworth, exit into Golden Square near the loo block and go into the Market Square, past HSBC Bank (on the right) and the town hall (on the left). Head towards the church along **Lombard Street**, turn right at the end by Charles Barry's splendid **obelisk/lamp standard**, then right into Bartons Lane. Go down to a path junction with a big view ahead over the estate. Go ahead: you can see the line of the old London Road, rising up the spine of the hill, to the right of the hedgerow and up to the wooded summit of Gog and Magog hill.

The path heads down the left side of the field to an old stone bridge (it's easiest to arc out to the right and back rather than going straight down). It is not very defined on the ground, but keep to the hedgerow on your left uphill. Look behind for a **fine view** of Petworth town and house. In winter you may see polo ponies grazing in the fields.

After a stile by a gate, the hedgerow ends: continue in the same direction (following waymarkers for the Serpent Trail), passing to the left of a small recently planted enclosure of trees. A red roofed building comes into view with a power post below and just to the left of it – the stile is found just to the left of the power post.

❷ The path carries up a woodland strip known as Lovers' Lane and emerges on a track corner by a sign for **Brinkshole Heath**, an area of bracken, birch coppice, holly and pheasant rearing. Go forward (keeping to the right) and follow marker arrows (initially with a field close by to the right). After the field ends on the right you can glimpse Goanah Lodges (also known as **Gog and Magog Lodges**) to the right, near the power post on the right). Keep forward at the next two track junctions, then go sharp right 70 yards later, heading towards the Lodges. If you look back here towards Petworth you see a remarkable **vista of Petworth House**. The route then bends left shortly before the Lodges and leaves the woodland, descending, with a fine view of the South Downs.

❸ Just after some barns on the left, keep forward over a stile where the track bends right, and now follow the path down the middle of the field, passing to the right of the nearest, lone tree. Cross a stile, turn right along pavement by A283 for 30 yards, then cross the road carefully to take signposted stile opposite. Walk to the far bottom corner of the field, to find a gate and stile, leading down through a tiny field with gate to a road in the hamlet of **Byworth**. Note the numbers into 370s – this is still that Petworth estate paint and numbering; the cottages are variously tile-hung, stone and half-timbered.

❹ Turn right along the road, then by an old cottage on left sporting Hovis sign (where the road bends right; the Black Horse Inn is a few yards further on left along this road); take the signposted footpath down a driveway to the left. Carry on down to cross a stream (by a stone slab bridge marking the supposed site of a **holy well**), carry on along a fenced path and, on entering a field, turn left along its bottom edge, passing some ponds on your left.

❺ At the next path junction go left downhill to cross the stream by a bridge. Turn right at a T-junction of paths (10 yards up) on the other side, then through a kissing-gate and half left at the next junction (30 yards later), on a path rising towards houses. At the top of the slope, go forward at a crossing of paths, on a path between fences, with houses on your right.

❻ Emerge at edge of Petworth, with **New Grove House** (where Grinling Gibbons stayed) in view to your left. Turn right along the road, past **Percy Terrace** with its tall chimney stacks, Rosemary Lane and the **Petworth Cottage Museum** to reach the town centre.

Black Horse Byworth GU28 0HL ✆ 01798 342424

🕾 www.theblackhorsebyworth.com. Just outside Petworth, and on this walk in an extremely pretty estate village. The garden is a lovely place to sit and enjoy the food or one of their four real ales.

Into the Low Weald around the upper Arun

North of Amberley, the downland landscape rapidly morphs into the watermeadows around Pulborough. Watermeadows are often confused with any general bog-standard flat field, or any standard boggy field – but there's a key difference. Systems of sluices and water-filled ditches can control when the whole lot is deliberately flooded to enrich the farmland with super-fertile river silt. Thus at certain times of year the whole valley is a splashy-looking wetland: it can look at its absolute best in winter. The profusion of bird and plant life makes this a prized pocket of countryside. I first heard about it through the piano music of John Ireland (1875–1962), who lived for many years in Sussex and wrote a hauntingly pastoral Downland Suite for orchestra. His *Amberley Wild Brooks* is a gorgeous and undeservedly unknown impressionist piece full of watery ornament. The tract of land after which it is named merges into the meadows of **Pulborough Brooks RSPB Reserve**, of year-round interest for its wildlife.

⑰ Loxwood

For a good part of the 19th century you could have travelled by boat from London to Arundel, by way of Weybridge, Guildford and Pulborough and using the 23-mile Wey and Arun Junction Canal that linked the rivers Wey and Arun. The canal closed in 1871, and gradually turned into a wilderness, and its glory days were rapidly forgotten. Today the Wey and Arun Canal Trust (*www.weyandarun.co.uk*), formed in the early 1970s by a band of enthusiasts, has embarked on a huge programme of restoring it while keeping its rich range of wildlife habitats; weeds have been cleared, bridges and locks rebuilt, and stretches made navigable.

The best vantage point for this impressive industrial relic is from the bridge by the Onslow Arms on the southern edge of Loxwood (there's a large public car park just behind the pub). The eastward stretch of the canal (on the pub side of the road) has been restored and boat trips run at weekends and on bank holidays from mid April until October. On the other side of the road you can see a restored lock, and further along is the Devil's Hole, an abandoned oxbow section of canal that was created as an attempt to bypass a slope. Nature soon takes over as you proceed this way, and the canal water eventually disappears. Another notable stretch of this canal is at New Bridge, west of Billingshurst.

They're always on the look-out for volunteers to help the project: all ages, 16 to 75, and all levels of skill welcome. See the website for details.

⑱ Nutbourne Vineyard

There are not many places in Britain where you can stand in a windmill tasting wine from grapes grown yards away and look out to a glorious view. Nutbourne Vineyard (*Gay St, Pulborough RH20 2HE; 01798 815196; follow the brown signs from the A283 just east of Pulborough*) is one: the tasting room is in a sail-less tower mill, and the distant view of the South Downs escarpment is one to drink in at leisure. Bridget and Peter Gladwyn admit they weren't looking for a vineyard when they started property-hunting in the area a few years back, but the scenic qualities of this one (which they then enlarged) persuaded them to take up wine production. They have backgrounds in catering – Peter runs the prestigious Just St James' restaurant in London. Bridget took a viticulture course at Plumpton College near Lewes, and had considerable help from Nyetimbers vineyard nearby. Their three boys help with the harvest, spraying and digging holes.

You can just turn up and wander round yourself for no charge, and try a free tasting of their excellent wines – *Sussex Reserve* ('dry, fragrant, with delicate citrus fruit characteristics') *Blush* (an 'aromatic, summery rosé'), *Bacchus* ('crisp and fresh with an elderflower bouquet') and sparkling *Nutty Brut*. For pre-arranged groups there are tours at a set price. 'We tell them about growing systems, what happens on the build-up to harvest. We go round the lakes, meet our llamas and alpacas. Then I set up a tasting and a buffet supper.' For the October harvest they get in local pickers, and bird-deterring goes big time: 'plastic hawks, anything that floats in the air, glittery things and bird scarers'.

⑲ Pulborough Brooks

One of the most accessible parts of the water meadows of the Arun Valley, this large RSPB reserve (*Wiggonholt, Pulborough RH20 2EL; 01798 875851; www.rspb.org.uk*) just south of Pulborough is one of Sussex's great wetlands, but also includes an area of small copses and hedgerow-lined fields; it is home to at least 160 species of birds, butterflies, insects and mammals. The natural wetlands have been carefully managed and nurtured to provide a thriving wildlife haven, by controlling the flooding on the wet grassland, grazing cattle, cutting hay and cleaning out the ditches to maintain the right conditions for wetland birds and plantlife. The woodland areas have partly been coppiced, and heathland has been regenerated by removing scrub, bracken and conifers and planting heather seed to provide more habitat for birds such as nightjars.

You can hire binoculars at the visitor centre, where chatty volunteers are on hand to explain what to look for. They're at pains for visitors not to feel out of their depth; one explained to me 'it gives me a real buzz to see kids full of enthusiasm having spotted an adder or a dragonfly'. Introductory talks and walks are held year round. In winter there are huge numbers of wintering duck, geese and swans here. Summer is particularly good for butterflies and dragonflies, and in the evening you may hear owls and nightjars, while spring sees wading birds breeding here. The walk around the reserve is a scenic pleasure in itself, with watery views extending towards Pulborough village, and fallow deer often in evidence. Strategically placed hides make excellent vantage points and the café is good value.

⑳ Hardham

This tiny village, off the A29 just southwest of Pulborough, has Roman origins as a road station on the Roman route known as Stane Street; Roman bricks and tiles from a nearby camp have been reused in the building of the **church of St Botolph**. Thought to be of Saxon origins – some of its round-arched windows may date from then – this remarkable building has the earliest near-complete set of medieval wall paintings of any English church. They were created around 1100, and although they have faded it is still possible to pick out the details, including the Torments of Hell on the west wall, the Nativity on the south wall and the Flight into Egypt on the north wall. Clearest of all is the Picasso-esque depiction of Adam and Eve on the west wall of the chancel. The fact that up to 1866 the whole lot had been covered over with plaster for many years has probably kept them looking relatively fresh.

Beside the A283 west from Pulborough and spanning the River Arun, **Stopham Bridge** is perhaps Sussex's most venerable span, built in stone in 1423 to replace an earlier wooden structure. Its central arch was raised in 1822 to allow boats to pass beneath. The bridge is closed to traffic, which now crosses the modern adjacent  bridge; there is an area where you can park and walk across. Further north, a house called Brinkwells (not open to the public) near **Fittleworth** was where Sir Edward Elgar took refuge from 1917 to 1921 and wrote his piano quintet, string quartet, violin sonata and part of his cello concerto.

The lower Arun Valley

The Arun wiggles its way sluggishly through one of the largest surviving systems of watermeadows in Sussex between **Amberley** and **Arundel**. Arundel Castle is what most tourists come to look at, and formidably impressive it is too, but many miss what lies close by – including some treasured bird reserves, and one of the most absorbing ways of finding out about the industrial past in the form of the **Amberley Museum**. A well presented museum in the Old School at **Storrington** (*www.storringtonmuseum.org*) covers local history in the area; it is free, but only open on Wednesdays and at weekends.

South of Arundel is less special, but you might like to venture out to the beach south of **Climping** for one of those rare stretches of undeveloped Sussex coast; it's between Littlehampton and Middleton-on-Sea (the latter being on the easternmost arm of Bognor Regis). The beach, backed by low dunes, is a refreshing place for a stroll, with the hamlet of **Atherington** being the best starting point, and it's pretty nice for a swim if you don't mind the pebbles. You get a good idea how a lot of the undeveloped Sussex seaside must have looked before the 20th century.

㉑ Parham House and Gardens

As you approach through the deer park via the main driveway, what is immediately apparent is the setting of this Elizabethan mansion beneath the South Downs (*Storrington, near Pulborough RH20 4HS; 01903 742021; www.parhaminsussex.co.uk; open Easter Sunday–30 September, Wed, Thu, Sun and Bank Holiday Mon, plus Tue and Fri in Aug; house open 14.00–17.00, gardens 12.00–17.00 Tue–Sun and bank holiday Mon; teas, lunches, garden shop with home-grown plants*). The house in its full glory only appears at the last minute; it dates from 1577 and has always been a family home, although the family do not live in the part of the house that you see. The panelled, plaster-ceilinged Great Hall has changed little over the years, and the smaller rooms contain choice examples of needlework, paintings and furniture. At the top of the house the Long Gallery has a fascinating array of curios and an exhibition about the Pearson family and the wartime evacuees.

The glorious **walled garden** can be visited separately. From the driveway you can just get a glimpse of it over the walls, which give not only privacy but also protection against the salt-laden winds blowing up from the sea. The natural soil is almost entirely sand here, but centuries of careful composting and manuring have created a fertile paradise inside. The garden layout dates from the 1920s, but the planting was transformed from the 1980s. The garden has been described as a series of interlocking pictures, woven into each other with a tapestry-like effect. The opulent mixed borders are planted in a 'wild and woolly' style in the English Romantic tradition and supply the cut flowers for decorating the House. In one corner the Wendy House is a favourite feature of the gardens, a child-scale house set into a brick wall. It was built in the 1920s for the Pearsons' three daughters, and has two storeys, a fireplace and a wooden parquet floor.

Parham's **events** include the Sussex Country Fair in mid June and a garden weekend in July and autumn foraging in October; there's also a programme of day **courses** linked to Parham themes such as embroidery, flower arranging and the history of the house.

Even when the house and gardens are closed, simply strolling through the **estate** is very enjoyable. The deer park and woodlands shelter over 300 deer, herons (nesting in the northwest part of the estate), woodland birds, and many rare insects and lichens. This is very much a landscape evolved over many generations by the owners (currently the Barnards) and estate team at Parham. Some of the ancient oaks in the park date back 600 years. The 1987 storm devastated much of the estate, bringing down many trees in its wake – some 80,000 trees and saplings came down, and 20-odd years on you can still see the damage to many of those which survived. Fortuitously this turned out to be the making of the estate as an important wildlife sanctuary. From that time on they have deliberately allowed any fallen or cut wood from ageing or damaged trees to decay and a new ecosystem has grown up up.

Some years back I spoke to Richard Edwards, then the Parham Estate Manager, who had vivid memories of the storm. 'You could hear the wind coming up like an express train roaring, and a barn next door collapsed and we didn't hear it. It took us three days to cut our way out of the Park. You couldn't see the drive – it was all covered with trees. In the end we hired a helicopter to assess the damage. We had to bring in contractors from Scotland and Yorkshire and the Gurkhas to clear the trees. When we replanted we could leave wider spaces between the plantations to make sunny corridors for butterflies so there were some good effects.'

Each year between February and May herons return to the heronry on the northwest side of the estate to breed. The trees are also, rather unusually, the home for greylag geese, who nest well out of foxes' reach; woodland birds include nuthatches, tree creepers, nightjars and all three species of woodpecker. Winter sees cormorants and mandarin ducks on the estate. At Parham they're also rather proud of being one of a very few release sites for **field crickets**, which are bred at London Zoo and have taken to the well-drained, sandy soil and south-facing slopes You might hear these now very rare insects during late afternoon or early evening in May and June when they 'sing' at the entrance to their barrows to attract a mate.

Near the house entrance is an 18th-century **dovecote** – where several hundred pigeons and doves kept for their eggs, meat and feathers nested. Close by, a door set into a grassy slope marks the entrance to the **ice house** – ice from the lake when it froze in winter was brought here by a chain of estate workers. The underground chamber, insulated by the earth around it, was cool enough to keep ice cold all summer; it would have been full of grit, leaves and worse though, so was not put directly into food and drinks. It's now a protected habitat for bats.

On the downland side of the house, the **church** is thought to date from Tudor times but was rebuilt in the 1800s and furnished with box pews made of yew wood. The family pew has a private fireplace and the 14th-century lead font is a rarity for being inscribed with lettering. Beyond lies an idyllic **cricket pitch**, used by the local team; in former days the estate mustered enough workers to form a team themselves.

There has been a **fallow deer herd** since 1628: unusually, they are rather darker coloured than you may see elsewhere. There are over 300 of them, with seven does to each buck. Fawns are born in June and hidden in clumps of grass by their mothers for two or three days until they are strong enough to walk. Never approach one (if the fawn smells of human the mother will reject it), and keep a safe distance from rutting bucks in October when you may hear them clashing antlers. The estate has to manage the herd to keep the numbers down, balanced between does and bucks and generally healthy; there's a humane cull by shooting each year in February and September. If this was not done, the condition of the herd would deteriorate and more bucks would be injured through rutting. The most oft-shot beast is beside the house in the form of an iron 'target stag' on wheels which came from Lady Emma Barnard's family home in Ireland. It would have been pulled by ropes and used for shooting practice.

High fliers

Adjacent to the Parham estate, the **Southdown Gliding Club** offers gliding instruction every weekend and on Wednesdays. Beginners can take a two-day or five-day course, or have a trial lesson in which you're towed up and then the engine is switched off and the controls are handed over to you until the instructor takes care of the landing. It's a strange, marvellous sensation of being over the landscape, at a normal maximum speed of around 50 knots; vertigo, curiously, is rarely a problem. The situation by the South Downs assists gliding considerably, allowing the aircraft to 'hill-soar'. This is historic gliding terrain: it was from Amberley Mount on June 27 1909 that the world's first recorded soaring flight by glider was made, in a glider made by a French artist José Weiss who was living in Amberley; the pilot was just 17.

Parham Airfield RH20 4HP ☎ 01903 742137 ✆ www.SGC1.org. You can take a trial lesson of 20–30 minutes for £90; two further lessons within a three-month period thereafter for £75. Weather permitting it is always possible to turn up on the day and get a lesson (they have a booking scheme for Fridays in summer).

㉒ Amberley

Ranged around a grid of quiet streets is this improbably perfect-looking village where thatch predominates on the rooftops and the stone walls are set off by a parade of carefully tended cottage gardens (with an 'open garden' event in June on even-numbered years). It always astonishes me that it's not better known. The Old Bake House, Old Postings and Old Brew House hint at a more industrious past, but thankfully the village is still very much a living community, with two good pubs, lots of local organisations, a school, a village shop stacked with Sussex produce and an excellent tearoom. Probably founded by Bishop de Luffa (founder of Chichester Cathedral), **St Michael's Church** has vestiges of a wall painting but is more striking for its Norman work, with a huge chancel arch bearing palm-tree ornamentation, and a rare iron hour-glass stand above the pulpit. Close by the church in a former United Reformed Chapel is **Amberley Village Pottery** (closed Wednesdays), where a showroom at the back has local-made jams and chutneys as well as ceramics.

Beyond the church a dead-end lane slopes down to the marshy dragonfly-populated flats of the watermeadows known as **Amberley Wild Brooks** ('wild' deriving from 'weald'), where the formidable curtain wall of **Amberley Castle**, now a very upmarket hotel, towers over a scene vaguely suggestive of some little lost paradise somewhere in rural France. You'll see a track (very muddy in winter, beware) heading north across the Wild Brooks, which was nearly drained and converted into conventional farmland some years back, to much (thankfully successful) local protest; there aren't a great many public footpaths hereabouts, and it's well worth the docile wander along this track a couple of miles to **Greatham Bridge**, a series of wonky arches dating from the 16th century and an idyllic picnic spot on the river banks, with fleets of Bewick's swans patrolling the Arun. Above the village, the Downs are virtually treeless, and the views along the South Downs Way is quite terrific, with **Amberley Mount** making a rewarding objective.

Close by Greatham Bridge, **Greatham Church**, a simple Norman building, has been restored but is remarkably untouched overall: no road leads to it, just a grassy track, and it's lit by oil lamps and served by a harmonium.

Amberley Museum

Allow yourself most of a day for this fascinating, large-scale and extremely unusual industrial museum adjacent to the South Downs Way (*Amberley Station, BN18 9LT; 01798 831370; www.amberleymuseum.co.uk*). It's variously a huge industrial relic, a nature reserve, a community of craftspeople and a collection of all sorts representing industry in the Southeast over the centuries. It occupies a chalk pit where chalk was quarried from the 1840s to the 1960s and burnt here in the kilns to make lime for mortar and for agricultural fertiliser – then the biggest operation of its kind anywhere in the country. For most of that period it was run by Pepper & Son, whose name is still emblazoned on the gates by the main road. Thanks to massive volunteer efforts it opened to the public in 1979. The kilns and site railway now form part of the site.

This has to be one of the most serendipitous museums I've seen. Much of the pleasure of being here is just nosing around the huge array of all things industrial, much of it organised into a series of display buildings, and full of curios of various periods to chance upon – a phone box with a stamp machine integrated into it, a brickyard drying shed, an ancient AA box and a bodgers' camp recreating the world of itinerant pole lathers who made furniture in the Chiltern woods up to the 19th century. Above all it gives the impression of being a real industrial site, and a lot of it is work in progress, with all manner of restorations taking place. Among its contents are some great rarities, including Britain's only working steam crane, which on occasions is put through its paces to lift items and load them on to wagons.

Of the museums-within-the-museum, some are tiny like the bagmender's shed, others seriously time-consuming such as the Electricity Hall with its wondrous selection of antique appliances, the transplanted Southdown Bus Garage with its vintage buses and advertising boards promising trips to Michelham Priory or Bodiam Castle, and a Connected Earth Telecommunications Hall comprising 'the most complete collection of telephone instruments and overhead line insulators in the country'. Vintage buses and narrow-gauge trains take foot-weary visitors round the site.

The chatty staff help make this a day not to rush. They are true aficionados: one maintains the extraordinary collection of wirelesses, while others make a living working on the site, repairing bicycles in the Cycle Repair Shop, carrying out woodturning, making stained glass, creating traditional besoms from silver-birch twigs or heather, or operating the print works where they'll show you the hot metal process, explain the vintage presses and print you out a certificate or sell you a print. Weekends are often the liveliest times to visit, with numerous special events, many centred around transport themes – vintage cars, motorcycles, buses and so on.

The site has an unexpected physical beauty, with its once gleaming white chalk cliffs now atmospherically overgrown with all sorts of species. Wild orchids are here in abundance, and there are 129 types of fungi, 24 species of butterfly and peregrine falcons nesting in a secret spot on the cliff. The tunnel in the quarry harbours four species of bats, and you can follow a trail up to the top of the White Pit for a view over the South Downs. The museum depends on voluntary effort and has an army of some 400 volunteers who spend their days on all sorts of restoration and other tasks.

Food and drink

Two useful pub options, one in the village and one just outside. The **Black Horse** (✆ *01798 831552*), right in the centre, has a spacious garden, while the **Sportsman's Arms** (✆ *01798 831787; turn right by the Black Horse, and it's ¹/₂ mile along the road*) has a conservatory with a magnificent view of the Amberley Wild Brooks, as well as Sussex beers like Harveys and Dark Star. Both places offer bar meals. The independent **village shop** has home-made sandwiches and local pork pies as well as Sussex produce.

  Amberley Village Tearoom The Square ✆ 01798 839196. Thoroughly cheerful village-centre tearoom in a converted 17th-century slaughterhouse (with old meat-hooks in evidence), with plenty of rustic character and a front courtyard with tables, pots of flowers from the garden, and a woodburner for chillier months. Homemade cakes made by Sue and her family, biscuits and orange cordial, loose-leaf tea, clotted cream teas, local jam, specially roasted coffee, speciality teas and a general emphasis on locally sourced or fairtrade products – all served in or on items made in the village pottery. Two dogs, two more aloof cats and maybe a friendly blackbird are on the premises. Closed Wed, and weekdays in winter.

㉓ Arundel

With its castle and cathedral crowning an abrupt rise in the downs, this most pleasing of small towns has a French look to it from a distance. The castle deserves plenty of time in itself, but there's much pleasure to be had from a walk up the main street, and into the handsome side streets – such as Maltravers and Tarrant streets – along the river and through Arundel Park (free access), the wider estate of the castle itself. A day here passes very pleasantly, with a potter around the town's shops, a visit to the castle and Wetlands Centre, a walk around the river and a swim in the scenically sited Arundel Lido.

The **rail station** is slightly out of things, but less than ten minutes' walk to the centre; it does involve crossing the unpleasant A27 by traffic lights and then wandering along a suburban road, but soon gets better. For **parking**, the best bet is to turn off the A27 at the easternmost of the two roundabouts, then turn right as soon as you cross the river – there's lots of free parking along Mill Road (right along to the Arundel Wetland Centre and beyond, and you can get into Arundel Park from here), which saves you parking in town.

At the top of the town, vertical, spiky and flamboyant, the 19th-century **Roman Catholic Cathedral** designed by Joseph Hansom (of hansom cab fame) sets off the skyline alongside the castle in a recreation of the French Gothic style of the 1400s. The dedication is to St Philip Howard, the 20th Earl of Arundel (1557–95), who is portrayed in a 1986 stained-glass window with his wife and dog, and whose remains are here too. He was once a favourite of Elizabeth I, fell from her favour after rediscovering his Catholic faith and died after being kept in the Tower of London for 11 years along with his faithful dog.

Along Mill Road, Arundel continues with its Little France look: a shady avenue invites picnics, and off it is a tea garden by a very prettily kept putting green. At the town end, near the bridge and ruins of a priory, **Arundel Boatyard** (*01903 882609; www.rivearuncruises.com*) runs 45-minute cruises along the river to the Black Rabbit pub just north of town, from which you can either return on the boat or wander back alongside the road. They also hire self-drive motorboats by the hour, for up to six people. Near the opposite bank is the **Arundel Lido** (late May to early September), where the castle provides a choice backdrop for swimmers, sunbathers and paddlers. Lidos are something of an endangered species, and this one – opened as the Fitzalan Pool in 1960 following a donation of land by the Duke of Norfolk to celebrate the 21st birthday of his eldest daughter – nearly became history after closure by the council in 1999. A group of dedicated locals recognised its very special qualities and set up the charitable Arundel and Downland Community Leisure Trust to rescue it. The paddling pool was the first stage of the rescue act, and then the main pool was reduced in size to 25 metres (with a 5-metre splash pool at one end) and heated. The crowds of people here on warm summer days testify to its lasting popularity.

Arundel Museum's History Store currently operates from a portacabin within Mill Road car park, until such time as they find a permanent home; only a fraction of what they have is shown, on a rotating basis (free entry).

Arundel Castle

A startling sight from whichever way you approach it, Arundel Castle (*01903 882173; www.arundelcastle.org; open Apr–Oct, Tue–Sun and bank holiday Mon*) looks almost too good to be true. Its battlemented form sprawls across half a hillside above the little town in a grand gesture of feudalism. What you see is largely Victorian, but that hardly detracts from its emotional impact. It is thought to have inspired Gormenghast, the sprawling universe of a castle in Mervyn Peake's novels, and has been used for the setting of various films including *The Madness of King George.*

The big restoration work was carried out in the 1870s–90s by the Dukes of Norfolk, whose ancestors have owned it since 1138. All is improbably smooth, grey stone, complete with battlements and turrets. If you ignore the obvious 19th-century details it gives a very good impression of how a medieval castle might have looked when new. And in any case, the Victorian revamp is very much part of its character.

Few other houses have such a long continuous occupation. It was founded on Christmas Day in 1067 by Roger de Montgomery, Earl of Arundel, one of William the Conqueror's associates. In the 16th century it passed to the Howards of Norfolk, who were Royalists in the Civil War and temporarily lost it to Cromwell in 1643. In that conflict the defences were destroyed, and the castle lay in ruins. Several rebuilds followed, including an extravagant revamp by Thomas Howard, the 8th Duke, and apartments, art and furnishings added by the 13th Duke.

Within the structure is the mechanism for the portcullis and the original medieval keep, giving a tremendous view over the coastal plain (when it was built, the sea would have been much closer). In contrast to the austerity of the oldest part, the residential portion of the castle has almost too much for the eye to take in. It all conjures up a great sense of dynastic continuity, with family portraits and photos from various centuries up to the present. The cavernous

Great Hall accommodates an entertaining array of seemingly unrelated bits and pieces – a sedan chair, lion-skin rug, portraits of cardinals, a sleigh, and German silver figures of an orchestra with nodding heads. Another room has three Canalettos, while the spare rooms still used for guests boast high Victorian comfort with baskets of logs, armchairs by the fire, great deep baths, and Turners and Constables displayed on the walls. Electric light was installed in the 1890s – all the switches and lamps are of gothic design and are quite a feature in themselves.

The Dukes of Norfolk never renounced their Catholic allegiance; several were executed for treason and had land confiscated, yet they have remained second in the nobility ladder. One of their number presented a whole series of tasty female relatives to Henry VIII, including Anne Boleyn, her sister Mary and Catherine Howard; eventually even Henry lost patience and that Norfolk ended up being executed for plotting.

Accessed through the castle grounds, the family's **Fitzalan Chapel** is Catholic yet backs on to the Church of England parish church, with which it connects – a unique arrangement arising from the Dissolution: a metal grille and glass screen separate the two parts of the building. In 1977 it was opened for a combined service for the Week of Prayer for Christian Unity, the first time the whole building had been used for a combined act of worship since 1544; it has only been opened half a dozen times since. Among the family tombs within is an extraordinary cadaver sculpture of a decomposing corpse, depicted beneath the effigy of the 7th Earl who died in 1435.

WWT Arundel

Opened in 1976 on a marshy wetland of old watercress beds and beautifully tucked away by the river, under the shelter of the castle and its hanger of woods, this is one of nine Wildfowl and Wetlands Trust (WWT) sites across the country (*WWT Arundel Wetland Centre, Mill Rd, Arundel BN18 9PB; 01903 881525; www.wwt.org.uk*). It's a wondrous little world unto itself, a place to slow down, look, listen and thoroughly immerse yourself in the wildlife of this important reserve for wild birds and other wetland species, and allow birds to feed out of your hand. You do get a feeling of being part of the wider landscape though, with the castle and downs in view and the occasional train trundling across in mid-distance.

Electric boat tours are included in the price, and take up to eight people a time: these silent craft get close up to species, and close enough to the reeds for them to tickle you as you glide by. With so much that is easily spotted – including rare ducks and kingfishers – and binoculars available for hire, this suits the beginner as much as the aficionado, and disabled access is excellent, with wheelchair-accessible paths and boats; special events (booking necessary) include art workshops and 'sunrise safaris' by boat. The photographer Robert Plummer runs wildlife photography courses several weekends each year. There are also opportunities for volunteers; see the website for details.

At the entrance, the restaurant gives a fine panorama of the water (although it will be out of view for a period while they de-silt it). The reception area has a board announcing the day's events and lists of recent sightings. Before heading off on the boardwalks through the jungle-like reserve, you can buy special duck food here, which dutifully sinks in the water so ducks have to dive for it, and an observation chart that points out what you might see. Among the hides is a thatched camera obscura built by landscape artist Chris Drury, and rather like a miniature Sydney Opera House made out of reeds. Collection birds are kept under cover of netting, mostly to prevent other creatures getting in; they include the only two bronzewings on the WWT's nine reserves. Less glamorous are the corrugated sheets around the place which serve as grass-snake habitats. Each snake's markings are different, and each one they've found here is named after a staff member.

Most children are likely to be very happy here. As well as a Meadow Maze and a play area, there are a number of activities; Pat Warren, who showed me round, said the children particularly love feeding ducks by hand and pond dipping (available weekends May to September and daily during school holidays). The latter is a fascinating way of seeing a microscopic world open up – children take samples of pond water and the results are flashed up on a screen via a microscope; when I looked in, one small girl was very proud to have found a caddis fly lava and a water boatman.

Dormice in the Wetland Centre

The centre's ground manager Paul Stevens told me about an unexpected new arrival at Arundel in the form of the rare, internationally protected hazel or common dormouse, which first appeared in 2005. 'Before I started here, one of the ground staff was strimming the bank and found a hibernating mouse that didn't wake up. When we got someone to look at it, it had disappeared, but the fact it didn't wake up seemed to point towards a dormouse. It wasn't until I came here in 2008 that we started surveying for dormice and we had immediate success: within a month of putting up survey tubes we found two dormice making their haven there. Finding dormice in the reserve was unexpected as their usual habitat is associated with coppiced woodland. They have been found on different habitats, but to find them on a wetland was fantastic!' How many are there, and

can you see them? 'It's very difficult to gauge how many; we've seen at least seven individuals. They're very hard to see, sleeping six months of the year and being nocturnal, but they're all over the site.' Only registered handlers like Paul are legally permitted to touch this rare species.

Spring brings out the most eye-catching plumage, while late spring and early summer are the peak time for young birds, and further into summer the wetland wild flowers are at their best. During August birdlife quietens down, but dragonflies and butterflies are prolific. Autumn and winter bring migrant birds, and you have a better chance of seeing kingfishers in winter, when you might also witness birds sliding on the ice.

The reserve is constantly evolving. In 2005 they began a successful programme to increase the numbers of water voles in the valley; these were becoming very rare, and in 2009 trumpeter swans hatched two eggs, one of which survived – the first time trumpeters have bred here for 18 years. When I last visited, Sir Peter Scott Centenary Hide had just been created, with the aim of putting visitors in the heart of a breeding colony of sand martins; the centre expects all 300 holes will be full by 2016.

Walks from Arundel

The most straightforward stroll from Arundel is along the canalised River Arun from the bridge near the priory ruin and Mill Road car park. Paths lead on either side of the reed-fringed river; if you keep on the town (west) bank and walk with the river on your right, you can loop round just south of the Arundel Wetland Centre and back to the road after 1¹/₂ miles. Either return along the road to the start, or carry on through the gateway into Arundel Park (opposite and slightly right), where paths lead either side of **Swanbourne Lake**, an ornamental feature, at the far end of which the landscape becomes increasingly rural and less park-like; beyond the far end turn sharp left on a rising track, through a gate and turn right over the grass past Hiorne Tower and follow the estate road to the left to reach the top of the town again.

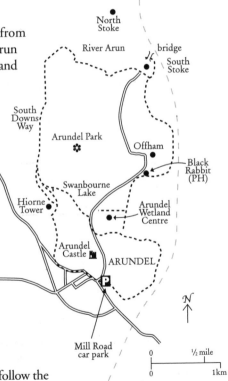

The South Downs Way takes a satisfying cross-section through **Arundel Park**, which undulates very pleasantly before dropping steeply through South Wood to the river; you could either carry on along the river to Amberley station for the train back to Arundel (a total of 5 miles) or walk back via South Stoke and the riverside path. Between South Stoke and North Stoke, the **suspension bridge** was happily rebuilt in 2009 after the original bridge had suffered storm damage.

The council intended to replace it with a bog-standard span but an Amberley villager had connections with the Gurkhas and persuaded them to organise a group of soldiers to set up a camp and rebuild it. One villager described it to me: 'It ended with a fantastic party with Indian food and Gurkha families and locals, and the Gurkhas performing their Kukri knife dance. The Gurkhas loved the project, which was a wonderful training job.' The bridge is now officially renamed the Gurkha Suspension Bridge.

Food and drink

Arundel has some renown for its independent food shops, including a chocolatier, a fishmonger, a butcher and an excellent deli/wine merchant. In 2010 the town held its first very locally focused **Arundel Food Festival** (⌖ www.arundelfoodfestival.org.uk) during a week in October; it's given a contemporary edge with its educational and thought-provoking events, from wild food foraging, to vineyard and allotment visits. There's an excellent choice of cafés and eating places in town, including the ultra-traditional **Belinda's** at 13 Tarrant Street, with homemade cakes as well as full meals, and the much more contemporary Italian **Osteria** at 41a High Street (downstairs from Pappardelle) where you sit communally at long tables – very conducive to friendly chat. Arundel Boatyard's **Riverside Tea Gardens** enjoy a position right by the river.

> **Pallant of Arundel** The Square ☎ 01903 882288 ⌖ www.pallantofarundel.co.uk. The tradition of food shopping here stretches back to 1905, when Denton's Stores operated. After changes in owners, Jonathan Brantigan and Mark Robinson have made it something akin to what perhaps it was in those early years, with quality local goods as well as items from further afield. As well as ham on the bone, their deli counters feature tasty pies, quiches and antipasti, and there is an impressive stock of cheeses from Sussex and beyond. The many local offerings here include Nutbourne Vineyard and Nyetimber wines, smoked salmon, free-range eggs, bread and cakes, preserves and chutneys.

Shopping

Plenty of scope for browsing, with several antique shops and centres. For outdoor equipment, **Pegler's** has a comprehensive range in its three shops at 18 High Street and 67 and 69 Tarrant Street. **The Old Print Works** in Tarrant Street houses a number of interesting retailers, including **The Walking Stick Shop**, with many variations on the walking, cane and shooting stick theme (and most of them individually made) – among them handles made of glass or silver, or wood carved as a lion's head, as a duck or as Sherlock Holmes, plus many traditional styles too. There are a couple of **bookshops** – **Kim's** (10 High St; secondhand and antiquarian) and **The Book Ferret** (34 High St; eclectic range of new books).

㉔ Burpham

A real backwater of a village, Burpham (pronounced Burfam) is on the sleepy side of the Arun. St Mary's Church has some notable Norman work in the form of its mid-12th-century arches, one displaying zigzag decoration, the other carved with grotesque humanoid and ape-like heads.

Behind the **George Inn** (*01903 883131*), a deservedly popular dining pub, an apparently bland recreation field edged by a bank which drops steeply on all sides provides a clue to the village name: *burh* (or *burgh*), denoting a fortified Anglo-Saxon settlement, and *ham*, or a homestead. For this is a **burgh**, or fortified settlement – one of 30 established by Alfred the Great in his kingdom of Wessex as he embarked on the first spate of town-building in this country since the departure of the Romans, when trading effectively collapsed. The burghs were protected against Danish incursions, and included some re-occupied Roman towns such as Winchester and Chichester, and others such as Lewes – which may have had Roman origins or may have been Alfred's innovation; some of these became administrative centres with their own coin mints. Burpham was never an important town though. At its peak it would have been a fortified village, and as Arundel eclipsed it, Burpham dwindled into obscurity, leaving the fortified site around the flat area known as the Wall Field (or the War Field) in strikingly good condition.

㉕ Climping

Climping Beach, between Middleton-on-Sea (effectively the easternmost part of Bognor Regis) and Littlehampton, is on a rare section of undeveloped coast, popular with families. All pebbles at high tide but with a strand of dark sand at low tide, it is at the end of a dead-end road with old flint walls concealing a car park, snack bar and toilets and not much else, which is just how its fans like it. The pebbly bays between groynes feel almost like private rooms. There are saltmarsh meadows to the west.

It does get massively busy on warm days here, and tailbacks along the small approach road can be tediously long. A handy car-free way of getting here is from Littlehampton station: leave the town on the river side, cross over the bridge, from where you get a view of the town's various boatyards, and follow the road (initially called Rope Walk) parallel to the river for a short mile to the beach. Just inland from the estuary mouth here are the overgrown remains of a fort dating from 1854, and thought to have been refortified in World War II.

Food and drink

West Beach Café Rope Walk BN17 5DI ✆ 01903 718153. At the Littlehampton end of the beach on the west side of the mouth of the Arun, this beachside eaterie has won architectural awards, and the fish and chips aren't bad either, alongside a good choice of other simple fishy delights. Open daily in summer; weekends and holidays in winter. On the town side in Littlehampton there's also an architecturally remarkable **East Beach Café** (✆ *01903 731903*), inspired by driftwood. At both, the seafood has attracted rave reviews and the fish is from sustainable sources.

BRIGHTON AND
ITS HINTERLAND

3. BRIGHTON AND ITS HINTERLAND

The most densely populated strip of coast in the southeast is a proverbial mixed bag, and it's not an area in which I could promise sense of place wherever you go. But Brighton and Hove, as they are jointly called nowadays, celebrate being different with great aplomb, and I find there's much pleasure picking one's way through their less likely-looking further reaches as well as the more trumpeted aspects of one of the country's most rewarding seaside resorts. If you are a connoisseur of local museums, Worthing, Hove and Brighton together have a notable trio. Worthing's archaeology and costume stand out; Hove's has a great tearoom after you've perused the very early silent films of the 'Hove pioneers'. Brighton's, as you'd expect, is wonderfully eclectic. For complete unexpected quirkiness, Shoreham takes some beating with its Art Deco airport, Norman church architecture, maritime/local history museum and jaw-dropping assemblage of houseboats.

Inland are some of the most visited parts of the South Downs: Ditchling Beacon and Devil's Dyke get the crowds, but I prefer to walk over to the Chattri War Memorial, Cissbury's prehistoric ramparts and flint mines or Jack and Jill Windmills, or to savour the immediate sense of tranquillity found in those innumerable folds in the landscape. Steyning is a town with plenty of Slow attributes, and is handily placed for walks up to Chanctonbury Ring, one of those rare features on the Downs that are identifiable from a distance. Further north, the Low Weald has some notable moments, with the headquarters of the Sussex Wildlife Trust at Woods Mill and the Downs Link cycle route heading north to Surrey. Just off the A23, Hickstead is the centre for showjumping, with crowds of 15,000 drawn to the British Jumping Derby Meeting held over four days in late June.

Getting around

The Brighton and Hove conurbation isn't much fun to drive around, even less to park in (especially central Brighton), but public transport is good, and parts are cycle-friendly.

Trains

Arriving by train still conjures up a sense of occasion: Brighton station opened in 1841, but what distinguishes it dates from 1882 when the huge, curvaceous shed was added, 597 feet long, with a handsome roof of glass and iron spanning two and a half arches.

Quick services whisk you from **London to Brighton** in around an hour, from Victoria, London Bridge and London St Pancras via East Croydon and Haywards Heath; the London Victoria services also stop at Clapham Junction. On the **Hastings to Brighton** line, very frequent trains run via Eastbourne and Lewes to the east, and it's extremely scenic the whole way, slicing spectacularly through the South Downs in the final section from Lewes before arriving over a grand viaduct looking over Brighton. Sit on the south side of the train for the best views. Direct services run from **Portsmouth to Brighton**, but the journey seems interminable with its frequent stops. Shoreham, Chichester and Fishbourne are the most useful for Slow tourists on this line; although it follows the coast it barely glimpses the sea, though you do see Shoreham Airport, Lancing and Arundel from a distance.

Buses

It isn't easy to work out the intricacies of the Brighton and Hove bus network, even when armed with a decent bus map. However, there are very handy **CitySaver tickets** with scratch-off dates, giving freedom of travel on Brighton & Hove buses throughout the conurbation, and including Steyning, Shoreham, Lewes and Seaford too; validity is for a day, a week, a month or longer. You can buy them on the bus, slightly cheaper from post offices and selected shops or very slightly cheaper still online through www.buses.co.uk. Many Brighton buses end up in Churchill Square (near the clock tower), right outside the shopping centre and very central. Endearingly, many are named after well-loved local figures, such as the comedians Max Miller and Arthur Askey, and the inveterate Lewes conservationist and champion of cyclists' causes Elisabeth Howard.

Buses make the car-free option quite feasible if you want to get on to the **South Downs**. At weekends in summer the hourly 79 bus goes from the Old Steine, then past Brighton station (stop A) and up to **Ditchling Beacon**. For **Devil's Dyke**, the 77 bus departs hourly at weekends and daily in July and August from Brighton Palace Pier (stop N), via Churchill Square (stop H) and Brighton station (stop E).

Cycling

Brighton and Hove have a cycle path along the sea front, much of it a painted area on the pavement, on to which pedestrians inadvertently stray. A free Brighton and Hove city-wide map shows the routes. Dedicated cycle paths run alongside the **A23** northwards and the **A27** to Lewes – useful, but not much fun. For off-roading, the **South Downs Way** has magnificent stretches – I particularly savour the ride from Lewes to Shoreham via the South Downs Way, leaving it at Beeding Hill (just southeast of Upper Beeding) and swooping down the traffic-free lane to the edge of Shoreham, from where you can get the train back. From Shoreham to St Martha's Hill near Guildford, the largely unsurfaced **Downs Link bridlepath** (Regional Route 79) is a particularly enjoyable 37-mile ride through the low Weald along an old railway track. Busy north–south A roads rather break up the possibilities for quiet ambles around the lanes, although the **Ditchling/Plumpton area** has some lovely, unproblematic cycling.

Bike hire

M's Cycle Hire ☎ 07852 986165 ⊕ www.m-cyclehire.co.uk. A mobile cycle hire service based in Shoreham; they'll deliver and pick up bikes free of charge anywhere between Chichester and Lewes (so you could get a bike delivered at Amberley and ride to Brighton and get it picked up at the other end, or ride a stretch of the South Downs Way); helmet, lock, lights and tool kit are provided. Guided bike rides too.

Accommodation

Note that many Brighton hotels require a two-night minimum stay at weekends.

Cavalaire 34 Upper Rock Gardens, Brighton BN2 1QF ☎ 01273 696899 ⊕ www.cavalaire.co.uk. A five-storey Victorian terraced house (originally a home for retired clergy) with a contemporary edge: strong splashes of colour nicely offset the neutral tones. The ten thoughtfully equipped rooms are a mixture of standard, superior and de luxe; breakfasts feature smoked salmon, omelettes, vegetarian dishes and maybe pancakes and waffles. From £65 for a single to up to £160 for a de luxe room with a four-poster bed.

Five Hotel 5 New Steine, Brighton BN2 1PB ☎ 01273 686547 ⊕ www.fivehotel.com. Simon and Caroline Heath have been at pains not to make this look like a B&B – there's a refreshing lack of signage, and the décor is tastefully plain, contemporary and simple, with local artwork on the walls; 'we try to be as eco as we can'. Breakfasts feature local and organic produce, much from Standean Farm, and everyone sits down together to eat at a long table and tends to get chatting to each other. The house was built in 1795 and is in a quiet Kemp Town square with a sidewise peek at the sea. Around £50 a head.

George IV 34 Regency Square, Brighton BN1 2FJ ☎ 01273 321196 ⊕ www.georgeivbrighton.co.uk. In one of Brighton's most elegant Regency squares, this bow-fronted building faces the remains of the West Pier, with sea views from four of its eight bedrooms. The Balcony Room has a positively filmic view, with chairs set out on the little balcony. Furniture tends towards Edwardian. £70–£125 for a double, £95–£150 in Balcony Room; breakfast extra.

Nash Manor Horsham Rd, Steyning BN44 3AA ☎ 01903 814988 ⊕ www.nashmanor.co.uk. Run by May and Liz Esler, mother and daughter, who for years ran a nursing home, this is in tranquil and expansive grounds outside Steyning. As well as a general B&B, May and Liz offer breaks for carers, who can come for the day or up to four nights while a charity looks after the person being cared for. Reflexology and aromatherapy sessions and various workshops, such as painting, walking or yoga. The house is mostly Edwardian, thoroughly modernised and spotlessly kept. B&B is £40 single, £70 double. Gold Award in the Green Tourism Business Scheme.

New Hall Small Dole, near Henfield BN5 9YJ ☎01273 492546 ◈ www.newhallcottage.co.uk. Two self-catering cottages near Woods Mill nature reserve: Dairymaid's Cottage, sleeping five in three bedrooms, and the more spacious Garden Cottage, sleeping two with a folding bed for two more. These adjoin a large Georgianised hall, with amply spacious grounds, full of daffodils in spring, and a gorgeous walled garden for children to play in, and idyllically peaceful; croquet available. Within strolling distance of the Downs Link, for walks and cycle rides (with cycle hire available nearby in Southwater). They also have their own fishing permit for the Adur valley and their own hives – guests get given a pot of honey on departure. £250–£500 per week.

Paskins Town House 18/19 Charlotte St, Brighton BN2 1AG ☎01273 601203 ◈ www.paskins.co.uk. Run by the Marlowe family, this is two Victorian houses knocked into one in a quiet corner of Kemp Town, a short walk from the sea. They pride themselves on organic breakfasts, with most food sourced locally, and some from exotic recipes picked up on their travels. The 21 rooms are in a range of styles, maybe art nouveau or Indian. Mostly £70–£90 double, and a four-poster room for £135. Well behaved pets and children welcome.

Tourist information centres

Brighton Royal Pavilion Shop ☎0906 711 2255 ◈ www.visitbrighton.com.
Horsham The Causeway ☎01403 211661.
Worthing Chapel Rd ☎01903 221307.

Worthing and the west

Although they haven't the visitor pulling power of Brighton and Hove, these mostly western pockets of the conurbation offer some surprisingly rewarding areas of interest.

① Goring Gap

Not to be confused with the rather more famous Goring Gap in the Thames Valley, this does take a bit of seeking out, round residential roads and on to Marine Drive. Say a brief prayer to the gods of planning that this little chunk of coast was never developed thanks to a local authority policy to conserve gaps between settlements in West Sussex – 22 gaps have been created since 1970, and in that time 95% of that land area has been retained as countryside. You can't see any sprawl inland either, so there's the illusion of the distant Downs merging into an untampered coastal plain. The Gap itself is a broad agricultural strip fringed by a spacious lawn at the coastal end, so it gives a good idea of how the whole

Sussex coast looked before it was built over. The usual shingle beach with groynes is what you expect in these parts; modern development is screened by a long line of trees known as the Plantation on the east side, while to the north the Ilex Way, an avenue of 400 holm oaks planted in the 1840s along a carriage road for Goring Hall, extends from St Mary's Church in Goring to Ferring.

North of Ferring and sandwiched between main roads and suburban fringes, **Highdown Hill** is another isolated tract of rural Sussex and is owned by the National Trust: rising 261 feet, it gives a view over the built-up stretch of coast, extending in clear conditions eastwards to Beachy Head and westwards to the Isle of Wight. Lumps of an Iron-Age hillfort are in evidence. The OS Explorer map marks the Miller's Tomb just to the east – this belongs to John Olliver, an 18th-century miller turned smuggler who used to set his sails at a certain angle to signal to other gang members whether the coast was clear of customs men.

② Worthing

Worthing hit the big time when fashionable visitors came from Brighton in Regency days, and its success was pretty much ensured in 1798 with the arrival of the convalescent Princess Amelia, youngest daughter of George III. In August 1895 Oscar Wilde stayed with his family here and rapidly penned the comedy *The Importance of Being Ernest*, naming one of its main characters Jack Worthing. The handbag joke, incidentally, has a piece of railway snobbery that is probably lost on modern audiences – when Jack attempts to justify his being found as a baby in a handbag ('A *handbag?*') at Victoria station it was on the Brighton line, which was considered the 'posh' side as opposed to the distinctly less salubrious London, Chatham and Dover Railway section of the station.

Worthing isn't really a prime seaside resort nowadays, and there's not a lot there compared with the likes of Brighton, but it does some seasidey things extremely well, such as Macari's, a Worthing ice cream institution for over half a century, and the highly revered Fish Factory. Some its places of entertainment are of considerable style: the **Connaught** (doubling as a theatre and cinema) and the **pier** are elegantly Art Deco affairs, the latter with a theatre at its near end, while also on the sea front the **Dome** is one of the country's oldest cinemas, opened in 1911 and full of period detail inside. **Worthing Museum and Art Gallery** (free; closed Monday), a five-minute walk from the station, has very good sections on 19th and 20th-century costume, toys and the history of the town, as well as a sculpture garden. It also has one of the best public collections of archaeology in Sussex: as well as an early ferry boat from Hardham, dated to 1030–1220, it has some notable treasures. Among them is the Patching Hoard of 1997, which includes 23 gold Roman coins unearthed by a metal detectorist, happily on display locally after it was initially supposed they would end up in the British Museum. Virtually next to the museum and opposite the main street from the Connaught, **Ambrose Place** is as sweet and perfect an example of white, balconied Regency seaside architecture as you'll find anywhere in Brighton or Hove; note the detached house gardens across the street.

Food and drink

Fish Factory 51 Brighton Rd ☎01903 207123. Freshest fish and chips; open all day.
Lime Café St Paul's Centre ☎01903 368967. Small café in a handsome former church functioning as the community arts centre in the middle of town next to the museum. Fairtrade tea and coffee, and light snacks.
Macari's Restaurant and Café 24–25 Marine Parade ☎01903 532753. Offers 24 flavours of home-made ice cream and light lunches. Right next to the Dome.

③ Shoreham

Although it's perhaps not enticing at first sight, there are good reasons to linger in this long-established port. New Shoreham – the 'new'

denoting the Norman settlement that succeeded the Saxon village at Old Shoreham further north as the Adur silted up – enjoyed cross-Channel trade with Normandy in early times, and in the 20th century was the prime arrival point in Britain for sherry and port from Iberia. It has enough old buildings surviving for an absorbing walkabout, with beach-cobble fronted houses along Church Street leading to **St Mary de Haura Church**. Built in 1103 on a grand scale, it is one of Sussex's most impressive Norman churches: ruins in the churchyard of what was the nave indicate its former size. The Norman work is seen in the lower part of the tower and transepts, while the choir and upper part of the tower display transitional elements. In New Road, on the other side of the churchyard from Church Street, **P&A Butchers** has a fetching period shop front, with Art Nouveau tiles and stained glass depicting farm animals. Close by, facing the waterfront, **Marlipins Museum** (*open Apr–end of Oct, Tue–Sat*) partly occupies a 12th-century building with a striking façade chequered alternately with flint and Caen limestone. Within is a wide array of material on local and maritime history, with ship models, archaeology and fossils. Upstairs are displays on Shoreham Beach's own film industry, set up here in 1914 and drawn by the clarity of the light. Fire destroyed many of the studio buildings in 1923, and the rest were later demolished.

Across the footbridge over the Adur and accessed from a narrow concrete walkway just above the shore is Shoreham's big surprise – perhaps the most eye-opening assemblage of **houseboats** in the country. Originating from 1945 as housing for those who had lived in railway carriages and shacks in what was called 'Bungalow Town' on Shoreham Beach, they are now desirably bohemian homes. They are made from a strange list of retired craft, among them a coal barge, an ammunition lighter, a minesweeper, a 1905 passenger steamer and a 1941 torpedo boat, and have been variously adapted with DIY improvements and sunny gardens filled with potted plants and frequented by contented cats and dogs. *Verda*, built in 1929 as the Portsmouth–Gosport ferry, has been ingeniously extended by the addition of a coach split lengthwise and added to either side; this in turn links to *Venture*, a World War II motor gunboat, adorned by a dissected mustard-coloured Reliant Robin. The catalogue of dwellings slowly evolves; sad remains of former residences may be visible in the mudflats.

Further upriver is **Old Shoreham**, where the restored Saxon and Norman church of St Nicolas is the major landmark; it has striking 12th-century stone carving at the crossing. Just across the road and hidden from view is Shoreham's much-loved wooden **tollbridge**, originating from 1781 and largely rebuilt in 1916 but eclipsed by the opening of a new bypass in 1970. Demoted to use as a bridleway, it deteriorated and was deemed unsafe in 1997; its future looked very bleak indeed with a huge sum of money required to avoid it rotting into history. Local campaigners kickstarted a bid to save the bridge, and happily the Old Shoreham Community Trust helped raise the money in partnership with West Sussex County Council. The bridge was faithfully restored and reopened in August 2008. The Shoreham to Guildford **Downs Link** cycle and walking route goes straight past it.

You can cross over the tollbridge to the west bank and turn left (or walk up through fields from the houseboats) to **Shoreham Airport**, one of the Art Deco treasures of Sussex and the oldest licensed airfield in the country. Officially opened in 1911, it gained its terminal building in 1936 and still evokes the days of early aviation – the departure board in the elegant main building refers to private flights, although not so long ago there were scheduled services to France. A curious relic of its wartime days can be glimpsed on the north side of the airfield, where a camouflaged brick-built training dome is one of only five remaining: it was used for teaching aircraft recognition by means of projecting images on to the inside of the dome and changing the lighting to simulate different times of day. In August the Royal Air Forces Association (RAFA) holds an **airshow** here with flying and static displays of military and historic aircraft. Adjacent to the terminal building, the **visitor centre** has a fascinating stash of aviation memorabilia, including models of some of the earliest craft, among them Harold Piffard's 1910 biplane, which made the first flight from here, and the Valkyrie monoplane which in 1911 made the world's first registered freight flight, delivering a box of lightbulbs from here to Hove Lawns. Airport tours take in the terminal building, main hangar and the Sussex Police Helicopter Unit (*01273 441061; www.visitorcentre.info; a couple of weeks' notice usually required*). The good-value café in the terminal building and the terrace outside make vantage points for watching planes landing.

103

Shopping

Locals claim Shoreham's farmers' market (second Saturday of the month) as the best in Sussex. At other times, you might find excellent fish stalls by the road to Worthing, with very seasonal offerings at reasonable prices.

④ Brighton and Hove

A small ill-built town, situated on the sea coast, at present greatly resorted to in the summer season by various persons labouring under various diseases, for benefit of seabathing and drinking seawater, and by the gay and polite on account of the company which frequent it in the season, unlike a few years ago no better than a mere fishing town inhabited by fishermen and sailors.
Gentleman's Magazine, 1766

Exuberant, quirky and even outrageous, Brighton is arguably the liveliest seaside resort in Britain. Outwardly it gives the impression of anything but Slow, so instead of trying to cover each and every aspect, I have focussed on a selection of attributes that show off Brighton-ness to best effect. And of course Hove-ness: the two places merge to form the city of Brighton and Hove – Hove lying to the west of Brighton – and it needs local knowledge to determine where one ends and the next begins.

Let's start with **Richard Russell**. He was a successful Lewes doctor and an astute businessman who in 1750 published his paper *Glandular Diseases, or a Dissertation on the Use of Sea-Water in the Affections of the Glands*; it was written in Latin, so may not have been great bedtime reading. He trained at Leiden and studied the European concept of spas; he was one of a group of doctors who had the idea of using seawater instead of a spa water. To this end he prescribed seawater cures for his patients and encouraged wealthy people to visit Brighthelmstone, as it was called then, and to where he himself moved in 1753. The idea was to bathe in the sea, inhale the sea air, partake of treatments such as a pill made of crabs' eyes, cuttlefish bones and woodlice, and imbibe pints of seawater.

His prescription indicated the length of time the patient needed to spend in the water. Patients were wheeled out to the sea in bathing machines – actually little cabins on wheels, towed by horses – and immersion was effected with the aid of 'dippers' who engaged in the task of submerging the body completely; the victim would emerge spluttering from the ordeal by dunking. Attending to the needs of the thalassotherapy-seekers gave the fishing community an important new source of income.

Russell is sometimes heralded as the inventor of the seaside resort, but the trend of going to Brighthelmstone to recuperate dates from the 1730s. It was wealthy local people who recommended Brighton to their friends, who with Russell and other locals helped make Brighton a success. From 1783, the Prince of Wales, the future George IV, came because the resort was popular with his uncles and friends, and developed a lodging house into the Royal Pavilion. He revelled in the Brighton social scene, and was much caricatured by the political cartoonists of the day.

From the 1790s the town's population boomed. A contributing factor to this was the army who were periodically in residence from the 1790s to 1815; it was believed that a Napoleonic invasion might be attempted in the shallow bay on which stood Brighton. Officers often brought their families with them and soon the little town was transformed by commodious squares and elegant crescents. Many of the Regency buildings survive today, making this one of Britain's most rewarding examples of **seaside architecture**. Somewhat less celebrated are its highly distinguished 19th-century places of worship; not all of them are open outside services – it is a pity for instance that the Middle Street Synagogue, reputed as one of the finest in Europe, is rarely open – but you can usually look into the spectacular trio of **Anglo-Catholic churches**: St Michael's and All Angels, St Paul's and St Bartholomew's.

If you want to savour the many details, the excellent Pevsner Architectural Guide *Brighton and Hove* by Nicholas Antram and Richard Morrice picks out the landmark buildings and features 11 architectural walks, area by area.

Brighton revived after a very quiet, recession-hit period in the 1830s; Queen Victoria didn't really care for it, due to the lack of privacy at the Royal Pavilion, remarking 'there were far too many of the wrong sort of people, and they were all staring at me'. From 1841 onwards the railways brought the masses, and Brighton's fortunes soared. Along the sea front various contrivances were devised to extract money from pleasure-seekers. Seaside amusement arcades, a concept imported from America, sprang up. Brighton's fame spread; other seaside resorts named Brighton were built as far away as New York and Melbourne.

It has for long had a seamier side; even the Brighton Museum celebrates the resort's role as a venue for a dirty weekend. This famously was the place a couple could get 'a Brighton quickie' divorce. The husband would hire a private detective to observe him signing into a hotel, with a hired 'mistress' acting the part, as 'Mr and Mrs Smith'. A chambermaid would ever so accidentally open the door to see the couple, and the deed was done.

Graham Greene in his novel *Brighton Rock* depicted the Brighton underworld with its teenage gangland leader Pinkie and his innocent waitress girlfriend Rose, and John Boulting's 1947 film noir of the novel marvellously used the Brighton backdrop; the 2011 remake was filmed in Brighton and Eastbourne. The bank holiday weekend clashes on the seafront between mods and rockers started in 1964 and inspired the film *Quadrophenia*.

Brighton has long been a place of sexual liberation and, around the 1970s at a time when homophobia was rife, gays felt relatively comfortable visiting for a weekend of pleasure. Now, as the undisputed gay capital of Britain, Brighton hosts the biggest Pride festival in the country, and there's plenty in the way of gay pubs and clubs, and gay-friendly accommodation. Much of the action revolves around Kemp Town and St James's Street, and the spending power of the pink pound partly accounts for the city's eclectic shopping and eating out. To find out on what's on in gay Brighton, see www.realbrighton.com.

Another key to Brighton's distinctiveness is its high proportion of young people, thanks in part to the existence of its two universities – the University of Brighton and the University of Sussex. Although their main campuses are out of town at Falmer, the students tend to come into Brighton itself for nightlife and so on, and quite a few like it so much they end up living here.

The seafront

The beach is clean but isn't the most wonderful on the south coast, being composed of pebbles (reputedly 614 billion of them) with a bit of sand exposed at low tide, but provides some shallow bathing. The city's long-held status as lotus-eating capital of Sussex has imbued the whole seaside scene with a terrific atmosphere. Few coastal resorts have such architectural set pieces along their seafront as do Brighton and its neighbour, Hove. The first element is the cream-stucco frontages, which date from Regency times: the finest include Brunswick Square at the Hove end, Regency Square near the old West Pier and Lewes Crescent in Kemp Town in the far east.

At first glance, the seafront looks handsomely uniform, with stucco buildings on one side, and the esplanade with its trademark aquamarine and white lampposts on the other: but a walk from end to end reveals that the seafront changes in character from one moment to the other. The pivotal point, and best place from which to admire the seafront, from Shoreham power station's chimney in the west to the Marina in the east, is **Brighton Pier** (formerly Palace Pier), an exuberant example of late Victoriana, exactly a third of a mile long, completed in 1899. The far end has a funfair, continuing a tradition of rides on the pier stretching back to 1938. Though it has evolved with the years – the clock tower and entrance pavilion are postwar additions – the balustrades, two entrance kiosks and basic structure are original. In fact the kiosks originate from Brighton's very first pier, which this structure replaced: it was called the Chain Pier, built in 1823 like a suspension bridge, and primarily intended as an embarkation point for packet boats. It doubled as a promenading ground and thus can be considered among the very first seaside piers in the world. In the mid 19th century an early version of the booze cruise would depart from here, as visitors took the boat out to foreign waters and enjoyed tax-free alcohol.

London to Brighton Veteran Car Run

The longest-running car event in the world (emphatically a car run and not a race), this simply has to be seen to be believed, with up to 600 beautifully preserved and miraculously still working pre-1905 vehicles brought in from various parts of the globe given a run by their owners in front of an admiring audience of up to a million. It starts at sunrise from London's Hyde Park on a Sunday morning in early November: you'd have to be very keen to get there for the beginning. Fortunately, Sussex has it easier – the run stops by in Crawley, and carries on through Cuckfield and Burgess Hill to end up at the seafront in Brighton, on Madeira Drive. Not all of the entrants make it, but most get there eventually – giving a tremendous free show of the vehicles along the seafront until late afternoon. The car run goes back to 1896 – at a time when petrol would have been bought at a chemist's shop – to celebrate a change in the law whereby drivers could dispense with the red-flag-bearing attendant who walked in front, and zoom along at a brisk maximum of 14mph. The effervescent 1953 comedy film *Genevieve* is about two rival motorists who complete the run in their 1904 vehicles, a Darracq nicknamed Genevieve and a Spyker (both now retired to museums in Holland), then race back to London for a bet, to the exasperation of their womenfolk: 'I don't know what it is about these silly old cars. The moment people get in them they start behaving like idiots!'

East of Brighton Pier

Just across the road from the pier on the east side, **Brighton Sea Life Centre** (*01273 604234*) is one of the nationwide chain of aquaria that feature all manner of marine life. The highlight is the walk-through tunnel with sharks and giant turtles swimming around you and overhead; they're at their liveliest during feeding times, and it's worth planning your visit accordingly. So far this sounds reassuringly familiar for anyone who has enjoyed similar places elsewhere, but architecturally this is the most interesting aquarium in the country (and the oldest one anywhere still in operation). The largest in the world when opened in 1872 at a cost of £130,000, this was the creation of Eugenius Birch, better known for building seaside piers, including Brighton's sadly defunct West Pier. His Aquarium in Brighton was deliberately given subterranean qualities to convey an impression of life under the ocean. After a new entrance with stone kiosks and a sun terrace was added in the 1920s, it suffered a chequered history. It was requisitioned in World War II, hosted (in its ballroom) the very first Rhythm and Blues venue in Britain, and in the 1970s operated as a rather tacky Dolphinarium, but has a new lease of life as part of the well-run Sea Life Centre chain. The building retains many of its original Victorian tanks within the main crypt-like aisled hall, with its almost ecclesiastical Gothic vaulted ceiling. It was a wonder of the age, and is still pretty eye-opening; the granite columns have colourfully painted capitals carved with depictions of sea life. Thereafter the

Victorian period charm disappears, but there's plenty else, beginning with a simulated Amazonian maze set up with deliberately disorienting mirrors and abundant sound effects, followed by the main tank which you can view from above in the Auditorium (the former ballroom) via glass-bottom boat tours (extra admission payable) as well as from the walk-through glass tunnel, where sharks, giant turtles and other species glide overhead. Throughout the day there's an hourly programme of tours, talks and feeds, on the half hour; the turtle feeds at 11.30 and 14.30 and the shark feed at 16.30 are particularly popular.

Beneath the esplanade is one of Brighton's unsung (and endangered) treasures, the extraordinary **covered promenade** of 1889–97 along Madeira Drive, all cast iron and open fronted, providing a shady, sheltered walk and dating from the days when a tan was definitely to be avoided; it runs beneath the sea wall for half a mile. Towards the end, an exotic shelter, given the full pagoda-style treatment by the architect, served as a lift from shore level to the top of the esplanade and has recently been restored after years of neglect.

Running along the entire extent of Madeira Drive, **Volk's Electric Railway** (*www.volkselectricrailway.co.uk*) has been in operation since 1883 – the world's oldest electrically operated commercial railway (there was an earlier industrial electric railway outside Berlin, so the claims that it was the very first electric railway aren't quite valid); it now runs from the Brighton Sea Life Centre to Black Rock, near the marina. The track is narrow gauge and carriages are engagingly scaled down. This was the creation of Magnus Volk, an electrical engineer whose house was the first in Brighton to be installed with electric lighting, and who as a result won the contract to install electric incandescent lighting in the Royal Pavilion. At first the railway ran just a quarter of a mile from the Aquarium to the Chain Pier (which was adjacent to where the Palace Pier now stands), but later was extended westwards. The public loved it, but it was at the mercy of the elements: accordingly, it was raised on to a wooden viaduct for its entire length in 1886. In 1894 Volk turned his attention to another sea-front mode of transport that would enable people to travel on to Rottingdean. The snag was that the cliffs formed too much of a barrier, so he opted for a route through the sea itself, and created the *Pioneer*, an astonishing contraption comprising a large tram-like cabin raised on tall supports that ran with its wheels on tracks in the chalk bedrock beneath the sea: 'A Sea Voyage on Wheels' proclaimed the poster of what became dubbed the 'Daddy Longlegs'. Volk's grand scheme opened in 1896 but operated for only a week until a huge storm damaged it; repairs were made and services resumed, but the project faltered through technical problems and this unique passenger service closed a few years later; in 1910 the remains of the passenger car were carted off for scrap.

Near the eastern terminus of the railway at Black Rock, Brighton's **naturist beach** is clearly signed and screened by a slight rise in the shingle.

A brave new world ensconced beneath the cliffs on the east side of Brighton, **Brighton Marina** doesn't feel like Britain at all – but a futuristic grid of apartment blocks and waterside views. It reminds me of the set of *The Truman*

Show, the 1998 film about the man who doesn't realise he's the subject of a reality TV show and has his every move watched by millions of Americans. A Walk of Fame remembers Brighton celebs, past and present, in Hollywood Boulevard style, with plaques set in the boardwalk. There's outlet shopping, multi-screen cinema, a bleak car park and a big branch of ASDA, and it's geared to walking rather than driving in. The craft in the marina add a splash of colour, and eastwards Peacehaven Heights look wonderfully wild.

Developed by Thomas Kemp in the early 19th century, the eastern district of **Kemp Town** didn't take off quickly and was eclipsed in success by the areas further west towards Hove. Kemp overreached himself by trying to build carcasses of houses, and much of it remained uninhabited till the 1850s, by which time the façades were somewhat out of fashion. Kemp engaged Charles Busby and Amon Wilds as architects to develop countryside into 250 houses. His plan includes the majestic curves of Lewes Crescent, representing seaside architecture at its very grandest.

If you can find them open, two Kemp Town churches deserve seeking out: **St John the Baptist Catholic Church** in Bristol Road, built in the 1830s and with a particularly fine show of memorials, and **St George's Church** in St George's Road, a high-quality Regency Greek Revival-style preaching box opened in 1826. Opposite the latter the Royal Pavilion-inspired, tent-domed **Sassoon Mausoleum** (now the Hanbury Club) was built by and for the Jewish philanthropist Sir Albert Sassoon, who died in 1896.

West of Brighton Pier

The shore-level promenade immediately west of the pier beneath the esplanade represents the liveliest part of the seafront with a range of little businesses set up in the arches beneath street level, and a magnificent 1888 merry-go-round, fully restored and with its real fairground organ operating. Beyond a little **Artists' Quarter**, booths advertise tarot, clairvoyant and palmist services, one with dozens of testimonials to Prof Mirza, the 'Great Mystic of the East'; a couple of places are filled with **antique slot machines** of the 'haunted churchyard' and 'what the butler saw' variety. Brighton's fishing industry still lands and sells fish and shellfish here – one of the great little institutions is **Jack and Linda Mills, Traditional Fish Smokers** under the arches, who offer fresh crab sandwiches, smoked fish and fish soup; just over the boardwalk is the minute smokehouse where the fish are smoked in the traditional way most days each week. The tiny, volunteer-run **Brighton Fishing Museum** (free entrance) chronicles Brighton's fishing community from the early days; the largest exhibit is a 27-foot clinker-built punt boat of a type typical to Sussex, while an adjacent room has a few poignant relics from the sadly defunct West Pier.

All you can now see of the **West Pier**, directly opposite Regency Square, is an island of skeletal iron. This was Britain's only Grade I listed pier, last in use in 1972 and very splendid, but neglected and just when things looked rosy for its restoration it burned down. It has now lost its listed status, but is much valued

as a roosting ground for starlings in winter; they turn up here from Scandinavia and feed up to 20 miles away. Though in decline nationally, the numbers here are healthy in the extreme: the birds form a huge cloud that changes shape as they move around in a process known as 'murmuration'. At dusk with a winter sun lighting up the skeletal remains of the pier and the starlings in full murmur mode this is one of the great wildlife sights of Sussex. Soon its landward end may be marked by a 600-foot-tall, slender viewing tower called the **i360**: at the time of writing, most of it had been made in Holland. If and when it is installed, the views over the Downs and far beyond will be second to none.

The concrete brutalism that is Brighton Centre and the Odeon next door combine to get my prize for Brighton's ugliest development; the former is where the political party conferences are held. It was in 1984 that Patrick Magee, a member of the IRA, planted a bomb at the adjacent **Grand Hotel**, intending to kill the then prime minister Margaret Thatcher and her cabinet; the bomb caused huge damage, and killed five, including the MP Sir Anthony Berry, and severely wounded others. The building was massively damaged, but not irreparably so, and its flamboyantly Victorian interior was restored much to what it had been. Just inland, the very top of **Sussex Heights**, at 334 feet and with 24 floors the tallest residential block in all Sussex, has been home to a nesting pair of **peregrine falcons** since 1998; the nesting box subsequently provided for them is visible from the street on the north side, and often one peregrine may be seen perched outside, or its piercing high call may be heard. The peregrine is the fastest known living creature, and has been recorded swooping down at around 150mph. One wonders how many passers-by below are aware of the aerial mayhem caused by this rare bird (with a UK population of 1,500 pairs) when a couple of pigeon feathers drift down into the street as a peregrine snaffles a tasty meal.

The Hove end is really worth a walkabout for its magnificent examples of seaside Regency architecture. The **Brunswick** district was completed by 1828 and inhabited by local moneyed classes and visitors. Things were made more attractive by the fact that in Hove there wasn't a tax on coal. It was built as a new suburb, with views of the Downs behind imposing architectural set pieces in the forms of Brunswick Square, and a little further west, Adelaide Crescent (completed in the 1850s).

It was successful in attracting people as soon as it was built and developed rapidly. Brunswick Square has its own little festival in summer, and 13 Brunswick Square, the **Regency Town House**, is occasionally open for tours (*01273 206306; www.rth.org.uk*); the strikingly deep cream hue to the stucco in Brunswick was revived in recent years by an astute planning officer's enforcement of an ancient covenant. This square leads into **Palmeira Square**, begun as Palmeira Crescent in the 1830s by Decimus Burton, who also with his father James developed St Leonards, on the west side of Hastings. The style here is more pared down than Brunswick Square, and leans towards the Italianate. The **Montpelier** district extends inland and has some exuberant canopied terraces that were all the rage in the early Victorian period.

Further on **Hove Lawns** is a long-established place for kite-flying, and you see parasailers and windsurfers on Hove Lagoon (see below).

Seafront sports

The beach is all shingle, with some low-tide sand: buggies are available for hire for wheelchair users, to get access across the pebbles to the shore. As well as swimming, the Brighton and Hove beachfront is full of scope for activities, with windsurfing on Hove Lagoon, surfing on Shoreham Hotpipes (or the Marina for more experienced surfers), basketball, a sand pitch for volleyball or other beach sports, a petanque piste and marker posts for joggers on Hove seafront. The city is the main place in Sussex for surfboard hire.

The Lanes and North Laine

Inland, North, West and East streets enclose the old town, including the old area of twittens known as **the Lanes**. This is a prime area for shopping and eating, though the days when it had interesting junk shops are long gone, eclipsed by more upmarket jewellery and clothing retailers. In East Street you might see palmists or neck-and-shoulder masseuses set up stalls, while Duke Street has chocolate shops (including Choccywoccydoodah, which takes great pride in its window displays) and the Colin Page antiquarian and secondhand book store.

East of that, the **Old Steine** (confusingly pronounced either Steen or Stine, and sometimes spelt Steyne) was originally a damp area once given over to grazing and sloping towards the sea where nets would be dried out on the beach, and where capstans were used to haul boats up (one capstan survives, near the Fishing Museum). It was considered the 'centre' of town in the early resort days, when it became the strolling ground, a place to see and be seen – Brighton's own *passeggiata* area, shops selling lace and bonbons to tourists. A model in the Brighton Museum and Art Gallery hints at its former charm. Although a lot of the Regency buildings have survived, it's too much a whirl of traffic to walk through for pleasure now.

Often confused with the Lanes (which are closer to the sea), the **North Laine** and the area to the east were developed from the 1850s on what had been agricultural strips from medieval times in an area of market gardening: the roads today mark the lines of the agricultural strips (or the access tracks between them), making a very striking fossilised pattern of what has otherwise long vanished. Portsea in Portsmouth and parts of Worthing developed on similar lines.

The North Laine is effectively a set of streets, one leading into another – Bond Street, Gardner Street, Kensington Gardens and Sydney Street. Brighton's answer to Camden Lock market in London, this is a funkily anarchic parade of commerce with the likes of Neal's Yard Remedies, Oxfam and Amnesty bookshops, Infinity Foods, Red food 'vegan cake here!' and Shared Earth Fair Trading Company. Some of Brighton's most enjoyable shop browsing is along here, and though it's all very well known to locals the area is easily missed: to find it from the rail station, turn right under the canopy of the station, then immediately sharp left down Trafalgar Street, which heads down through a steep subway-like road tunnel adjacent to the bowels of the station frontage. Soon after you will see Sydney Street leading off to the right, marking the northern extent of the main North Laine axis. Jubilee Square, around the handsome new library, has sparked a revival in a previously drab corner at the southern end.

In the above-mentioned railway station netherworld and housed in the former Bass Charrington beer store, the Tardis-like **Brighton Toy and Model Museum** reveals a nostalgia-inducing stash of items. The owner Chris Littledale told me 'it all started with my obsession with model trains, going back to when I was a child – I've been collecting ever since; there were so many things I had to find a home for.' All the trains are his, but he has had numerous loans and donations of vintage teddies, dolls, puppets, toy castles, toy theatre, model soldiers and the like. He showed me his prize pieces, a display of German model trains; they stand by a station bookstall from the 1920s in pristine condition, complete with minuscule copies of Punch and Ideal Home and a train indicator next to it. A vintage model railway layout is the centrepiece, depicting an entire town, with a bowling match in progress; in it there are toy cars, taxis and a bridge (one of the rarest items in the whole museum). Some very interesting bits and pieces are for sale in the foyer, including old bits of Hornby train sets and the like – from about £5 upwards.

The North Laine nearly got bulldozed for a relief road a few decades back, and north of it you can see where some redevelopment took place. It's worth persevering through this to Ann Street to find **St Bartholomew's Church** (1872–74, by the otherwise unknown architect Edmund Scott), barn-like, brick and vast, with no spire or tower, or side aisles, and with a nave taller than Westminster Abbey's. Inside it is reminiscent of Westminster Cathedral with its bare brickwork, adorned with a quartet of onion-domed confessionals, and rich decoration in the form of Byzantine-style mosaics and Arts and Crafts metalwork. This is a notable place to see very high-quality late 19th-century and early 20th-century interior work by nationally recognised designers.

West Street meets North Street later at the conspicuous **clock tower**, erected to celebrate Queen Victoria's golden jubilee in 1887 and doubling as an elaborate signpost pointing to Hove, The Sea, The Station and Kemp Town. It's appealingly OTT, with mosaics of Victoria, Albert and the Prince and Princess of Wales, while female figures denoting the four seasons sit at each corner. This is otherwise not Brighton's most gloriously architectural corner, though in West Street, **St Paul's Church** is an exceptional early Victorian church by R C Carpenter with a spectacular and individualistic spire rising to octagonal bell-stage and a simple interior with stained glass by Augustus Pugin.

The Royal Pavilion

Most memorably entered through the magnificent arch of the William IV Gate on the north side of the grounds, the Royal Pavilion (*03000 290900; open daily*) is a quite startling sight, flamboyantly over-the-top and bristling with domes and minarets. As an Indian fantasy, it's actually something you'd never encounter in India, and within it is more Chinese-inspired, the most complete example of the *chinoiserie* style anywhere, beautifully restored and furnished much as it was in the heyday of the Prince Regent, the future George IV. After the relatively pale and restrained entrance hall, guests would be conducted through the salmon-pink and blue Long Gallery to the astonishing Banqueting Room, with its huge crystal and mirrored chandeliers, held in the jaws of dragons, glittering above a table laid out for a feast. They would be invited to inspect the Great Kitchen, where food was prepared in a high-ceilinged room supported by columns with palm-leaf capitals, and entertained afterwards in the hot, scented atmosphere of the Music Room with its great dome lined with 26,000 hand-gilded cockle shells.

By the 1750s, Russell's sea cure was drawing numbers of wealthy people to the town, among them the Duke of Cumberland. In 1783 his nephew, the 21-year-old George, who became Prince Regent in 1811 during George III's decline into insanity and king in 1820, was recommended to try the Russell treatment to ease his swelling neck glands. So he went to stay with his uncle there. Whatever he thought of the sea water, the prince greatly took to Brighton's social life, the theatre and the races, in defiance of his frugal father. He very soon opted to rent a plain Georgian lodging house on the fashionable strolling ground of the Old Steine, which improbably evolved into one of the most engagingly eccentric royal palaces in the world. Its transformation began in the form of the Marine Pavilion designed by Henry Holland in 1787, with a rotunda added. Shortly the prince's devotion to riding and racing horses managed spectacularly to upstage this, as he had an Indian-style stable building constructed nearby during 1803–08. John Nash was engaged in 1815 to adapt the pavilion in similar style. By 1823 it was complete. As was the prince's wish, it was very public, right in the middle of things: when concerts were held inside, the prince often would have the windows opened so that the promenaders outside could hear.

Some observed at the time that it was 'far too handsome for Brighton', and predicted that it would be a ruin in 50 years. And indeed things were not always rosy for the Pavilion. Almost from the start, the innovative iron frame of the added-on structures began to decay in the wet and salt air, and leaks led to extensive dry rot. Queen Victoria, who came to the throne in 1837, found the Pavilion too small for her burgeoning young family and regretted its lack of sea views: in 1850 it was sold to the town of Brighton, but not before the Crown Estate had stripped out all the furniture, wallpapers and other decorative features, right down to the hearths and the wires for the bell pulls. Refurbishment was carried out – and the lavish ceilings of the Music Room, Banqueting Room and Saloon were restored to how they had been, but other rooms that had been stripped bare were decorated in all manner of ways. Then in World War I it was used as a hospital for some 4,000 convalescent Indian soldiers: when they came round and found themselves in this place, some might have thought they were hallucinating, but one described it as paradise: 'it is as if one were in the next world'. In gratitude the Indian government donated the gate at the south entrance to the gardens. Following 1918, a huge project to restore the Pavilion's Regency authenticity was carried out through much of the 20th century, with Buckingham Palace returning many of the original furnishing and decorations. An arson attack in the Music Room in 1975 was a major setback, and just when it was finally repaired, the Great Storm of 1987 sent an architectural stone ball crashing through the dome, embedding itself in the floor and damaging the costly new hand-knotted replica carpet. Some attribute the Music Room's misfortunes to bad *feng shui*; apparently its décor's combination of dragons and snakes would produce reactions of superstitious horror in China.

Meticulous restoration has once again left the Royal Pavilion looking quite remarkably good: even for those jaded by country-house visits, it simply has to be seen to be believed. Upstairs, the Queen Adelaide Tearoom has a pleasant terrace overlooking the gardens.

The **gardens** surrounding the Pavilion are presented as they would have been in Regency times: a naturalistic effect with trees and shrubs arranged around snaking paths through shaggy grass, cut to the length it would have been scythed by hand: adorned with antique gas lamps, this space has become a favourite sitting place within central Brighton, not that it's that big. Most weekends there are events here, often with a band playing.

The Indian-style former Royal Stables now house the **Dome Theatre**, with its adjacent Riding House now functioning as the **Corn Exchange**.

Bon appetit?

One of the greatest banquets ever prepared at the Royal Pavilion was for the Grand Duke Nicholas of Russia, in 1817. Among more than 100 dishes were 'the head of a great sturgeon in champagne', 'a terrine of larks', 'a pyramid of lobsters with fried parsley', and 'the Royal Pavilion rendered in pastry'. Since no more than 30 guests ever dined here at one time, the servants that night must have been very well fed.

Brighton Museum and Art Gallery

Entered through the Pavilion gardens, Brighton Museum and Art Gallery (*closed Mon*) is one of the city's great free attractions. It is entertainingly eclectic, with displays of art and costume (including George IV's breeches and shirt); you enter through the furniture gallery where some eye-catching pieces include very fine Art Deco and Art Nouveau furniture and two sofas with a difference, one in the form of Mae West's lips (by Dalí, c.1938) and another in the form of a gigantic baseball glove (inspired by the baseball player Joe Di Maggio). Images of Brighton looks at a range of aspects of the resort, including its gay scene and the seamier, dirty weekend side, and has models of the Old Steine as it was in 1804, and of Brighton's two vanished piers: the West Pier and the Chain Pier. Henry Willett, one of the founders of the museum, was an ardent collector, and his extraordinary assemblage of ceramics depicting social history themes makes up the display of Mr Willett's Popular Pottery – which he grouped into 23 subjects such as pastimes, statesmen and music. The display of Brighton Life includes oral histories from Brightonians and the frontage of 'the only cork factory on the South Coast', an antiquated shop that existed for exactly a century in Gardner Street in the North Laine before its closure in 1983. Upstairs, the café makes a good lunch spot.

Inland and westward from the centre, and into Hove

Between Seven Dials (to the north), Dyke Road (east), Western Road (south) and Boundary Passage (west), **Montpelier** and **Clifton Hill** areas constitute one of Brighton's most rewarding strolling territories, and one missed by many visitors – a hilly residential area of white-stucco Victorian terraces, all immensely characterful with unexpected twists and vistas. In all it has 351 listed buildings, among the most striking being Montpelier Crescent of 1843–47 by Amon Wilds and sporting the trademark 'ammonite capitals' (a visual pun on Wilds's Christian name; at the top of the columns are representations of ammonite fossils), the bow-windowed frontages of Temple Gardens, the Arts and Crafts houses of Windlesham Road, and the streetscapes of Clifton Road and Powis Villas.

In the southeastern corner of this area, **St Nicholas' Church** was the old parish church for Brighthelmstone, very much safely up the slope and on the edge of things; although the church was comprehensively rebuilt in the 1850s it still has a rustic feel to its hilly churchyard, and gives you the impression you're on the

Downs (as technically you are). Tombstones here mark some of the great Brighton characters including the famous 'dipper' Martha Gunn, and the immensely long-lived Phoebe Hessel (1713–1821) who had dressed up as soldier so she could be with her lover; they both served in the West Indies and Gibraltar. Just below the church is the collegiate-looking Wykeham Terrace, used at one time as a refuge for repentant fallen women and prostitutes: a very attractive Gothick confection in grey and white, with castellations and a tower.

Only open on Saturdays but definitely worth seeking out, its red brick contrasting strikingly with the white stucco of the area's domestic architecture, **St Michael and All Angels Church**, Victoria Road, is one of the greatest Victorian churches anywhere. It was built in 1858–61 by G F Bodley and later enlarged with cathedral-like proportions to designs by William Burges, who memorably embellished Cardiff Castle among others. The stained glass in this Anglo-Catholic incense-filled church is the finest of this period in Sussex, with designs by William Morris, Edward Burne-Jones, Philip Webb, Peter Paul Marshall, Charles Kempe and Ford Madox Brown: the man on duty who lends out binoculars to visitors told me 'from the east window in the south aisle which forms the original church, if you make a clockwise tour of the building you've got a complete history of Victorian stained glass.' He pointed out the window for which Dante Gabriel Rossetti's wife was the model and urged me not to miss the Lady's Chapel with its stained glass of the Flight into Egypt by Burne-Jones and the Three Marys at the Sepulchre by Morris. He also showed me the particularly quaint carved misericords – which feature a grasshopper atop a snail, and one frog shaving another (yes, really).

Further inland in Dyke Road, the **Booth Museum of Natural History** (*03000 290900; free; closed Sun morning and Thu*) dates from 1874 when Edward Booth presented his collection of stuffed-bird dioramas to the public.

Mathematical tiles

The black shiny bricks you see here and there in Regency Brighton aren't bricks at all, but so-called mathematical tiles – thin clay veneers that were all the rage in this corner of Sussex in the late 18th and early 19th centuries. Royal Crescent, in Kemp Town, is the longest frontage of mathematical tiles anywhere. The tiles appear in other colours too (and sometimes have been painted over). Lewes has the shiny black variety, as well as brick-coloured versions that take some spotting, and were tapped on over timber frontages to make the houses look more trendy. You can spot them throughout Lewes' High Street: look out for bow-windowed frontages where the tiles aren't quite flush and the building corners are covered over with wooden boards; the mathematical variety is slightly shorter than normal bricks.

The term 'mathematical' appears to be a piece of Georgian pretension, alluding to an age of discovery when all things scientific were deemed very cool.

In the churchyard at Brightling, 'Mad Jack' Fuller's pyramidal mausoleum is the aptly eye-catching memorial to a Georgian squire who dotted his estate with follies. (RA)

Eccentric Sussex

The area's many idiosyncracies are an enduring part of its appeal.

Sussex's widespread Bonfire celebrations are a joyous riot of nonconformity, complete with marching bands, burning torches and fancy dress. (PR/D)

No-one knows the age of the Long Man of Wilmington, a huge figure cut into the chalk escarpment, and its purpose is a mystery too. (AG/S)

A cruise out on a rigid inflatable from Eastbourne is an exhilaratingly wind-blasting experience and gets unbeatable views of Beachy Head. (TL)

Yurts, like this one at Wowo near Sheffield Park, combine the back-to-nature appeal of camping with creature comforts – even in deep winter. (W)

Activities

Part of the character of the region is the wealth of ways to enjoy the moment, whether by paddling a canoe, riding a horse or watching a craftsperson at work.

Among many traditional wood crafts encountered in the Weald is the art of using a pole lathe to turn wood. (ML/SC)

You can explore a tranquil corner of Sussex at a llama's pace at the Ashdown Forest Llama Park. (AFLP)

Experts say the South Downs escarpment is among the best places in the world for paragliding, a sport that is not difficult to learn and gives a remarkable perspective of the landscape. (TL)

Wild Weald

North of the Downs, the scenery could hardly be more different, with expansive watermeadows, hidden, intricate greens and landscapes, and tree-fringed hammer ponds.

Spring typically sees Wealden woods graced with vividly hued carpets of bluebells. (W)

The greensand country north of Midhurst in West Sussex has unexpected moments of rugged grandeur. (TL)

Home of the fictional Winnie-the-Pooh characters and haunt of the real Christopher Robin and his parents, the Ashdown Forest is a wild, heathy expanse, fiendishly easy to get lost in. (DBP)

Eridge Rocks, a miniature sandstone cliff, extends for half a mile through woods and bamboo thickets and is one of several prized challenges for rock climbers in the vicinity. (DBP)

In the meadows of the Arun Valley, Pulborough Brooks RSPB Reserve has a shimmering, watery beauty and attracts huge numbers of birds, butterflies and other wildlife. (RW/FLPA)

COPYHOLD HOLLOW BED & BREAKFAST

Copyhold Lane, Lindfield, RH16 1XU

01444 413265   info@copyholdhollow.co.uk

www.copyholdhollow.co.uk

RUBENS BARN

East Dean, West Sussex PO18 0JJ

01243 818187

info@rubensbarn.co.uk

www.rubensbarn.co.uk

"Rubens Barn is the perfect idyllic escape –
perfect in every way" Joseph Fiennes

Nestling in the South Downs and only 7 miles from historic Chichester, this 17th century flint barn is an exclusive romantic retreat with a tennis court, hidden within the majestic Goodwood Estate.

Rubens Barn is a luxurious self-catering accommodation (sleeps 4) surrounded by farmland and forests ideal for walking and cycling, located 1 mile from the Star and Garter pub in East Dean.

Relax and enjoy the welcome breakfast hamper, complimentary "White Company" toiletries, and fluffy white bathrobes.

A beautiful, eight bedroom house in the historic Cathedral grounds

A stay at George Bell House offers the convenience of a city centre location within the tranquil setting of the Cathedral precincts. An ideal location from which to explore the historic city of Chichester with its beautiful Cathedral, galleries and shops.

- Bed & Breakfast rates available
- Table d'hote menu
- All rooms en-suite
- Limited parking available
- Rooms to be booked in advance

For further information regarding availability and tariffs please contact reservations on 01243 813586 or email bookings@chichestercathedral.org.uk

Come Yurting at Meon Springs Yurt Village

"Outdoor living with indoor comforts"

- A beautiful location for a unique short break in a Mongolian Yurt.

- Lots of fun and loads to do for all the family (including the dog).

- Located on the South Downs Way in Hampshire.

See more at www.meonsprings.com Or call Alison or Jamie on 01730 823794

Since then, galleries of insects, fossils and ecology have been added making this one of the most notable displays of its kind. Jeremy Adams, one of the curators (now semi-retired), explained to me that in the 1850s Booth was one of the pioneers of the concept of dioramas or ecological displays that illustrate the whole ecology of birds rather than just exhibiting birds by themselves. Of its hundreds of such exhibits, about 300 date from Booth's time. 'The Booth Museum is known as the birthplace of dioramas, and the Smithsonian copied the concept from us. Booth's aim was to have one of every British bird – a male, a female, a juvenile and any plumage variation. He didn't quite make the full list but made a very good start.'

On Preston Drove in the Preston Park area, **Preston Manor** (closed Monday) is a highly evocative mostly Edwardian country house now lapped by comfortable suburbia: it's run by the city council, and guided tours take you back through the centuries. The assorted family trappings and domestic gadgets of yesteryear, pictures, sonorously ticking clocks and servants' hall vividly recreate Edwardian life for the privileged classes.

Hove, mainly Victorian in character, was traditionally rather more sedate and relaxed than Brighton, but the nuances are fading and the transition between Brighton and (as it's jocularly known) Hove Actually is hard for all but locals to discern. Hove tends to be popular with media types, and reputedly has the highest proportion of Apple Mac owners in the country.

Sussex County Cricket Club play at Hove. It's rather a ramshackle sort of ground, with a very appreciable slope and surrounded by blocks of flats, and the pavilion side-on to the playing area, meaning the best views are on the roof of the gym, on a terrace grandiosely known as the Gilligan Stand. The southern end is known with wonderful simplicity as the Sea End.

Hove Museum and Art Gallery (*free; closed Sun morning and Wed*) at 19 Church Road occupies a grandiose villa. Outside is the supremely ornate Jaipur Gate, carved from teak and sent by the Maharasjah of Jaipur to London for the Colonial and Indian Exhibition in 1886, and installed here 40 years later. Inside the museum is an eclectic collection of art, changing exhibits, a Wizard's Attic of toys and an excellent display about early Hove and environs. Perhaps best of all is the room about the early pre-Hollywood movie industry in Hove that was pioneered by James Williamson and George Albert Smith. The two were members of the Hove Camera Club, and began making films in the late 1890s. You can sit in a seven-seater cinema in the museum and watch a medley of their efforts – comic or melodramatic miniatures with titles such as *Mary Jane's Mishap – or Don't Fool with the Paraffin,* and *Our New Errand Boy,* some of it not that far removed from music hall acts, but sometimes with a touch of special effects wizardry that must have been astounding to early audiences. Note the everyday streets of Hove that served as a backdrop, and the children and pets of the film-makers that inevitably end up in the action. The mini show also includes some shots of everyday life along the Brighton seafront in various decades of the 20th century, and a magic lantern narration relating tales of woe and awe.

In the outer reaches of the city, near the junction of the A27 and A293, a camera obscura within **Foredown Tower**, an Edwardian water tower, gives a unique view of the Downs. It is a starting point for country walks, and the countryside centre here hosts nature and astronomy activities. The camera obscura is open at weekends and bank holidays in March–October; for information phone 01273 292092.

Food and drink

Traditionally Preston Street (inland from the old West Pier), St James' Street in Kemp Town and the Lanes have been the prime places for eating out, but it is now easy to find places all over town and prices don't vary hugely. For inexpensive **wholefoods**, three among several in the North Laine are Food for Thought (*16 Kensington Gardens ☎ 01273 674919*), Bill's (*100 North Rd ☎ 01273 692894*) and Kai Organic Café (*52 Gardner St ☎ 01273 387575; everything on offer is certified as organic by the Soil Association*). Aloka (*14 East St ☎ 01273 823178*), an alternative spa therapy/yoga centre, crystal and cosmetics shop and appetising vegetarian/vegan café all rolled into one has some amazing ice creams.

For **fish and chips**, there is one place you must, must visit though it's a bit away from the tourist mainstream: Bardsley's in Baker St (*☎ 01273 681256; closed Mon*) has been in the same family since 1926; the fish is the freshest and the chips perfect – they do seafood platters and grilled or fried fish (cod and haddock weren't on the menu when I last visited, but the bass, calamari and scallops were excellent). Not at all posh, but very efficient, and plenty of tables (including a private area at the back full of Max Miller memorabilia); note this is now unrelated to other chippies in town of the same name. For **freshly smoked fish** (including soup and sandwiches) the celebrated place is Jack and Linda Mills' Traditional Fish Smokers under the arches on the beach near the Fishing Museum – well worth the (frequent) queues.

Brighton's rather good on backstreet **pubs**. For beers, it's hard to beat the Evening Star (*55–56 Surrey St, a couple of minutes' walk from the rail station ☎ 01273 328391*), with a comprehensive collection of the local Dark Star Brewery's ales, other real ales from all over the country, real ciders, unusual lagers and bottled continental beers; no food to speak of, but a great place for the beer or cider connoisseur; regular live music. Tucked away in a street-corner location in the North Laine and just off the Old Steine, the Basketmakers' Arms (*Gloucester Rd ☎ 01273 689006*) is a very amenable Fuller's pub with good-value pub grub and Sunday roasts; the walls are plastered with old tins, beermats, old advertisements and posters. Two notable historic pub interiors are in the Lanes at the Cricketers (*Black Lion St*) and by the Theatre Royal in the Colonnade (*New Rd*).

Food shopping highlights include Infinity Foods in the North Laine (*25 North Rd; wholefoods, and very good bread*), Choccywoccydoodah in the Lanes (*24 Duke St; they take great pride in their all-chocolate window displays, featuring the likes of kittens, teapots, roses and all*) and Archer's butchers in Hanover (*128 Islingword Rd; fine organic meats and tempting pies*).

Brighton and Hove have a good array of markets. **Jubilee Square**, by the handsome new library in the North Laine, hosts various markets, including a crafts market in the run-up to Christmas. **Hove Farmers' Market** (*Ralli Hall, Denmark Villas, Hove, first Sunday of month, 10.00–14.00*) is veggie only, just round the corner from Hove station. Churchill Square hosts an **Italian Market** every Wednesday, and there's occasionally a food market held outside the **Theatre Royal**. Near the Hove Museum and Art Gallery at 214 Church Rd, the **Grasmere Farm Shop** has local Sussex foods, including cheeses, meats, smoked garlic and the like.

The **Brighton Spring Harvest** in March and the **Food Festival** in September are the largest events of their kind on the south coast, with markets and food-and-drink events.

Being entertained

Pleasure-seeking is what Brighton is all about. Here are some suggestions for starters:

All Saints recitals Free lunchtime classical recitals of chamber and instrumental music, every Thursday at 13.00, May–Sep. An excellent opportunity to bask in the architectural glories of All Saints, Eaton Rd, Hove.

Brighton Comedy Festival Held mostly at the Corn Exchange and the Pavilion Theatre within the Dome during most of October, this features big names among stand-up comedians.

Brighton Festival and Fringe Takes place throughout May and is one of Britain's leading art festivals. Visit during that month and you can hardly avoid stumbling into something arty. The House Festival (🖰 *www.aoh.org.uk*) features artists' open houses throughout the Brighton and Hove area.

Brighton Little Theatre Clarence Gardens, off Western Rd. Amateur theatre which has been going since 1940 and puts on ten to 12 productions each year.

Duke of York's Cinema Preston Circus. The oldest purpose-built cinema in the UK, and a Grade II listed building, this Edwardian picture palace opened in 1910 and is part of the excellent Picturehouse chain. Going here is always an occasion; Brighton's London Road station is handy.

Komedia 44–46 Gardner St. Right in the North Laine, the top venue for comedy and cabaret.

Marlborough Theatre Prince's St 🖰 www.drinkinbrighton.co.uk/marlboroughtheatre. Upstairs at the Marlborough pub. Wonderfully intimate and atmospheric 50-seater place dating back to 1794 that served as a ballroom and gambling hall.

Theatre Royal Just across from the Royal Pavilion, this beautifully preserved theatre has a Georgian core. The gorgeous adjacent theatre bar (with its main entrance on the street) called The Colonnade is full of theatrical memorabilia.

Tours

MP3 tours are downloadable for a small fee from the Visit Brighton website, under 'Tours'.

Blue Badge Tours Official Blue Badge guides can take you round Brighton; see the Visit Brighton website, under 'Tours'.

Brighton Ghost Walks Creepy ambles round the Lanes with tales of apparitions and chilling happenings, every Thu, Fri and Sat evening 19.30, outside Druid's Head pub, Brighton Place; ☎ 01273 328297 ⚲ www.ghostwalkbrighton.co.uk.

Brighton Sewer Tours certain dates May–Sep; booking essential; ⚲ www.southernwater.co.uk and search 'Brighton sewer tours'. 'We are walking anti-clockwise under the roundabout by the pier – if traffic drives over the manholes, they will rattle. Please do not look up otherwise you'll get dirt in your eyes.' Absolutely fascinating, this 300-mile netherworld of brick tunnels is a Victorian engineering marvel, built in the 1860s at a time when the crude sewerage system, consisting mostly of outflows on to the beach, was threatening to destroy the appeal of Brighton as a health-promoting resort. The problem didn't go away entirely though, as flash floods often caused the overflow to gush out into the sea. So in the 1990s the largest project of its kind in Europe was undertaken to make a 3-mile stormwater tunnel, where excess water can be stored 100 feet down and then pumped away. The tour starts from an unpromising-looking door beneath the Palace Pier – arch 260, next to a door advertising tarot readings. You begin with an explanatory film, and then don hard hats and latex gloves. You might spot rats and other nasties, but it is not as smelly as you might imagine, and all the walking is along (fairly) dry, brick overflow tunnels – following the trickle of an underground stream at one point. It's very hard not to expect Orson Welles to appear along the way, accompanied by the zither strains from *The Third Man*. You end up scaling a ladder and popping up through a manhole in the middle of the Old Steine Gardens.

Brighton Greeters ⚲ www.visitbrighton.com. One of the pleasures of travelling is meeting local people, and the Brighton Greeters scheme puts local people in touch with visitors. This is a relatively recent service whereby volunteers who live in the city meet you and show you round. The scheme is also available in Winchester. You book up through the website and choose a theme that interests you. When I tried this, I was contacted by Marilyn, a retired history teacher, who met me at the Brighton Visitor Centre by the Royal Pavilion Shop. She told me that it's totally volunteer-led, and that other Greeters are similarly mostly active retired: 'We're not professionals. We do it because we want to do it and don't take tips. The market we're expecting is from overseas, especially singles who want to meet a friendly face.' Three hours passed very fascinatingly, leaving me hoping that this scheme will spread elsewhere across the country.

Water activities

The Brighton Watersports Company Beachfront, west of Palace Pier ☎ 01273 323160 ⚲ www.thebrightonwatersports.co.uk. Kayak hire and lessons, wakeboarding, waterskiing, parasailing and surf lessons, watersports equipment.

Lagoon Watersports Centre Hove Lagoon, The Kingsway, Hove ☎ 01273 424842 ⚲ www. hovelagoon.co.uk. Powerboat driving, windsurfing, sailing and water skiing. See also box feature on windsurfing.

Ross Boat Trips Pontoon 4, Brighton Marina ℂ 07958 246414
🖰 www.watertours.co.uk. Offers 45-minute boat trips and 25-minute zips in a rigid inflatable along the Brighton sea front as well as fishing trips.
SailnetUK Pontoon 19, West Jetty, Brighton Marina ℂ 01273 628648
🖰 www.sailnetuk.com. Sailing and powerboating activities for all levels, from beginners upwards. Family-run, with self-catering accommodation that actually sits on a floating jetty in the marina.

Windsurfing for beginners

Standing on water attached to a board and a flimsy-looking sail may look like a recipe for extreme dampness, but the experts reassure me that windsurfing is a very steep learning curve and that total novices are actually windsurfing within half an hour, though becoming an expert obviously takes longer. Hove Lagoon Watersports give two-day courses for complete beginners (two lots of four-hour days) on Hove Lagoon, a former Victorian boating lake. The shallowness of the water and the sheltered conditions make this one of only three places in Sussex to learn windsurfing (the other possibilities are Princes Park Lake in Eastbourne and, at low tide only, in the sea at West Wittering). Super-fitness isn't essential by any means, and if you just stay on the lake you don't even need to be able to swim. It is a pretty thorough work-out though and seemingly uses every muscle in your body. The age range is eight upwards; when I spoke to them they had a 75-year-old active member. Three-hour taster sessions are very good value and include a go at windsurfing as well as kayaking and paddleboarding.

East of Brighton

⑤ Rottingdean

For many years this refuge from bustling Brighton enticed artists and writers to settle. The old centre is still appealingly villagey, with gracious old houses around its green, pond and the Rudyard Kipling flint-walled rose garden – despite the heavy, slow-moving traffic that nudges its way between the coast and the A27.

The pre-Raphaelite designer and artist Edward Burne-Jones moved here in 1880 and joined together three properties to form North End House, by the green. He is buried in the nave of St Margaret's Church, in which he designed a notable set of stained-glass windows. In 1897 his nephew Rudyard Kipling arrived from Torquay with his wife, two children and a third on the way, to take up Rottingdean residency at The Elms. He was thus among an extended family that included his favourite aunt, Georgie (the wife of Burne-Jones), and his cousin Stanley Baldwin, the future prime minister, a frequent visitor to his inlaws who lived in a nearby house called The Dene.

Kipling made numerous family excursions by car into the Sussex countryside, which had a profound effect on him, and recorded that the cousins took their families in farm carts 'into the safe clean heart of the motherly Downs for jam-smeared picnics'. During his time here he penned his *Just So Stories* and the village's notorious smuggling links were encapsulated in his poem *A Smuggler's Song* ('Watch the wall my darling, while the Gentlemen go by'). Eventually Kipling tired of the sightseers from Brighton, who would arrive by double-decker bus and could peer over his garden wall, and he left in 1902 for the Wealden seclusion of Bateman's near Burwash (see page 218).

Another artist, William Nicholson, visited to create a woodcut portrait of Kipling and was so taken with the village that he moved into the former vicarage, renaming it The Grange; it is now the volunteer-run **Grange Museum and Art Gallery** (*01273 301004; closed Wed; free*), with works by Sussex artists, and rooms dedicated to Kipling and Burne-Jones as well as local history; there is a tea garden too, serving snacks and light lunches. On the west side of the village tar-black Rottingdean smock windmill (1802) – also known as Beacon Mill – stands just above the coast on a grassy miniature South Down surveying a satisfying panorama all round.

⑥ Saltdean

During the 1930s Brighton began to expand eastward, and Saltdean promoted itself as the 'Coming Resort'. Although it is hardly the sort of place you would now go on holiday, it contains two magnificent examples of Art Deco in the form of the Saltdean Lido and Ocean Hotel. The Lido is the greatest example of its kind to survive. Built in 1935–38, this was perhaps inspired by the De La Warr Pavilion in Bexhill (see page 234). Designed by R W H Jones it has two storeys, with a café with curved metal windows on the upper storey, very much in the spirit of contemporary airport design. It was arranged with changing rooms below and sun terraces above. Alas, the pool was threatened with closure at the time of writing and seemingly destined to be turned into apartment blocks, though thankfully its listed status will save the buildings themselves from the bulldozers.

More Art Deco awaits in the form of the Ocean Hotel (also by Jones, and now flats), which was once home to Butlins. Look out too for a group of modernist houses just above the lido.

Beneath the cliffs is the concrete undercliff walk to Rottingdean, where cycling is allowed so long as pedestrians are given priority, making an enjoyable level traffic-free route. There's also a beach, accessed by a ramp, where lifeguards are in attendance during summer, and a small café is usefully positioned.

⑦ Peacehaven

Conceived in 1914 as a garden
city by the sea, Peacehaven
never quite lived up to the
aspirations of its pioneer, Charles Neville.
'A seaside home for £350' exclaimed a
poster in 1929 'Have your own
seaside home on the South Coast
– it will pay for itself. Live on the
glorious South Downs for
HEALTH AND HAPPINESS.
Every site commands views over
Sea and Downs.'

He engineered a brilliant publicity machine to kick things off: a competition to name this new resort was posted in the *Daily Express*. Some 80,000 entered, and thus Neville had his own mailing list: the winning entry got £100 cash, and then there were 50 offers of building plots supposedly offered for free. When it transpired that the 'free' plots required a conveyancing fee of £50 each, the Express's editor successfully sued Neville. Nevertheless the scheme had caught the public eye. People who had never ventured to the south coast before came out to look at this new utopia-by-sea. The winning name, New Anzac on Sea, paid homage to the Australia and New Zealand Army Corps ('Anzacs') who had had such a disastrous episode at Gallipoli during World War I; ultimately the name Peacehaven was preferred as something without associations of tragedy; a sensitive move considering that quite a lot of the punters were servicemen returning from the war.

Then Neville laid out roads, erected houses and sold building material to those who wanted to construct their own homes; supplies were then very short, but they managed to acquire buildings from a decommissioned army camp at Seaford. Early days in Peacehaven were indeed pioneering: a grid of tracks dotted randomly with shacks of wood and asbestos. It grew and improved; a 300-seat Pavilion Theatre appeared in 1923 and staged Gilbert and Sullivan performed by Peacehaven Operatic Society, the year after the creation of the Peacehaven Hotel with its sunken Italian gardens.

Not a great deal from those early days survives now, apart from the grid layout, landmark concrete 'pylons' on the road bearing the Peacehaven nameplate, and a handful of much-adapted properties. A lot of the rest has been rebuilt into a neat suburbia, but it surreally has a distinctly un-British feel – it could almost be somewhere in the US. On the seafront, the lawn-fringed unmade road by the coast offers a nice enough stroll, from the globe-topped obelisk that marks the point where the Greenwich Meridian leaves Britain's south coast; there are two access points (both east of the obelisk) to the foot of the sheer, chalky cliffs, and a concrete walkway along the bottom.

Away from the coast

Head northward from the coastal towns and you are soon into some very accessible and unspoilt country, especially away from the main roads. Sompting and Lancing lie close to the nastily busy A27, which heads eastwards past the campuses for the universities of Brighton and Sussex, and the newly completed football stadium at Falmer. The brick and concrete University of Sussex opened in the 1960s to designs by Sir Basil Spence, and is a rare 1960s building that is listed Grade I. It's in a rather beautiful sloping site, with a lantern-shaped chapter house and curving arches echoing the shapes of the Downs; its architectural merits might win over the most cynical anti-modernist, though its pitiful over-abundance of steps won't endear it to wheelchair users. Stanmer Park, near the universities, is a municipally owned country estate around a Georgian mansion, with free access to paths across 200 hectares of farmland and woodland.

⑧ Cissbury Ring

Sussex tots up 27 Iron-Age hillforts, of which this is easily the most impressive, and it contains a much earlier flint mine. Viewed from Google Earth, Cissbury is one of the most prominent features of the South Downs, with still-massive ramparts that take a good 20 minutes to walk around even at a brisk pace. There's a car park at its foot, at the end of a dead-end road leading up from Findon on the A24; but to make more of a walk of it, you could start beneath the car park at Chanctonbury Ring (see page 129), itself within strolling distance of Steyning and bus connections: from Chanctonbury there are plenty of easy bridleways crossing the arable plateau of the Downs, though it's a bit too intensively farmed to rank as one of the great walks in the area.

As a hillfort, the site dates from about 350BC: it surveys the coast from Beachy Head near Eastbourne to the east to Culver Cliff on the Isle of Wight to the west. In its day the ramparts would have been built up with a timber stockade; this protected the community, who lived in thatched round houses, and their livestock.

If you turn right along the ramparts you reach one of the largest of the ten known **Neolithic flint mines** in England. There's no sign announcing this, but it's an obviously disturbed, bumpy area within the ramparts, where between about 4500BC and 2300BC, people mined for flint. Using antlers for picks, they dug down through a series of shafts, all of which have been filled in, but the bushy hollows give the game away. It's a mystery why these folk went to such efforts to mine flint, when there was plenty of the stuff lying around on the surface – particularly good quality along parts of the coast. It's possible that there was some ritual attached to the perilous task of crawling into a hole and mining flint, or perhaps the mined flint had a certain prestige value assuming you knew someone had gone to all that effort. Archaeologists have found something that looks like graffiti etched into walls of some shafts, and rather more sinisterly some skeletons – one of a woman – who might have been performing some rite of passage; they were buried with some partly worked flint axes.

How to spot a worked flint

Present in abundance on England's chalklands, flint was the prized material of the pre-metal age. Extremely hard yet easily shaped, with the capacity to cut, bore or scrape, it was employed for a great range of purposes, including scrapers, knives, arrowheads and axes for felling trees.

The South Downs is one of the most renowned sources of prehistoric flintwork, and if you get your eyes trained, it's possible to spot flakes that were worked by prehistoric people thousands of years ago. By the flint mines in Cissbury there's quite a large concentration (though bear in mind that as it's a Scheduled Monument you can't dig here or take anything away – just look on the surface where the heritage-oblivious rabbits have unwittingly unearthed items). What you will find are predominantly waste flakes, not tools: they were chipped off when the flint knapper was making some object.

Top hints for spotting a worked flint are:

Colour: look for white flints. When a flint is newly broken, the broken part is black; over many centuries it gets a patina from the surrounding subsoil, which here is the white chalk (in other places you might be looking for grey, bluish, brown or – confusingly – black flints).

Shape: ignore the chunky bits, and look for thin slices.

Platform and face: there will be a flat 'platform' where the flint was struck, at right angles to the smooth (originally inside) face. Beneath the platform on the smooth face (which was the side of the flint joined to the larger bit of flint before it was struck) there's a little bulbous lump called a 'bulb of percussion'. This face will have a series of ripples that appeared like shock waves when the flint was struck. Sometimes you may even find evidence that the flint was 'retouched' along one edge to make it usable as a tool – for example as a 'scraper' for removing bark from a branch or flesh from a hide.

Scars: on the back, or dorsal, side there may be long bevelled facets where other bits of flint were knocked off.

⑨ Sompting

One very striking oddity here: St Mary's Church has a tower unlike any other in Sussex, but of a type commonly seen in the Rhineland of Germany. Rising 100 feet, it is of a type known as a Rhenish helm, with a four-sided, shingled, pyramidal cap. Its origins are clearly Saxon, and it dates from around 1000, although the timber within it has been radio-carbon-dated to the 14th century. Elsewhere are numerous Norman features, including the chancel and the characteristic rounded arches in the north transept. As Rhenish helms go, this is the oldest to be found anywhere in the country.

⑩ Lancing College

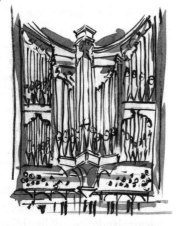

More ecclesiastical wonders await within this celebrated independent school, in the largest college chapel in the world, visible for miles for anyone striding along the South Downs Way or journeying along the A27. Begun in 1868 to the design of R H Carpenter and William Slater and open daily 10.00–16.00 (Sunday 12.00–16.00) it is built of Sussex sandstone. The chapel is a spectacular gothic revival edifice, lofty and ethereal, with its vaulted stone roof rising 90 feet and giving it cathedral-like proportions. Clear windows bathe the interior in natural light and illuminate tapestries designed at the William Morris workshops and richly carved stall canopies originally from Eton Chapel. At the west end, the rose window contains 30,000 pieces of blown glass and was the largest stained-glass window since medieval times.

Lancing College has a strong musical tradition: Benjamin Britten composed the *St Nicolas Cantata* for its centenary in 1948. This work is an enduring favourite of choral societies, and was conceived so that it could be performed by amateurs, with the addition of a professional tenor and string quartet to lead the other strings in the orchestra. The great tenor and Britten's lifelong partner Peter Pears attended the school. The college concerts, including lunchtime recitals, are open to the public.

⑪ Coombes

A Guy Fawkes ram
Brings forth an April fall lamb.

Tucked under a fold of the Downs and north of the A27 and Lancing College, the tiny hamlet of Coombes gets very busy in spring, when **Church Farm** (*BN15 0RS; 01273 452028; www.coombes.co.uk; farm tours during lambing, mid-Mar to mid-Apr, plus some Suns during school summer holidays, but see website or phone to check*) runs farm tours during the lambing and calving season, with up to 10,000 visitors coming over the weeks. It is a long tradition, stretching back to 1979, when this became the very first farm tour in the country, and gives a privileged insight into life and work on a Sussex farm. You are taken on a tractor and trailer right up to the top of the Downs, looking far over the Weald;

you'll hear about what you're looking at, how the farm is run, and how dew ponds are important and how they are formed.

Five generations of Passmores have farmed these 1,000 acres since 1901, the original family bringing their cattle from Devon. They had dairy cows until the 1950s, and in the following two decades turned to intensive farming in a period where food production was paramount. They now farm sheep and beef cattle and have arable fields with wheat for bread flour, animal feed, cakes and biscuits, and barley for animal feed and brewing beer.

Jenny Passmore told me that her father, Dick, received an MBE in 1992 for his farming and education efforts in the field of conservation. 'The conservation areas begun in the 1950s are always called "Dad's follies" – people didn't do conservation then. He was always progressive, and deliberately left areas for conservation for birdlife and flowers, planted trees and left an area we call the "bank of flowers" – this we graze sensitively to keep the scrub down. We get scabious, cowslips, orchids, poppies, clover and lots of butterflies like chalkhill blues.'

The South Downs is one of Britain's Environmentally Sensitive Areas (ESAs), in which farmers get subsidies in return for adopting agricultural practices that enhance landscape, wildlife habitats and areas of historic value. 'In 1987, the first year of the ESA, we joined the scheme – we're not allowed to use spray or fertiliser on the grassland, but manage it with sheep and cattle grazing and we 'top' the stinging nestles and thistles. We do use sprays and fertilisers on arable fields, where we grow wheat and barley; without doing this the crops wouldn't grow, as the Downs are so flinty and poor that we just wouldn't get a crop otherwise. Also if there's a disease in the area, we spray against it.'

'We have 800 ewes (Welsh mules) and rams (Charollais). We go to Breconshire, in Wales, in October, to buy replacements, near my brother's farm in the Llanthony valley. Welsh mules are a good breed that produces good twins and meat; the wool is a by-product – the price is half the cost of the shearing. My 16-year-old son Andrew has a shearing certificate, and Plumpton College students come here to learn.' The Passmores have 80 pedigree Sussex cattle: chocolate brown, but officially described as red. 'They're good, hardy animals, they rear their own calves, which stay with us till October. They produce a nice marbled beef – we used to have Limousin and Charolais cattle, which were leaner, but tastes have changed.'

Jenny says she loves the diversity of farming. 'The seasons and animals are always changing. In winter the animals stay out – the cows until Christmas and the sheep till the end of February. We end up with 1,200–1,400 lambs. We sell most of them and buy in replacements because you can't cross daughter and father. The beauty about lambing and calving is that everything's new. We calve and lamb at the same time. It's tiring but fun.'

Trevor Passmore runs **coarse fishing** here throughout the year on two ponds – Passies Pond and Match Lake – for carp, roach, tench, chub, rudd, bream and perch, with instruction and equipment available. Church Farm also hosts the

Glastonwick Beer Festival, on the first weekend of June, with music, poetry reading and other entertainment in addition to 80 real ales and numerous real ciders.

Accessed through a field just above Church Farm, the Norman **church** is seemingly oblivious of the passing of the ages: no electricity, no heavy-handed Victorian restorations, just a beautifully simple, untampered-with medieval building, with remains of 12th-century wall paintings uncovered in 1949 which include Christ in Majesty over the chancel arch, the inside of which bears some well preserved geometric abstract decoration. The bell could well be as early as 1100 and is thought to be the oldest in Sussex. The pews seat around 60, but over a hundred might squeeze in for the service on Christmas Day morning, followed by coffee in Church Farm's barn. On Rogation Sunday in May, the congregation process around the fields in a blessing ceremony with readings and singing.

The best station to cycle from is Shoreham, from where you can pedal along the traffic-free, entirely level Downs Link until it joins the South Downs Way, then turn south along the lane to Coombes.

⑫ Steyning and Bramber

Just west of the Adur, these two join together. **Bramber Castle** (free access) comprises merely the toothlike ruin of its gatehouse and chunks of curtain wall, in what is a favourite picnic ground for local families. Built as a motte and bailey, Bramber dates from the castle-building days of the Normans following the Conquest. Remnants of the outline of the foundations of the guardhouse and living quarters can be discerned next to it, but architecturally this is perhaps not one of the great castle moments of Sussex. At its base, the church built to serve the castle took a battering in the Civil War but still functions. Towards the river **St Mary's House** (*open Thu, Sun and bank holiday Mon, 14.00–18.00*) is a conspicuously historic half-timbered 15th-century house, originally a hospital for pilgrims. Its panelled interior features 16th-century parquetry overmantels, and the gardens contain rose beds, herbaceous borders, pools and topiary. Its Victorian music room, resplendent with stained glass and gothic detailing, stages numerous concerts and recitals.

Steyning is a handsome small town, in medieval times a prosperous port but doomed by the silting up of the river. Its High Street looks thriving enough nowadays, though, with proper food shops, as well as a bookshop doubling as the box office for professional chamber concerts and recitals organised by the Steyning Music Society. An impressive array of old buildings survive from its heady days, especially in Church Street, which is quite a treat for the eyes with its exceptionally well preserved jettied timber-frame houses and imposing brick facades. Near the library an absorbing stash of informatively captioned local history is on show in the free museum.

Opposite, St Andrew's Church was built by Norman monks from Fécamp in the 11th to early 12th centuries: within its lofty interior, massive dog-toothed arches and Norman windows survive from the early days. In the porch is an extraordinarily little-sung ancient curio in the form of a stone slab inscribed with primitive, possibly pre-Christian markings; for centuries this was placed face down and served as a step into the churchyard. It seems very possible that it is an idol from a pagan cult adhered to by locals until the arrival of St Cuthman in the 8th century. He reputedly arrived while carrying his mother in a wheelbarrow, only for the the strings around his shoulders to break here at Steyning, where he was persuaded to stay, and eventually built the church and converted locals. In a typical gesture of defiance of old ways, the stone seems to have been placed at the entrance so that Christian worshippers would effectively be disdainfully stamping out the pagans. The stone, which may give Steyning its name, meaning 'people of the stone', was only rediscovered in 1938. In the churchyard a modern sculpture of St Cuthman shows him doing his stuff with the evil stone – his foot rests on top of it. In spite of his endeavours, he was ousted as favoured saint here when French monks rededicated the church to St Andrew in the 12th century.

Steyning (and a car park further west, just beneath the Downs and signposted off the A283) makes a useful starting point for walks up on to the Downs, notably taking in **Chanctonbury Ring**, a prominent clump of beeches that is one of the most identifiable features on the escarpment. The Great Storm of 1987 wrecked it, and it is a fragment of how it previously looked, but is slowly regenerating itself and appears a good deal healthier than it did some 20 years back. It occupies the site of a Romano-British temple on the location of an earlier hillfort, and excavations after the storm revealed archaeology beneath where the trees had been. The dew pond at the top is a beautiful spot for a picnic, and the chalky tracks over the intensively farmed rolling plateau make for easy wandering right over to Cissbury.

Food and drink

Steyning Tearooms 32 High St ☏01903 810064. On the corner of Church St. Cosily friendly tearoom with very appetising snacks and cakes.

Sussex Produce Company 50 High St ☏01903 815045
⌂ www.thesussexproducecompany.co.uk. Among Steyning's admirable High Street food shops this is a super fruit and veg shop (next to the fishmonger's); they have a vegetable box scheme, buy from small-scale local growers and sell Fairtrade products too.

⑬ Woods Mill

The headquarters of the Sussex Wildlife Trust, this is where you can find out more about the trust's reserves, activities and courses. Free to access, the reserve around the 18th-century watermill is used heavily for educational purposes, but is a beautiful and richly diverse place in its own right, with a wheelchair-friendly trail of just under a mile lacing its way through coppice woodland, past a dipping pond frequented by water boatmen and dragonflies, across meadow land and around a reedy lake. Mike Russell of the Trust told me 'I'm very keen on stopping and listening. Woods Mill is one of the best places for nightingales – there are four types here. This is the essence of slowing down; as dusk comes, everything else goes quiet. The reserve demonstrates the richness of the ordinary.'

⑮ Devil's Dyke

Kite fliers will be very happy here on the escarpment looking out across the Weald. The ramparts of an Iron-Age hillfort crown the top of the slope at this most satisfying of viewpoints. Sadly a good many visitors probably miss out on what is actually the 'Dyke' itself – a deeply incised dry valley owned by the National Trust and formed during the last ice age. You can reach it by walking round the south side of the Devil's Dyke Hotel (actually a pub) from the escarpment, and along the road a few yards until the head of the valley appears on the left.

So named because of a legend that the devil gouged it out in a fit of pique, it has a few visible remains of the concrete footings of what was Britain's first cable car, built in 1894. This wasn't the only novelty way up: from Poynings a funicular railway made the ascent, and a railway line climbed its way up from Hove. It's still a particularly accessible spot on the Downs, easily reached by frequent buses from central Brighton at weekends and daily during July and August. The 1¹⁄₂-mile walk up from Poynings is extremely satisfying: along the bottom of the dry valley all the way to its head.

⑭ Ditchling and Clayton

Ditchling village was home to an artists' colony in the 20th century; it included Eric Gill and Edward Johnston. Gill's name as a calligrapher lives on in the form of the 'Gill sans' font, though his incestuous relationship with his daughters hardly endears him to posterity, while Johnston invented the sanserif font adopted by London Transport and still used for their very effective lettering on maps and tube-station signs. The story of this colony along with much other local history is told in the excellent **Ditchling Museum**, in a former school near the church. The annual London-to-Brighton Bike Ride – Britain's biggest event of its kind – saves its toughest moment for near the end with the ascent of **Ditchling Beacon** (814 feet), a favourite viewpoint capped by discernable ramparts of an Iron-Age hillfort. The site was donated to the National Trust in memory of a 21-year-old pilot shot down in the Battle of Britain: a finer memorial is hard to imagine.

Just beneath the downs at **Clayton**, the pre-Conquest **church of St John** has one of the finest series of wall paintings in Sussex, depicting the Fall of Satan, the

New Jerusalem and other scenes, painted in the 11th century. Across the A273, **Clayton railway tunnel** has a spectacular castle-like portal – which you can just see by peeping over from the road. The tunnel witnessed what was at the time the worst-ever train collision in Britain in 1861 when three northbound trains crashed into each other after the first had stopped because of a red flag being waved by a signalman; the mayhem resulted in 176 people being injured and 23 deaths. Charles Dickens was very likely prompted by this event to write his short supernatural story of 1866 *The Signal-Man*, about a signalman apparently haunted by the future spectre of himself. Above, on the Downs and most easily reached from the dead-end road leading up from the A273 just south of Clayton, two windmills known as **Jack and Jill** (*www.jillwindmill.org.uk*) preside over the scene as they did when last in full use in 1906. Jack is a brick tower mill, in private ownership, but Jill, a wooden post mill, is open most Sunday afternoons between May and September. Jack resulted in the invention of the rotating gun turret for naval ships by Captain Cowper Coles': his daughter and naval-officer son-in-law lived in the windmill, the technology of which germinated the idea.

West of Clayton, **Wolstonbury Hill** is a rare separate peak in the South Downs. Capped by prehistoric earthworks, it is often bypassed by walkers because it is not on the South Downs Way, and although it is sandwiched between the A23 and A273 you can neither see nor hear the the roads from the top. The National Trail officer for the South Downs Way, Andy Gattiker, told me that it is a favourite spot of his: 'Its subtle detachment makes it special and gives it a 360-degree view you don't get from other viewpoints. You can see the undersides of the scarp, both to the east and to the west.'

Food and drink

Ditchling Tearooms Ditchling ℃ 01273 842708. In the middle of Ditchling, opposite the church, this popular tearoom gets lots of touring cyclists ('we had a hundred in the other week'). It received an award for the largest scones in the south and also does takeaway pizzas on Fri and Sat nights; cream teas, all-day breakfasts, light lunches; sit inside, or in the back garden.

Jolly Sportsman East Chiltington, BN7 3BA ℃ 01273 890400. Very peacefully placed in a hamlet at the end of a narrow lane and located east of Ditchling and northwest of Lewes, this dining pub enjoys a strong reputation. Its dining rooms have a fresh, contemporary feel, and the sense of style extends to the food too, which is cooked and presented with considerable flair. The garden, play area and terrace look out to the South Downs, and the bar has an authentically pubby character, with real ale, farm cider and an excellent wine list.

Ridge View Wine Estate Fragbarrow Lane, Ditchling Common BN6 8TP ✆ 0845 345 7292 🖰 www.ridgeview.co.uk. North of Ditchling off the B2112, this highly regarded winery offers tastings and sales of its wines. In 2010 the winery won the Decanter Trophy for Best Sparkling Wine in the World, beating prestigious French champagne growers in the process. Occasional tours (see website); shop open 11.00–16.00 Mon–Sat.

A walk from Ditchling Beacon

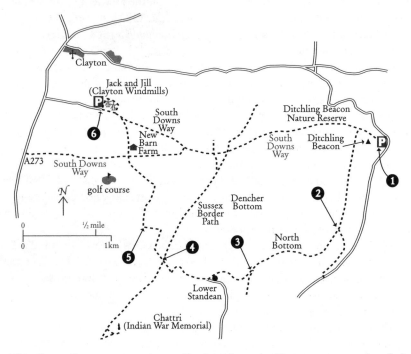

This five-mile route gets you really deep into the Downs scenery that feels miles from anywhere, into the secretive folds, ancient-looking dry valleys and rolling cornfields speckled with poppies and skylarks singing above, then Brighton suddenly appears as a reminder how close it is, before the finale along the much more frequented South Downs Way, with those endless views over the Weald, the Surrey hills and Black Down. On the way you can take a detour to the Chattri War Memorial and you pass by the Jack and Jill Windmills.

The **Chattri War Memorial** was erected to honour 'the memory of all the Indian soldiers who gave their lives for their King-Emperor' on the site of the funeral pyre of the 53 Sikh and Hindu soldiers who fought for Britain on the West Front during World War I and died after being brought to Brighton for hospital treatment. In its downland setting looking over Brighton, the Chattri – 'umbrella' in Punjabi, Urdu and Hindi – was created of Sicilian marble by a Mumbai designer, its canopy supported by eight columns. In June there is a memorial service held here, with a sizeable turnout from local dignitaries, Indian soldiers in spectacular formal dress and the British Legion. The detour to the Chattri adds an extra mile but is very easy walking.

Start: Ditchling Beacon National Trust car park, at the very top of the road signed to Ditchling from the A27 (buses from Brighton station and Old Steine on Sundays and bank holidays, plus Saturdays April–October; discounts available if you hold a rail ticket to Brighton or Hove); pay and display (free if National Trust parking sticker is displayed). You could also use a free (and larger) car park at Jack and Jill Windmills reached from the A273 and start the walk at point **6**. No refreshments en route, but often an ice-cream van in Ditchling Beacon car park.

1 Take the path at the back of the car park, by the National Trust sign for Ditchling Beacon. Follow the South Downs Way for 200 yards up to the top then down a little, until turning left through a gate signposted Heathy Brow. This soon drops and later runs between fences.

2 After ½ mile along this path, reach a gate at a three-way signpost and bear half right along the bottom of a dry valley called North Bottom; you later see another remarkably unspoilt dry valley – Dencher Bottom – away to the right. After a fence joins on the right, cross it at the signposted gate and continue along it a further 150 yards.

3 You need to take care to bear right at a waymarker (indicated as point 39 on the Downs on Your Doorstep walk), up a stony track, leaving the valley floor. 100 yards later, bear left to leave the track (this wasn't at all obvious initially when I was last here) and walk alongside a line of trees which curves round to the right. Just after a fence begins on the left, take the signposted gate on the left – this bends right and leads down to a track by Lower Standean farm buildings. Turn right along the track, out of the farm. Pass a lone brick-and-flint barn up on the left, avoid a minor track to the left soon after and keep on the main track up to a gate. The route (now clearly waymarked as the Chattri and the Windmills walk) bends left, then right.

4 At a four-way bridleway junction in the next field (indicated as waymark point 13 on the Chattri walk), the route ahead, along the field edge, is the continuation, but first detour left through the gate to see the **Chattri War Memorial**. After ½ mile, go through a gate, and go down to the left a few steps to the Chattri, beyond another gate. Return to point **4** and turn left along the field edge. The path goes through a gate and bends right uphill between

Sheep on the Downs

Traditionally the Southdown breed were, as the name implies, the sheep of the South Downs. Sheep have probably grazed the Downs since Neolithic times, although the early beasts would have looked very different. Gilbert White in *The Natural History and Antiquities of Selborne* (1773) describes sheep on the west of the Adur valley as horned with smooth, white faces and white legs 'but as soon as one passes over the river heading eastwards the animals become hornless, have black faces and speckled legs. Shepherds tell you this has been the case since time immemorial'. The speckled type became the norm of Southdown sheep through careful selective breeding by one John Ellman of Glynde, who saw the scope for producing a hardy strain of sheep that could flourish on downland vegetation. Other farmers paid huge sums for the services of Ellman's ram, and he and other landowners founded the Sussex County Agricultural Society. In the 19th century, Southdown sheep became big business, with the annual wool fair at Lewes bringing in up to 30,000 of them; they were exported worldwide, allegedly as far as the Andes in Peru.

A sharp demise followed, intensified by the need in World War II to give over some areas to tank training. Southdowns are now quite a rarity – in 1798 around 150,000 grazed the Downs between Shoreham and Eastbourne; by the 1950s this number was down to 25,000 on the Downs between Brighton and Eastbourne; today barely a tenth of that number is found across the entire country, and the Southdown has been declared a Rare Breed. The old Southdowns' fatty meat has gone out of favour, though Terry Wigmore, who has a flock of 30 Southdowns at his farm at East Dean (the Seven Sisters Sheep Centre; see page 182), told me you need that fat to make the most of the special taste. Instead a breed of sheep known as mules are ubiquitous across much of Britain – they produce saleable meat and a ewe reliably has two or three lambs.

Despite a recent upturn in knitting as a hobby, the prices sheep farmers get for their wool are derisory. A fleece of the finer wool types is worth only around 90p, meaning that meat production is always the reason for having sheep nowadays.

On some of the Downs, hardy sheep breeds – notably Orkneys and Herdwicks – have been introduced to keep down the amount of invasive scrub that threatens grassland species. Herdwicks, brought in from the Lake District where they perform a crucial role in maintaining the landscape, have a very coarse wool that copes with the harsh Cumbrian climate. Their fleeces sell only for around 8p each.

The Sussex Wildlife Trust has been instrumental in operating grazing schemes, centred on Southerham Farm, by the Trust's reserve on Malling Down near Lewes, where it manages a flock of 1,000 sheep, including many rare breeds, as well as a small number of cattle.

fences, then left around a field. You can see **Jack and Jill windmills** to the right and **Wolstonbury Hill** straight ahead.

❺ 200 yards later turn right at a path junction in the middle of the field. This drops and bends left around the end of a golf course. Keep forward at a four-way junction, on the South Downs Way, past New Barn Farm. Turn left at the next junction on the track down to Jack and Jill car park (or turn right on the South Downs Way if you don't want to make the short detour past the windmills).

❻ Go right through the car park to see the windmills, and turn right at the end of it on a path that loops round to join the South Downs Way. In the distance you can see a third windmill beyond Ditchling. Turn left on the South Downs Way, and follow it all the way to Ditchling Beacon – after about ten minutes with nothing much happening the views open up gloriously, and you pass several **dew ponds**. The highest-located building you can see away to the right is Brighton racecourse.

Dew ponds

With the lack of surface water for cattle and sheep to drink on the permeable chalk, dew ponds are very much a characteristic of the South Downs landscape, and may originate from Saxon or even prehistoric times. These small ponds, high up and sometimes marked by a few trees, are manmade: layers of straw and clay form an impermeable lining on the chalk or lime base, with a top layer of rubble as a protection from beasts' hoofs. Contrary to what was formerly thought by some, the act of animals walking round the dew pond actually helps reseal the bottom of the pond and prevents cracking and the growth of pond weed. A farmer explained to me 'If the animals are healthy, then the pond is healthy.'

N

| 0 | | | 4 miles |
| 0 | | 5km | |

A275

A26

A22

⑨ Bentley Wildfowl and Motor Museum

⑩ Farley Farm House

HAILSHAM

① LEWES

A27

⑧ Glynde

⑭ Michelham Priory

Middle Farm

⑮ Arlington Reservoir

A22

② Spring Barn Farm

③ Kingston

A27

⑪ West Firle

⑫ Charleston

⑬ Berwick

⑯

④ Rodmell

South Downs Way

Alciston

Drusillas

⑰ ✝ Wilmington

River Ouse

A26

⑱ Alfriston

Lullington Church

⑤ NEWHAVEN

PEACEHAVEN

A259

Cuckmere River

㉒ Combe Hill

⑥ Tide Mills

Seaford A259

⑲ Friston Forest

⑦

Exceat

㉑

Seaford Head

East Dean

Cuckmere Haven Seven Sisters

⑳

Birling Gap

㉓ Beachy Head

LEWES DOWNS TO BEACHY HEAD

4. LEWES DOWNS TO BEACHY HEAD

Sussex's most sublime stretch of coast is within this small chunk of the South Downs, comprising the cliffs between Seaford and Eastbourne. But it's a relatively brief affair; if there's one place above all that needs to be savoured slowly, this is it – browsing a rockpool at Cuckmere Haven, munching a sandwich and spotting Bronze-Age flints on turf clifftops, or drinking in the view of the wavy profile of the Seven Sisters from Seaford Head. Westwards, a huge shingle beach lines the low-lying coast all the way to Newhaven, a clean and inviting sweep of shore that makes one of the best swimming spots hereabouts.

Inland, the Downs have some really quiet moments: even though this is one of the most thoroughly thumbed parts of the national park, there is plenty for escapists. The ever-nasty but useful A27 disappears from view and earshot completely as you ascend into the world of skylarks either side of the Cuckmere valley near Alfriston; the South Downs Way encounters a primeval moment above the enigmatic Long Man of Wilmington, Britain's tallest chalk hill figure above the head of Deep Dean, a secretive dry valley unaltered by modern agriculture, its slopes too steep for the plough.

Lewes gets a trickle of canny tourists but apart from the spectacular exception of bonfire night in November is never particularly overrun. Sloping, neighbourly, enticing, nonconformist, ancient, distinctive – it stimulates plenty of adjectives. It is my own town, and if I had to single out a favourite landmark view I would say it is the prospect down School Hill, past Harveys Brewery with its periodic malty aroma wafting over passing shoppers, to the Downs above. Art and music are big in the vicinity: many musicians working at Glyndebourne Opera House are based in town or around, and opera-goers often stay over and discover the town's many pleasures. Lewes also makes an obvious base for those on the trail of Virginia Woolf, who lived nearby at Monk's House in Rodmell, and her bohemian sister Vanessa Bell and her entourage at Charleston near the estate village of Firle. Anyone keen on the Charleston set should also beat a path to Farley Farm House at Muddles Green for one of the entertaining and erudite Sunday tours of the former house of surrealist painter Roland Penrose and the photographer Lee Miller, where Picasso once visited.

Getting around

Trains

Your options by rail aren't bad at all. Lewes is the hub, with frequent services to Brighton, Eastbourne, Hastings, Seaford and London Victoria.

Lewes to Seaford: A strange little branch line that keeps going by virtue of the ferry at Newhaven. **Southease** is a tiny, rural halt slap bang on the South Downs Way, so it is ideal for walkers or cyclists: westwards you head through Southease and up to the top of the Downs above Kingston and Iford, and can also get to Virginia Woolf's house at Rodmell (best to avoid the main road above Southease by turning right as soon as you cross the river and walk along the Ouse until a track heads west to Rodmell); or eastwards up to Itford Hill, Beddingham Hill and Firle Beacon, from where you can drop down to Firle, Firle Place and Charleston Farmhouse for a very full day's walking and cultural sightseeing. **Newhaven** station is on the other side of the harbour from the fort (a 20-minute walk, grotty at the start but better once you're off the main road). **Newhaven Harbour** is useful for nothing apart from the ferries. **Bishopstone** is handy for the beach (five minutes' walk), along which you can walk west to Tide Mills or east to Seaford. **Seaford** is very slightly further inland, but useful for the east end of the beach and the stroll up on to Seaford Head for the view of the Seven Sisters.

Lewes to Eastbourne: Just one stop after Lewes is **Glynde**, the sort of place you can imagine in an Enid Blyton story: a classic little Victorian country station right in the middle of the village and virtually adjacent to the Trevor Arms (which is on the right as you come out of the station). Ideal for a wander up Mount Caburn and back down to Lewes (turn left, then left at the road junction and immediately right opposite the tea shop, and the path leads straight up; just over three miles, but easily extended). From Glynde you could also walk to Firle fairly easily, but the A27 noise spoils it and despite a traffic island it's not pleasant to cross. Cyclists may like to dismount here and to get access via Firle to the Old Coach Road or the South Downs Way. The next stop, **Berwick**, links up nicely with a weekend bus service known as the Ramblerbus that gets you into the Cuckmere Valley (see *Buses*, below); note that Berwick village is a mile's trudge down a busy road and over the A27. **Polegate** is useful for cyclists, as the station is close to the Cuckoo Trail and to the tranquil, marshy farmlands of the Pevensey Levels (see pages 224 and 233).

Buses

Newhaven to Eastbourne: Buses from Brighton to Eastbourne run frequently (every ten minutes; every 30 minutes on Sunday) along the A259 to get you to rail stations at Newhaven, Seaford and Eastbourne: this is very useful particularly for point-to-point walks along the coast, such as from Friston along the Seven Sisters to Cuckmere Haven then inland along the valley to Exceat. For the Seven Sisters Country Park, get off at Exceat – not really a village, just a bus stop and a few buildings at a wiggle on the A259 just where it is about to rise eastwards. Beachy Head has services from Eastbourne on Sundays.

Cuckmere Valley – Berwick rail station to Seven Sisters: At weekends and on bank holiday Mondays the extremely useful Cuckmere Valley Ramblerbus takes a circular route hourly from Berwick rail station and links in all the key places in the valley: Drusillas Zoo, Alfriston, High and Over, Seaford, Exceat/Seven Sisters Country Park, Litlington, Wilmington and back to Berwick rail station. That gives a lot of permutations for bus-assisted walking routes and car-free sightseeing.

Cycling

My wife Anne and I have created a **cycle map** for Lewes and District. Available free from tourist information centres and other points, or downloadable from www.cyclelewes.org.uk (click on Routes, then on either town map or district map). The roads down the Ouse Valley from Lewes are not good news for cyclists, but there are better alternatives, notably the network of quiet lanes north of the A27 east from Glynde. Off-road, you can take the **Cuckoo Trail** (see page 166) between Eastbourne and Heathfield, much of it along a former rail trackbed and easily reached from Polegate station; or the **Old Coach Road**, an unsurfaced track beneath the South Downs from West Firle to Alfriston. For an energetic day's off-roading along the **South Downs Way**, the section from Lewes to Eastbourne is recommended.

Bike hire

M's Cycle Hire ☎07852 986165 ⌂ www.m-cyclehire.co.uk. A mobile cycle hire service; they will deliver and pick up bikes free of charge anywhere between Chichester and Lewes. Helmet, lock, lights and tool kit are provided.

Seven Sisters Cycle Company Next to Seven Sisters Country Park Visitor Centre, Exceat ☎01323 870310 ⌂ www.cuckmere-cycle.co.uk. Mountain bike hire ideal for Friston Forest and the Seven Sisters Country Park.

Accommodation

For the Lewes area in general, there's a useful list of B&Bs not affiliated to the tourist office but of a good general standard: see ⌂ www.lewesbandb.co.uk.

Beachy Head Holiday Cottages East Dean BN20 0AA ☎01323 423906 ⌂ www.beachyhead.org.uk. Three different beautifully updated and quietly located traditional flint-and-oak 18th-century self-catering cottages adjoining each other in the old part of East Dean village, a stroll away from the village green and the Tiger Inn, and within walking distance of the Seven Sisters, Beachy Head and Friston Forest. Beachy Barn sleeps six, Giddy Cottage sleeps four, and single-storey Chestnut Lodge sleeps five. Part of the Green Tourism Business Scheme. Weekly prices from £360; weekend and midweek lets available.

Belle Tout Lighthouse Beachy Head BN20 0AE ☎01323 423185 ⌂ www.belletout.co.uk. Not cheap, but an utterly dreamlike location right on the cliffs between Beachy Head and Birling Gap, with unrivalled views of the sea or downs from each of its six characterful rooms, and one of the two bedrooms is in the lantern room. The smallest room, Keeper's Loft, is the former lighthouse keeper's bunk room. Enjoy complimentary wine and nibbles each day, inside or outside. Prices from £155 for two adults sharing; minimum stay two nights.

Danny Cottage Winton St, Alfriston BN26 5UJ ☎ 01323 870406
🖰 www.dannycottage.co.uk. Quaint thatched and beamed self-catering cottage (formerly owned by the National Trust) quietly located on the very edge of the village, ideal for walks on to the Downs, and a ten-minute stroll from the shops and pubs. Three bedrooms, sleeping six, two bathrooms, lots of antiques and far from a standard rental cottage in character. Central heating and a log-burning stove make it snug for winter visits. Large, well maintained garden edged by woods populated by badgers. £600–£950 a week; short lets available off season. Dogs welcome.

Foxhole Campsite and Camping Barn Seven Sisters Country Park, Exceat BN25 4AG ☎ 01323 870280 🖰 www.sevensisters.org.uk. Nicely tucked away, towards the beach at Foxhole (no car access). I've mountain-biked here over from Lewes and put up my tent, so I could get up early on a heavenly summer's morning and have the beach at Cuckmere Haven to myself; highly recommended. Space for 20 tents; April to October only. £4.50 per adult (£6.50 in the camping barn).

Millers 134 High St, Lewes BN7 1XS ☎ 01273 475631
🖰 www.millersbedandbreakfast.com. At the top end of the High Street on St Anne's Hill, Tony and Teré Tammar's 16th-century house is sympathetically furnished with antiques, and with four-poster beds in each of its three double bedrooms; the room at the back has views over the garden, one of those secretive Lewes spaces you can't see from anywhere else; there is also a resident cat. Two rooms for breakfasting in; the larger one has a splendidly ecclesiastical harmonium as well as framed samplers embroidered by Teré. B&B is £95 double, £85 for single occupancy; slight reductions if staying more than one night.

Netherwood Lodge Muddles Green, Chiddingly BN8 6HS ☎ 01825 872512
🖰 www.netherwoodlodge.co.uk. 'You should be hailed as a national treasure' wrote one visitor in an appreciative card to Margaret Clarke, the friendly and enthusiastic owner of this B&B, tucked away in a little hamlet next to Farley Farm House and within walking distance of the excellent Six Bells pub at Chiddingly. Her single-storey house makes a relaxing retreat; its double room overlooks her meticulously tended English garden, with its roses, scented flowers, lavender hedge and fuchsias. Breakfast features items like fresh blueberries or apricots, home-made preserves and organic eggs. From £50 per person.

Old Whyly London Rd, East Hoathly, BN8 6EL ☎ 01825 840216
🖰 www.oldwhyly.co.uk. As soon as you turn off the road, you are into ancient parkland, as you near the house along a gravel drive lined with venerable oaks. This is a superior and elegant B&B (with dinner available on request) in a fine country house, squared off in Georgian times but with medieval parts too. Rooms are restrained, immaculately presented, well proportioned and light, and furnished with

thoughtfully chosen antiques; family portraits adorn the imposing hall around the staircase. Sash windows look out on to quintessentially English grounds, with lawns, herbaceous borders and a pergola, and there's a hedge-sheltered heated swimming pool as well as a tennis court. The Wealdway passes directly by along the driveway just outside. £90–£140 double or twin.

Spring Barn Farm Kingston Rd, near Lewes BN7 3ND ☎01273 488 450 ✆ www.springbarnfarm.com. Simple camping field in a downland valley beneath the Kingston ridge, adjacent to the farm park with its animal collections, adventure playground, farm shop, restaurant and children's activities, making a super place for families to stay. I have heard of people from Lewes who spend the weekend here with their children, making a journey of less than two miles – you can't get much Slower than that. For prices see website.

Tiger Inn East Dean BN20 0DA ☎01323 423209 ✆ www.beachyhead.org.uk. Four doubles and a twin room above a well-run village pub, right on the traffic-free village green. The rooms have been tastefully refurbished to a high standard in a blend of traditional and contemporary and are all en suite; three of them overlook the green itself. Excellent location for exploring the Seven Sisters and Beachy Head. £90 per room per night.

Wilmington Priory Wilmington ☎01628 825925 ✆ www.landmarktrust.org.uk. Apart for annual open days, this is not open to the public, but what a place to splash out on a self-catering escape (£1,000 or so for three nights, sleeping six). Next to the car park for the Long Man, this was a Benedictine foundation belonging to an abbey at Grestain in Normandy, then became a farmhouse and is now let by the Landmark Trust as holiday accommodation. It's a wonderful mishmash of periods and styles, and bits of it are in ruins including the former Great Chamber.

Tourist information centres

Lewes 187 High St ☎01273 483448.
Seaford 37 Church St ☎01323 897426.

Lewes and the lower Ouse Valley

The National Park spreads just north of Lewes, where the land rises. Southwards the Ouse meanders towards the sea, and in winter the valley is often speckled with partially flooded fields. Quarrying has left some striking cliff edges above the valley; on the east side of Lewes, peregrine falcons can often be seen above the sheer chalky drops. The unclassified road heading from Lewes Prison down to Newhaven bypasses a string of villages, notably Rodmell. Southease is an unexpected haven of tranquillity with its sloping triangular green below the church, while a rare bottle-shaped brick kiln – the only one in Sussex – marks the entrance to one-street Piddinghoe, the easiest access point for the riverside path.

① Lewes

Ensconced on the River Ouse as it flows between the South Downs, Lewes has a character unlike any other town in the southeast. It's remarkably hilly and squashed together by its setting, with a Norman castle crowning an imposing hillock and the South Downs dominating the view as you look down its main street. Its array of historic buildings is remarkable for both quantity and variety – along the main High Street and down School Hill, across the river into Cliffe, and down the hillside to the south to the Southover district, with its supremely handsome shop-less High Street.

The main axis runs along a shelving ridge for about a mile, lined for the most part with notable buildings – variously tile-hung, brick, weatherboarded, with mathematical tiles (see page 116), stone-fronted and flint cobbled. Leading from this are the narrow lanes known in this part of Sussex as **twittens**; some date back to Saxon times and all of them are worth exploring. **Pipe Passage** (named for the manufacture of clay pipes in a tiny, now overgrown kiln), by the site of what was once the West Gate, leads along the former sentry walk above a high chunk of town wall; the sail-less windmill here was briefly owned by Virginia Woolf. Across the High Street, cobbled **Keere Street** drops steeply southwards – at the bottom another section of town wall faces Grange Gardens and Southover High Street lies just beyond.

Lewes has kept itself remarkably free from the cloned town-centre look, thanks in part to its preponderance of independent shops; these include Harveys Brewery Shop and Reeves, the latter reputedly the world's oldest high-street photographers, at 159 High Street since 1858. This has some of the original equipment in the studio at the back, as well as glass slides of the original photos stretching back to the early years.

The town has for long had a tradition of nonconformity – comedian Mark Steel described its essential character as 'stroppy' – and on 5 November (or the day before if 5 November falls on a Sunday) celebrates **Bonfire**, the hugest and most clamorous Guy Fawkes night in the country. If you visit Lewes in the weeks preceding, you'll see hoopy-jerseyed 'bonfire boys' selling bonfire programmes or generally at large in the town centre. The event features races with tar barrels, laying wreaths at the war memorial, a mammoth procession with bonfire society members of all ages in elaborate, hand-made costumes, marching bands, effigies and satirical tableaux stuffed with fireworks and destined to be exploded, and bonfire boys dropping lit 'rookies' (commercial bird scarers) that detonate with ear-shattering noise. Bonfire societies from all over Sussex – who have their celebrations on other weeks (see box on page 216) – join in the main procession, apart from the Cliffe Bonfire Society, who for historical reasons march separately. After that, the Lewes societies – Waterloo, Commercial Square, Cliffe, Southover, South Street and Borough – march off with burning torches to their various bonfire sites for their own displays. The organisers always stress that this is an event for the town and not really for outsiders; nothing is timed to precision, and although no one will be turned away the event is not actively promoted. Nevertheless huge crowds come in anyway, and hotels get booked for the event years ahead.

Quite what Lewes Bonfire is all about is open to a lot of debate. Its origins are undoubtedly anti-Catholic, including commemorating the burning of 17 Protestant martyrs outside Lewes Town Hall in the 1550s and the installation of William of Orange as a Protestant monarch. The Cliffe Bonfire Society put up banners proclaiming 'no popery' in Cliffe High Street and ceremonially burn an effigy of the Pope who was installed at the time of the Gunpowder plot. That said, there are Catholic members in the bonfire societies, so it doesn't do to try to read too much into it, and I reckon it is essentially a community celebration of 'a Sussex man won't be druv'. Other similar celebrations took place in other southern English towns but died out or were suppressed; in Lewes the organisation into formalised bonfire societies in the 19th century probably saved the day.

So Sussex

Very much attuned to the Slow concept, Nigel and Maria Greenwood run **So Sussex** (*www.sosussex.co.uk*), a business in East Sussex that tailor-makes visits to the countryside, particularly near Brighton and Lewes. 'We explore Sussex off the beaten track and use outdoor activities as a way of learning about, enjoying and appreciating the countryside,' explained Nigel. 'We're locals and we show visitors aspects of an area they're unlikely to see, so they really get under the skin of Sussex. I love seeing people catch their first fish or being astonished as the landscape suddenly opens below them from the top of the Downs. So Sussex caters for individuals or groups (including corporate groups and schools), on such activities as mountain bike rides, walks, fishing trips, bushcraft skills and mushroom forays. Maria is Swedish and got Nigel into the mentality of hunter-gathering for edible mushrooms: 'on a mushroom walk we choose the venue and the timing according to when the mushrooms are most likely to be at their best – we teach what's edible, where the mushrooms are likely to be, and even explain how they can be used in dyeing.' So Sussex can pick you up wherever is convenient (from a railway station for example) and hire bikes for you, and should you wish can include a visit to a country pub as part of the day out.

Lewes Castle and its precincts

The castle crowns a steep-sided artificial mound within a dry moat. William de Warenne, the brother-in-law of William the Conqueror, built the first castle on nearby Brack Mount (see page 145) to show in no uncertain terms who was in charge. This was soon replaced by a simple motte and bailey on this main mound, to be rebuilt stronger and larger around 1100, with angled towers added in the first half of the 13th century.

Castle Gate, the little cobbled street that leads to it from the High Street, is spanned by two contrasting arches – the imposing Barbican, complete with portcullis slot, was built in the early 14th century primarily for show; beyond it the simpler, rounded arch is Norman. You can wander up this street for free and peer into the castle precincts (though a lot of visitors can't believe this is a public road), but of course the views are much more revealing from within (you pay at Barbican House, opposite). Lewes Castle is owned by Sussex Past, the commercial arm of the Sussex Archaeological Society (*www.sussexpast.co.uk*).

The **castle grounds** were partly beautified into a pleasure garden by Thomas Friend, who acquired the site in 1726, and by his successors, and Lewes Castle's gardens became an early tourist attraction. At the bottom, the gun garden has some quaintly irrelevant bits and pieces: a Crimean-era Russian cannon, a huge, rusty 300-year-old anchor from Newhaven and by the old stocks some handsome railings made in the Weald and intended for the area around London's St Paul's Cathedral. A path climbs up, giving access to the rooms over the Barbican itself, where you get the chance to try out a replicated crossbow and medieval crane, and children (or adventurous adults) can try on medieval costumes. Further up the path reaches a higher garden and from the very top plaques help to pick out the landmarks, which extend over the rooftops and long, narrow medieval back yards as far as the sea at Newhaven.

Your ticket into the castle also gets you into the **Barbican House Museum**, with displays of archaeology and local interest, and a very painstakingly created model showing the town as it was in the 1880s. Some 100 locals made this remarkable artefact in the 1980s using old photos and architectural plans as source material. Commentary backed up by spotlighting and projected images (every 30 minutes, on the half hour or hour) gives an excellent introduction to the town. The museum shop includes a good selection of local history and archaeology books, with a secondhand section too.

Further up Castle Gate you are still in the castle precincts. On the right a grassy space marks the site of the former tilting yard (a practice ground for jousting and the like), which since at least the 18th century has been a **bowling green** – Britain's oldest. It's not exactly a level playing field, and the participants, often out there at weekends, never wear whites. The great Thomas Paine was himself a member, and when curiosity got the better of me I asked a friendly member if I could make a guest appearance one Sunday morning. Pete showed me the selection of woods in the tiny pavilion. These are much smaller than modern woods but no two are exactly the same size or weight and most have been patched up over many years of use; some are 18th century, which makes one wonder which ones Paine might have played with. Pete picked two reasonably similar-sized ones that would suit a beginner, and helpfully pointed out the lumps, bumps and 'valleys' on the green. I still lost massively, but managed to avoid steering my woods into the flowerbed, which alongside various other bowling misdemeanours attracts a fine of a princely 5p.

At the end of the bowling green by railings and a descriptive plaque, benches provide a look-out point towards the **site of the Battle of Lewes**, which took place in 1264 on the Downs just above the town's modern fringes. This was effectively the first triumph in establishing parliamentary democracy: Simon de Montfort gathered an army of barons and Londoners and defeated Henry III, forcing him to sign the Mise of Lewes, which resulted in the very first meeting of parliament at Westminster the following year.

The castle precincts are one of only two such sites in Britain to feature two castle mounds, Lincoln being the other. You can see the second lump, **Brack Mount**, looking over the Lewes Arms although there's no public access. An occupant of adjacent Brack Mount House in the interwar years was novelist Alice Dudeney whose diary was kept under wraps for many decades as so many local people still living were acerbically described. It's a fascinating picture of the town at that time, and though Mrs Dudeney was a bit of a snob her diary has proved more enduring than her mostly forgotten novels.

Southover

In the Southover district on the south side of the historic centre of Lewes, **Grange Gardens** is a public park which makes a gorgeous retreat in summer. An ancient mulberry tree on a zimmerframe arrangement of wooden props casts shade over picnickers. A lot of stone from Lewes Priory (see below) ended up here, some of it in the form of Southover Grange, the Cotswoldian-looking house now owned by the council and which was the boyhood home of the diarist John Evelyn. More stone arches and bits of column and other carved masonry were used to create a garden wall. This screens a wonderfully colourful garden where bedding plants are installed for a few weeks and then ripped out; it's a bit of an indulgence but very much cherished by Lewesians – the council once proposed cutting costs by planting something more herbaceous and permanent but were met with howls of protest. A tiny kiosk operates from a hatch and serves large mugs of tea and coffee and slices of homemade cake and other snacks.

Southover High Street is another architectural treat for its entire length, with all manner of villas and ancient town houses along it including the very London-like Priory Crescent. A gateway on one side of the crescent is a relic of **Lewes Priory**, a Cluniac house founded by William de Warenne and his wife Gundrada between 1078 and 1082. Longer than Chichester Cathedral, and set in a walled precinct approaching the size of a medieval town, its great church was blown up during the Dissolution. The remains stood until the 1840s when the London-to-Brighton railway was built right through them; in response, incensed local antiquarians formed the Sussex Archaeological Society, one of the earliest bodies to protect ancient buildings, including Lewes Castle and Anne of Cleves House. The substantial remains of the monks' living quarters were recently restored by the Lewes Priory Trust and now form Priory Park, an absorbing and always-open free visit rivalling many paid-for heritage sites. It's best reached by taking Cockshut Lane, off Southover High Street, and turning left just after the railway bridge. Clever reconstruction drawings on eleven panels round a trail help make sense of the stonework. The most prominent structure is one of the largest surviving medieval loo blocks in Britain, with individual cubicles for dozens of monks to sit simultaneously, perched high over what was once a running stream. Nearby is a small monastic herb garden, tended by local schoolchildren, with each plant meticulously labelled, and a little further on is a curious grassy mound (yes, another one), not thought to be as ancient as the two at the castle. It overlooks Lewes' football stadium, quaintly named the Dripping Pan, a rectangular basin dating from the time of the Priory.

One house in Southover you can see inside, and a fine example of a tile-hung, timber-framed 15th-century Wealden hall house, is the **Anne of Cleves House** (like Lewes Castle, owned by Sussex Past; joint tickets with the castle are available), a venerable old place which has somehow survived the centuries remarkably intact. It was given by Henry VIII to Anne of Cleves as part of her divorce settlement, but she probably never actually set eyes on the building. Since the 19th century it has belonged to the Sussex Archaeological Society who keep it as a likeably miscellaneous museum. As well as a creaky upstairs room with a barn-like roof and period furniture, the building contains a prized collection of Wealden-made iron artefacts, including firebacks and bootscrapers, and an ancient octagonal table of 'Sussex marble'. Allegedly the knights who murdered Thomas Becket in 1170 rested their weapons on the table and it twice hurled the whole lot off. The Lewes Room is a fine stash of local interest, particularly for three very well known paintings: of Thomas Paine, of Lewes Bonfire as it was in the 19th century with masked men in smuggler outfits and a 'no popery' banner, and of the Lewes Avalanche in 1836. The last of these depicts the worst avalanche in British history in which nine people

Local hero

A mural in the market tower, near the Town Hall, depicts famous Lewes resident Tom Paine (1737-1809), who once worked as a Customs Officer here and lived at Bull House in the upper High Street. He was a controversial republican thinker who went on to inspire both the American and the French revolutions and write *The Rights of Man*. He became a French citizen after the revolution but was thrown into prison and only narrowly escaped the guillotine himself when he opposed the execution of the King. The Tom Paine Trail, for which there's a free leaflet available in the town, takes a stroll around 17 sites in Lewes connected with Paine.

perished after a 15-foot ridge of snow formed on the cliff above South Street and then tumbled down; the dress of a two-year-old girl who was dug out of the snow and lived another 74 years is on display. The pub standing on the site is named the Snowdrop – not after the flower but after the natural disaster.

Unobvious Lewes

The High Street and castle are what visitors see, but it's all too easy to miss out on the less conspicuous pleasures of the town. Lewes is full of surprise **vistas**, several of them preserved for posterity by the campaigning efforts of its residents. One of the best is from the far side of the **Paddock**, a hilly recreation ground which occupies a dry valley just below the castle precincts: walk up to one of the strategic benches for the view of the castle and town that features on numerous greetings cards – the whole thing could easily have been ruined in the 1970s by the insertion of a proposed, totally monstrous relief road right through the middle of the Paddock. Adjoining this little park is the actual horse-inhabited paddock itself, and beyond that **Baxter's Field**, with its backdrop of the castle and Malling Down; when it came up for sale a few years back, locals wasted no time in organising a trust and buying it as a public space for posterity; Lewes can count itself extremely fortunate to have rural views of this calibre in the middle of a town.

Another prize viewpoint is up **Chapel Hill**: walk down the High Street over the bridge and into Cliffe. At the very end a somewhat Cornish-looking street called Chapel Hill, with slate-hung cottages, rises abruptly on to the Downs (for a longer walk you can carry on up to the golf course, turning right at the club house and follow the path that eventually climbs up to Mount Caburn). Soon you look down on the whole town from a path raised above the road; immediately beneath the chalk cliff-face drops nearly vertically to the river. The spiral feature formed in the reedbeds on the far bank is a heart-shaped creation by landscape artist Chris Drury on the **Railway Land nature reserve**, itself accessed from the High Street – take the side road on the east side of the bridge, past a pet shop; beyond an old level crossing gate you enter the reserve, which leads out on to the water meadows of the Ouse valley. Yet again, Lewesians came to the rescue when a few decades back a supermarket wanted to plonk itself here on this wasteland of former rail yards, so instead the town gained a nature reserve and retains another chunk of rurality minutes away from the town centre. A rich wildlife habitat, it is now used for ecological, educational and community projects.

That same community spirit of standing up for what you believe in is also exemplified in the form of the **Pells Pool**, the oldest open-air swimming pool in the country – near the river, in the part of town known as the Pells, conspicuous for its L-shaped canal-like duck pond amidst the trees. Opened in 1860, the pool is almost Olympic size; fed by spring water, it can be distinctly bracing but has none of the smack of chlorine associated with indoor pools. A few years back the council wanted to close it and turn the space into a nice, neat

The Lewes pound

During the freefall of the pound sterling in late 2008, one monetary unit in Britain soared, though not in terms of conventional exchange rates. The Lewes pound, launched in September that year, was intended to boost the fortunes of local shops. It's really a token: you swap the conventional sterling for the Lewesian variant at the Farmers' Market or at other outlets (or ask for them in your change) and then spend them at participating retailers. Within only weeks of its launch, collectors round the world were trying to get their hands on them, and they were going for as much as £40 on Ebay. The Lewes pound organisers offered to sell Lewes pounds for 99p for a while on Ebay in order to stop this happening (only I've just had a look on Ebay and someone's trying to flog a £1 note for £100; good luck to him). In the end it probably didn't matter much, as it put the town on the map and everyone was talking about this new 'currency'.

In such a nonconformist town you'd hardly expect the Queen to be put on the banknote (even if it were legal to do so). So as quasi-monarch, local hero Thomas Paine has his wise head depicted on the currency. No one's going to argue with that, not in Lewes.

Currently some 160 local businesses take the Lewes pound. So what's it really for? Patrick Crawford, one of the people who run the scheme, told me 'It's about supporting Lewes, about supporting Lewes traders, and about keeping money circulating in Lewes. The grand scheme is that the circle helps to help local suppliers and local employment. And people get to hear about Lewes. If we can encourage people to visit Lewes and to visit local shops because of the Lewes pound this benefits Lewes.' I'd add that although it's hard to quantify the benefits, it's something that Lewesians are rather proud of too, though admittedly I tend to keep a few in my wallet to show to incredulous outsiders and don't often get round to spending them.

It's issued in denominations of £1, £5, £10 and, bizarrely, £21 – 'because we can' explained Patrick, and because it symbolises the fact that 5% of the money we issue goes into Live Lewes, a fund that will be used for local projects.' The present issue of notes is valid till 2014.

and completely unwanted car park, but Lewes wouldn't stand for it of course, and the inevitable action group formed itself; a photo appeared in the Guardian, people pledged money and time, and a trust took over. It's now a cherished spot on those hot summer afternoons, when half the town seems there, yet the pool's so large that the water doesn't feel too crowded.

The footbridge known as Willey's Bridge near the Pells marks the start of walks up river on the Ouse Valley Walk and out of town: it immediately becomes rural. A recommended wander is as far as **Hamsey**, where you turn right along the road to the remote, beautifully primitive, electricity-less medieval church – it is usually locked but the key is available from a nearby house in the village. The ancient pews here are staggeringly uncomfortable; presumably the shallowness of the seat was intended to stop the congregation nodding off during services.

For one of the several ways to sample Lewes life behind the scenes, visit during **Artwave** in late August to early September when artists – and there are a lot of them in Lewes – open their houses for free to show the artworks for sale within. The free monthly magazine *Viva Lewes* is one of the best-written and most insightful of its kind I have seen anywhere. Its local angles to some extent inspired this Slow series of books; one of the cover designers also created the covers of the series.

Harveys Brewery

Known reverently by locals as Lewes Cathedral, this brick and mock-Tudor-cum-gothic pile is the only Victorian brewery of its kind surviving in the southeast. The Harveys brewing tradition spans two centuries, and has been on this site since 1838, with the present structure dating from the 1860s. Harveys is one of those companies that everyone in Lewes seems to revere: the brewers donate money to local causes, they use local hops from suppliers who would otherwise have gone out of business, they take a pride in using English malt only, and put on a terrific series of seasonal ales – each one highly distinctive – including Copperwheat for the balmy harvest days of September, Bonfire Boy for November, a Porter brewed to an 1859 recipe for March, a dark, sweet Old to warm you through winter, and a lethally strong Christmas Ale that's almost like a barley wine in character.

Their Sussex Best Bitter is a masterpiece: the head brewer Miles Jenner, who lives in the Georgian brewers' house that adjoins (and obviously predates) the brewery, told me that one of the hardest things to brew is a less strong ale: this one's only 4%. You could use the same recipe and come up with a totally different tasting beer. The liquor – that's what they call the water that's drilled by artesian well right beneath the brewery – is one of the elements; another is the yeast that gives it that distinctive, almost metallic aftertaste. Harveys nearly lost it in the flood of 2000, when the Ouse burst its banks and the water came almost up to the ceiling. It was very touch and go, and Shepherd Neame (in Kent) would have helped them out by giving them some of their own brewer's yeast, but then Harveys would have never quite tasted the same again.

Miles has all the right attitudes in my book: he confesses to giving a daily prayer of thanks to the existence of the Campaign for Real Ale, thanks to which many small breweries like this might have disappeared in the big-brewery takeover days of the 1970s and 1980s. Should you be so lucky to get on a brewery tour – the bad news is that the waiting list is usually two or three years – you'll find a marvellously untouched factory where even the paint colour is original, and the manager's office almost Dickensian.

To sample the wonderful ale, pop into **Harveys Brewery Shop** in Cliffe High Street – where they sell bottles of most of their seasonal products, as well as some very classy wines, and Best and one or two others straight from the barrel. The brewery tap is just across Cliffe High Street: the **John Harvey Tavern**, where they keep several Harvey varieties in perfect condition. The **Lewes Arms**, tucked behind the castle, and the **Dorset** (in Cliffe) are among places in town where Harveys is consistently excellent.

In 2007, Greene King, who used to own the Lewes Arms, tried to remove Harveys from the beers they served and faced an extraordinarily hostile campaign from locals – ending with picketing, petitions, interviews on Radio 4's *Today* programme, and final, totally humiliating climbdown by the brewers, who've since sold it on to Fullers (who stock Harveys on condition that the one Harveys pub in London sell Fullers; a very neat solution). Another indication of the passion Lewesians feel about Harveys is an incident in the 1990s when one night someone set fire to empty cardboard boxes outside the Harveys Brewery Shop and the shop burned down, destroying most of the brewery's archives in the process: no one found the culprit, but the 'Cliffe Ars(e)onist' was duly burned in effigy at that year's Lewes Bonfire celebrations.

Food and drink

Lewes **farmers' market** takes place on the first Saturday of the month in the precinct, and there's a very good smaller market on Friday mornings in the market tower (near the Crown Inn). Fresh fish and organic meat are on sale in the **Riverside**, an old converted building by the bridge in the middle of town. Opposite and over the bridge by Harveys Brewery is the **brewery shop**, (see above), which also sells Harveys beer glasses, aprons, bags and other Lewes-oriented souvenirs. Close by are several good options for a meal or delis for picnic items, like **Bill's** in Cliffe High Street at the top end of town, in Westgate, is the combined café and colourful Polish pottery shop **Baltica**, which serves hearty and authentic Polish dishes. For interesting beer and cider, try the **Gardeners** (*Cliffe High St; no food*); the **John Harvey**, just across from Harveys Brewery and its excellent shop, has all the Harveys seasonal ales fresh from the brewery and the food's good value.

> **Bill's** Cliffe High St. No reservations, and you sit at long tables with everyone else. There's often a long queue to sit down, and the comfort couldn't be more basic. Yet this is a hugely and justly loved institution, started by the eponymous Bill after his greengrocer's shop was washed out in the Lewes floods of 2000. He used produce from his shop in a variety of wholefood dishes, fruit smoothies and the like; gradually the café part of the shop has taken over the greengrocery, which has gone distinctly upmarket, and a new branch has opened in Brighton.

Lewes Arms Castle Ditch Lane ☎ 01273 473152. This is the place where everyone meets up after an archaeology lecture at the town hall, after a stoolball match in the Paddock, after a rehearsal for whatever musical the Lewes Operatic Society are doing next, so it's nearly always full of convivial chat. Fullers and Harveys real ales, and a decent choice of very reasonably priced main courses (and they use real pastry for their pies). Has a tiny terrace abutting the ancient mound known as Brack Mount. They do a very adult panto in March, and also host the likes of the world pea-throwing championships (record = 38.7 metres) and the extremely wet dwyle-flunking event (involving a lot of splashing about of stale beer as one participant attempts to lob a dishcloth soaked in stale beer at the others who stand in a ring around him or her).

Pelham Arms High St ☎ 01273 476149 ✇ www.thepelhamarms.co.uk. At the top of the High Street in the St Anne's area, and a very good bet for pub food; excellent Sunday roasts, nicely cooked vegetables and ample portions.

Pelham House St Andrew's Lane ☎ 01273 488600 ✇ www.pelhamhouse.com. An architecturally interesting hotel, often with art exhibitions inside, and a splendid 16th-century panelled room. As well as being the top eating place in town, it makes a great spot for tea or coffee – sit on the back terrace if it's fine.

Shopping

Several **antiques** centres are dotted around the High Street, the two largest being Cliffe Antiques Centre in Cliffe and the Fleamarket in Market Street. Gorringes auctioneers (✇ www.gorringes.co.uk) hold weekly Monday auctions in a characterful iron shed between the rail station and Grange Gardens (viewing on Friday and Saturday mornings); more select antiques are periodically auctioned at their other salesroom at 15 North Street. Wallis & Wallis (✇ www.wallisandwallis.co.uk) have regular auctions of toys and militaria at West Street.

Lewes is stuffed full of **galleries and craft shops** with the most rewarding browsing grounds being along the main street, in the Hop Gallery (in the old Star Brewery building by Fisher Street and opposite the Lewes Arms) and in the Needlemakers (a former hypodermic needle factory, very imaginatively converted, between Market Street and Fisher Street). Another excellent place is the Sussex Guild Shop (*Southover Rd* ☎ *01273 479565; with entrance also in Grange Gardens*) with a varied selection of traditional and contemporary crafts.

② Spring Barn Farm

Just outside Lewes and open all year, this family-run sheep and cattle farm (*Kingston Rd, near Lewes BN7 3ND; 01273 488450; www.springbarnfarm park.co.uk*) is in a great little rural spot in a downland valley, and includes one of the most likeable farm parks I have seen; it is not at all overdone. You pay admission to go to the farm park area, where contented-looking goats, alpacas, donkeys, hens, rabbits and ducks occupy a series of areas on a steepish slope; you can buy feed for the smaller animals from goat size downwards, and there are 'meet the animal' sessions. Just below these are areas for activities such as pedal go-carts, a zip wire and gigantic jumping pillows, with a play barn inside too, and events include Easter egg hunts and lambing, a summer maize maze and Halloween. The farm's own beef and lamb, chutneys, cakes, pies and garden veg are all available in the farm shop, along with produce such as beer, apple juice and cheeses from Sussex. The restaurant opens all day, with a wood burner making it very cosy in winter. There's also a camping field (see page 141).

③ Kingston

This is a spreading village with an old centre, set beneath the Downs. The prominent Y shape of chalk tracks on the escarpment includes the **Juggs Road**, an ancient route supposedly so called because womenfolk used to carry baskets or 'juggs' of fish along it from the coast to Lewes. The pub in Kingston is called the Juggs, and has a very cosy main room with a huge open fireplace. If you want the feeling of your feet taking you cross-country from Lewes to Brighton, there's no better way to go. From the Swan Inn in Southover, the Juggs Road begins as a small road, crosses a very high bridge over the A27, then peters out into a track along the spine of Kingston Ridge – a mini South Down.

Along here you'll find a very beautiful six-sailed weatherboarded **windmill** – at least I hope its sails are installed by the time this book is published. Not all is what it seems. As I was putting finishing touches to this book it was still being completed, as an exact copy of what stood there until 1916 and was known as Old Six-Sweeps. On 28 March of that year it collapsed in a mighty blizzard, and many of the bits and pieces were rapidly carted away. Foundry owner John Every took an interest in the fallen mill, and removed the unique triple canister mill-shaft to the private museum, mainly of Sussex ironwork, that he had set up at the Phoenix ironworks.

The first I heard of it was when the present owner asked the Mid-Sussex Field Archaeology Team to field-walk and then excavate the site to locate the foundations, in preparation for his bid to get planning permission to rebuild the mill on the same spot. For a few days the ploughed field was full of archaeologists and soon they found the brick and concrete footings. While field-walking we picked up all sorts of bits of mill – my most spectacular find was a huge chunk of millstone I prised out of a hedgerow with a rake.

This mill is planned to generate its own electricity: the surplus goes into the national grid. Happily it (instead of the very much less wonderful County Hall in Lewes) now dominates the view from the top of the downs above Kingston, thus nicely bucking the trend for the decline of windmills over the past hundred years in the Sussex landscape.

④ Rodmell

A parade of vernacular architecture awaits at the village of Rodmell: the Old Rectory with its handsome flint frontage; Deep Thatch Cottage, a long weatherboarded structure beneath a massive thatched roof; and then **Monk's**

House (*Rodmell BN7 3HF; 01323 870001; www.nationaltrust.org.uk; open Apr–Oct, Wed and Sat 14.00–17.30*), the 'unpretending house, long and low, a house of many doors' described by Virginia Woolf in her diary in 1919. She and her husband Leonard came here that year and it became their country base while visiting her sister Vanessa Bell and entourage at Charleston. The lean-to greenhouse became 'Leonard's Crystal Palace'; his writing desk retains letters, pens, bundles of magazines and albums of 78s. In the orchard at the end of the garden is Virginia's summer house that she used as her 'writing hut', with a bottle of green ink laid out at the ready on her desk.

In fact green is very much the theme of the interior. Virginia Woolf had a passion for the colour, which gives the house a strangely underwater feeling.

In 1941, driven into depression during the dark years of the war, she committed suicide in the Ouse. It's quite a long walk along the flat track to the river; the last things she saw must have been Lewes Castle, away to the left, and Mount Caburn, ahead, with the Woolfs' former house of Asham not far ahead. She filled her pockets with heavy stones and plunged in. You can trace Virginia's last steps by following the stony track just left of Rodmell's car park (where the road bends left beyond Monk's House) to the River Ouse, from where there are views of Lewes Castle and Mount Caburn.

Food and drink

Abergavenny Arms Rodmell ☎ 01273 472416 🖥 www.abergavennyarms.com.
Usefully placed for the Ouse Valley on the main road through Rodmell, and offering decent-value pub food; has a small area for sitting outside. Note the marvellously unchanged blacksmith's shop across the road.

⑤ Newhaven

Better known as a cross-Channel port, with ferries to Dieppe in Normandy, Newhaven is not a pretty place at all, with mounds of scrap metal and huge, partly derelict sheds looming large, but there's appreciable atmosphere with a distinctively salty whiff among the fishing jetties, marina and harbour. I find the town has an infectious sense of place. Property is cheaper here than in the likes of Brighton and Lewes, and there's been a mild influx of artists into town of late.

A swing bridge intermittently brings traffic to a halt on the main road that rings the town far too close to its old centre. From there the road along the west side of the harbour area leads out to the West Beach, sandy and very alluring at low tide but unfortunately and controversially inaccessible at the time of writing for health and safety reasons. Fishermen set up rods on the harbour breakwater, itself a bracing stroll, built in 1890 to prevent the build-up of shingle that had previously hindered the flow of the Ouse and necessitated a cut to be made through it, with a 'new haven' established at the new river mouth. To the west of the breakwater, a large, rather wild shingle beach is backed by the crumbling cliffs of Peacehaven Heights.

Newhaven had a military role for many years. During World War I it became the port through which troops and supplies were sent to Europe, and during the latter half of that war the town was designated a Special Military Area. In World War II, the ill-fated Dieppe raid of 1942 was launched from here, in which large numbers of Canadian military personnel stationed in town perished or were taken prisoner.

Newhaven Fort (*01273 517622; www.newhavenfort.org.uk*), above the harbour and dating from 1859, is the largest fortification ever erected in Sussex, and was very much working up to 1945. Restored after years of dereliction, it now houses an excellent museum evoking the two world wars, with much more to look at than first meets the eye as you enter the courtyard. Two hours would probably be rushing it: the historical material is voluminous and well presented, with World War I displays in the former officers' quarters, exhibits on the Dieppe raid and D-Day landings and a recreation of a blitzed house complete with sounds and smells. Energetic children will enjoy clambering up grassy slopes, exploring gun emplacements and descending through a labyrinth of stepped, gloomily lit tunnels that drop to shore level. The busy event calendar includes plenty at weekends, such as outdoor theatre, concerts, shows and (in mid September) a Battle of Britain commemoration.

Newhaven's spectral station

Arrive at Newhaven by cross-Channel ferry and you step off and wander to the run-down terminus that is Newhaven Harbour station. Only last time I stepped off after crossing from Dieppe I hesitated, and wondered what that dead-looking, unnamed station-like relic was, right next to the ferry terminal a few hundred yards before Newhaven Harbour station itself. Months later I discovered this is one of Britain's lost and very strange stations: Newhaven Marine. Stranger still, it is still functioning yet no trains run from it. Never officially closed, it theoretically has a train to Lewes five evenings a week, yet this is not advertised in any timetable. Moreover it supposedly connects with a ferry that doesn't exist either. Currently the train leaves at 20.15, but in 2008 this was 18.52; and until August 2006 a real empty train departed from this spectral terminus. Which I suppose could mean you could buy a ticket from it for Lewes, find the train doesn't arrive and then claim a taxi ride instead.

Thanks to my friend Nicky Gardner, editor of *hidden europe* magazine, who told me about this wonderfully strange railway curio.

⑥ Tide Mills

Though it doesn't look an obvious place to stop off, the concrete track from a small car park south of the A259 between Newhaven and Seaford leads to a bracing beach with added interest – an eerie area of shingle and ruined flint walls that seems at first sight like an abandoned monastery. These are the

remains of the once-immense **Bishopstone Tide Mills**, which dominated the corn trade hereabouts from the 1760s until they closed in 1883. Nicely presented information panels bring them to life. People carried on living here until the workers' village was demolished in World War II – the ruins were used by Canadian troops to practise street fighting. Further out on the shingle are the remains of a World War I seaplane base and a 1930s hospital for disabled children, now colonised by a range of seashore plants such as sea kale and yellow horned-poppy. The derelict military railway running along the shore here was used for testing the first armoured train, in 1874.

⑦ Seaford

Once a thriving medieval port, Seaford has long since seen its harbour silted up; its oldest streets are now inland around the church.

Its special qualities lie along the shore, one of the nearest beaches to London, and certainly one of the most inviting despite the shingle, yet one that never gets seriously crowded.

The shingle beach runs several miles from Bishopstone along to the start of the cliffs at Seaford Head, backed by a hotchpotch of very vaguely Mediterranean-style 20th-century buildings that don't seem to belong in England at all. It couldn't be more different to Brighton and it would be difficult to find anywhere to spend money without leaving the seafront. Even the parking is free. You can also reach the beach from Bishopstone or Seaford stations.

In summer you'll see toddlers paddling, cross-Channel ferries coming and going and sub-aqua divers waddling over the beach. Towards evening the fishermen set up camp and the barbecues begin to sizzle.

Seventy-four **Martello towers**, erected during Napoleonic times to counter the threat of invasion by France, are dotted along the coast from Sussex to Kent, but this one, the most easterly, at Seaford, is one of the very few to open its doors to the public. You have to time it though: the comprehensive local history collection only opens on Sundays and bank holidays, plus Wednesday and Saturday afternoons in summer. It is far larger inside than seems possible from outside; among the kitchen bygones, retired typewriters and historic radio and TV sets is a model of Seaford station as it was in 1926. The name Martello, incidentally, is seemingly a mistake: the towers are modelled from Mortella Point Tower in Corsica, which was attacked by the British in 1793 and 1794, and its rounded form impressed as a formidable defence.

A cycle path leads out of Seaford along the seafront and through a landscaped country park area in **Ouse Estuary Nature Reserve** – home to the internationally protected great crested newt.

Seaford Head rises abruptly at the east end of the seafront, taking you up into another world. As you look along the base of the crumbling chalk cliffs from the end of the esplanade, a pong of kittiwake droppings will greet you – a huge colony of these seabirds occupies these cliffs. The climb up along the cliff from here leads you past perhaps Sussex's most scenically placed golf course, then suddenly Cuckmere Haven and the Seven Sisters spread themselves ahead: one of the great coastal scenes of southern England. Further down you find the group of former coastguards' cottages that provide the foreground for the most photographed version of that view. Just above them, steps lead down to a fascinating, potentially ankle-turning rocky foreshore. If you want the view without the climb, find the obscurely located car park reached via a maze of residential roads around the easternmost part of Seaford: South Hill Barn at the top of the hill marks the spot.

From the Ouse to the Cuckmere

Not a nice route if you whiz along the A27, but a different, slower, easier world once you are away from it. The South Downs' knack of looking far larger than they really are is seen to spectacular effect here, with the steep grassy escarpment rising abruptly from the bewitching one-street villages of Firle, Alciston and Berwick, where grazing sheep look absurdly oversize on the slopes. The 'Old Coach Road' – an unmade track for walkers, cyclists and horse riders – makes an unproblematic way to see the Downs from beneath and to link the places, or to combine high and low levels by travelling the other direction on the South Downs Way along the top.

If you want to make a car-free day of it, Glynde station is useful; although the first bit out and across the A27 is an uninspiring start if you're on foot, it soon gets better. Firle is within a half-day's walk of the other places.

Dead-end roads, or 'bostalls' to use South-Downs-speak, lead up from the top from Firle to a point between Beddingham Hill and Firle Beacon and from a crossroads near Alciston to what's known locally as Bopeep (after a long-abandoned chalk pit of the same name). From either of these little car parks there's marvellous elevated walking, with the sea in view, and it's all preposterously easy: you could wander along the South Downs Way in slippers. In fact I've accompanied a wheelchair-bound friend up here for her first-ever sample of the Downs at high level.

⑧ Glynde

Every front door painted in a drab rusty red: the whole village is still owned by the Glynde estate that built it. It's not conventionally chocolate-box stuff, but a real rural community of somewhat stark terraces evoking a pit village in the middle of the Sussex countryside. After the railway was built in 1846, mining begun in chalk pits nearby, to produce lime from three kilns set up in Glynde itself. It hasn't quite lost that working-class atmosphere: it's a place where the cricket team thrives and everyone knows each other. They maintain a healthy rivalry with that distinctively smarter estate village, Firle, a short distance away across the A27. It's not every day you find a village with its own pub, tearoom, forge, paraglider school, railway station, stately home and – just a mile up the road – its own opera house.

Glynde Forge, in the village centre, marvellously evokes the pre-motor age. Bearing the date of 1907 by its quaint horseshoe-shaped doorway, this was meticulously copied from another smithy (now a garage) at the Kent village of Penshurst after the estate manager at Glynde happened to see it and decided it was what Glynde needed. Terry Tyhurst has been at Glynde since 1996, and has transformed an empty shell into a very retro-style place of work; his dog Lucy snoozes in an improvised bed beneath a work bench. Terry makes railings, waterwheels, gates, lanterns and – his favourite – weathervanes, but steers away from horseshoes. He is always happy to chat to anyone who pops in to have a look round, and it's usually open at weekends as well as weekdays, though there's seldom anything set out for sale. Hanging over a pair of brick-built hearths there's a fascinating array of horse bits, stirrups, a wartime stirrup pump, a shoe stretcher, weather vane templates, some gas torches, latch bars, bits of spectacularly rusty bikes and a framed photo of his predecessor.

Mount Caburn

Just above Glynde village you'll see the lumpy outlier of the South Downs known rather pompously as **Mount Caburn**, a 15-minute walk up the path opposite the Little Cottage Tearoom on Ranscombe Lane. Topped by an ancient hillfort and with a sweeping view of the Downs and sea, it's full of mystery – in Neolithic times there was a huge yew forest here, and Iron-Age occupants dug a series of 164 pits and for some reason put deposits in them – dog bones, boar's tusks, potins (Iron-Age coins), weaving combs and deliberately broken tools and weapons. The pits may have been used for grain storage, followed by ceremonies involving the burial of special symbolic objects. We would expect there to have been a population nearby, though there is little sign of habitation on Caburn itself. I've helped on a dig up here a couple of seasons and discovered that it can get beastly cold even in July – so I doubt anyone lived here year round.

So archaeologists are still trying to work out what it's about, and whether it was indeed reoccupied in Norman times as an outpost of Lewes Castle, forming a look-out to scan the vulnerable coastal approach. During the very late Iron-Age and Roman period Caburn seems to have lost significance and become an agricultural site. It's a hopeless place to defend, as you keep losing sight of people if you wander around the top – hillforts aren't all thought to be primarily defensive anyway. The hill dominates the landscape to the south and east but is less prominent from the north. This suggests it was a focus for the landscape to the south and east, which would have been more watery than today.

Paragliding on the Downs

When the thermals are doing the right things, you'll see often see swarms of multicoloured **paragliders** hovering over Mount Caburn and around Firle Beacon. Glynde has two places where you can learn and teaching takes place all year; you just need warm windproof clothes and supportive boots.

Tim Cox teaches beginners and experts at **Sussex Hang Gliding & Paragliding**. His enthusiasm for the sport is certainly infectious, and after chatting with him for a while I was sorely tempted to try something I'd always thought of as merely suicidal.

'There's nothing like free flight. Have you ever had a dream about flying? You step off a hill – and instead of falling you fly.'

I ask him to rate the best places for flying in the world. In fourth place are the Atlas Mountains in Morocco, third Tenerife, second the Alps, and first, yes, the South Downs. 'Because of the way the South Downs are formed it's probably one of the best and safest places in world to paraglide, and over the years this area has become the epicentre of paragliding. The South Downs are superb, with ridges you can pootle along even in winter. We teach complete beginners to fly – so you can turn up here and in a day would be doing your first solo flight. We take you out to one of our flight sites, we teach you how to take off and land at very low levels, just a few inches up, and we do some gentle flights down some inclines; when you feel confident we creep you up a little bit, then when you can satisfactorily fly the glider and land it we'll get you up a few metres – once you've done that we'll get you up quite high.'

Tim says you don't need to be super-fit. 'As you get more experienced you can do cross-country flights – like today someone went from Brighton to here (25km). You can steer the glider, any way you want to go. I've got from Devil's Dyke to Pevensey and on to Polegate.'

I signalled my apprehension. Tim said 'It's a bit like learning to ski – if you go hell for leather on a black run on day two, you'll hurt yourself; if you choose nice weather to fly in and have good equipment and proper tuition, it's safer than cycling.'

It's a steep learning curve and you can become a competent private pilot after about ten days of instruction. 'People are usually amazed at their progress – on day one they can't quite believe what they've done. If you're reasonably fit and can climb a flight of stairs, then you can fly. The oldest person we had last year was an 82-year-old who went off to India, and last time I heard he was 12,000 feet up in the Himalayas.'

Paragliding schools

Airworks Glynde station ☎01273 858108 🖰 www.airworks.co.uk.
Sussex Hang Gliding & Paragliding Tollgate (A27 just out of Glynde), Beddingham, BN8 6JZ ☎01273 858170 🖰 www.sussexhgpg.co.uk. Tuition for a full day starts from £125.

Just north of the village, **Glynde Place** (*01273 858224; www.glynde place.com*) is a rather un-grand country house from the front; plonked next to a Palladian-style temple-like church, the house looks more the part from the back, with imposing Tudor flint gables and brick chimneys, and a sweeping view across meadows and towards Firle Beacon. You need to time your visit if you want to get in – it's open only two or three afternoons a week and only in summer, but the family history of the inter-related Morleys, Trevors and Brands is interestingly explained in what is still a very much lived-in country house, and there's the ubiquitous set of old masters brought back from the Grand Tour. The Tearoom (also open to non-visitors) has a cobbled courtyard shaded by fruit trees.

Glyndebourne

North of the village, beyond Glynde Place, is **Glyndebourne Opera House**, home to Britain's top country-house opera company, and one of the major employers in the area – one reason Lewes is full of rather accomplished musicians. It all started in the 1920s when the owner of Glyndebourne, John Christie, began to stage concerts and amateur opera excerpts in the Organ Room for friends and family. Through this he met his wife, Audrey Mildmay, a professional singer, and the idea of an opera season developed. In 1934 they opened the first theatre, built on the former kitchen garden; its successor, sublime both acoustically and aesthetically, is a fitting venue for one of the great opera festivals in the world. The summer festival (May to August) features long intervals when opera-lovers dressed in evening finery set up lavish picnics in the grounds; tickets are horribly hard to come by. In October, there's a shorter season where tickets aren't quite so pricey and you might just strike lucky. The first time I went to Glyndebourne, to see a wonderful production of *Cosi fan Tutte*, my group walked over the Downs from Lewes in dinner garb, cagoule, walking boots, brollies, the lot – carrying our posh picnic in rucksacks. It poured relentlessly all day; the only others braving the outdoor picnic at the interval apart from our party were an elderly couple who'd arrived by helicopter and were being served by someone who seemed to be their butler. And on another occasion the very first words I heard someone say as we made our way in were 'And how are your pheasants this year, Jeremy?' Actually it's not at all universally snooty; in Lewes I'm very much aware what a remarkable range of people have been to Glyndebourne. But it's all a world apart from Glynde – both places have the same first six letters, but there the similarity ends.

><<<<>>>><

Food and drink

Trevor Arms ✆ 01273 475381. In the middle of the village, the Trevor is nicely unpretentious, hardly a gastro-pub, but serving good-value, voluminous pub nosh and decent Harveys; you can eat in the village-hall-like dining room, in the bar or on a cheerfully unkempt large lawn beneath the Downs.

⑨ Bentley Wildfowl and Motor Museum

An eclectic and offbeat visit awaits at this country house and estate (*BN8 5AF; 01825 840573; www.bentley.org.uk*). It is essentially the 20th-century creation of Gerald and Mary Askew – Gerald farmed, bred horses, gardened and collected wildfowl. Inside the long, low Palladian **house**, the Askews' love of wildfowl is illustrated by the collection of bird paintings by Philip Rickman in the Chinese Drawing Room; unfortunately Gerald didn't live to see this room completed. He also used antique wallpapers, and copied the chimneypiece in the Bird Room from a Palladio villa (Villa Maser).

The **wildfowl collection** sets one marvelling at what the bird keepers have achieved. It was begun in 1962 by Gerald when he returned from a visit to the Wildfowl Trust at Slimbridge with twenty pairs of wildfowl. They now have 125 species of wildfowl – or to state it even more impressively, there are only 22 species they don't have. Within a series of naturalistic pens, each labelled with the species you can see, are highly exotic-looking geese, ducks and swans numbering well over 1,000, in addition to flamingoes and cranes (which don't count as wildfowl).

On a totally different theme is the constantly changing display of lovingly maintained **vintage motor cars and motorbikes** from the early days of motoring, lent by various owners and mostly in working order; look out for Vehicle Event Days that take place here from time to time.

Having been influenced by seeing other local gardens such as Sissinghurst and Charleston Manor, the Askews remodelled the **garden** into a series of outdoor 'rooms' enclosed by yew hedges, and featuring old species of roses and rare shrubs. Elsewhere the grounds have been imaginatively embellished in recent years, with **'living willow'** tunnels and arbours, and 12 acres of mixed woodland dotted with **woodland sculptures**. Archaeologists have recreated **ancient buildings** in the woods too, including a Bronze-Age hut and a sunken Saxon building. These small, rectangular structures are recessed into the ground and are common discoveries on Saxon sites. It is not yet known why they were sunken: one theory is that there was a floor suspended above the hollowed-out space, another that it was a cool place for storing food. Some have been found with holes for loom posts and clay weights showing that they were used for weaving – though they must have been rather dark for working in.

The **shop** includes crafts made by members of the Sussex Guild, as well as bird-related items, and the old stable block houses a café which offers lunches and cream teas, and has outside seating.

In mid-September, the **Weald Wood Fair** takes place in the grounds. This huge three-day festival celebrates the use and importance of wood, from forest to final form with all things wood: there are hedge-laying and other demonstrations, story-telling, seminars, activities and the chance to meet a host of people from wood designers to archaeologists – all enough for a very full day. And you can come away with all manner of crafts, local produce, sculpture and furniture. A frequent shuttle bus operates from Lewes station during the event.

Just to the south on the B2192, **Raystede Centre for Animal Welfare** (*The Broyle, near Ringmer BN8 5AJ; 01825 880472; www.raystede.org*) is a centre for rescued animals, but in addition to those seeking a new pet attracts plenty as a free attraction in itself, with wildfowl lakes, picnic areas, a dog play area, exotic birds, an equine barn and a café.

⑩ Farley Farm House

It's an almost startling experience to pass from the very ordinary-looking farmyard off the village street into a garden filled with sculpture and then to what is probably the most surprising farmhouse you will ever see (*Muddles Green, near Chiddingly BN8 6HW; 01825 872691; www.farleyfarmhouse.co.uk; tours on first and third Sun of month Apr–Oct, and on certain other weekends during local arts festivals; pre-bookable extended tours approximately monthly*). Home from 1949 to British surrealist painter and art promoter Roland Penrose and his American wife, photographer Lee Miller, the house has been kept largely as it was by their son Antony Penrose, who conducts the extended tours in person.

A brick-floored corridor leads to a well appointed 1950s kitchen – where a tile painted by Picasso is cemented into the wall rather off-centre above the aga stove, and three of his lithographs hang over the table where Lee Miller, an accomplished cook, used to set her guests to peeling potatoes. In the dining room the great fireplace alcove is joyously decorated in golden yellow and shows the nearby Long Man of Wilmington chalk carving (see page 168) as a sun god. Works by Roland Penrose range from a Magritte-like image of his wife-to-be to a blackly humorous representation of himself in old age as a dried-up toad with hip pain, his world reduced to a cube supported by London taxis.

Seen along with Charleston (see page 164), Farley Farm encapsulates the influences on British modern art through most of the the 20th century. Penrose himself was a key figure, bringing Picasso's *Guernica* on tour to Britain in 1938, and co-founding the Institute of Contemporary Arts. But where Charleston presents an art-centred domestic world apparently remote from politics, the malign effect of World War II is palpable at Farley Farm. Lee Miller worked with surrealist photographer Man Ray in Paris, and became a photo-journalist with the US army in 1944. She was long haunted by her experiences covering the liberation of Buchenwald and Dachau concentration camps, which revived a personal childhood trauma, and never quite recovered the sunny personality indicated by her pre-war portraits. Life at Farley Farm and developing a new interest in imaginative cooking provided some respite, and the couple hosted many giants of the modern movement: she photographed Picasso by the village sign and greeting the farm bull. Antony Penrose's children's book *The Boy Who Bit Picasso* recalls his childhood friendship with the artist, while cleverly introducing the concepts of modern art to youngsters.

Food and drink

Six Bells Inn Chiddingly BN8 6HE ☎01825 872227. Unpretentious and welcoming village pub with good-value food, open fires and weekend live music, little changed since Lee Miller photographed willowy Vogue models there in the 1950s.

Events

Chiddingly Festival ⌨ www.chiddinglyfestival.co.uk. Late Sep–early Oct. A long-established village festival featuring an eclectic and inclusive mix: perhaps an original performance inspired by life at Farley Farm, pantomime, storytelling, a beer festival, poetry in the pub, jazz, comedy, bell ringing and belly-dancing or morris-dancing workshops.

⑪ West Firle

Turn off the busy, bland A27 and you're suddenly transported back a century here. The Firle Estate own pretty much everything at West Firle (or call it plain Firle), and the village street is a classic, with estate cottages fronted with flint. In summer, village cricket matches provide a bucolic scene, all very perfect even for those without the slightest interest in the game. Round the corner from the Ram Inn, very handily placed for walks along the foot of the Downs and up to the top of them, the church has Gage family monuments and some highly striking modern coloured stained glass by John Piper, one of the foremost painters and stained glass designers of the 20th century.

The Gages are the folk who have owned **Firle Place** for half a millennium. Some of the ancestors had dodgy associations: the house was begun in 1530 by Sir John Gage whose roles included being the Constable of the Tower of London, where he presided over executions of Catherine Howard and Lady Jane Grey, and over the imprisonment of Elizabeth. His son supervised the burning of the Lewes Martyrs in the 1550s, so can't have been too popular in Lewes. Far less nasty folk came later – most famously the horticulturalist Sir Thomas Gage who acquired Reine Claude plum trees from monks in France only to completely lose track of what were called by the time they arrived, so they were called 'greengages' instead.

In the 18th century, to the Tudor core of the house was added a crisp-looking stone facade of Caen stone which had made a very slow journey from Normandy – brought over to England for the building of Lewes Priory just up the road. When the Priory was dissolved in Henry VIII's time, it was robbed of much of its material, some of which ended up here. Perhaps it's something to do with the stone, but to me the house is reminiscent of a French chateau, at least from outside. Curiously, it could hardly be less conspicuous in the wider landscape: you see nothing as you come up the sweeping arc of the carriageway, until the last moment when it appears, snuggled beneath the Downs, with gardens rising beyond. Some windows have been blocked out, but for symmetry rather than window tax.

The 18th-century remodelling extended to the inside: all is light, airiness and space, with a cream and gold drawing room and some wonderfully intricate plasterwork. It's clearly very much still lived in, with board games, art books and a Dansette record player in evidence along old masters that include family portraits by the likes of Gainsborough. The Long Gallery has gorgeous views over the park. The collection of Sèvres porcelain is said to be of national importance; very sadly burglars swiped one million pounds worth one night in 2009. Let's hope they've got it back by the time this book is in print.

The house was used for the filming of the 1997 movie *Firelight*, directed by William Nicholson. When I attended a showing of this in Lewes Film Club a few years ago, the self-deprecating director told us 'you people who are about to watch this film are a very rare sect', and explained how the premier in London was attended by a mere handful of people – the kiss of death was the New York critics who proclaimed it an 'art film' whereas Nicholson said it was more of a mainstream melodrama about a governess and a young child. Anyway, I found it highly watchable, particularly memorable for its views of the Firle estate in the snows of 1996. The Great Hall has the second largest Van Dyck in the country; for the filming of *Firelight* they were unable to move it out, so the painting became a very distinctive backdrop.

If instead of forking left into the village you carry straight on, the road leads you steeply up to the top of the downs, where the metalling ceases. You can park at the end of the road, where the South Downs Way crosses, and stroll along the top. To the left it leads to the trig point at **Firle Beacon**, where a prominent grassy lump that is a Neolithic long barrow surveys a scene over Seaford, Newhaven and the English Channel to the south and far over the Weald in the other direction, towards the heights of the Ashdown Forest. Closer at hand, just beneath the scarp, Firle Tower is an estate folly (let as holiday accommodation) and Arlington Reservoir appears as a strangely regular-looking lake.

Middle Farm

Right beside the A27 near Firle, this has fair claim to be Britain's very first farm shop (*near West Firle BN8 6LJ; 01323 811622; www.middlefarm.com*), opened in 1960. It's also home to the National Collection of Cider and Perry, with the largest choice of ciders and perries anywhere in the country. As well as the bottled varieties, they have an astonishing array of cider barrels ranged in order of taste – dry at the left end, medium in the middle and sweet to the right, and you can sample them before you buy. From Sussex they have Matthew Wilson's English Organic from Oakwood Farm at Robertsbridge, and John Batcheldor's JB cider from West Sussex. They stock their own cider and apple juice too, and you can also bring your own apples in and they'll juice them for you. The residual pomace is fed to animals, including geese, which are fattened up for sale for Christmas.

Visitors can also meet the animals at the 'open farm' and watch the milking, see the chickens, ducks, spotted pigs and donkeys, and follow a nature trail.

⑫ Charleston

A modest pebbledashed farmhouse set just below the South Downs, Charleston (*West Firle BN8 6LL; 01323 811265; www.charleston.org.uk; open Apr–end Oct; guided tours Wed–Sat, with extended tours on Fri; stewarded rooms with no guided tours on Sun and bank holiday Mon; café; May literary festival*) was for more than 60 years the cherished retreat of the circle of artists, writers and intellectuals known as the Bloomsbury Set, who have remained enduring objects of fascination as much for their unorthodox relationships as for their creative talent. The first arrivals, in 1916, were Virginia Woolf's artist sister Vanessa Bell, her lifelong painting partner and occasional lover Duncan Grant, and Grant's current male lover, writer David Garnett – Vanessa's husband Clive Bell joined them at weekends. Virginia and Leonard Woolf had a series of homes in the area, ending up at Rodmell (see page 152). Grant and Garnett, as conscientious objectors, had been directed to do farm work, which they found nearby.

Amid this Bohemian enclave, a regular guest was economist and Treasury adviser John Maynard Keynes: after World War I he wrote his denunciation of the Versailles Treaty, *The Economic Consequences of the Peace*, here. Following his marriage to a Russian ballet dancer – a move which shocked the Bloomsbury Set considerably more than their free-thinking lifestyles might have suggested – he leased **Tilton House**, a few fields away, which is now run as a centre for food-oriented courses and yoga-type retreats (*www.tiltonhouse.co.uk*).

Bell and Grant's art was influenced by French post-impressionists like Cézanne and Matisse at a time when the British had scarcely even heard of the impressionists. One story goes that in 1918 Keynes left a freshly acquired Cézanne temporarily in the hedge after he was dropped off at the end of the road with too much luggage. The artists developed highly individual styles completely at variance with the modernist minimalism which became fashionable during the interwar period, adorning walls and furniture with bright, splashy designs and pictures, and creating endearingly homespun details like beaded lampshades based on pottery colanders and woollen fringes to cover radiators. But as they never owned the house, the décor was done cheaply and not intended to last. After Duncan Grant's death in 1978 the fragile interiors could easily have been obliterated, but the Charleston Trust raised more than a million pounds to buy the house and commence restoration. This was immensely complex: in the dining room, restorers – including Angelica Garnett, Bell and Grant's daughter, who had created some of the original works – found eight layers of wallpaper ravaged by damp. Their huge achievement is to have re-captured the lived-in appearance and atmosphere of Charleston as it was in the 1950s.

The colourful, densely packed cottage-style garden has also been restored, and the site shop sells pottery, textiles and furniture inspired by Bloomsbury designs. More of Grant and Bell's work can be seen at nearby Berwick church (see below), which they were commissioned to decorate with wall paintings in 1941.

⑬ Berwick

One of the string of delightfully unspoilt villages alongside dead-end lanes running towards the Downs – only this one has a difference. During World War II Vanessa Bell and Duncan Grant put their own very individual stamp on the otherwise typical rural **church of St Michael and All Angels**, illustrating the life of Christ against a background of the South Downs as they looked during the war. The decision by the Bishop of Chichester to allow these pacifist, radical, free-thinking bohemians to transform the building in the heart of war-torn Sussex certainly raised a few eyebrows but nowadays brings great numbers of appreciative visitors. The Bloomsbury Set used themselves, their friends, their children and local people as models. If you've just been to Charleston, the almost outrageously multi-coloured pulpit decorations will be instantly recognisable. However unusual now, the idea of a church covered in wall paintings echoes medieval times, though the details –including a soldier, airman and sailor – are clearly 20th century: look out for their hair styles for instance. Their model for Christ (over the chancel arch) was the artist Edward Le Bas, who gallantly let himself be secured to an easel at Charleston in a crucified position and was fortified with brandy during the ordeal. Sussex cameos are everywhere in the pictures, among them the South Downs, shepherds' crooks (of the type made for many years at Pyecombe, near Clayton), a Sussex trug full of fresh produce and the pond at Charleston.

A short walk or bike ride taking the path at the end of the road towards the Downs and turning right on the chalk track known as the Coach Road brings you to **Alciston** – turn right at the wooden bench on a grassy triangle. Around the church cluster the village's medieval remains. The massive tithe barn here is at 170 feet one of the longest in the country and would have been used for storing parishioners' compulsory contributions of a tenth (or tithe) of their produce to the church authorities. The roof is reputed to contain 50,000 tiles. A ruined medieval dovecot is in the complex of buildings near the church. You can retrace to the Coach Road and continue to West Firle (see page 162).

Food and drink

Both Berwick and Alciston have invitingly placed traditional pubs:

Cricketers Berwick BN26 6SP ☏ 01323 87046 🖰 www.cricketersberwick.co.uk. A very lovely setting beneath the Downs, with a cottagey garden (road noise just audible) and pleasantly rambling and relaxed inside, with half-panelled walls, low ceilings, cricket bats hanging up, rustic benches and old wooden tables.

Unpretentious, good home cooking, Harveys Best and seasonal beers. Look out for 'toad in the hole' here – an old Sussex pub game that involves throwing 'coins' on to a sloping lead platform aiming for a hole.

Rose Cottage Alciston BN26 6UW ☎ 01323 870377
⌂ www.therosecottageinn.co.uk. On the village's single street, nicely relaxed, with small rooms warmed by log fires, its own resident parrot and some seating outside, with ducks and chickens in a little paddock. Organic produce features in the reasonably priced food, and they serve Sussex beers like Dark Star and Harveys.

Cuckmere Valley: from Hailsham to the sea

⑭ Michelham Priory

Founded as an Augustinian monastery in 1229 and now run by Sussex Past (the Sussex Archaeological Society's commercial arm), this bears no resemblance to a religious house now: dissolution in 1537 was followed by the demolition of the church, whose outline is marked by stones in the lawn, but part of the range was adapted into the house that stands today (*BN27 3QS; 01323 844224; www.sussexpast.co.uk*). Inside the contents include kitchen equipment, an 18th-century child's bedroom and a set of tapestries created for the owner in the 1920s and 1930s.

Cuckoo Trail

You pretty much always see cyclists along this hugely popular walkers'/cyclists'/horseriders' trail which runs for 11 traffic-free miles between Heathfield and Polegate, with an extension to Eastbourne, along a  defunct railway (apart from the odd, well signposted diversion through quiet streets), which saw its last train in 1968 and which was named after the Sussex legend that the first cuckoo of spring was always heard at Heathfield Fair.

The trail slopes downhill very gently from north to south, but is easy enough in either direction. Part of the National Cycle Network and opened in 1990, it's ornamented with carved benches and chunky sculptures made from recycled materials. I always think it feels like an optimistic vision of the future, where people commute around on two wheels instead of four. Don't expect scenery, by the way: it's largely between hedgerows and viewless.

Google 'Cuckoo Trail' to find East Sussex County Council's free leaflets showing circular walks and rides on the trail.

For those arriving by train, Polegate station is ideally placed.

The interest here is partly the exquisite atmosphere of the site itself, surrounded by England's longest water-filled moat and entered through a huge medieval gatehouse that looks like somewhere in rural France. An area is devoted to archaeological reconstructions and experimental archaeology; look out for medieval and other history-themed weekends and country fairs when it particularly comes to life.

Just outside the grounds, Michelham's watermill grinds flour to continue a milling tradition that dates back to 1434 or perhaps even earlier. The volunteer millers will lead you through the whole process. They sell their own stoneground flour, which makes excellent bread.

Elsewhere on site are a café, a picnic site and play area, a little rope museum that commemorates an aspect of the industrial history of nearby Hailsham, and the aptly named Elizabethan Great Barn, an agricultural storage barn dating from 1597–1601, and now used for wedding ceremonies, receptions, and other functions (it's sometimes possible to peek inside).

⑮ Arlington Reservoir

A footpath circles this very artificial-looking reservoir. It's not a bad place for a cobweb-removing stroll, but hardly worth crossing the county for. Its geometric shape fools no one, and one wishes it was a bit more raggedy-edged. The 1960s constructors unwittingly ignored the archaeology. Since then it has been discovered that various Roman roads converge on the site of the reservoir, and as there are other Roman remains in the locality it is assumed it may have been built on the site of a Roman town.

And while on the subject of Roman leftovers, the strikingly rectangular grid of roads just to the west of here around **Ripe**, **Chalvington** and **Laughton** has very early origins. The historian Ivan Margary, an authority on Roman roads, believed the area was 'centuriated' – divided into rectangular blocks using Roman measurements, and given as plots to retiring soldiers (a sort of Roman Peacehaven). Archaeological finds suggest there was certainly Roman activity; this was a huge grain-growing area, exporting via Pevensey. However the latest thinking is that the Roman road/track system was itself based on earlier straight drove roads which could date back to the Bronze Age.

At **Bates Green Farm** in Arlington, Rob Bookham makes fresh and dried pasta with regional English flour. He takes his pasta-making skills into schools and gets the kids to have a try, and by the time this book is published his pasta workshop for children should be up and running at the farm. Rob is a familiar face among the stallholders at local farmers' markets. I've bought his delicious hard, grating cheese many times (though seldom have the self-restraint to keep it for grating); this is the stuff that isn't allowed to be named after its more famous Italian counterpart, any more than Sussex wine producers can call their sparkling wines Champagne, so it's called instead Sussex 'farmers' ham' which sounds just a little like 'Sussex parmesan' if you say it quickly. He also does a 'Sussex charmer' – using a cheddar and parmesan recipe to create a creamy cheddar with a subtle zing of the cheese we can't call parmesan, all very well-rounded for eating. In spring you could combine your visit with a bluebell walk: see box below.

Food and drink
Bookham Fine Foods Bates Green Farm, Tye Hill Rd, Arlington BN26 6SH
☎ 01323 636110 🖰 www.bookhams.com.

A bluebell wood to end all bluebell woods

Nothing unusual there, you may think – bluebells grow everywhere in the southern counties. But time it right in this part of East Sussex and the purple-blue carpets seem like some psychedelic excursion. The place to come to is Bates Green Farm near Arlington. Here for a glorious four weeks in mid April to mid May the farm opens its woodland estate in cooperation with two neighbouring farms, charges admission and sells teas, coffees and other refreshments for good charitable causes. John McCutchan, the farmer, has been doing this since 1972, when he started fund-raising for an outdoor swimming pool at a local primary school. It's quite remarkable for the quantities of blooms and of the folk who come to see it (up to 18,000 each year), mostly from East Sussex but some from further afield. Good for wood anemones too, and the wood has always been maintained to encourage bluebells – it is left empty of people for the rest of the year. John says it's worth phoning or checking their website before coming to see if the bluebells are out.

Eight signed trails lead round, but just following the crowds is easy enough. It all adds up to a gorgeously good-natured social event, with local produce on sale too: fruit juice, eggs, ice creams, preserves and chutneys. May it last for ever.

Bates Green Farm Tye Hill Rd Arlington BN26 6SH ☎ 01323 485151
🖰 www.bluebellwalk.co.uk.

⑯ Long Man of Wilmington

No one has the faintest idea what this colossal carved man is doing here on the escarpment of the Downs, how old he is or what he's carrying in each hand – or if he's actually standing in a doorway. From the A27, carry on along the main street of Wilmington, past the Giant's Rest pub, through the village and past the church with its ancient yew (see opposite).

At the southern end is a free car park with an information panel about the Long Man.

Across the road, a footpath leads alongside the road for a distance before heading to the base of the hill figure. You can turn left here, along the track at the bottom of the downs, then take a path up across the steep escarpment (note how little sense you can make of it all upside down, with all the clever tricks of perspective in operation).

Measuring 235 feet from foot to head, the Long Man is the largest hill carving in Britain, an iconic image, much used to symbolise the South Downs. He has been variously explained as a fertility symbol, though he has a conspicuous lack of manly attributes (some argue because he in fact has his back to us); a surveyor of ley lines (holding two staffs); a religious image from the Bronze or Iron ages; a Roman figure, similar to many depicted on Roman coins; an Anglo-Saxon representation of Odin with two spears, as on the 7th-century Finglesham buckle; and a medieval Christian image of the Good Shepherd associated with Wilmington Priory. Or he could be even earlier.

What we do know is that in the 19th century the carving was re-laid in bricks and its shape got somewhat distorted; it's now outlined with white-painted concrete blocks. Perhaps the greatest mystery is that there are no written records of the figure existing at all before 1710. Recent archaeological work suggests it isn't as ancient as frequently supposed: it could well date from the Tudor period, when post-Reformation landowners taking over monastic sites like nearby Wilmington Priory sometimes literally put their own mark on the land with such pagan-looking figures.

In 1700 the Wilmington estate passed to Spencer Compton, Speaker of Parliament, who adopted the title Baron Wilmington, and the Long Man first appears on a map he commissioned in 1710. There's a good view of the figure from the Priory, and Compton's map-maker/surveyor would have had the skills to lay it out. It's feasible that at a time of heightened interest in ancient monuments, Compton decided to add a new one with secular, even pagan, associations, to 'his' landscape.

But all that doesn't preclude the possibility that there has been a Long Man in one form or another for much longer than that, as it has certainly been tampered with over time. Some are sure it is Neolithic and functioned as a solstice indicator.

St Mary and St Peter Church, at the south end of Wilmington's unspoilt single street, has what is thought to be the oldest tree in Sussex – a huge yew, gigantically propped up but still very much alive. A certificate in the porch dates it as 1,600 years old and requests 'Please do all you can to prolong the life of this venerable member of your local community.' Inside, a very beloved medieval window depicting bees and butterflies around the figure of St Peter was sadly destroyed by fire in 2002, but has been replaced by a painted glass window created by Paul San Casciani in 2004. He partially recreated the original, with the addition of a phoenix symbolising its return from the ashes; surviving bits of the original window have been incorporated into the bottom of the new one.

⑰ Lullington church

Blink and you'll miss the turning for this isolated, improbably minute 13th-century place of worship: a small signposted path leads past it from the road between Wilmington and Litlington (about 400 yards after the road begins to drop if you're coming from Wilmington). Alternatively you can reach it by walking up from Alfriston, by crossing the footbridge to the left of the church, carrying straight on over a road, and on for another quarter mile.

In the league for church superlatives it might get the prize for being the country's smallest, at about 13 feet square. Before chunks of it fell down, it was much more of a normal size; all that now remains is a fragment of the chancel. There's a harmonium, and no electricity. It has 23 chairs but a congregation of a dozen would make it feel positively crowded.

⑱ Alfriston

It's worth timing a visit to avoid the excesses of summer and weekend tourists that fill the very handsome main street of this largest of the Cuckmere valley villages.

Apart from the deluge of visitors, it has no jarring note. Virtually all of it is 18th century or earlier. A memento of Alfriston's smuggling days is incorporated into the facade of the 16th-century **Star Inn**; a ship's figurehead in the form of a red lion, pilfered from a wreck off the Sussex coast by the notorious Alfriston gang member Stanton Collins (see page 176) in the early 1800s.

Alfriston's village sign was unveiled in 2000 by local resident and erstwhile Chancellor of the Exchequer Lord Healey.

Right in the middle of things beneath a horse chestnut tree stands an ancient **market cross**, weathered into what's now not much more than a stone pillar, which has got knocked over by lorries more than once; one smashed into the Market Cross Inn a few years back and caused an almighty mess.

On the Tye, or village green, another item of street furniture takes the unusual form of a collecting box made out of an unexploded 1940s mine. Across from here, the beautifully spacious **parish church**, the 'cathedral of the Downs', dating from 1360, is well away from the road on the Tye and within a circular churchyard. Inside, it is unusually wide and light. I can think of few other churches that have actually gained a musicians' gallery in recent years; in 1995 this was added to provide extra space – there's a lively programme of musical events here.

Pretty much contemporary with the church is the adjacent **Alfriston Clergy House** (*01323 870001*) with small diamond-leaded windows beneath a massive thatched roof. In 1896 the newly formed National Trust paid just a tenner to rescue this ancient timber-framed Wealden yeoman's house of around 1350 from a state of spectacular decay; it was the Trust's very first purchase anywhere, though it didn't open its doors to the public for another 81 years. Clearly the Trust recognised the house's rarity value. Inside you can see a photograph of its alarming condition in 1893. Happily it has been painstakingly restored. The main hall is very much as it was 650 years ago: there's no chimney, just a central fireplace from which the smoke drifts surprisingly unchokingly up through the high ceiling. Its floor is made of rammed chalk mixed with milk, a traditional and surprisingly durable surface. When the modern craftsmen first had a go at it, this didn't quite come off. They realised they were using pasteurised milk, and only the unpasteurised version solidified properly. The cottage garden has old rose varieties, lilies, clematis and poppies giving directly on to a wilder landscape of river reeds. Raised vegetable beds are edged with lavender.

The bottom left corner of the green (as seen from the main street) leads to a long footbridge over the Cuckmere – and starting point for the **kissing-gates walk** (which goes up one side of the river and returns on the other).

Food and drink

You're almost falling over places to spend money and eat in Alfriston – with three pubs and various places for teas or snacks. The excellent **Alfriston Village Stores** has fresh bread daily, pasties, local produce and a good deli section, and it's also open on Sundays: plenty of very useful fuel for walkers and cyclists.

Badgers Tea House ☎01323 870849 www.badgersteahouse.com. Sip tea from bone china and tuck into home-baked cakes and scones in this enjoyably unpretentious 500-year-old cottage (which was a bakery from the early 18th century until 1933, so they're continuing a fine tradition), or sit out in the tranquil, pretty walled yard at the back. They use proper ingredients and free-range eggs. Checked tablecloths and bentwood chairs set the tone.

George ☎01323 870319 www.thegeorge-alfriston.com. Pleasant old village inn, open all day, interesting choice of food using local produce, and a large, secluded garden.

Ye Olde Smugglers Inn (formerly the Market Cross) ☎01323 870241. Refreshingly unprecious 14th-century village local right by the worn stump of the market cross itself. Pub nosh, decent beers including Harveys and Dark Star, as well as real cider; garden. Note the vintage, utterly lovely Cyclists' Touring Club sign outside.

A walk from Alfriston

The area bounded by Alfriston and Litlington to the west, Westdean to the south, Jevington to the east and Folkington (pronounced Foe-ington) and Wilmington

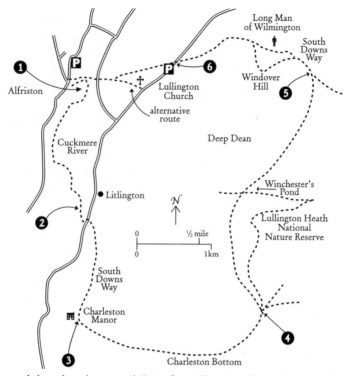

to the north has abundant possibilities for walks. For all-round views the seven-mile route mapped here is one of my favourites and is well signposted throughout.

Start in: Alfriston, main village street, by the Star Inn.

❶ With the **Star Inn** on your right, follow the street for 50 yards, and go left by the United Church of St Andrew and opposite The Apiary. You'll see the church across the Tye (village green to the right), but continue ahead between flint walls and then forward on a track, soon crossing the footbridge over the Cuckmere. On the other side, turn right downstream (signposted South Downs Way to Exceat) to follow the Cuckmere south to Litlington. You later see the **Hindover White Horse** carved into the hillside beneath High and Over (see page 175).

❷ After ³/₄ mile, just after passing Litlington away to the left, you go through a kissing gate into a semi wooded, reedy area. About 150 yards later, turn left shortly before the next footbridge, into Litlington; the **Harrow** (to the left) makes a useful pub stop. You might also like to peep inside **Litlington Tearooms and Gardens** (also to the left), possibly the oldest tea garden in existence; this dates from the early decades of the 19th century when visitors arrived by horse and carriage on their day out. A few remnants of those days survive, and although it's obviously evolved with the times it retains a fetching assemblage of ageless sheds and summerhouses around tables and chairs set out on two terraces, one gravel and the other grassy.

Turn right along the village street, then 50 yards later take the next turning left where the road is about to bend right at the end of the village, go past the village hall and immediately right on the South Downs Way. This rises up through a field, and then follows the right edge of a field downhill.

3 At the bottom cross a stile and turn left on a track inside woodland, skirting the grounds of Charleston Manor (to the right), at the end of which bear left (where the South Downs Way continues ahead up steps) along the beautifully peaceful valley of **Charleston Bottom**. You later enter a semi-wooded area by a gate; after five minutes' walking, keep forward at a marker post with a blue arrow, ignoring tracks to the left and right.

4 At a track junction where there are two gates ahead, do not go through the gates but go sharp left uphill on a track that immediately bends right through the forest. As you emerge into the open, go over the first track crossing. Down to the right is **Lullington Heath National Nature Reserve**, where the cohabitation of species suited variously to chalk grassland and acid soils throws up some unusual botanical neighbours such as heather and salad burnet. At the next track junction, where the view opens out to the left, take the track ahead (to the left of the nature reserve sign, which itself is by the entrance to **Winchester's Pond**, a dragonfly haunt). Carry straight on through a gate, gently uphill and soon alongside a fence on the left.

5 Just before you reach a point above the head of the valley, the South Downs Way joins from the right. A delectable view now opens on the left, over the dry valley of **Deep Dean** – a good indication of how much of the Downs must have looked before modern agricultural methods. With the sea in the background, this panorama for me epitomises the South Downs.

Go through a gate; the South Downs Way leads all the way back to Alfriston, but I prefer beyond the gate to turn right, along the fence, and soon directly above the steep escarpment. You'll see the **Long Man of Wilmington** (see page 168) from above – not the familiar view, and it makes little sense, but shows how ingenious its creators were in dealing with foreshortening and working on an extremely steep site. Beyond it, **Wilmington Priory** is in view at the near end of Wilmington village.

Soon, rejoin the South Downs Way, and keep left on it, down to the left of a covered reservoir.

6 At the road, either take the South Downs Way opposite (it's quicker to then cut a corner by crossing the stile on the left after 50 yards and then crossing the field directly towards Alfriston church), or if you want to see the almost comically tiny **Lullington Church** turn left along the road and then right on a path after 300 yards, past the church (up to the right). Carry on down the path, across another road, along the path opposite and slightly to the right and to the river at Alfriston.

Drusillas

It would be hard to find any child or indeed accompanying adult who wasn't

fascinated by something at this particularly intimate-scale zoo (*BN26 5QS; 01323 874100; www.drusillas.co.uk*). Mice live in a Mouse House like a doll's house, tiny monkeys look as curious about the visitors as the visitors are about them and children can go through a tunnel to look at the meerkats through a clear dome right inside their enclosure, and greet the snoozing ring-tailed lemurs; elsewhere there are otters, pigs, macaques and penguins, and some very innovative play areas including an interactive maze called Eden's Eye. Drusillas has an accent on learning too – there's a rogues' gallery of confiscated illegally traded objects like crocodile shoes – and they carefully place labels at child level.

As a family attraction Drusillas is very much cherished by many locals, quite a few of whom have season tickets.

Perhaps the most enriching Slow experience of all is to become **Keeper for a Day**, where with some expert supervision you get to help out with the cleaning and feeding for the whole day. It's very hands on, with mucking out straw for pigs, scattering feed for the meerkats and chucking sprats for the penguins. Not surprisingly such a close-up encounter of the animal kind is hugely popular for all ages and as there's a maximum of one 'keeper' per day the slots get booked up months ahead.

Drusillas began in 1922 as a simple thatched tearoom named after the founder's wife, and has evolved, expanded and metamorphosed. On the way out, you see the original tearoom: you can just about imagine its old mock-Tudor chintziness, but really that's not what it's about nowadays. Look out too for (or perhaps avoid) the seriously purse-emptying menagerie that awaits in the furry animal gift shop.

Visitors can eat and drink at the restaurant or café, or bring their own picnics.

English Wine Centre

Some 160 of the classiest English wines are on offer at this shop run by Christine and Colin Munday (*Cuckmere Barns, Alfriston Rd, Berwick BN26 5QS; 01323 870164; www.englishwine.co.uk*). The wine buyer, Matt Thomas, told me 'We have the largest collection of English wines in the country. We're not region-specific – if it's good, it's on the shelves.' So how does Sussex fare in the viniculture stakes? 'Around here we have the same sort of structure as Epernay, where Champagne comes from, with underlying chalk which makes the vines stretch their roots and produces wonderful grapes. The quality has improved massively over the past 15 years. There's more, particularly sparkling wine – Nyetimber are heading for one million bottles in production.' Matt's Sussex favourites include Limney from Rotherfield as well as Ridgeview, Breaky Bottom and Nyetimber.

Who's buying English wine nowadays? Matt says the home-grown factor is important, but there's definitely a generational divide. Younger people are often keen to try it but older people are often cautious: 'You have to tend to bend their ear to it a bit – they may have tried it 15–20 years ago and think it's dreadful; once they try it again, they're on your side. It has a loyal following – almost a cult following I'd say.'

And how about England versus France at wine? 'We have a French chap who runs an English-language school in Brighton and he brings people here to show them how good the wine is. They are astounded by the quality. In a blind tasting, English sparkling wines come out a lot better than French ones. Nyetimber particularly trounces the French at their own game. Non-vintage champagnes are comparable to our bottom-end (pricewise) sparkling wines. But it's a boutique industry in England; there are no tax breaks, land is very expensive and there are no co-operatives.'

They have a small restaurant at the back – a civilised lunch stop with local ingredients; prices are on a par with decent-value pub fare. On the menu might be beetroot and apple soup, slow-roasted loin of free-range pork seasoned with thyme and juniper, and homemade banoffee pie or a Sussex cheese platter.

Also on offer are tutored wine tastings. These take two hours with a minimum of two people, though it often works better with larger groups as you get more feedback. The session starts with the background on how English wine production has evolved, how to taste and what the wine taster is looking for, followed by a light-hearted tutored tasting of a range of eight wines. You start with a sample of sparkling wine, three whites, a rosé, two reds, and a dessert wine. Then comes lunch – maybe local sausages, seasonal vegetables, homemade soda bread and regional cheeses – accompanied by a glass of English wine of course.

High and Over

The road south from Alfriston climbs up past this viewpoint – which sometimes gets garbled into 'Hindover'. A very special view over the Cuckmere's meanders extends from here. Just below where you stand is the **Hindover White Horse**, seen to its best effect from across the valley near Lullington. The horse was carved in 1838 by the Pagden brothers – James Pagden of Alfriston was also a Sussex county cricketer and beekeeper who pioneered a method of artificial swarming. He made rather more of bees than he did of cricket: though his playing career spanned 23 years, he played only two first-class matches, one in 1835 for the MCC, and one in 1858 for Sussex; his four innings featured not out = 1, highest score = 1, total runs = 1, and he didn't bowl a ball. His former house, the Old Apiary, is in the main street in Alfriston. He was the author of the snappily titled *£70 a year, How I Make it by MY BEES and How a Cottager or Others May Soon do the Same*.

⑲ Friston Forest

You can wander where you like along the paths and rides of this forest, one of the few substantially tree-covered expanses of the East Sussex South Downs. Trees were planted here from 1926 over an underground reservoir constructed a few years earlier to serve Eastbourne on the understanding that planting a forest on top would keep the groundwater clean. Actually it turned out to be quite unnecessary, but the forest has become a prized amenity, and is now managed for leisure use. This is a calming, sheltered place that is lovely to wander into when the weather is unruly, and it also makes a satisfyingly contrasting inland leg to the circular walk along the Seven Sisters. It isn't bland plantation-style uniformity by any means, with a nice mix of beech, Scots pine and Corsican pine on the whole, and fritillary butterflies, adders, roe deer and badgers.

There's free access to the paths and tracks, subject to felling operations, with useful starting points from Seven Sisters Country Park on the southwest corner and from car parks on the Friston–Jevington road to the east. Colour-coded **walking trails** lace the forest. With enough serious up and down, **mountain bikers** are kept very happy here: 'if you can find your way to the downhill track, the descent is a real buzz with jumps and drops on the way down' pronounces an online guide for off-roaders. Two mountain bike trails – green (easy and level, 4¹/₂ miles) and red (technical, 7 miles) start from behind the visitor centre.

You can pick up a free map of the cycle trails from the Cuckmere Cycle Company (*next to Seven Sisters Country Park Visitor Centre; 01323 870310; www.cuckmere-cycle.co.uk*) – which has cycle hire. At the visitor centre they give out a map showing **orienteering** points. This was the first permanent orienteering course set up in the South Downs – it is suitable for walkers, runners, bikes and people with disabilities. It would take several days to find all the orienteering points (red-and-white-topped posts), but even novices can pick up several within a few hours.

A smugglers' coast

The cliffs hereabouts have a heady history of illicit money-making in centuries past. Locals made a good income plundering the contents of wrecked shipping driven against the cliffs: these folk included the Seaford Shags, a very rough lot who might well have finished off any survivors before helping themselves to the swag. Cuckmere Haven was for long the hub of smuggling activities for duty-free or illegal goods. Typically cargoes of brandy and gin were brought close to the shore in barrels known as 'half-ankers' and then retrieved at low tide. The preventive officers had the desperate job of trying to stop the trade, and were hopelessly outnumbered and often vulnerable to bribery. The notoriously violent Alfriston Gang wrought havoc in the area, using the Cuckmere River to bring goods into the village for distribution inland. Things ended for the gang in the 1830s when its leader, Stanton Collins, was transported to Australia for sheep rustling.

Surrounded by the forest, the remote-feeling village of **Westdean** seems to be a complete retreat from the modern world. Next to its partly Norman church stands a rectory dating from the late 13th century and one of the oldest inhabited buildings in Sussex. There's no parking in the village, so walk up the signposted route from the Seven Sisters Country Park car park. On the east side of the forest, Jevington church contains a stone carving (dating from around AD950) of Christ stabbing a beast, depicting the triumph of Good over Evil.

⑳ The Seven Sisters

One of the glorious things about this highly cherished stretch of completely unspoilt coast is how it never quite looks the same from one day to the next, thanks to natural lighting effects. In spring sunshine it can seem surreally bright, and the cliffs can take on a pinkish hue at sunset, while under sea fog the full septet partially disappears into an ominous grey nothing.

The 'Sisters' are a wavy series of 500-footer cliff-edge summits, with dry valleys in between. To be precise, there are eight hills, with seven dips in between. Once this chalky landscape extended across to France, until some 8,500 years ago the English Channel broke through, leaving a sheer wall of chalk. Sea erosion is constantly chopping the coast back at the rate of a yard a year, although intermittently much larger chunks fall away; in a hundred years several more metres will have been snipped off. Unlike the not very White Cliffs of Dover, the unprotected Sisters and neighbouring Beachy Head really are white – a result of constant eroding back by wave action and through fissures in the bedrock. After a cliff fall, the debris protects the cliff edge until it's eroded or washed away – during which time caves form, then fissures form through the rocks and the caves collapse. You can often see evidence of recent rockfalls on the shore beneath the patently crumbling cliffs.

Why they are called Sisters isn't that clear, but it may be a name dreamt up by sailors who tended to give female names to quite a lot of things. There are indeed seven, though some reckon seven and a half, and as the sea is eroding back extra ones will develop: we'll eventually have eight. Half of the Sisters (three and a half of them to be precise) are within the Seven Sisters Country Park – but there's free access to pretty well the entire area of the Seven Sisters, so this designation doesn't make much practical difference if you're out walking the whole caboodle.

There are nine different habitats here, including chalk grassland, vegetated shingle, saltmarsh, scrub and intertidal zone (or foreshore). Most unusually for this part of the world, the estuary has a lagoon. Viper's bugloss, blue and pink and growing to spectacular heights, is a common sight on the clifftop turf, alongside chalk milkwort, bastard toadflax and round-headed rampion, and the downland supports a range of butterflies, including five species of blue and the marbled white. This is very good bird-watching territory, especially for spring and autumn migrants, waders and winter ducks.

Cuckmere Haven, at the western end of the Seven Sisters, is the only estuary in Sussex to be undeveloped. Only in World War II it didn't always look as if it was quite like that: a mock town with the valley lit up was created to dupe enemy bombers into thinking this was Newhaven, on which they set their coordinates. This resulted in them dropping bombs east of central London. Other wartime relics that have survived here include pill boxes and concrete 'dragons' teeth' tank traps in the form of concrete blocks just inland from the shingle beach. At the Seven Sisters end of the tank traps is the D-shaped foundation of an anti-aircraft battery. One of the pill boxes is now a bat hibernaculum, while another is an unusual cylindrical type and was recently restored. One visitor whom staff at the country park met not so long ago had been, when in the Home Guard aged 14, on duty here in one of the pill boxes with a World War I veteran. Together they formed a force of two, ensconced with a thermos flask and waiting for the enemy, with the master plan: 'when the Boche arrive, we'll set the guns up and fire every bullet we've got down the valley, then run like hell and hide in the forest'.

A bone of contention locally has been the decision by the Cuckmere Estuary Partnership, formed of members of local councils and heritage agencies including English Nature (now Natural England) and the National Trust, to restore this valley to a naturally functioning estuary, thus reducing the need for costly engineering works. In the long term it would mean the area would revert to salt marsh, but this is likely to take many years. It is undeniably very beautiful as it is; but if the area were already salt marsh and a plan was being drawn up to turn it into what it is now, there would surely be objections too.

Rockpooling beneath the Seven Sisters

Robin Thorpe, a ranger at the Seven Sisters Country Park, pointed me in the direction of the joys of low-tide rockpooling and encountering a constantly changing microcosm. 'Find a good-size rock pool and you'll typically see crabs, bearded rock things that use their bearded bits as sensory organs. You might find strawberry sea anemones (which look like strawberries) or red and green-blobbed beadlet anemones, which grow big – they're global warming indicators. Devils crabs – or velvet swimming crabs – are so called because they have red eyes – they're the most vicious things you'll find, and might swim across a rock pool and chase you off. My favourite are porcelain crabs – these live on the underside of rocks, are very hairy and are the size of a little fingernail; they're slow and elusive; most people miss them completely. I also like seaweed – several types are edible and a lot of them beautiful. I've made very tasty sugar kelp crisps and carrageen mousse from the stuff.'

A few tips: watch the tides, and be extra careful on the slippery rocks; summer is particularly good as there is greater diversity of rockpool life. If you have a bucket for looking at what you find, make sure there is water in it. Never prise anything off a rock, such as a limpet, and replace any stones you've turned over. Periodically there are guided rockpooling events in the Seven Sisters Country Park.

Beachy Head and the Seven Sisters walks: variations on a theme

Plenty of permutations exist here, from easy saunters lasting half an hour to more demanding explorations taking most of the day. Getting lost is not a problem, except in Friston Forest where you'll certainly need to follow an OS map. You have to pay to use car parks at Alfriston, Birling Gap and Seven Sisters Country Park, but you can park free a bit further east at East Dean. The bus service along the A259 is quite outstanding, with up to six buses an hour in summer: the Beachy Head loop though is only hourly in summer and during Sundays in winter.

The map here and directions below show a long (8-mile) walk taking in all the Sisters and short (3-mile) circular walk that starts the same way then cuts off at Crowlink, giving a walk along the eastern Sisters. Both start from the free car park in East Dean, giving a great pub (the Tiger Inn) for the beginning and end of the walk, and a good tearoom at Seven Sisters Country Park (by the visitor centre) mid way.

❶ Turn right out of the car park to leave it on the village side, and emerge on the village green by the Tiger Inn; go up the green and turn right on the road in front of the Thai Terre restaurant and delicatessen. After 50 yards, where the road bends right, turn left on a concrete track, past

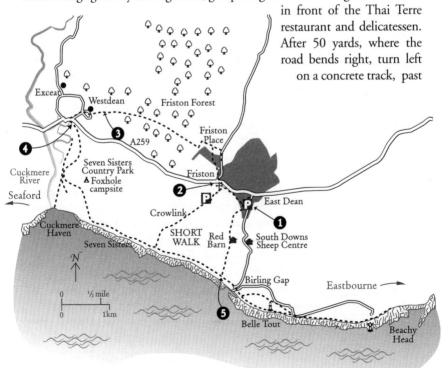

a National Trust sign for Farrer Hall, through a gate. Walk up the field to the top, then through a gate and Friston churchyard, at the far end of which emerge by the road junction.

❷ For the 3-mile walk, turn left along the road to Crowlink, past the small car park and then down the track past Crowlink house itself. From there, drop across the grassy slopes by any route towards the clifftops and turn left along the top of the Seven Sisters. Pick up the walk again at point **❺**.

For the 8-mile walk, cross over the main road by the pond and take the signposted woodland path opposite on the far side of the grass triangle, immediately bearing right, dropping and crossing a field towards stile over a wall. Go over a road, up steps and take the obvious path ahead across another field. Turn left on the metalled road (or follow the path immediately parallel on its right side), and left again as the route skirts two sides of a rectangle around Friston Place. Then when the driveway joins from the left from Friston Place itself, turn right up a track (signposted Westdean, blue waymarker) leading through the forest. Keep forward in a straight line all the way, ignoring all side turns; you later go along a field edge then re-enter the forest. Finally as the track drops, keep forward as the left fork goes through a barrier, and descend through another barrier, past a cottage.

❸ Enter Westdean village. Follow the road to the left around the village (though you may like to look at the church and medieval rectory to the right first),

Clifftop alternatives for walkers

Instead of following the circular routes I have described you might prefer to follow the clifftops all the way and to return by bus (frequent buses along the A259; if you want to start at Beachy Head, services are more limited – see page 138). For the **main clifftop walk along the South Downs Way** (8¹/₂ miles), start in Eastbourne, and walk up to Beachy Head, then along the cliffs westward, past Belle Tout lighthouse, and down to Birling Gap. This part of the walk is really much better in this direction, as otherwise it's an uphill slog west to east up to Beachy Head. Then carry on from the track behind the loo block at Birling Gap, past a line of houses and along all of the Seven Sisters. From the last Sister you have a choice of either dropping down to the Cuckmere Valley near the beach at Cuckmere Haven and following the obvious concrete track to Exceat, or taking the down-and-up route of the South Downs Way. At Exceat is the Seven Sisters Country Park Centre, with loos and the Exceat Farmhouse Restaurant; from there very frequent buses take you back to Eastbourne, Seaford or Brighton. An **extension to Seaford rail station** can be made by taking the waterside path along the straight cut of the Cuckmere to Exceat Bridge, and then heading back to the coast on the west side of Cuckmere Haven. Then climb up Seaford Head, and follow the cliff edge (looking behind for the most famous view of all along the length of the Seven Sisters), and drop down into Seaford.

then by Pond Cottage and a phone box turn left on a track, up a flight of steps (signposted Cuckmere Haven). At the top, cross the steps over the wall and drop down to the car park and buildings at Exceat.

❹ Cross (with great care) the A259 and carry along the Cuckmere valley to the sea – either along the concrete track or closer to the river. Where the concrete track bends left at a signpost, carry on through the gate and along the left-hand fence (signposted to the beach). Shortly before the beach, a steep path leads up to the left on to the Seven Sisters, but first carry on a short distance and explore the beach at Cuckmere Haven ahead. Climb up the path and follow it near the cliff edge for two miles. A prominent red-roofed barn (the Red Barn) later comes into view inland.

❺ Just above the hamlet of Birling Gap by the last Sister, turn inland over a stile, rising up over the open grassland (there's no defined path on the ground) and past the Red Barn (which comes back into view), keeping alongside the dwarf woodland on the right. 400 yards later, find a signposted path dropping to the right into East Dean. At the first houses, go through a gate and follow the road into the village centre by the green.

㉑ East Dean

With its free car park and idyllic village green, East Dean makes the perfect point to start a walk on to the Seven Sisters or Belle Tout. Fronting on to the green are the Tiger Inn and a useful coffee shop, the Hikers' Rest. In 2006, local landowner Charlie Davies-Gilbert and gardener Roger Green set up the village's own **Beachy Head Brewery** in a former farm building as part of farm diversification away from arable crops. Above the village, a walk up the grassy field known as Hobbs Eares leads to Friston's **church of St Simon and St Jude**, with its Saxon tower. I always admire its ingenious centrally pivoted tapsel gate – a design seemingly unique to Sussex – designed both to keep cattle out and to make it easier for coffin bearers to get through. The first such gate is thought to have been made by one John Tapsel of Mountfield, near Battle; other examples are found in Pyecombe (near Clayton), Kingston-near-Lewes, East Dean and Coombes (near Shoreham by Sea). In the churchyard, a simple (presumably 20th-century) grave marks an unknown body, marked starkly 'Washed ashore', close to four World War II graves to similarly anonymous naval sailors. Inside the church are Tudor monuments to the local Selwyn family, and a memorial to the composer Frank Bridge, a teacher of Benjamin Britten, who died at Eastbourne in 1941; look too for graffiti in the porch, scratched by medieval pilgrims. **Friston Pond**, just above the church and by the A259, was the first pond in the country to be designated an ancient monument.

Fields in this valley are unusual for the area in that they have flint walls. These were created by a landowner as a local employment scheme after the Napoleonic wars.

Seven Sisters Sheep Centre

You may find it hard to tear your children away from this utterly charming farm attraction just south of East Dean (*BN20 0AA; 01323 423302; www.sheepcentre.co.uk*), and adults might well fall for it too. It's a proper family-run sheep farm, so it's not open all year round; only in spring and late summer, and only in the afternoons on weekdays. Here is the largest selection of sheep you'll see anywhere in the world, with 55 of the total of 63 British breeds on display, including rare old breeds seldom seen out in the English countryside. The lambing season from March to early May is a particularly good time to come, and children can bottle-feed the lambs, but later on in summer it reopens and there's plenty to experience with daily shearing and displays of sheep-milking, and around the farm you'll encounter pigs, chicks, goats and rabbits. Plenty of feeding and animal-petting opportunities await, as well as tractor rides and a very agriculturally rustic playground including defunct tractors. There are a range of fleeces for spinning, and the ewes' milk is made into cheese and yoghurt which is on sale. You can adopt a sheep, and give it the name of your choosing (provided that name hasn't already been used).

Terry Wigmore, who runs the farm, is a shepherd turned livestock manager. He took on the derelict 17th-century barn in 1988 – a handsome structure sporting roof timbers which were recycled from old barges and from Birling Gap shipwrecks – and after buying 20 British milk sheep nurtured his interest in rare breeds.

Food and drink

East Dean has a weekly farmers' market 10.00–12.00 in the village hall on Wednesday. At the top of the village green, Frith and Little is a useful deli for picnic items. By the clifftop at Birling Gap, the Victorian colonial-style 'hotel' has a 1930s roadhouse interior of a type that is almost endangered, and is run as a National Trust café, exhibition area and shop.

Hikers Rest Coffee and Gift Shop East Dean BN20 0DR ✆ 01323 423733. On the village green by the Tiger Inn; open daily for cream teas, light lunches and sandwiches.

Tiger Inn East Dean BN20 0DA ✆ 01323 423209 ✆ www.beachyhead.org.uk. Open all day, this has a picture-book position at the bottom of a sloping, cottage-lined village green. Long and squat, it is ancient-feeling and little changed inside, with a stove in an inglenook, well-used old wooden furniture and a stuffed tiger's head. Plenty of space to sit outside on the village green too. Tasty bar food and local real ales, including the village's very own Beachy Head Brewery ales. Also has very pleasant accommodation (see page 141).

㉒ Combe Hill

A grand viewpoint marking the northeastern culmination of the Downs, this sprawling hill is most easily reached via Butts Lane, which climbs from Willingdon, a suburb of Eastbourne; a car park at the top makes for a straightforward stroll along its flat top – a favourite ground for dog walkers and kite fliers. The grassy humps mark what is termed a Neolithic causewayed enclosure, one of the very earliest constructions in Sussex (built around 3200BC), surrounded by a ditch in a series of segments, with access points or breaks through it. Such features are of unknown purpose, but this is thought to be a place of ritual rather than a dwelling. What is less cryptic is a small but prominent dressed stone by the track up from the west side, from the downland village of Jevington: it is actually a sad remnant, which somehow made it up here, of Barclay's Bank in Eastbourne, bombed to bits in World War II.

㉓ Birling Gap and Beachy Head

The wind-battered hamlet of **Birling Gap** marks the point at the eastern end of the Seven Sisters. Steps lead down to the shore by the row of coastguard cottages; like the rest of the hamlet they are threatened with collapse as the cliffs become undermined by weathering. The decision has been made – not without local controversy – not to bolster them up with hugely costly and unsightly sea defences. The beach is a wild, rugged place, good for rockpool browsing and with sublime views of the cliffs from below; the submerged jagged flinty rocks make beach shoes a good idea if you are swimming.

Eastwards from here, it is a short stroll past **Belle Tout**, the former lighthouse that perches near the edge of the cliffs: it was built in 1832 and decommissioned 70 years later. In 1999 it was famously moved back on rails from the cliff edge by a few yards, an operation that was seen on TV across the world. Now a very superior and characterful B&B (see page 139), the lighthouse was used for target practice by Canadians in World War II which didn't do it a great deal of good; it was restored as a home in the 1950s, hence its strange hotchpotch of ages and styles. In the 1980s the BBC filmed the mini series of Fay Wheldon's novel *The Life and Loves of a She-Devil* there. Beneath it on the inland side, a striking Iron-Age earthwork runs near the foot of the hill.

Continuing eastwards, the South Downs Way touches on a bend in the road where you can look down to the vertigo-inducing view of Beachy Head Lighthouse, at sea level beneath **Beachy Head**, which at 530 feet is the tallest sheer chalk cliff in Britain. In exceptionally clear conditions the view can extend as far as Dungeness in Kent to the east and westwards to Culver Cliff on the Isle of Wight. The lighthouse itself was built of some 3,500 granite blocks imported from Cornwall, which were cut to size and lowered from the clifftop. It was painted with its distinctive red and white stripes in the 1950s; its 400-watt light rotates constantly and can be seen up to 20 miles away.

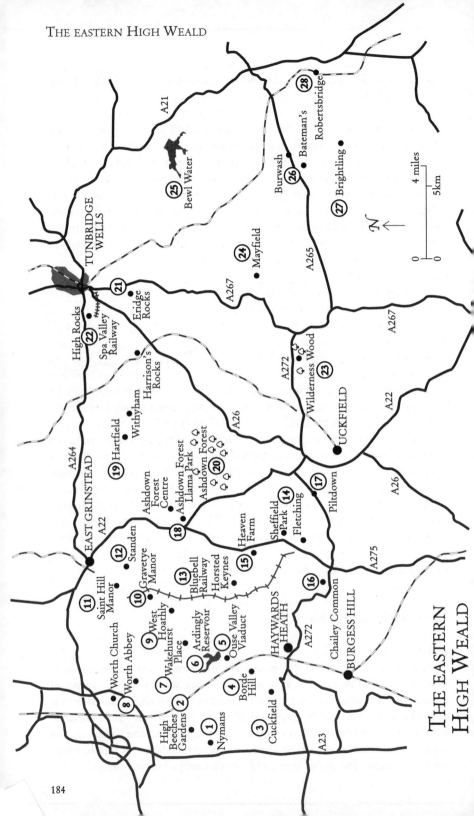

THE EASTERN
HIGH WEALD

5. THE EASTERN HIGH WEALD

E ast Sussex doesn't geographically extend north to south for any great
distance, but this northern strip of sandstone scenery feels a world away
from the more visited South Downs and coast. You need to get high up
to piece together this remote-feeling and strangely impenetrable landscape of
copses, hammer ponds, larger woodlands and sandstone outcrops. From
churchyards such as those at Turners Hill, West Hoathly and Cuckfield you
look over the tree tops towards the South Downs, bare-sloped and orderly.

You can get similarly grand views from some of the big estates that harbour
world-class gardens such as Standen – itself my favourite Arts and Crafts house
open to public view – and Borde Hill. Others of these great horticultural
creations are more tucked away and secretive. Come here in late spring or early
summer and the rhododendrons and azaleas put on a dazzling show. Nymans
perhaps outdoes them all for sheer theatricality. Wakehurst Place and Sheffield
Park are two vast and justifiably famed National Trust gardens. The latter, also
celebrated for its stupendous autumn foliage, is most memorably reached by a
vintage steam train on the Bluebell Railway. Among other architectural
hallmarks, Horsham slates, hipped gables, medieval 'Wealden halls', pantiles
and timber frames are seen in a plethora of ancient buildings in numerous
villages – among them Mayfield, Burwash and Rotherfield.

Parts of this area have a distinctly un-Sussex look. The Ashdown Forest is a
large lowland heath that has almost a moorland character, carefully preserved by
conservators for many years and almost a mini national park in itself.
Wandering deer stray on to the lonely roads, clumps of Scots pines punctuate a
skyline that might be in northern England, and Winnie-the-Pooh aficionados
tackle a daunting maze of paths in search of literary landmarks. Further east
Eridge Rocks is one among several rock outcrops in the vicinity that wouldn't
look too out of place in the Peak District, although the luxuriant growths of
bamboo hint at something more exotic.

Getting around

Public transport

Getting around without a car is feasible for some areas but not always
straightforward. The network of trains doesn't get you to the key places of
interest, and for the most part you are restricted to convoluted bus journeys.
One of the more accessible **gardens** is Sheffield Park, thanks to the Bluebell
Railway, which is linked by bus services to the main line at East Grinstead. On
the line from London Victoria to Brighton and Lewes, Haywards Heath station
is within walking distance of Borde Hill Garden, and a bus service heads north

past Wakehurst Place (though services are sporadic). From Crawley station, two-hourly bus services (Monday to Saturday only) get you to Handcross for Nymans garden and to East Grinstead rail station via Three Bridges station via West Hoathly and Standen. The **Ashdown Forest** is not at all well served; your best bet may be to take the bus (hourly; two-hourly on Sunday) from Haywards Heath or East Grinstead and get off at Wych Cross, at the junction of the A275 and A22 near the Ashdown Forest Llama Park, and explore the paths immediately south of the A22. Useful rail stations for **walks** are Eridge (for a walk taking in Eridge Rocks and Harrison's Rocks; see page 211) and Balcombe, from which there are some excellent possibilities eastwards taking in Wakehurst Place, Ardingly Reservoir and the Ouse Valley Viaduct.

Cycling

Very good cycling is here in abundance, but so are the hills. If you keep clear of the main roads, there are plenty of quiet lanes north of Haywards Heath and Uckfield. Note that off-road cycling isn't permitted on the Ashdown Forest, except on the few bridleways that exist. The area north of Heathfield is outstanding too, but there is a lot of up and down in and out of small valleys.

Accommodation

Copyhold Hollow Copyhold Lane, Borde Hill, Haywards Heath RH16 1XU ☎ 01444 413 265 ⌨ www.copyholdhollow.co.uk. Just round the corner from Borde Hill Garden, this tile-hung house stands by itself on a quiet lane, with a hedgerow in front thought to date back 1,000 years and to be the oldest in Sussex. Three characterful ensuite bedrooms, exposed timbers, a half-tester bed in one room, a cosy sitting room with a huge fireplace, and uneven walls and ceilings everywhere ('we don't do right angles' says the owner Frances Druce). A spring-fed stream tumbles through the two-acre gardens, all surveyed from a tree house; beyond, a deer fence bounds woodland which guests are welcome to explore. B&B £100 for two; £55 single; no dinner but guests are welcome to bring their own picnic supper.

Dernwood Farm Dern Lane, Heathfield TN21 0PN ☎ 01435 812726 ⌨ www.dernwoodfarm.co.uk. A very special eco-friendly, low-impact, wild camping experience, in a field surrounded by ancient, semi-natural woodland, coppiced to create bio-diversity. You leave your car at the farm and take your belongings in a wheelbarrow or on a trolley. The woods are full of interest: bluebells, primroses, anemones and orchids – they open from Good Friday to the end of May for bluebell walks – and a fallow deer herd is often at large. Camp fires are encouraged (logs for sale), but no amplified music or bongos, so the owls may be the only sound at night. Amanda, who runs the camping business, is fascinated with the woodland archaeology and will help you spot the appreciable remains of the iron-making activity that existed here in Tudor times, including charcoal-burning platforms and sawpits. The on-site farm shop sells meat from the farm's own pedigree Sussex beef herd, pigs and free-range chickens. The Vanguard Way runs close, and the Six Bells at Chiddingly is not far away. If you're coming without a car, get the bus from Lewes, Berwick or Uckfield to Horam or Golden Cross and they'll pick you up from there.

Holy Well Barn Keysford Lane, Lindfield RH16 2QT ☎01444 484438 ⌂ www.holywellbarn.com. Right at the very end of a long driveway, this has sweeping views from the most peaceful of rural positions – the occasional toot from the nearby Bluebell Railway might be the only thing to disturb the birdsong. From here you can walk along a choice of footpaths: 45 minutes will get you to the Sloop Inn, which has a good garden. The neatly laid out and very pretty B&B (just the one bedroom, so perfect privacy) is in a separate building at the back of the converted barn and has under-floor heating and a sitting area upstairs. £100 for two.

Wilderness Wood Hadlow Down TN22 4HJ ☎01825 830509 ⌂ www.wildernesswood.co.uk. £30 per night camping in family-run sustainable woodland, with trails, slow food, woodland courses and more. See page 215.

Wowo Wapsbourne Manor, Sheffield Park TN22 3QT ☎01825 723414 ⌂ www.wowo.co.uk. Oodles of space on the Cragg family's farm here, within walking distance of Sheffield Park station (so you could arrive in true Slow style via the Bluebell Railway): you can bring your own tent or stay in a luxurious Mongolian yurt (from £112 for three days midweek for two to £250 for a weekend for six) or bring your own tent; they don't allow caravans (apart from camper vans) or amplified music, radios or bongo drums; compost loos. For an extra fee you can join activities like bushcraft – where you learn such skills as tracking animals, knifecraft and building a simple shelter – and wild food foraging. I met Kristen from the Red Tipi company, who hires out tipis across much of Sussex, and was setting up her own for her family's week's camping here. 'It's just a big space – there's rope swings, there's streams, there's mud – it's just free-range children really.' It can be noisy at times, but never rowdy – 'just kids laughing and having fun' said Alice Cragg. On Saturday evenings there's free soup for all, and they have acoustic music – for kids and then adults. Note if you want to stay in a tipi, you need to book through Red Tipi, ☎01273 858406 or 07971 216075 ⌂ www.redtipi.co.uk; they also supply a box of camping supplies. Tipis have a stove that can keep you toasty warm all night even in winter. Minimum stay two nights at weekends. From £10 a night for adults, £5 children (double at weekends).

Tourist information centres

Burgess Hill 96 Church Walk ☎01444 238202.
East Grinstead Library Buildings West St ☎01342 410121.

Wealden gardens and the Forest Ridge

① Nymans

A more romantic garden than this would be hard to envisage (*Handcross RH17 6EB; 01444 400321; www.nationaltrust.org.uk; garden open daily all year; house open daily Mar–Oct except Tue*). Some 500 feet above sea level and on light acid loam, it is a secretive 30-acre series of spaces that entices the visitor round from one surprise to the next, very much more intimate than the likes of Wakehurst Place or Sheffield Park. In late

spring and early summer its colour is quite startling. Paths continue into the more naturalistic park and pinetum.

It was begun by Ludwig Messel who acquired the property in 1890 and brought in plants from around the world – he made a heather garden, sunken garden, raised pergola walk and pinetum, and planted azaleas and rhododendrons; his work was continued from 1916 by his son Leonard who planted the notable collection of rare magnolias and eucryphias and invested in plant-collecting expeditions in the Far East and South America, while his wife Maud created the rose garden, with old-fashioned varieties. Leonard also rebuilt the Victorian house in neo-Jacobean style only for it to be largely destroyed by fire, leaving all but one end a roofless ruin that has become part of the landscape in itself, complemented by sculptural topiary. After the National Trust took over in 1954, the Messels continued to oversee operations.

② High Beeches Gardens

'He's seriously glamorous – there's just something about him; he simply glows on a sunny day' said Sarah Bray, owner of this glorious 25-acre woodland and water garden just east of Nymans (*High Beeches Lane, Handcross RH17 6HQ; 01444 400589; www.highbeeches.com; open late Mar–end Oct except Wed, 13.00–17.00*). She was pointing out an acer, a riot of autumn colour in mid October, that to her stands out as a favourite. From the top with its vista to Devil's Dyke on the South Downs, the site slopes down through an intricate series of semi-open spaces between the trees; there are rhododendrons, champion trees, rarities from the Far East, a magnolia garden, redwoods and a pond reflecting giant rhubarb. 'We also have one of the best acid wildflower meadows in the southeast. It hasn't been cultivated in at least 60 years; we just mow it once a year. In late spring it's a mass of orchids, daisies, vetch, hay rattle and cowslips.'

Nothing remains of the original house that was reduced to a shell in 1942 after a Canadian plane carrying propaganda leaflets bound for Nazi Germany crashed into one of its chimneys. Sarah's parents, who live next door, bought

High Beeches at auction in 1966, after the death of Colonel Loder; he created this, the first of the local gardens laid out by the Loder family – the others are Leonardslee (closed in 2010, to the great consternation of many garden-lovers; let's hope its new owners open it up one day) and Wakehurst Place. As well as the landscape, the open spaces between the trees and the views, she rates the sense of continuity here as one of the garden's special attributes – Eric Stockton was the gardener here from 1927, and after the auction he was re-engaged and carried on until his death in 1979.

Food and drink

High Beeches Tearoom Open even to those not visiting the garden; all year except Wed. Lunches, cream teas and light refreshments. The walled garden just outside is inviting.

③ Cuckfield

A very unspoilt large village/small town on the brink of the subtopia of Haywards Heath, Cuckfield is thought to take its name from the cuckoo, used as the village emblem. No single building stands out, but it is very pleasant to stroll around. The spacious churchyard has an expansive view of the Downs; among the gravestones is an unusual 1840 survival in the form of a wooden rail to commemorate Sarah Tulet, a faithful servant to one Mr Sergison. Within the Queen's Hall in the High Street the Cuckfield Museum (*01444 473630; free; open Wed and all day Sat, plus Fri mornings in summer*) has 200 years of local history museum, with old photos and examples of local clockmaking.

A dinosaur discovery

A quarry at Whitemans Green, just north of the village, was where the Lewes-based geologist and palaentologist Gideon Mantell began investigations of the fossil beds in 1819. Three years later his wife found some quite gigantic teeth; other experts pronounced them to be variously parts of a rhinoceros or a fish, but Mantell realised they were from the Mesozoic era (67–250 million years ago), which we now know was the dinosaur period. He realised they were from a vast creature that measured some 60 feet in length. The similarity to iguana's teeth – which they outsized by a factor of 20 – led him to name his hitherto undiscovered beast the *iguanadon*.

④ Borde Hill

Successive generations of the Stephenson Clarke family have developed this enchantingly diverse garden (*01444 450326; www.bordehill.co.uk; open most of late Mar–mid Sep and Oct half term*), which belies its proximity to Haywards Heath (actually only 30 minutes on foot from the rail station, though one might be tempted to get a taxi). Totally rural and blissfully tranquil, it surrounds a late 16th-century mansion built by Stephen Borde. The current family have been here since 1893, when Colonel Stephenson R Clarke created a ha-ha and planted shrubs and exotic and specimen trees. There is a host of rare tree and plant collections – many are the original or the only ones in Britain, and were

gathered on plant-collecting expeditions to exotic parts, particularly China but also other parts of the Far East and South America. The garden also contains 82 champion trees – that is, the greatest in girth or tallest of their kind in the British Isles. A further distinguishing feature is the rural views in various directions over the Weald, including the Ouse Valley Viaduct (see page opposite).

I was shown round by Eleni Stephenson Clarke, the Greek Cypriot wife of the great-grandson of the founder of the garden. She is passionate about this mini paradise, has an encyclopaedic knowledge of what grows where, and began the Jay Robin's Rose Garden – with its prized collection of David Austin roses – and Mediterranean garden (both designed by the eminent horticulturalist Robin Williams). She also developed the Italian Garden (on the old tennis court), with its rectangular, lily-filled pool and box hedging. Eleni walked me past the Garden of Allah, with its massive rhododendron sutchuenense from the forests of central China, a wildlife pond that encourages newts and dragonflies, and the Victorian greenhouses that have been restored with grant money from the Heritage Lottery Fund. A lot of visitors, she remarked, confine themselves to the garden and unfortunately miss out the magnificent woods, carpeted with springtime bluebells; the canopy of trees has Himalayan proportions.

Like the other local gardens, this is utterly spectacular in May and June when the rhododendrons and azaleas are in bloom, and the roses present glorious shows of colour during summer. During July and August they have musical events including Brass Bands and picnics in the grounds. They are keen to attract families with children: there is a maize maze, an adventure playground and in August various activities such as go-karting, crafts, a magician and face painting.

Eleni confesses she was overwhelmed when she first saw this place, certainly quite unlike anything in Cyprus. Happily their son is keen to follow on in his forbears' footsteps and to carry on developing the garden.

Food and drink

Jeremy's Restaurant and Elvira's Café Borde Hill Garden 📞01444 441102 🖰 www.jeremysrestaurant.com; 📞01444 458845 🖰 www.cafe-elvira.co.uk. At the garden entrance, but accessible without paying the entrance fee, these two excellent eating establishments are run by husband and wife respectively. Jeremy's goes for bold flavours, and locally sourced modern European cuisine (also open in the evenings). Both have alfresco dining possibilities.

⑤ Ouse Valley Viaduct

Not far from Balcombe, the insignificant Ouse is spanned by one of Britain's grandest railway viaducts, built in 1841 to carry the London to Brighton railway. If you approach by rail, you only get a hint of its architectural bricky swagger as the train briefly emerges into the open and passes fanciful pavilion-like structures at either end of the 37-arch, 95-foot-high and 450-foot-long viaduct.

To see it in its full glory, take the footpath that leads from the road. You're looking at 11 million Dutch bricks. Each pier has a huge oval void within it – which saved the need for millions more bricks – and by looking through all the oval spaces you gain a surreal view into a tame infinity.

There's a similar viaduct at Brighton, but as it curves there's no such nether-vista as that of Balcombe's structural wonder.

⑥ Ardingly Reservoir

A surprising feature in an area not well endowed with large expanses of water, Ardingly Reservoir extends across 198 acres – enough water to fill 15.9 billion drinks cans – and feeds the River Ouse. Its V-shape positively graces the Wealden landscape, and footpaths around the southeast and northwest sides make an attractive strolling ground. The obvious starting point is from the car park beneath the dam at the south end; from there a trail heads past one of the reservoir's bird hides: kingfishers and great crested grebes may put in an appearance. Day fishing permits are available here through the **Ardingly Activity Centre** (*www.ardinglyactivitycentre.co.uk*), which also runs a programme of watersports including sailing, windsurfing and canoeing courses. They also hire out two-person kayaks for £15 an hour; no experience or tuition required – and no danger of capsizing.

In June, the **South of England Show** (*www.seas.org.uk*) takes place at the showground on the B2028 just north of Ardingly, over three days. It's easily the biggest event of its kind in the region, attracting tens of thousands of people: all sorts of country-related happenings, with show-jumping, a cattle parade, a Young Craftsman of the Year competition and such exhibits as an EcoVillage and a tableau of Victorian poultry-keeping. Frequent buses run from Haywards Heath station (small charge). There's a two-day Autumn Show and Game Fair in early October featuring all sorts of rural crafts, sports and food-and-drink stalls. The showground also hosts the region's largest **antique fairs** (*www.iacf.co.uk*) with up to 1,700 stalls, held over several days at various times of year; on Wednesdays a free hourly courtesy coach runs every hour to and from Haywards Heath station.

⑦ Wakehurst Place

Be prepared for quite a lot of walking around this richly varied and hugely important semi-naturalistic garden (*Ardingly RH17 6TN 01444 894066; www.kew.org/visit-wakehurst; www.nationaltrust.org.uk*), which spreads into a deep woodland valley and is of year-round interest. Managed by the Royal Botanic Gardens at Kew, it occupies a large country estate around an Elizabethan mansion (which itself is not open to the public). The land is owned by the National Trust but has been leased to Kew since 1965. As a horticultural creation it owes its beginnings to Gerald Loder, who planted it from 1903 to 1936, after which Henry Price took over. It has national collections of skimmia, hypericum, betula and nothofagus. The daily guided walks led by volunteer guides are well worth catching, and the events calendar includes courses such as photography, flower arranging and fungus forays.

Expansive and with more to take in than anyone could in a single visit, the site has a secretive nature, with no far-ranging views to speak of, and this whirlwind global tour of plants gets wilder as you proceed, beyond the island beds of more familiar perennials, round the sandstone crags of the Himalayan Glade, where you can appreciate the hilliness of the site to the full. Its northern extremity merges into the Loder Valley Nature Reserve, a woodland, wetland and meadowland haven for Wealden wildlife, with entry by free permit (restricted to 50 permits a day; no pre-booking), where badger watches are periodically held using special hides.

In a contemporary pavilion-like structure at the top of the site, the Millennium Seed Bank is a project aiming to conserve the world's wild plants through the storage of seeds, enabling species to be kept alive for hundreds or even thousands of years. It was begun amid predictions that half of the species on the planet could disappear in a century; currently they have seeds of 24,000 plant species, which once gathered are stored at a constant minus 20 degrees Celsius in seed banks at Wakehurst and in the country of origin. More than 30 countries have been involved in what has been described as 'one of the most significant international conservation initiatives ever' and has already secured for posterity the vast majority of native flowering species found in the United Kingdom. Within the Seed Bank you can look straight into the areas where the scientific work is being done.

There are two **cafés**, one at the entrance and the larger one inside the former stable block (perhaps designed by Wren).

⑧ Worth

Two very different religious establishments exist a couple of miles apart under the name of Worth. **Worth Abbey** is a modern Benedictine community of some 22 Catholic monks, where the TV documentary series *The Monastery* was filmed (you can watch it on their website www.worthabbey.net) in which five outsiders sampled the world of cloistered living for 40 days to see if the monastic tradition would offer anything to them. Monks spend four hours a day in prayer and gather for worship in the striking 1960s Abbey Church six times a day. They observe a strict rule of silence from 21.30 until after breakfast the following day – one monk described the silence as 'like a wonderful spiritual bath which we invite you to get in to relax your spiritual muscles.' There is an Open Cloister programme for men and women who want to experience a day or longer in this monastic community through a variety of events, including some for people who have never been on a religious retreat before. If you're just curious to look in casually, there is free entry to the site.

On the highest ground is a range of Tudorbethan stone and black-and-white buildings, once known as Paddockhurst and designed by Anthony Salvin in the 1860s. After the death of its owner Lord Cowdray in 1927, monks from Downside Abbey near Bath acquired the site and established a school there. The circular Abbey Church is tucked into the slope, while part of the Paddockhurst grounds have been restored to form a Quiet Garden open to all for contemplation.

To the north is the old village of Worth, at the fringes of Crawley. Soon after the northbound B2036 crosses over the M23, turn right into Church Road (signposted as the National Cycle Network). Here within earshot of the motorway and approached from the lychgate by a narrow avenue of limes known as the Ten Apostles, the **church of St Nicholas** is one of the finest surviving Saxon ecclesiastical buildings in the country. Edward the Confessor founded the present church, possibly as a centre for the court to worship while on hunting trips in the surrounding forest, but the site may have already been a minster, or early centre for Christian missionaries. The footprint of the church is identical to the original Winchester cathedral, which was built in the 8th century. Inside, the chancel arch is – at 22 feet high and 14 feet wide – one of the largest Saxon arches anywhere in England. As you enter at the west end, look for the two blocked-in Saxon arches opposite each other on either side of the nave. Strangely tall and narrow, these are characteristic of Saxon church-building and are said to have been for knights on horseback to ride through and pay their respects without dismounting – like an early drive-thru church. In 1986 a workman's fire destroyed the Victorian roof, but this was by no means a complete disaster. The uncluttered design of the replacement is more in harmony with the form of the original Saxon timbers, and the acoustics are much improved, ideal for the many concerts that are performed here.

Food and drink

Red Lion Lion Lane, Turners Hill RH10 4NU ☎ 01342 715416. An enjoyably unchanged, chatty rural local, run by the same people for many years. In an old tile-hung building looking over the village, it is just the place for a drink or for unpretentious home-cooked food; children and dogs are welcome, and there's a garden.

Tulleys Farm Turners Hill RH10 4PE ☎ 01342 718472 🖰 www.tulleysfarm.com.

Northeast of Worth Abbey and west of Turners Hill, this has been a pick-your-own operation since the 1930s, with soft fruit throughout the summer. Also a farm shop and lots of children's activities – a giant maize maze, adventure play area, tractor and barrel rides, farm animals and a seasonal Easter egg hunt.

⑨ West Hoathly

This unspoilt backwater of a village has an extraordinary **churchyard**, falling in terraces down a precipitous slope, and looking towards the breach in the South Downs around Lewes. Opposite the churchyard is a conspicuously handsome manor house of 1627, symmetrically gabled and with mullioned windows.

What really makes West Hoathly worth seeking out is the **Priest House** (*01342 810479; www.sussexpast.co.uk; closed Mon (except bank holidays and in Aug) and winter*). This is a marvellously untouched 15th-century timber-framed cottage of the 'Wealden hall' structure – originally a buttery, pantry, and upper chamber at either end, and a hall 23 feet long and 27 feet high (an open room with no chimney but with smoke from the fire going upwards through the ceiling). It's the same kind of arrangement as the much more visited Clergy House at Alfriston (see page 171), but with considerably more to see inside. Unlike the Clergy House, where later changes have been stripped away to reveal the original, this has its later additions: chimneys and a central ceiling were added around 1580, but little has changed since then, apart from the division of the house into two cottages in the 18th century. Antony Smith, the curator here since the late 1980s, lives in one part.

Despite its name, the building has nothing to do with priests, originating as an estate office for Lewes Priory. It might well have been forgotten were it not for its rescue by local man John Godwin King, who acquired it in 1905, restored it and opened it as a museum three years later. He gave it over to the Sussex Archaeological Society in 1935; many items from his collection of artefacts are still inside.

As you enter the house, notice the iron doorstep, made of local waste iron, and the Ws scratched into the front door: these are anti-witch devices (the iron being there because witches were supposed to be deterred by cold iron, and the W for Virgo Virginum, or Virgin of Virgins) and Antony will point out others inside, including circles, flower shapes and Ms, over the fireplace and elsewhere. 'They're not that rare,' he explained, 'but what is unusual is to find this many in one place. That iron doorstep is probably unique.' The normal sort of thing to do if you didn't want witches coming in was to fill a bottle with nails, iron and urine, but the practices varied; Antony told me that another house locally has a cat's paw embedded in the mantelpiece, and that it's not uncommon to find similar marks on church doors.

There's a square piano of 1776, built when Beethoven was only six and Mozart was 20 (CDs of it being played are on sale); a curator once found a man playing it without permission, and realised it was Richard Burton, here with Elizabeth Taylor (according to Antony, 'the only visitors ever who put their address in the visitors' book as 'Hollywood'). Upstairs are some fine examples of samplers and embroidery, and a handkerchief embroidered with 65 signatures of Suffragettes imprisoned in Holloway in 1912. Very fortunately it was rescued in the 1960s by Antony's predecessor. 'It was about to be put on a bonfire with all the other remnants from a jumble sale. The custodian here obviously saw what it was, plucked it off the fire, and it's been here ever since.'

Antony's tasks also include attending to the garden, kept in the style of a Victorian cottage garden, rather than a medieval one, which would be less spectacular anyway. 'The plants are in control; I try to referee occasionally.'

><><><

Shopping

Plaw Hatch organic farm shop Sharpthorne, RH19 4JL. The outlet for a mixed organic farm owned by a charitable trust and using live-in farm apprentices; it is part of a cooperative with Tablehurst Farm in Forest Row. From their dairy herd they produce cheeses, yoghurt, cream and unpasteurised milk; they also grow their own organic fruit and veg and have laying hens, sheep and pigs. East of West Hoathly; closed Sun and bank holidays.

Horsham slates

The Priest House has a fine example of a roof made of Horsham slates. Also known as Horsham slabs, they are very local to the Weald – used since Roman times and coming from a series of sandstone quarries in the Horsham area. The natural cleave in the rock produces slates of different sizes and thickness; roofers (who were known as 'stone-healers' in medieval times) took advantage of this variation to create distinctive gradation patterns where the larger slabs are laid at the bottom, and become increasingly smaller towards the top. Various reasons exist for this, one being that the larger ones, which are typically three feet square, are easier to lay but harder to carry up to the top. It also makes sense in that the wall at the bottom provides support for the larger ones, and there are fewer joints for water to percolate through further down. Overall, though, it was probably done as a display of craftsmanship too.

⑩ Gravetye Manor

Frustratingly in this delectable scenery, the network of rights of way is limited, so it's hard to get to the heart of it. But just north of West Hoathly the estate around the luxurious Gravetye Manor Hotel is luscious, deep country (*RH19 4LJ; 01342 810567; www.gravetyemanor.co.uk*). You can take a forest walk from

Vowels car park, on the road towards Kingscote station on the Bluebell Railway, while Gravetye Manor itself has a **perimeter walk** around the estate, open on Tuesday and Friday only: follow the sign for the hotel from the road, and before you reach the hotel entrance gates there is a small parking area on the left. Walk towards the hotel, and turn right before the gates – the trail is marked by yellow-notched posts; walk 200 yards along the estate road, past a house and then left through an ornamental iron gate. The trail takes you down to the lake at the bottom and gives you tantalising glimpses of the garden from a distance.

Designed by the great landscape gardener William Robinson, who lived here from 1884 until his death in 1935, it has been restored after being neglected for many years. Robinson was a passionate advocate of gardening with hardy plants and wild flowers, with layouts becoming more natural-looking and wild further away from the house, in reaction to the artificial style of Victorian horticultural creations with dense bedding of hothouse-reared annuals. A white wisteria pergola and gorgeous herbaceous borders are set against the weathered stone of the Elizabethan manor house, and the orchard is strewn with daffodils. For a closer, leisurely look at it all, treat yourself to afternoon tea at the hotel, or an overnight stay.

⑪ Saint Hill Manor

Glorious gardens, sloping down to a lake, with a fine manor house: it sounds like all the ingredients for a typical country house visit. Only this isn't. Saint Hill Manor (*RH19 4JY; 01342 317 057; www.sainthillmanor.org.uk; free tours daily, 14.00–17.00, on the hour*) is the national headquarters of the Scientology movement in this country – the controversial organisation established by the late L Ron Hubbard and which lists Tom Cruise among its followers. It's certainly worth a look, even if Scientology most definitely isn't your thing – it's free to enter and take a tour, or you can stroll round the grounds at leisure.

I wasn't at all sure what to expect when I ventured in here. It was a hot, sunny day and the place felt like some hugely endowed university campus in California. The collegiate part of it is the 'castle', actually built in the late 20th century in a curious and somewhat surreal retro style, all stone, battlements and gothic windows. There's a spacious reception whose staff will happily arrange for a free tour. The guide took me to the little building where they give students 'purification programmes' – a rigorous schedule of up to three weeks, consisting of exercise, saunas and dieting for up to five hours a day. It sounded a lot more Spartan than a spa treatment.

A little further down and overlooking the rhododendron-embellished grounds and goose-populated lake is the late 18th-century manor house which Hubbard bought in 1959, and where he lived and ran his Scientology empire. The library is devoted entirely to a set of his books with their trademark garish covers: he started off in science fiction and is the world's most published and most translated author of all time – 1,084 works in 71 languages. His office has been left as it was when he died, with a vintage dictating machine resembling an old-style record player, his two electric organs – a Wurlitzer and a very rare Mellotron, an early form of synthesiser – and desk complete with biros, stapler, a toy tiger and whatever other everyday bits happened to be there at the time. But the room that really drops the jaw (perhaps not for the right reasons) is the Monkey Room – with a quite bizarre mural painted by John Spencer Churchill, Sir Winston's nephew, for the former owner in 1945. Created for the American Ambassador's monkey-adoring wife, it depicts 145 monkeys of 20 species all sketched at London Zoo but given human roles – variously playing instruments in a bandstand, parading in clothes or diving into a swimming pool.

⑫ Standen

For me this is the most pleasing and enjoyable National Trust house in the southeast. An Australian globetrotting friend who rapidly notches up National Trust properties when in England announced to me that he'd like to visit Knole House in Kent. I suggested that we ought to add on Standen (*RH19 4NE; 01342 323029; www.nationaltrust.org.uk; closed winter weekdays, Tue all year and some Mons*), of which he'd never heard – so almost as an afterthought after visiting the impressively gloomy Knole House we cheered ourselves up by taking in this one, which he liked much more. Unlike most country houses, it's on a small and liveable scale with an almost contemporary lightness about the décor, though unmistakably in the style of its time.

The house is the Arts and Crafts masterpiece of Philip Webb (1831–1915). He was a close friend of the hugely influential designer William Morris, with whom he founded the Society for the Protection of Ancient Buildings in 1877; in 1858 Webb had completed Morris's Red House at Bexleyheath (on the Kent edge of London, and also now owned by the National Trust).

Webb's clients for Standen were the Beale family – William Beale was a wealthy London solicitor married to Margaret; they had seven children and an entourage of servants. This was their country weekend retreat until his retirement, after which they lived here permanently. After the last of the children died at the age of 92 it was left to the National Trust. Webb was at the forefront of technology with the house built round a steel frame, central heating and electricity, yet he also deliberately created something that harmonised with existing buildings and the physical setting. He used local Sussex materials, including sandstone quarried from the estate, bricks and tiles from Keymer, and timber from nearby oakwoods.

The inside is what makes it special, a million miles from the usual Victorian country house. Upon completion in 1894, Webb continued advising Margaret Beale about decorations, and the family used the firm Morris & Co for much of the wallpapers, fabrics and furniture. It's the small details one remembers – gorgeous lustre-highlighted ceramics by William de Morgan, a 'Decego' historic loo, ceramics by Dante Gabriel Rossetti, textiles and drawings by Edward

Burne-Jones or the steel fireplace in the all-green dining room. Upstairs, Mrs Beale's embroidered bed hangings complement a bedcover by May Morris (daughter of the great William, whose wallpaper abounds here too) as fresh as it was when made in 1894 owing to its being stored away for a hundred years before being presented to the National Trust.

Webb, like William Morris, revered craftsmanship and the use of materials, and took much of his inspiration from nature. His architectural output was limited because of the detail he lavished on his projects, and his fastidious attention to detail was no doubt instrumental in the Beales engaging him in the first place. At Standen, elecricity and central heating were installed from the start (the house's electrical generator was in the long, low building near the current car park). Indeed, W A S Benson's electric light fittings are very much part of the character of the house – admirably the Trust have gone to pains to get the original style of lightbulbs manufactured; the light is feeble but at least it had the advantage over gaslight that it wouldn't threaten to asphyxiate the inhabitants.

The recently restored gardens are not huge but have a wonderful variety. They spread in a series of sloping linked areas along the hillside, looking over Weir Wood Reservoir.

The adjacent National Trust shop stocks reproduction William de Morgan tiles, Morris-pattern tea cosies and the like. The Standen Café is in a converted barn. Various activity days, talks, open-air theatre events and conservation demonstrations are held at the house.

⑬ Bluebell Railway

Named after the bluebells that bring a vivid splash of colour to the views from the window in spring, this is in many ways the very best of Britain's many heritage railways (*01825 720800; www.bluebell-railway.co.uk*). In 1958 the line from East Grinstead to Lewes closed, but within two years some passionate enthusiasts got their act together, and a stretch reopened in 1960, This was at a time when steam engines were still operating on the national BR network, making this the first of Britain's heritage railways. And being first on board, they acquired a lot of the best railwayana – in addition to some marvellously antique standard-gauge railway carriages and locos, an impressive array of station paraphernalia, including wonderful displays of enamel advertising signs. Kingscote station is done out in 1950s style, while Horsted Keynes evokes the 1930s and Sheffield Park is a recreation of a country station in the 1880s. They've done a good amount of work to get the extension ready to run to East Grinstead and thus to join up with the mainline, but blocking the line is an excavation that the council filled up with household rubbish which needs £2 million to remove.

The carriages mostly date from the 1930s and 1950s, but there is a 1913 observation car as well as even older ones from 1890, and they're constantly renovating others that will eventually come into service. Virtually all were from the southern region, and have been rescued from all sorts of uses – including as hen coops, bungalows, holiday homes and even aviaries. The enamel advertising signs – of the likes of 'Redfern's Rubber Heels', 'Venus Soap: stops rubbing' and 'Virol, growing boys need it', were mainly collected in the 1960s and came from auctions and from stations that were closing.

They welcome volunteers, skilled or unskilled, and will train people up for a range of tasks. A week's volunteering here would make a memorable holiday, and they even have accommodation in the sleeping cars on the sidings. You might start off cleaning and painting, then learn how to use a lathe, or make mortice and tenon joints. Not surprisingly the volunteers are passionate enthusiasts and the lifeblood of the whole operation. David, who was in the workshop restoring old carriages, said 'I'm a chartered engineer and am interested in seeing engineering artefacts preserved, especially steam locos, and getting them in working order. It can take ten years to restore one, and when you've finished it you really feel you've achieved something – I can say to myself "I've preserved the engineering heritage"'. Some volunteers get the plum job of driving engines; Brian told me about some of the challenges for a learner driver – like needing to have sufficient water in boiler to keep the steam up, not stopping too quickly and stopping at the right place. They may in the future resume engine-driving courses if they can find enough small engines for the role.

The lively events programme includes a big collectors' fair each summer, various wining and dining trips – on which some dress up in 1920s period costume – Santa Specials and Children's Fun Days. The full fare gives you unlimited travel for the day, and dogs are welcome; all the engines are steam-powered, though you might like to time your trip to coincide with the vintage carriages with their old luggage racks, original upholstery and period adverts. Buses from East Grinstead station take you to Horsted Keynes (see the railway's website for operating days); note there is no road access to Kingscote station.

In all the Bluebell Railway really recreates the feeling of proper travel through the countryside as it was in the steam era, and for the most part the views can hardly have changed in a hundred or so years.

⑭ Sheffield Park

A short walk up the main road (which has a footway) from Sheffield Park station, at the end of the Bluebell Railway, leads to this, one of the greatest of all English gardens (*TN22 3QX; 01825 790231; www.nationaltrust.org.uk; open daily except weekdays Jan–mid Feb; joint tickets for Bluebell Railway available*). Like many others in the Weald, this 120-acre garden and arboretum is renowned for its dazzling show of azaleas, kalmias, cherries, rhododendrons and other flowering shrubs in May and June, but the interest is year round, with carpets of bluebells and daffodils in spring. In particular, the autumn colours rival those you might find in New England, when maples, tupelo trees, swamp cypresses, birches and eucryphias and others combine to make an astonishing show of golds, reds, oranges and yellows. The four linked, broodingly silent lakes reflect the abundant and diverse foliage and shrubberies, providing exquisite vistas at every turn. High above stands the Gothic 18th-century mansion designed by James Watt for the Earl of Sheffield; it is now converted into very desirable flats.

The garden's master plan – including two of the lakes – was begun by Capability Brown in the 18th century, with further modifications in the 19th century. James Pulham, whose company specialised in water features and was responsible for some of the rock constructions in Brighton Aquarium, added cascades. In 1910 Arthur Soames acquired the property and added the magnificent collection of trees and shrubs, making the most of the sloping nature of the site.

The estate includes a historic cricket field, where Australia began their tour between 1884 and 1896 against a team captained by W G Grace and put together by cricketing aficionado Lord Sheffield. He financed the England team's tour of Australia in 1891–92 and was also the longstanding president of Sussex County Cricket Club, to which he made a large donation so they could purchase Hove cricket ground, still the club's home.

><><><

Food and drink

The Griffin Fletching TN22 3SS ✆ 01825 722890 🖥 www.thegriffininn.co.uk. In a lovely village street near the east side of the Sheffield Park estate, this warmly welcoming ancient beamed inn is one of the area's most celebrated dining pubs. The bar and restaurant food is not cheap but consistently good, with locally reared meat and vegetables from a market garden in the village; the Sunday barbecues in the garden are deservedly popular. Good wine list, and Harveys best among the selection of real ales. Booking strongly recommended. Open all day. They also have very comfortable bedrooms.

The Old Dairy Sliders Lane, Furners Green TN22 3RT ✆ 01825 790517 🖥 www.theolddairyfarmshop.co.uk; open Thu–Sat. Just south of Sheffield Park station is this farm shop run by the Barnard family, with all the produce grown on the site, as well as home-made pies and ready meals; occasional open days. Their old English pork sausages won top prize at the South Eastern Prime Stock Winter Fayre at Ardingly, among a field of 200 producers.

⑮ Heaven Farm

Just 1¹/₂ miles north of Sheffield Park, and south of Danehill, this 1830s farmstead turned Slow tourist attraction makes a very useful stopping point or a destination in itself, and is worth popping into just for the delicious rural, hilly views (*Furners Green TN22 3RG; 01825 790226; www.heavenfarm.co.uk*). The café (Stable Tearooms) is in the converted stable, though in decent weather you'll want to sit outside at the tables amid roving chickens (a sign warns you that they may nick your food), and children can sit on long-retired tractors. Within a barn, a little farm museum has a fascinating stash of bits and pieces related to farming life here over some 175 years: milking equipment, butter churns, craftsmen and countryside tasks, and the oasthouse where hops were dried by kiln. In spring the nature trail comes into its own with a magnificent show of bluebells; on the way are badger sets, an ancient iron-smelting 'bloomery' and the farm's own free-range wallabies.

The Heavenly Organics Food Shop has locally sourced produce, including cheeses and apple juice, and there's also a craft shop, aviary and campsite.

⑯ Chailey Common

Near the crossroads village of North Chailey, this is like a miniature version of the Ashdown Forest, a surprisingly heathery enclave in the rich green Sussex farmlands. Large enough to lose your bearings in, it's a very pleasant 450-acre strolling ground with a windmill in the middle. Species include blue marsh gentians, heath-spotted orchids, lizards and nightjars; it's a designated Site of Special Scientific Interest and local nature reserve. To find the car park, carry on north towards Sheffield Park and East Grinstead on the A275 from its junction with the A272, take the first left and the car park is a short distance on the left.

><><><><

Shopping

Townings Farm shop Plumpton Rd, North Chailey BN8 4EJ ☎ 01444 471352
⏚ www.towningsfarm.co.uk. They sell wool from their own sheep, home-grown pumpkins, farm-reared meat using their own sheep, pigs and cattle, and locally produced fruit and veg. Open Thu–Sat. They also have a five-van caravan site.

⑰ Piltdown

At the village of Piltdown, the Piltdown Man pub is a reminder of a spectacular non event. Perhaps the most celebrated archaeological fake of all time, the skull of what was known as Piltdown Man was hailed as a great find when in 1912 Charles Dawson claimed the discovery of the millions-of-years-old missing link between man and apes. There were some doubters, but many more swallowed every word Dawson and his entourage said. Only in the 1950s was it exposed as a crude archaeological hoax consisting of a human skull and an ape jaw: the teeth had been shaped with metal files and the bone had been painted brown to make it look old.

Born in 1864, Dawson became a solicitor (practising in Uckfield) and keen fossil collector – made a Fellow of the Geological Society aged only 21, he had several previously unknown species of dinosaurs and prehistoric plants named after him. He directed digs at Hastings Castle and Lavant caves. Somehow he developed his knack of making spectacular discoveries and was elected Fellow of the Society of Antiquaries at 31. Dawson lived in Castle Lodge in Lewes, which had been leased to the Sussex Archaeological Society, and which he deviously swindled the society out of by using Society notepaper to lead the vendors into thinking he was acting for the Society.

In the pre-1914 climate of jingoism and international arms races, Dawson's announcement that the earliest species was an Englishman struck quite a chord. But the Sussex Archaeological Society's annual publication, the *Collections*, made no mention of it even when the national press was ecstatic: Dawson never even gave them a lecture on it.

Various players have been accused of the Piltdown forgery, with Dawson the main suspect. Sussex archaeologist Miles Russell has recently looked at the case again and found a damning pattern going back as far as 1891 when he filed down a fossil tooth and claimed it came from a new species.

In 1893 Dawson published his first archaeological article, the astonishing discovery of a Neolithic stone axe still in its wooden haft, apparently found by a shepherd but which could no longer be produced. Then he produced a supposedly Roman statuette from Beauport Park (near Battle), in fact a modern copy in cast iron. At Lavant Caves, a medieval chalk quarry, various worked flints and antler finds turned up which suggested it was a Neolithic flint mine although there was no flint to mine. At Hastings Castle, it was strangely only Dawson who was able to recall outlines visible many years before, apparently of manacled human figures who had been chained up and left to die against the walls. And so on.

He started life as a reputable fossil collector, but his ambition seems to have got the better of him. Having become a Fellow of the Geological Society and Society of Antiquaries so young, it seems he craved a Fellowship of the Royal Society and a knighthood. In 1909 he complained to his friend and fellow excavator Arthur Smith Woodward that he 'was waiting for the big "find" that never seems to come along'. No doubt he would have got these honours if he hadn't died in 1916 at the age of only 52 – others associated with the site were knighted. Poor Smith Woodward retired to Sussex and spent the rest of his life digging fruitlessly at Piltdown.

Dawson's very pretty flint-fronted house next to Lewes Castle still stands. A memorial to Piltdown Man was erected at the excavation site, but is on private ground. His grave is in St John-sub-Castro churchyard in Lewes, but even his tombstone says nothing about his 'discoveries'.

Shopping

Old Spot Farm Shop Piltdown TN22 3XN ☎ 01825 722894

www.oldspotfarmshop.co.uk. Good selections of organic produce, meats and cheeses; closed Mon.

Stoolball

Right outside the window of my home in Lewes, the Paddock hosts a weekly summer game of that strangely Sussex pastime, stoolball. It's a variant of cricket, played by both sexes, organised into leagues over much of Sussex and into western Kent. Instead of wickets there are posts with flat boards on them - a bit like estate agents' boards, and instead of bats there are wooden paddles like antique table-tennis bats to hit the semi-hard rounders-style ball. After I moved to Lewes, I watched this weekly ritual from my house, then wandered down to the ground and asked the players to explain. 'So do you fancy a bat? The Lewes Arms have bowled us out already, and we're batting again to play out time.' Thus wearing quite unsuitable indoor clothes and open sandals I began my extremely short career batting for the Sussex Flintknappers' Stoolball Team.

Stoolball has had a strange ride through history. Its origins are murky, but it is certainly from pre-industrial England. The 'stool' may have been the wicket or the bat, or may have referred to a tree stump in a woodland clearing. It was known to have been played in Elizabethan times as a Shrove Tuesday game. In the 19th century it was taken up wholeheartedly, particularly in Kent and Sussex, by gentry and clergy, who organised female teams of upper-class ladies intermingled with village and farm women, with no barrier as regards age. The rules were first codified in 1867: it was seen as an ideal way for women of all classes to exercise and socially interact. The sport became organised into a Sussex Stoolball League in 1903; soon men sometimes joined in, playing left handed against or with the women.

William Grantham, a wealthy Sussex lawyer and landowner from Chailey, popularised the game further, partly as a way of lubricating his social contacts. As Sussex became a hospitalisation area for wounded soldiers in World War I, in 1917 he set up games of stoolball in the grounds of the Royal Pavilion in Brighton for officers whose injuries excluded them from more strenuous forms of sport: this proved a hit with patients and other hospitals in Sussex followed suit. As a member of the MCC he even got a demonstration stoolball match played at Lord's, and subsequently the game was even played on rough ground close to the trenches in the battlefields.

After World War I, Grantham revived the game for men and women and attempted to spread the sport further, promoting it in the spirit of reviving a folk tradition of old England. While playing, he donned the garb of a labourer of yesteryear – smock and beaver hat. It took off in Sussex in the 1920s at a time when such features of rural life were tangibly disappearing; by the 1930s stoolball was being played in the Midlands and northern England too, and he broadcast on television and radio, and travelled round the globe to the likes of Chile and Greenland, getting locals and expats to join in. Grantham fell out with what became the Sussex Federation, which adhered to 'Sussex rules' on positioning of umpires and allowing only 'clean' catches away from the body. Outsiders may find it astonishing as well as gratifying to learn that this quirkiest of pursuits still thrives.

Ashdown Forest and around

⑱ Ashdown Forest Llama Park

I heard that in Lewes a few years back some local person used their pet llama to carry home the shopping, and that the animal could sometimes be spotted in Tesco car park awaiting its porter duties. Intrigued whether llamas are really that practical and hoping that this wasn't a Lewesian myth, I rootled around for some background info at the Ashdown Forest Llama Park (*Wych Cross RH18 5JN; 01825 712040; www.llamapark.co.uk*).

Back in 1987 this enterprise started rearing llamas and alpacas for sale; about 100 beasts in all including five reindeer. It aims to give them a stress-free, sustainable environment to live in.

Linda Johnson started this as a hobby with a couple of llamas, and it's just grown and grown. What appeals to her about llamas? 'They have a really laid-back attitude to life, they're very inquisitive – and because no one has decided this is how llamas ought to look, they come in all shapes and sizes: you get woolly ones and ones with fluffy ears. They've got such quirky personalities and love interacting with people.' Currently Ralph is the public's favourite llama, and features on a postcard – when I visited in February he had a Valentine's card from one of his many fans.

Llamas have got an unfair reputation for ill-temper. Linda attributes this to llamas that have been pent up in cages in zoos and have felt pretty fed up with things. But give them their freedom and they're very amenable beasts; they may have tiffs with each other and spit inter-llama, but they very rarely spit at people and are fundamentally good natured. 'They're very sociable animals' says Linda. 'They're very sensible, and not stupid like sheep, and don't try to jump over fences.'

I didn't realise before I came here how different llamas are from each other, and from alpacas. The latter are distinctly more woolly, and tend to stand around looking beautiful, whereas llamas are kept in small working groups. Both are related to the camel: the feet aren't that different from those of their larger, humped cousins, and they have split upper lips too. But only the alpacas produce useful wool – in 22 different shades.

They've also got a few reindeer, which provide a special focus around Christmas, but the hub of the business is selling alpacas and llamas: they tend to be kept as field pets. Prices currently start at around £600. And here you can also walk with a llama – they've a special section of walking llamas that you can accompany for an hour and a half's stroll through the estate, and provide bits of carrot for your beast to nibble on the way.

The llamas and alpacas can cope with big fluctuations of temperature, but aren't that keen on extreme heat, so a shearer comes in to give them a trim for summer.

The gift shop (you don't have to pay admission to the park to visit this) has alpaca knitware and accessories, South American textiles and Pooh-related items, as well as toy llamas, and the café is useful after excursions on the Ashdown Forest.

⑲ Hartfield

In Hartfield itself the shop and tearoom **Pooh Corner** (*01892 770456*) is the area's one concession to Milne commercialism, but on the gentlest, most amiable scale; everything Pooh-related you might imagine is here, including pots of 'hunny' and the great books themselves. Best sellers in the shop are balloons, the books and Pooh alphabet letters. Alas they don't sell the Latin translation of the noble book – *Winnie Ille Pu* – any more, and the 'original' styling of the cuddly animals has been replaced by the Disney versions. Tut.

Here you can pick up the official rules for poohsticks in English and Japanese; a couple of Japanese students waiting at the bus stop had obviously found their way early on a chilly, dank winter's morning when I last visited, so there clearly are takers.

Elsewhere the **village** has enough to justify a small potter around. Church Lane leads off the main street by the Anchor pub, a former workhouse, to the quaintest of lychgates – beneath a jutting-out 16th-century cottage. Beyond the churchyard spreads the Croft, the village's open space, cricket, football and stoolball pitch combined. By the B2026 at the northern end, Hartfield's long-defunct railway station stands by the former trackbed which is now the 10-mile Forest Way (East Grinstead to Groombridge) – offering an undemanding, sheltered walk; there are no views at all in the section around Hartfield, though. I've used it on several occasions to walk on to Withyham (and then up through the Five Hundred Acre Wood and on to the Ashdown Forest heathlands). **Withyham** is little more than a roadside pub, the Dorset Arms, a very comfy looking rectory and a memorable church. The church occupies an unevenly sloping, idyllically shady churchyard full of wonky, calligraphic sandstone tombs. Inside, the tomb of the gentry occupies the limelight – a most lump-in-the-throat memorial to the Sackvilles' 13-year-old son, with weeping parents, a frieze of skull-bearing children and a heartfelt epitaph 'what mother would not weepe for such a son...'

Food and drink
Pooh Corner has a tearoom at the back of the shop; Hartfield has two pubs – the Anchor and the Haywaggon, as well as a village store.

Perryhill Orchards Edenbridge Rd, Hartfield, East Sussex TN7 4JJ UK ☎01892 770 595 🖰 www.perryhillorchards.co.uk. By the B2026 north of Hartfield, this farm shop sells its own apple juice, perry and cider from the adjacent orchard (tastings available), with a range of tastes to suit most palates; the startlingly sharp James Grieve apple juice will wake you up. I find the cider from the barrel consistently good, and it goes very well with fish.

St Ives Tea Gardens Butcherfield Lane, near Hartfield TN7 4JX ☎01892 770589. Virtually on the Kent border and signposted off the B2026, this marvellously unpretentious and wholly rural farm tea garden is approached by a long, bumpy road. It has tables set out informally in the shade of fruit trees, and different areas separated by pergolas with old-fashioned cottage roses clambering over them, and the terrace at the very bottom has huge views south to the Downs. Tea is served in pots and homemade sponges served on assorted pretty china cups and plates, as well as cream teas and simple lunches. Chocolate labradors doze on the terrace outside the farm kitchen where you can buy free-range eggs. There are also inside tables with a wood-burning stove in a converted barn. Camping is available in a field at the farm nearby.

⑳ Ashdown Forest

A very surprising place in the heights of the Weald: this is 'forest' in the old sense of the word, meaning a deer-hunting forest enclosed in the 13th century. It is a rare survivor of some 300 deer forests that existed in medieval times, including such areas as St Leonard's Forest in Sussex. In late summer it's an absolutely glorious purple and yellow sight of heather and gorse, and humming with bees. Or after rain it's the obvious candidate for a walk, as the water just drains away instantly in the sand.

Here and there you encounter a stream flowing a deep rusty colour – because of its high iron content. This was a busy place at the height of the Wealden iron industry, which was going strong in Roman times, and saw the opening of Britain's first furnace at Newbridge in 1496; this material supplied the Roman navy and the British navy (cannons for fighting the Spanish Armada).

It was enclosed by a fence, or pale, entered by hatches or gates (at points like Coleman's Hatch and Chelwood Gate). The peculiarly piecemeal shape of the forest today is the result of enclosures made 300 years back, which took parts of the original forest into private ownership. Centuries of activity of hunting and use by commoners have left the remaining area a heathland, though there's a fair amount of tree cover, especially further down the slopes. Lowland heath like this is internationally rare; it is a special haven for all sorts of flora and fauna, such as spiders.

The magic of Ashdown Forest

Dr Hew Prendergast, Director, Ashdown Forest Conservators

'A heath with here and there a few birch scrubs upon it, verily the most villainously ugly spot I ever saw' – hardly an extract from a tourist guide, and indeed it wasn't! By contrast, the same quality of Ashdown Forest that William Cobbett decried in his description of 1822 was admired, and in greater detail, by a Mr A E Knox in 1849: 'Nothing can exceed the picturesque beauty of certain portions of this district, eminences clothed with heather and gorse, and crowned with Scotch fir and holly, enclose valleys intersected by clear running brooks, whose course, here rapid and noisy, rushes over rocks and ridges of sandstone.' In the 1920s A A Milne saw much the same as he wrote about Winnie-the-Pooh and we can do so too today.

Part of the charm of the Forest is that it is so unexpected. In a Sussex countryside dominated by Downs, fields and woods, a sudden expanse of purple flowering heath, of free-range sheep and cattle wandering along the road, and views to distant horizons are more like the wilder west or north of Britain, of Exmoor perhaps or upland Wales. Yet London is scarcely over the horizon and Gatwick less than half an hour away. Added to this are miles and miles of walking (for it's all free and open access), lots of wildlife otherwise rare in the region (Dartford warbler, nightjar, marsh gentian...), archaeological lumps and bumps undestroyed by the plough, and a connection through the numerous deer with the distant Norman origin of the Forest for hunting. In short, Ashdown is a patch of wildness, even wilderness. Just a few minutes walk from any car park, and it can all be yours. Magic!

Hew Prendergast of the Ashdown Forest Centre told me that trees (especially the extra-persistent birch) are the biggest threat to this scenic microcosm. His team are charged with tasks of looking after visitors and protecting wildlife, and find chopping down trees is an emotive issue for some of the public, despite the fact that people have been doing this very activity for centuries. Since 1945 the amount of tree cover has increased from 5% of the total to 40%. Left to its own devices the whole area would become secondary woodland in fifty years.

The red deer have long gone, but fallow deer proliferate – hence the 40 mph limit painted merrily on the road surface, which is there for a serious reason: deer don't have very good road sense and there are an awful lot of them about. More scarce are the sika, roe and muntjac deer.

With its uncluttered vistas and strangely disorienting topography, the heath displaces you to a different part of the country altogether – a London friend who knew nothing about it when I took him there thought he'd just woken up in the moors of Yorkshire.

For **walking**, prepare to be confused. The soil is highly acidic, and there's no farming or settlement up here to speak of. It's a rather magical maze of a place.

The *OS Explorer 135* map is surprisingly useless here, as what few rights of way that exist are indistinguishable on the ground from the dense network of other paths, and you can wander at will. Much more user-friendly is the *Ashdown Forest* map at the unusual scale of 1:30,000, obtainable from the Ashdown Forest Centre. It shows all the firebreaks and paths, and I've found it plus a compass the only way of finding my way around. Strangely the handiest landmarks are the car parks, which are numbered and named on the map and at their entrances.

Picking out a route to recommend above all others is hard, as it's all very pleasant, and however carefully I try to map read, I never quite end up where I'm aiming for. Favourite starting points on the forest are Camp Hill (a prominent clump of trees on the west side of the B2026) and the village of Fairwarp on the south side of the Forest (from which you could try following the ever-so-discreet wooden marker WW posts denoting the route of the Wealdway. Or begin anywhere and aim to circle the high ground – you'll soon realise the Ashdown Forest is donut-shaped, and the hole in the centre is the Old Lodge estate (with few public footpaths).

Some very good free walks leaflets are available from the Ashdown Forest Centre and from www.ashdownforest.org (click on 'downloads', and find the walks); these include the two Pooh Walks from Gills Lap which take you past the Enchanted Place, Heffalump Trap, Roo's Sandy Pit, Milne Memorial and North Pole and skirt Eeyore's Sad and Gloomy Place. Another takes in the Southern Slopes and the Airman's Grave, starting from Hollies car park (TQ462286) and getting views of the South Downs. It might be worth printing them off at home in case they've run out when you get there.

Nutley Windmill, the only working open-trestle post mill in Britain (and one of only five such structures surviving in any form), is just outside the main-road village of Nutley – rather elusive, as you see it from a distance and then it disappears till the last moment. The easiest way to find it is from Nutley: take the A22 north, then turn east on the road towards Crowborough for a mile, until a car park appears on the left – the mill is a five-minute walk from there. Renovated in 1968 after 60 years of disuse, its age is uncertain; it's open free of charge most Wednesdays, in the afternoons on the last Sunday of the month, and on spring and August bank holidays.

Another feature to include in a walk here is the **Airman's Grave**: a walled enclosure marks the very spot where a Wellington Bomber crashed in 1941, killing its crew of six – it was on the way back from a raid on Cologne and got hit in the conflict, but struggling to make it on just one engine in atrocious weather conditions was unable to crash land and ended up here. A few years later the mothers of crew members set up a simple wooden cross on the site, and this was later improved with a stone cross. There's a ceremony on Remembrance Sunday each year, with poppy wreaths laid down and the Last Post bugled. Despite the name, no one is actually buried in the 'Grave'.

Ashdown Forest Centre between Wych Cross and Coleman's Hatch, RH18 5JP
☎ 01342 823583 ⌖ www.ashdownforest.org Headquarters of the Ashdown Forest
Conservators, which manages the Ashdown Forest. I once brought an American
visitor here who was amazed to find it devoid of gigantic fibreglass Pooh
characters; that it has remained so clutter-free and unchanged is thanks to the
Conservators in no small way. You can pick up books and the excellent but
otherwise hard-to-come-by *Ashdown Forest* map here. Also horseriders can get
permits for riding in the forest from the Ashdown Forest Riding Association
(currently £92 a year). The Conservators are raising funds for a substantial upgrade
to the Centre.

'Drawn by Me and Mr Shepard helpd'

Thus spake (supposedly) Christopher Robin on the map of the 'forest' at the
beginning of A A Milne's immortal quartet of children's books which began
with *Winnie-the-Pooh* in 1926, followed by *The House at Pooh Corner* (1928).
Simply penned with pine trees and sandy tracks, and variously marked 'Pooh
trap for heffalumps' and 'nice for piknicks', E H Shepard's map and the
illustrations that follow perfectly evoke the Ashdown Forest landscape. Some
names are only slightly changed: 'Hundred Acre Wood' in the stories is Five
Hundred Acre Wood in reality, not far from Cotchford Farm near Hartfield
where the Milnes lived. Galleons Lap is really Gill's Lap,
the 'enchanted place on the very top of the Forest'
(close to which is said to be where that Heffalump
trap was set), easily picked out nowadays by an
ice-cream van that's often in the car park at a
Y-junction of roads; just beyond, a
memorial stone to Milne looks north
across the Weald in celebration of what
his stories gave to the world. Poke around
further and you might find Owl's Tree or
'the North Pole'.

Easier to locate is the **Poohsticks Bridge** –
officially known as Posingford Bridge –
where Pooh, Piglet and Co invented the pastime
of poohsticks. The wooden bridge is a replacement of the 1907 original – the
Disneyland Corporation stumped up the cash for its rebuilding – but happily
it is identical to what you might remember from the illustrations. To find it turn
off the B2026 1½ miles south of Hartfield, and the Poohsticks car park is a
short way along on the right. The little walk leads through woodland and down
a track to the bridge, where there's a conspicuous dearth of anything resembling
a poohstick – so be sure to take your own supply of judiciously selected twigs.

Pooh, Kanga, Tigger, Eeyore and Piglet are now living in retirement in the
New York Public Library. Of these, Eeyore is said to be the most identifiable
and Piglet the least. Tigger and Kanga appeared on the scene later than the others

– Christopher Milne, in his highly readable autobiography *The Enchanted Places*, speculates these two may have been added partly for their literary potential. Roo was lost during Christopher Milne's childhood in a family outing from Cotchford Farm, and Owl and Rabbit never existed except in the creative mind of A A Milne. Shepard, who drew the original illustrations, drew Christopher Robin from life – unlike the animals, for which he used his imagination.

As a child I found the presence of Christopher Robin in the stories rather an irritating intrusion into a magical world. He seemed utterly wet and a weed. Having read *The Enchanted Places*, one gets the bigger picture. Christopher Robin was born in 1920; five years later the Milnes bought Cotchford Farm and came down for weekends from London, before moving in permanently. This must have been a very idyllic world for him to grow up in. His was certainly a happy childhood and at first he revelled in his celebrity status, though by the age of eight he dropped the 'Robin' and at boarding school he was not at all comfortable at being Christopher Robin; you can imagine the ribbing he must have got.

The Milnes' walks into the Ashdown Forest took them to a little valley with the stream shallow enough to paddle across; it was here that the 'North Pole' was discovered by Pooh and his associates.

Food and drink

The snag about pubs in the Ashdown Forest is they aren't brilliantly located for walks, being at the bottom of the slopes and often not well linked by paths. The most useful pubs include the **Foresters Arms** at Fairwarp (by a village green) and the **Hatch** at Coleman's Hatch (a gorgeous garden, and an attractive weatherboarded building, but no paths leading directly to it). **The Anchor** at Hartfield and the **Dorset Arms** at Withyham are away to the north.

㉑ Eridge Rocks, Harrison's Rocks

Quite a surprise in the gentle Wealden landscape, these are two lines of shapely greensand formations (free public access), both magnets for climbers – it saves them a hefty trip to the Peak District or West Country. They are in mixed woodlands that harbour woodland birds like great spotted woodpeckers and long-tailed tits; it is striking how trees cling to many of the rocks. Both sets of rocks are of soft sandstone that has been weathered into all manner of shapes, with fissures and bastions.

A variety of ferns, lichens and mosses – some rare – thrive in the damp conditions, the rocks absorb water and some are 30 feet high.

Eridge Rocks is Sussex Wildlife Trust land (*www.sussexwt.org.uk*), at Eridge Green; turn into Warren Farm Lane from the A26 by a small church; a track leads to a car park (grid reference TQ554355). Though tackling the rocks is definitely not for unequipped climbers, the walk along them is a delight – the views are rather better at Eridge, where the path goes beneath this strange inland mini-cliff for a fascinating half a mile, than Harrison's, but both deserve exploring. Eridge Rocks is designated a Site of Special Scientific Interest, with some rare mosses and liverworts, and a Regionally Important Geological Site, and is the only place in Sussex where you can see the Tunbridge slimy fern, if your eyesight is up to it (it is quite tiny). It forms part of a reserve owned by the Sussex Wildlife Trust and adjoins a larger forest called Broadwater Warren, an RSPB reserve. Graffiti scratched into the rock nearest the gate record that the trees were planted in 1811. There were also plantings of bamboo, which has gone somewhat out of control.

Access at Eridge was restricted for many years, and surreptitious climbing went on invoking the wrath of local gamekeepers, but the SWT now runs it and has lifted the ban. Its climbs of 15 to 30 feet feature challenges with names such as Sandstorm, The Crunch and More Cake for Me.

Harrison's Rocks was where the great Chris Bonington cut his climbing teeth – his introduction to rock climbing here is described in his book *I Chose to Climb*. The area was purchased by local climbers in the 1950s.

><><><

Food and drink

Huntsman Eridge Station TN3 9LE ☎ 01892 864258 ⌂ www.thehuntsman.net. Right by the railway station, this has a pubby feel to its unpretentious interior; no gimmicks or piped music, but appetising bar food from a menu that changes daily and uses lots of locally sourced ingredients; Badger ales and farm cider. Children are welcome and there's a garden.

A walk through Sussex's climbing country

For me this is one of the most enjoyably varied and surprising walks in the High Weald, with views of three of Sussex's sandstone rock outcrops that are the prime terrain for climbers in the Southeast. The opening section from Boarshead gets quintessential Wealden views straight away, and there's a very beautiful, shady forest (RSPB Reserve) beyond Eridge Rocks.

It's quite well waymarked, but as this is complicated country you do need to follow the directions or the OS map carefully. Most of the road sections are very quiet, apart from the crossing of the busy A26 twice (good sight lines along the road make this safe enough though).

I have started at a point that has plenty of roadside parking; there's also a small car park at Eridge Rocks, and a larger one at Harrison's Rocks. The Boar's Head pub just south of the start point is useful; there's also a pub at Eridge Green,

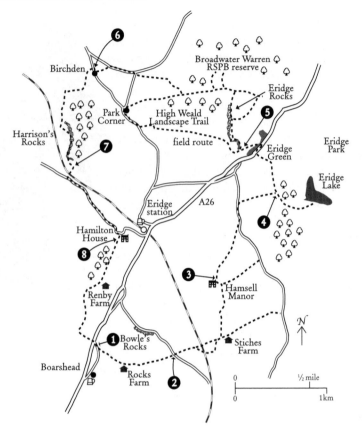

200 yards off the walk (reached by the footway along the A26). The Huntsman at Eridge station is the best food option. There's also a drinking fountain outside the loos at Harrison's Rocks car park.

By car: start at Boarshead (signposted, just off A26 north of Crowborough, turn into Boarshead Road, then immediately left at a T-junction, and follow this old stretch of A-road to where it ends. Plenty of roadside parking. Grid reference TQ535330.

By bus: buses 28 and 29 (Tunbridge Wells to Brighton via Lewes, twice hourly; hourly on Sundays) pass nearby. If you're using buses, it's better to start at Eridge Green, where the bus stop is right on the walk where it goes down the lane between the black-and-white mock Tudor building and the church. Join the walk at point **5**.

By train: Eridge (turn right out of the front of the station, take the first right and after 400 yards and join the walk at point **8**.

1 Facing the bollards at the end of the road, turn right by a tall wooden shed on a concrete driveway, which immediately bends right (tennis court on left), and passes house back gardens, with gorgeous Wealden views on your left. At a farm, the track deviates round it to the left as signposted, and then drops down the edges of fields, with views over the hedgerow of **Bowle's Rocks** – the first sandstone outcrop seen on this walk – and its adjacent dry-ski slope.

❷ At the bottom, go through a gate, cross a lane and continue on the path opposite and slightly to the right through another gate. This drops down alongside woodland, crosses a bridge and continues half right under a railway bridge, then rises up the right side of the field. At a break in the hedgerow on your right, go right to a group of buildings. Turn left on the driveway in front of the red-roofed house. Follow this as it drops and rises (passing two driveways joining to the left), and just after a pond away to the left, turn left at a T-junction where the view suddenly opens out ahead.

❸ After 50 yards turn right near Hamsell Manor (opposite the Coach House) on another driveway. This drops, and just as it is about to bend left, take a narrow path on the right side, crossing a small bridge and emerging into a field. Cross the field diagonally to a stile in the far right-hand corner, then go forward down a grassy track. Carry on down across a field, and down to its bottom right-hand corner and on to a road. Turn left along the road for 300 yards, and just before it crosses a stream and rises, take a path on the right, along the stream and at the bottom of fields.

❹ At the end of the third field, turn left on a path just inside woodland (if you want a viewpoint over Eridge Lake, turn right here – in a few minutes you emerge on to an open hillside with a glorious lake view over Eridge Park). Keep along the right-hand field edges all the way to the A26 at Eridge Green. Cross over carefully and turn right on the pavement for 100 yards then turn left (signposted Park Corner) by a bus stop (where you'll start if you're coming by bus) and take the lane between a black-and-white mock Tudor building and the church.

❺ Follow the lane to the entrance to **Eridge Rocks** on the right (marked by a sign; the first rock is just visible). From here you have a choice of routes – through the forest, or a more easily followed field route. In any case, you will first want to go through the gate and explore the rocks, which extend for nearly half a mile.

To continue through the forest, carry on past the end of the rocks, ignore a crossing-path and turn left at a T-junction in denser forest by a nature reserve map sign. This brings you into **Broadwater Warren**, an RSPB reserve rich with bird species: at dusk you might see a nightjar in summer in pursuit of moths or in spring a woodcock, while winter is the season for lesser redpolls, suspended from birch and willow trees to find seeds, or chattering from the trees.

Basically just keep to the main track and ignore side turns (two tracks to the right). After half a mile, where another track joins from the left, you see a field ahead and away to the left; carry on forward on the left-hand of two paths ahead, just inside the forest and alongside the field. Emerge on to a road, turn right and immediately left (in front of a house with a bull in chains depicted on its gable) at the T-junction. 100 yards before the Groombridge village sign turn left at a gate (signpost missing when I visited, but it's where the telephone wire crosses the road), and head up the field to a point between the two prominent gabled red-brick houses above. Turn right on the road for 50 yards.

For the field route on the waymarked High Weald Landscape Trail, avoiding the forest: take the rising path on the right immediately after the entrance to Eridge Rocks on the right; this rises to join a track. Turn right along it, then as soon as it emerges into the open, turn left along the middle of the field, with big views ahead. At the far end, the path bends right and left, drops slightly, crosses a footbridge and follows the right field edge to a road. Turn right along the road to the junction at Park Corner, then keep left at the road junction to the hamlet of Birchden.

6 Turn left into the lane with the Harrison's Rocks sign. After this enters woodlands, take a path signposted to the left (yellow arrow), dropping between banks. Cross over a track and take the waymarked path ahead (the car park, loos and a drinking water fountain are just to the right). The path emerges into a field, with the railway in view (maybe with some old rolling stock from the Spa Valley Railway); the railway later runs adjacent to the path. Just after a path goes off to the left into the woods, take a gate on the left by a sign for Harrison's Rocks and immediately turn right on the lower path beneath the rocks themselves. Later, where the rocks are about to curve away to the left, fork right to resume walking close to the railway.

7 After a house (Forge Farm), turn right on a lane in front of an oast house, over the level crossing, and then turn left at the T-junction. After ¹/₂ mile ignore a lane to the right signposted as a bridleway. The lane crosses a stream (white bridge parapets are more obvious than the stream itself), then 30 yards later turn right on a driveway by a grassy triangle.

8 After Hamilton House on the left (opposite which an attractive lake is glimpsed), this continues as a path, soon into a field: maintain direction ahead, passing beneath Renby Farm, then joining a track. Turn left at a junction of routes with yellow marker arrows, up a sunken track. Go over a stile and keep right on a house drive. At the end, within earshot of the A26, turn right on a narrow path. Cross the A26 with great care (fortunately the sight lines are very good) and take the path opposite up to the bollards at the end of the old road at the main starting point.

㉒ High Rocks and the Spa Valley Railway

More rocky wonders await just outside the western side of Tunbridge Wells in the form of **High Rocks** – there used to be a maze, bowling green and cold bath here in its 19th-century tourist heyday. The sandstone crags are crossed by 11 footbridges creating an aerial walk; a small fee is payable at High Rocks pub opposite. The **Spa Valley Railway** (*01892 537715; www.spavalleyrailway.co.uk*) stops here on the way from Tunbridge Wells West to Groombridge, a line that closed in 1985 and partly reopened from 1996. At the time of writing they were about to extend through from Groombridge to Eridge, glimpsing Harrison's Rocks on the way and giving the highly unusual experience of travelling on a heritage railway alongside a mainline track. Eridge station itself is on the line from London to Uckfield. The ride is on steam or diesel-hauled services; the oldest carriages are 1932, from the Metropolitan Railway; the others are mostly 1950s and 1960s vintage. The website has details of themed events, such as Thomas the Tank Engine days and 1940s or local food weekends.

㉓ Wilderness Wood

'Wow, that's like what we have in Canada!' exclaimed a Canadian guest of this close-to-nature woodland (*Hadlow Down TN22 4HJ; 01825 830509; www.wildernesswood.co.uk; admission charge for day visitors*). The owners of the child-friendly, dog-friendly 62-acre wood have enthusiastically embraced the slow, sustainable way. It's a campsite, but more than that, and you can come as a day visitor: the woodland is set up with activities and seasonally changing woodland trails such as one they had on forest folklore when I visited. For children there are gruffalo or bug hunts and courses on survival skills, while adults can learn willow weaving or take a 'death or dinner' fungi identification walk with an expert. If you own a patch of woodland, this is the ideal place to learn about the art of coppicing – Doug Stewart told me that within a weekend you'll acquire the basics: 'you'll learn the theory and how to cut what size of pole, and how to fell it safely. Coppicing is actually fairly simple; if you have a couple of acres, you can easily do it by hand.' The course starts with the theory, then moves on to cutting down and making roof shingles or fence stakes.

Camping is in several areas, with a small number of pitches in each (for ten to 15 tents); by the time of publication of this book there should hopefully be pre-pitched tents available too. In the evening you eat local, Slow food – with the emphasis on quality products; currently vegetarian all through the week and local meat at weekends for candlelit dinners. And of course they have a leaning towards the seasonal, such as a mushroom feast in autumn. Doug told me 'In our catering, we're looking at ethics and food miles– the quality and depth of experience are essential – every product we sell has a story behind the decision to sell it.'

They also make wooden products here out of locally sourced wood (mostly sweet chestnut and oak) – indoor and garden furniture, pergolas, trellises and stakes in particular, or you can buy the raw ingredients and self assemble. It's a far cry from IKEA, though.

Towards the Kent border

㉔ Mayfield

This is my nomination for the most perfect-looking Wealden village: Mayfield grew rich in medieval times on the iron industry – hence the Elizabethan cannon made in the local foundry and now proudly displayed in the High Street – and has survived the centuries remarkably well, with barely a hanging basket or pantile out of place.

The long High Street, with its raised brick pavements, has an eye-catching array of half-timbering, tile-hanging and cottagey front gardens; the most imposing are the 15th-century house known as Yeomans, Walnut Tree House, Middle House (a popular oak-beamed dining pub with lozenge-shaped panels in its Tudor façade) and the Old Brewhouse. The church opposite Middle House has two locally cast iron memorial slabs in the nave each to a Thomas

Sands – the one of 1708 very well crafted but the earlier one of 1668 spectacularly amateurish and wonky, and with some of the lettering the wrong way round. On the High Street by the entrance to the churchyard, a red devil depicted on the bottom of the village sign is a nod to the village legend revolving around St Dunstan, who is said to have had a forge in the village and to whom the church is dedicated. The legend relates that the devil assumed the disguise of a young girl and at tempted to seduce the saint who was then working at his forge; the plan didn't work and St Dunstan spotted the cloven hoofs beneath the skirt, tweaked the devil by his nose with red-hot

The Sussex bonfire tradition: but not in Lewes

Lewes is justly heralded as the prime place to see the bonfire celebrations on 5 November (see page 142). But what's less known is that the numerous other societies, mostly in East Sussex, start celebrating the bonfire season in September, and carry on each Saturday until late November. Many other societies come along on those days, and there are processions, bonfires and fireworks. In fact these are generally more manageable and family-friendly than struggling through the crowds in Lewes in an atmosphere that certainly doesn't suit small children. The usual running order roughly falls into months as follows, with all events on Saturdays. A full list of dates appears on www.bonfirenight.info.

September: Uckfield, Crowborough, Mayfield, Burgess Hill. Note the Uckfield and Crowborough events are really carnivals with processions but no bonfires or fireworks, even though they are run by bonfire societies.

October: Rotherfield, Hastings, Hailsham, Fletching, Firle, Neville Juvenile Bonfire Society (Lewes), Eastbourne, Staplecross, Littlehampton, Newick, South Heighton. Friday in late October: Lewes Bonfire Council Bonfire Costume Competition, Lewes Town Hall, with the costumes that will appear on 5 November on display.

November: Lindfield, Lewes (5 November, or on 4 November if 5 November falls on a Sunday). After 5 November: Battle, East Hoathly, Chailey, Rye, Barcombe, Robertsbridge.

pincers and lobbed him into a spring at Tunbridge Wells, which consequently gained sulphurous qualities.

Standing out among the tiles and half timbering is the Gothic stone façade of St Leonard's School, a Catholic girls' boarding school. This occupies the former palace of the archbishops of Canterbury; in 1617 it fell into the hands of the Baker family, who owned several local foundries, and has been a school since 1872. Its restored 14th-century Great Hall is its most notable survival.

During the reign of Queen Mary in the 16th century, four Protestant martyrs from Mayfield were condemned for their religion and burned at the stake in Lewes. Perhaps partly for that reason, Mayfield's bonfire society continues to thrive to this day in a tradition that commemorates each of the 17 victims from various parts of Sussex with a burning cross held aloft during the bonfire celebrations.

Food and drink

April Cottage West St. Just off the High Street, this quaint little tearoom has been in Mayfield for as long as I can remember. Teas from 15.00 only.

Rose and Crown Fletching St ✆ 01435 872200. By a triangular green at the bottom end of the village (a very pleasant few minutes' stroll down the hill from the High Street) and with seating out in front beneath a horse chestnut tree, this convivial, chatty weatherboarded pub welcomes children and has tasty food. They have a quiz night on Tuesdays.

㉕ Bewl Water

Bisected by the East Sussex/Kent border, this naturalistic and undeniably landscape-enhancing reservoir is the largest body of water in southeastern England. Completed in 1975, it drowned a landscape – as evidenced by the little, ancient, sunken lanes to nowhere that approach it and abruptly fizzle out at the shore. It provides water to the Medway towns, Thanet, Hastings and elsewhere, and doubles as a major hub of outdoor activities. The Round Reservoir Route – open to walkers and cyclists (and horse riders May to October) – makes a varied 12½-mile circuit of the lake, all nicely varied and alternating between patches of woodland and open ground. The lanes on the south side around Three Leg Cross and Ticehurst onward make good starting points, with a number of paths leading to the water's edge.

On the north (Kent) side, the dam and visitor centre are the main focus, where the Waterside Bistro and Bar makes the most of the views from a terrace and conservatory; here from the end of May to September and weekends in October (weather permitting) you can join 40-minute trips on the lake aboard the *Swallow* (*01892 89017*), try the zip wire (minimum age seven) or hydroballing – a literal walk on water by means of installing yourself inside a giant plastic ball and making your way around a purpose-built pond (all ages welcome, but participants must be under 14^1/$_2$ stone). For anglers, permits, tackle and boat hire are available from April to November, and there's a children's fishing pond for mini trout and coarse fishing.

Bewl Water The Estate Office, Bewl Water, Lamberhurst TN3 8JH
☎ 01892 890000 🖥 www.bewlwater.co.uk. See the website for links to all outdoor activities, including watersports at Bewl Water Outdoor Centre, cycle hire, fly fishing courses and events.

Learning woodcraft at Flimwell

The Woodland Enterprise Centre at Flimwell, near Bewl Water, hosts a number of day courses run by Plumpton College (*www.plumpton.ac.uk*). These include trug-making (see page 221), woodland skills, green woodwork and making hazel hurdles, chestnut gates or charcoal.

㉖ Bateman's

'Kipling strikes me personally as the most complete man of genius (as distinct from fine intelligence) that I have ever known.'
Henry James

Built along a ridge, the handsome village street of Burwash has tile-hung, timber frame houses in the typical Wealden tradition. A short distance below it is Bateman's (*01435 882302; www.nationaltrust.org.uk; house open mid Mar–end Oct, Sat–Wed; garden open further into winter; tearoom*), the 17th-century country house where the Indian-born author and 'poet of Empire' Rudyard Kipling (1865–1936) moved in 1902, three years after the death of his daughter, purchasing the house, its outbuildings, its 18th-century watermill and 33 acres of grounds. It was a cherished escape for the author, who had become a huge celebrity in Edwardian England, as creator of the *Barrack Room Ballads*, in which he encapsulated the feelings of the British soldier, and the *Just So Stories*. He had travelled much – including in the Far East – and after his marriage to Carrie Balestier in 1892 lived in Vermont where he revelled in the autumn colours. Prior to Bateman's, he lived at Rottingdean in Sussex, but the hordes of sightseers keen to catch a glimpse of the literary celebrity were becoming increasingly tiresome to him. At Bateman's he found privacy and seclusion: it was love at first sight. 'Behold us, lawful owners of a grey stone lichened house – AD1634 over the door', he recorded, 'beamed, panelled, with old oak staircase, and all untouched and unfaked. It is a good and peaceable place.' He adored being driven by his chauffeur along the Sussex lanes: his beloved 1928 Rolls Royce Phantom I is displayed in the garage.

Inside, the house is strongly evocative of Kipling's day, his book-lined study seemingly unchanged, with pen and typewriter at the ready. It is dark and rather snug, filled with mementoes of his time in the Far East. During his years here he wrote two connected collections of poetry and stories: *Puck of Pook's Hill* (1906) – the hill of the title is in view from the house – and *Rewards and Fairies* (1910), which contained the perennially popular poem *If*. He also wrote pamphlets in support of the aims of World War I, only to have his only son, John, die in the Battle of Loos in 1915. He continued to write into the last years of his life, but latterly his output declined in quantity and success. His wife survived him by seven years, and bequeathed Bateman's to the National Trust in 1939. Elsie, the only one of their children to live beyond the age of 18, died in 1976 and left the copyright of his works to the National Trust too.

The delightful grounds slope down to the River Dudwell and the watermill. Using money from the Nobel Prize for Literature which he won in 1907, Kipling laid out the pond, the rose garden and its yew hedges. In the watermill he installed a water turbine to drive an electric generator that gave modest lighting to the house.

㉗ Brightling

The sheep-grazed churchyard around St Thomas à Becket church here has the aptly curious memorial to that stalwart among Sussex eccentrics, 'Mad Jack' (John) Fuller (1757–1834), the local Georgian squire and ironmaster who is commemorated in the form of a 25-foot-tall stone pyramid; alas the popular legend that his skeleton was inside, dressed up

in a top hat and eating dinner-turned out to be a complete fabrication when the structure was renovated and opened in 1982. He wasn't at all mad in fact, but left his mark on the Sussex landscape in the form of many noble philanthropic gestures, purchasing Bodiam Castle so that it could be safeguarded for posterity, setting up Fullerian professorships in chemistry and physiology at the Royal Institution, and bestowing generous financial gifts upon the Eastbourne lifeboat. He funded the recasting of five church bells at Brightling and the addition of a new treble one, and commissioned the barrel organ in 1820 – the largest in the country to be in full working order.

The churchyard pyramid was the apt finale for a man who embellished the locality with some notable follies. On Brightling Beacon he erected the unexplained **Brightling Needle**, a 65-foot-tall obelisk that may or may not commemorate triumphs in the Napoleonic War, while his **Observatory** (visible from the road to Burwash) of 1818 originally housed a camera obscura, projecting an image of the surroundings on to a wall inside. Within his estate – Brightling Park – were a coade stone summerhouse in the form of a Grecian

Rotunda Temple, allegedly a venue for gambling and orgies (or perhaps not). The pointy-topped **Sugar Loaf**, seen on the road from Battle to Heathfield, is said to stem from a bet he made that he could see the spire of the church of St Giles, Dallington, from his house: when it transpired that he was wrong, he had this mock-up of a spire built to that he would win the wager. His 35-foot **Tower**, near the road from Brightling to Darwell Hole, was traditionally thought to have been built so he could watch the workmen's progress on restoring Bodiam Castle – but it is thought to date a few years earlier from his Bodiam phase, and it seems more likely that he simply liked adorning the landscape with viewpoints.

㉘ Robertsbridge

Another conspicuously handsome Wealden village, Robertsbridge has a sloping main street with the ubiquitous mixture of pantiles, half-timbering and weatherboarding. But a rather more startling surprise awaits at the fireplace business, **Mark Ripley Forge and Fireplaces** (*Bridge Bungalow, Robertsbridge TN32 5NY; 01580 880324; www.ripleyfireplaces.com*), run by Kay Ripley and her son John at their home just outside the village near where the road crosses the River Rother. The front yard is crammed full of Wealden iron, most notably a unique and rare collection of locally made firebacks. You can have a cast made of any of them for around £400–£500. Kay gave me a tour: the oldest ones are plain pieces of iron, then came simple ones with designs created by imprinting everyday objects and handprints into the sand moulds. Later designs were more elaborate and specially moulded, often with heraldic themes. She explained they have a much wider range of originals than you're likely to find anywhere else, and that her father-in-law started the collection after he settled here in 1920. 'The biggest fireback we have is the Ashburnham one – under that cannon,' she said, pointing to a cannon that originated from Woolwich Arsenal. At the back of her fireplace showroom is the former local museum, very sadly damaged by the floods in 2000: 'What made the museum special is that it belonged to Robertsbridge – 80 percent came from the village.' The Bruderhof community, a local religious group, turned up after the disaster and provided cakes and help; Kay said their kindness moved her to tears. She hopes that one day it might reopen.

Robertsbridge has its own **rail station**, on the line from Hastings to Tunbridge Wells, so it's only a matter of minutes from Battle (see page 251). A footpath leads you along the Rother for most of the way to Etchingham, the next station, three miles up the line towards Tunbridge Wells.

Food and drink

George High St ☏ 01580 880315. Stylishly modernised pub set up for dining and run by enthusiastic staff. Children welcome; some outdoor seating.

Trug-making, Sussex-style

Robertsbridge is a key manufacturer of cricket bats, made by the renowned Gray-Nicolls company. An unexpected by-product of this comes in the peculiarly Sussex industry making wooden open-topped containers known as trugs. Variously round, oval, rectangular or square, with a central carrying handle, properly made Sussex trugs are admirably sturdy and practical – useful for gathering fruit, carrying gardening materials or storing what you will.

The trug developed where there were no suitable materials to make baskets, so instead willow was used from marshy areas like the Pevensey Levels and sweet chestnut from the woodlands. As a concept the trug is probably very ancient indeed, and comes from an Anglo-Saxon word 'trog': documentary evidence shows that its present design is basically unaltered in some 200 years.

Charlie Groves (*www.thetrugstore.co.uk*) is the last full-time trugmaker in Sussex, based near Hailsham (north of Eastbourne). He told me that huge quantities of willow used to be burnt up after billets were extracted for the manufacture of cricket bats. Now he uses the remainder for trug making. He uses sweet chestnut for the frame and clefts of willow, which are soaked in water, as boards. Willow feet are added and a coating of linseed oil is applied. Charlie also gives day courses in trug-making at Flimwell (see page 218), near Bewl Water, through Plumpton College (*www.plumpton.ac.uk*).

EASTBOURNE, HASTINGS AND 1066 COUNTRY

6. EASTBOURNE, HASTINGS AND 1066 COUNTRY

W here the South Downs end at Beachy Head, a stretch of coast extends eastwards to the Kent border, comprising the most diverse seaboard in Sussex. While researching this book, I took a boat cruise from Eastbourne and strolled its gorgeous Victorian pier, tucked into fish and chips by the net houses of Hastings Old Town after an exhilarating walk over the adjacent sandstone cliffs, wandered through the cobbled streets of Rye and cycled my way along the unheralded coastline west of Bexhill's astonishing 1930s De La Warr Pavilion.

This region has numerous reminders of invasions both threatened and actual. Most famously it was the landing point of the Normans in 1066 in the last successful invasion of the mainland, from which they went on to defeat the English at what is now called Battle and change the course of English history. Then in medieval times it was a confederation of wealthy ports supplying naval craft and men to the monarch in return for certain privileges, including tax exemption and legal jurisdiction over criminals. These Sussex and Kent towns were known as the Cinque Ports, which originally numbered five, but the list later grew to include Hastings, Rye and Winchelsea. The area is instilled with a tremendous sense of the past, with Normans in evidence at Pevensey Castle (originally Roman) and Battle Abbey, and magnificent moated castles at Herstmonceux and Bodiam – the latter reached by the Kent and East Sussex Railway, and easily visited in conjunction with Great Dixter, the great 20th-century horticultural creation of Christopher Lloyd.

Camber Sands is by far the best beach in East Sussex, and a bike ride away from Rye. Some former coastal settlements now stand well inland as the sea has silted up over the centuries, leaving areas of rich, marshy farmland that have a quiet, brooding beauty – seen at its best around Rye Harbour nature reserve, the Royal Military Canal between Winchelsea and Cliff End and the Pevensey Levels.

Getting around

Trains

Eastbourne to Rye: Here the train is good news for coastal explorers. The line from London Victoria through Lewes to Eastbourne continues to Hastings and often finishes at Ore (a northeastern suburb). The first stop out of town, **Pevensey and Westham**, is within walking distance of Pevensey Castle, and east of Normans Bay the line runs very close to the coast and into **Bexhill**, just a few minutes' stroll to the De La Warr Pavilion. **Hastings** station is central, though a good ten minutes on foot to the Old Town. Trains continue from there east to

Ashford in Kent, taking you through **Winchelsea** (where the station is about a mile's walk along a quiet country road and up the main road into the village) and **Rye**.

Tunbridge Wells to Hastings: Inland, options by train are far more limited. The line from London Charing Cross to Hastings goes via Tunbridge Wells, and then winds a scenic route through the Weald via **Robertsbridge**, and probably more useful for most visitors, **Battle**, from which it's a 15-minute ride into Hastings.

Buses

The **Hastings to Lydd** bus (daily, hourly; two-hourly on Sunday) gets you into Winchelsea rather than having to slog up the hill from the rail station, and after it goes through Rye, takes you through Camber, where Camber Sands is the great beach hereabouts. Inland options are not great, although considerably better than train, and few services run on Sunday. For Tenterden (outside which is the Kent & East Sussex Railway to Bodiam), buses go from Hastings and Rye (not Sunday), or for Bodiam, you could get a bus from Hastings.

Cycling

The National Cycle Network has some quiet routes over the peaceful, flat and easily cycled **Pevensey Levels** between Polegate, Pevensey, Wartling and the western fringes of Bexhill. Currently you're forced on to the main road for some short but uninviting stretches between Bexhill and St Leonards, but Sustrans is developing an alternative coastal route with National Lottery funding. From **Eastbourne** Route 21 is mostly urban, around the eastern fringes of the town, then joins up with the **Cuckoo Trail** proper from Polegate to Heathfield. Along the **coast**, routes 21 and 2 are useful, taking in sections of road and seafront through Pevensey, Bexhill and Hastings, east of which it's appreciably hilly through Fairlight before dipping to shore level at Cliff End and heading on through Winchelsea and towards Rye. Further north in the High Weald, it can be very tough going, with a lot of up and down, although the scenic rewards are great; some of the main roads head along ridges, with not quite so much climbing but with more traffic to contend with.

Cycle hire

Rye Hire 1 Cyprus Place, Rye TN31 7DR ☎ 01797 223033; Sun and bank holidays ☎ 01797 227826.

Accommodation

Hastings Old Town and Rye both make appealing historic town destinations for a stay, though accommodation in their old centres is not in vast supply; there's a much wider array in Eastbourne and the resort part of Hastings.

Some accommodation providers in the 1066 Country part of Sussex are part of the Sussex Breakfast initiative, where the accent is on local breakfast fare, including dry cured and smoked bacon from pigs reared outdoors, dairy produce processed on local farms, seasonally produced fruit and any of over 60 different types of cheese made in Sussex. Intended to sustain rural communities, better the lot of farm animals and to produce tastier and healthier food, the scheme is intended to spread to other parts of Sussex.

Jeakes House Mermaid St, Rye TN31 7ET ☎ 01797 222828 ⌂ www.jeakeshouse.com. Former Quaker Meeting House, then Baptist Chapel, now a supremely elegant B&B in a house visited by numerous literary figures in times past. The bedrooms are gorgeously, individually styled. Two people sharing £90–£138; single £70–£79.

The Laindons 23 High St, Hastings TN34 3EY ☎ 01424 437710 ⌂ www.thelaindons.com. Chris Jackson moved from London recently and absolutely loves Hastings Old Town. Within her gracious Georgian coach house she has styled up the three bedrooms with impeccable taste: uncluttered, unworrying and utterly tranquil, with greys, off whites, luxurious Egyptian cotton sheets and grey striped carpets; within months of opening she received a five-star rating from the AA. The conservatory has super views of the East Hill and the open fireplaces are in use in winter. Don't be put off by the address – this is at the very quiet end of the High Street. £110–£125 per night; single occupancy £80–£90.

Mermaid Cottage Mermaid St, Rye TN31 7EU ☎ 01580 712046 ⌂ www.mermaidcottage.supanet.com. Self-catering cottage, sleeping five, on a famous cobbled street in the town centre. Open fire and courtyard garden. £350–£600 per week.

Simmons of Rye 68–69 The Mint, Rye TN31 7EW ☎ 01797 226032. Dating from the 14th century and skilfully blending antique and contemporary, in a lovely town-centre location. Locally sourced breakfast. Four rooms; B&B for two £115–£160.

Strand House Tanyards Lane, Winchelsea TN36 4JT ☎ 01797 226276 ⌂ www.thestrandhouse.co.uk. Just below the town, this 600-year-old former Wealden hall has neck-craningly low ceilings and delightfully wonky rooms, lots of timbering and character – all much cosier than its former days as the town's workhouse, later knocked through to take in a neighbouring building. With fish from Rye and meat from the organic farm next door, food is likely to have a very local theme, and they've won a Green Tourism Silver Award for their composting, energy and water-saving arrangements; ten bedrooms, each different, with tiny bathrooms ingeniously fitted in. Dogs welcome. Around £70–£135 for double or twin, from £55 single; special offers available.

Swallowtail Hill Hobbs Lane, Beckley TN31 6TT ☎ 0845 3372948 ⌂ www.swallowtailhill.com; booking through ⌂ www.canopyandstars.co.uk. Luxurious eco camping five miles north of Rye, in two five-metre bell tents (Apr–Sep) or in two shepherds' huts with stoves. The farm is run purely for sustainability and ecodiversity. There are free-range livestock, two wildflower meadows and semi-ancient woodland. As well as feeding the farm animals, you could drive a tractor, try longbow archery or perhaps learn woodland crafts. £315–£355 for a four-person bell tent for three nights over the weekend. No pets, but children of any age are welcome.

Swan House 1 Hill St, Hastings TN34 3HU ☎01424 430014
🖰 www.swanhousehastings.co.uk. Imaginatively and sensitively done, Brendan McDonagh's very civilised, central but quiet B&B consists of five individually styled ensuite bedrooms, including a suite, in Farrow and Ball colours, bare painted floorboards, stressed wooden furniture and trompe l'oeil effects such as doors resembling bookcases. The hub of it is a medieval house, rather grand by Old Town standards, with a spacious part oak-panelled sitting room (given over to guests' use) with a large stone-arched fireplace, and part of the building comprising a former 19th-century bakery. If the weather is fine you can have the delicious breakfast of locally sourced ingredients out in the back garden. £115–£145 double or twin; £70–£95 single occupancy. No under fives; two nights minimum stay at weekends. Brendan also has another Hastings B&B at The Old Rectory, Harold Rd, Hastings TN35 5DB (🖰 *www.theoldrectoryhastings.co.uk*), with eight rooms and a self-contained unit.

Tourist information centres

Battle Battle Abbey, High St ☎01424 773721.
Eastbourne Cornfield Rd ☎0871 663 0031 🖰 www.visiteastbourne.com.
Hastings Queens Square, Priory Meadow; also The Stade, Old Town ☎01424 781111 🖰 www.1066country.com.
Rye Rye Heritage Centre, Strand Quay ☎01797 226696 🖰 www.visitrye.co.uk.

The 1066 coast

① Eastbourne

Beneath the South Downs' spectacular termination, Eastbourne is on the coastal plain, but its western edges creep up to the chalky downland slopes towards Beachy Head. There's not a lot that is ancient about the town, although it has Saxon origins: well into the 19th century it wasn't much more than a dot on the map. By 1813 it was noted in *The Beauties of England and Wales* as having lately become 'a fashionable bathing place' but apart from a villagey cluster known as the Old Town, well inland around St Mary's church, you'll struggle to find anything pre-Victorian.

With the arrival of the railway in the 1840s things took off. Much of the resort was developed by the seventh Duke of Devonshire – the family that owns Chatsworth and prospered out of Derbyshire mining ventures – and this was done with considerable style that still graces the town today. Its plan is neat and organised: ample-looking streets, leafy suburbs and above all a little-blemished stucco-sporting period-charmer of a seafront, resplendent with flowerbeds that are in the best municipal seaside tradition.

The composer Claude Debussy came here to stay in the Grand Hotel in 1905 when his personal life was in turmoil: he was having an extramarital affair with one Emma Bardac, who was pregnant with his child. The couple managed to avoid the public gaze. He had recently completed his astonishing impressionistic masterpiece *La Mer* and worked on the final proofs here ahead of the first performance. It is often said that he wrote the music here, but this is not the case: 'The sea unfurls itself with an utterly British correctness', he declared, so evidently the scene was poles apart from the sonorous complexities of the three tone paintings that this, his most famous orchestral work, comprises. Yet some of his piano music might have been inspired by the town: *Reflets dans l'eau* may have been a result of his observations of sun and cloud in a pond in Devonshire Park, while buskers on the streets of Eastbourne are said to have inspired his marvellous little comic-grotesque piano prelude called *Minstrels*.

Rather unfairly, Eastbourne sometimes gets saddled with a reputation for dullness; 'it's a little English seaside place, silly as these places sometimes are,' remarked Debussy dismissively. But more than a century on from his visit, the town has kept its dignified, neatly prosperous look better than most seaside resorts. Towering above, **Beachy Head** (see page 183) looks positively mountainous and other-worldly. Paths zigzag their way up through the undercliff to the very top; or you can get one of the frequent buses, including City Sightseeing buses (Easter to end of October).

The **pier** is one of the most delectable you'll find anywhere, bristling with elaborate ironwork all picked out in blue and white. It houses a fully operational **Camera Obscura**, installed in 1901 and giving views of the surroundings which are projected by means of a prism on to a curved surface inside (best on a sunny day), a nicely low-tech ancestor of Google Earth that somehow holds its fascination by virtue of its sheer simplicity. In 2010 the pier was selected to feature as Brighton's Palace pier in the filming of *Brighton Rock*, starring Helen Mirren, Sam Riley and Pete Postlethwaite. Production designer James Merifield found Eastbourne's pier had far more period ambiance. 'We came to Eastbourne to recce the Grand Hotel, and looked east to see this incredible piece of architecture and we asked ourselves why are we not filming here instead of Brighton; here it already feels like we're the 1950s. So we had a wander down and went on to the pier, and it unravelled itself – it had the right feel and the right architecture with very few modern influences on the pier, and we found we had the right canvas.'

The extraordinarily long **prom**, choice terrain for rollerblading aficionados, heads westwards past the pier, the little **Lifeboat Museum** and a Martello Tower known as the **Wish Tower**, around which spreads an exotic 500-foot long border of palms and succulents. Nearby, the Holywell Tea Chalet serves outside winter months as the eastern terminus of a land train (the Dotto Train) which trundles along the seafront to **Sovereign Harbour**, Europe's largest manmade marina, very Docklands in feel, with ship-shaped apartment blocks and several waterside eateries for alfresco dining. Inland from here, reached by following the brown signs from Lottbridge Drove, is the very quaint **Eastbourne Miniature Steam Railway** (open March to September and weekends in October). This developed from a passion of Mike Wadey, fired by an interest in model engineering while working at the fire service: with the assistance of his family he set it all up in a year and opened in 1992. His locomotives are all one-eighth scale and meticulous recreations of famous ones from the past, bringing tears of nostalgia to some visitors. A particular favourite is the Southern Railways Schools Class locomotive *Eastbourne*, one of a number of engines that were named after famous schools. Passengers ride astride the carriages, based on 1930s and 1950s designs, on a circuit of nearly a mile through a restored landfill site comprising a five-acre lake and 6,000 trees planted through the legacy of an Eastbourne man. Eastbourne has four **theatres**, including the Victorian, very lovely **Devonshire Park Theatre**, and takes its onion-domed **bandstand** very seriously: amid a sea of deckchairs, it offers a very busy programme of concerts ranging from 1812 nights to film music or rock 'n' roll; fireworks in the evening in summer. My favourite Eastbourne interior is the **Winter Garden**, which stages various concerts and events; built in the spirit of the Crystal Palace; it's rather ramshackle from outside, but its period charms reveal themselves within.

Next to the Congress Theatre and backing on to the tennis courts of Devonshire Park is the crisp, **Towner Gallery** (*01323 434670; free; closed Mon except bank holidays; charge for special summer exhibitions; membership scheme available*), a sleekly modern setting for high-standard changing exhibitions of national and international art, as well as an annual historical art exhibition and more than 4,000 items from the permanent collection shown on a rotating basis – including a notable array of paintings by the incomparable Eric Ravilious, as well as works by Christopher Wood and Alfred Wallis, Picasso, Duncan Grant, Vanessa Bell and others. At 11.30 each day there is an excellent free building tour that includes a look behind the scenes in the Collection Store. The café on the top floor is a very calming space with views towards the Downs.

Eastbourne resident Milly Clark, one of the gallery assistants at the Towner, is thrilled with her town's latest art venue. She told me 'the new Towner has given me reason to talk of my home town with renewed pride – not many towns can boast of the range and quality of art always on show that Eastbourne now can. But I not only look on Towner as enabling me to access great art on my doorstep – I think it has refreshed the way I look at the landscape around me on a daily basis. With the collection's focus on landscape, and the extraordinary talent of Eric Ravilious on show, the art in the gallery has inspired me to go out into the Downs and think very differently of the environment I grew up in, and its eternal capacity to nourish the human spirit.'

Eric Ravilious

The colour of the landscape was so lovely and the design so beautifully obvious.
Eric Ravilious, while writing about the South Downs

The Sussex artist Eric Ravilious (1903–42) captured the character and beauty of the Downs landscape like no other artist. His paintings date from his rediscovery of the area in the 1930s where he grew up; when he was a boy his family moved to Eastbourne, where his father ran an antiques shop. In 1925 he began teaching at his old school of art in Eastbourne after studying at the Royal College of Art in London. He would take students to sketch the Saxon downland villages like Alfriston, Wilmington and Jevington.

In 1934 his friend Peggy Angus invited him to stay at her cottage – Furlongs – beneath Beddingham Hill on the Firle estate. He felt at home in an area he had never explored in detail, selecting familiar subjects like the Long Man from new angles. A perfectionist, he destroyed two thirds of his watercolours. He died in his prime in 1942 when as a war artist he flew to Iceland to draw planes of the Norwegian squadron and his aircraft went missing in bad weather.

His works have been described as the calm before the storm, done at a time that witnessed a revival in English landscape painting, spurred on by the uncertainty of the European political situation and the awareness of fragility of the national way of life. Often there is an element of ambiguity and mystique within the everyday in his pictures, and some seem to have a foreboding sense of imminent threat that all is about to change. In 1939 he painted a series of chalk hill figures, including the Long Man, whom he thought of as a giantess. These he considered 'symbols of Englishness and defiance as well as an evocation of the manmade in a natural setting.' The Towner in Eastbourne has the finest public collection of Ravilious paintings anywhere.

Cricket aficionados will almost certainly be familiar with one of his works: the woodcut depicting the duo of behatted Victorian cricketers that has graced variously the cover and title page of *Wisden* each year since 1938.

Further east along the seafront on Royal Parade is the Redoubt, a fine example of an early 19th-century circular fort. It now houses the **Military Museum of Sussex** (*01323 410300; open Apr to early Nov; closed Mon except bank holidays*) with military collections of the Queen's Royal Irish Hussars, the Sussex Combined Services and The Royal Sussex Regiment – the latter formed in 1701. Among the items featured is a display evoking life in front-line Eastbourne, a telescope that belonged to Winston Churchill and a scale model of the fort exactly as it was when in use.

For something bewitchingly potty, head inland to Cornfield Terrace, where a perfectly ordinary house is now **How We Lived Then: the Museum of Shops**. It's a fascinating nostalgia stash gathered since their childhoods by Jan and Graham Upton and now amounting to upwards of 100,000 retail and other bygones arranged into themed rooms. This was once their house, only they've kept the museum downstairs and created a flat above. There are packets of Hudson's Soap and Tristella Shredded Suet, draper's shelves full of lace, a wartime kitchen and sitting room, an ironmongers sporting adverts for Royal Daylight Lamp Oil, and quite a lot more. Thank goodness someone else has to dust it.

Boat trips from Eastbourne

For the best cliff views of all take a boat trip from Sovereign Harbour run by Pete Smith at Sussex Voyages, (*0845 838 7114; www.sussexvoyages.co.uk*). He offers several options on a 10-metre rigid inflatable, which skims along nippily at around 24 knots (30mph) along the base of the cliffs to Birling Gap, getting terrific views of Beachy Head and the Seven Sisters, or out to the remote Royal Sovereign Light Tower (built in the 1970s and often mistaken for an oil rig). He also offers a shorter trip to the pier and back, or an exhilaratingly speedy adventure trip that shows off the agility of the boat and on which you may get the chance to steer. On all trips he provides goggles, waterproof jacket and trousers to shield you from the appreciable spray and headwind. From the sea, the cliffs' crumbly qualities are much in evidence, and seals and porpoises are occasionally seen on the water. Once the craft is close to the cliffs, he stops to allow for photo opportunities.

Pete, a BSAC (British Sub Aqua Club) instructor who will take BSAC or PADI qualified divers out to top dive sites, rates the Sussex area particularly highly for diving. There are numerous World War I and II wrecks, which are habitats for abundant sea life, such as lobsters, crabs and sponges. 'There's a lot of history: two world wars have left a few hundred wrecks off this coast. With the diving that you have now, you can get to wrecks that are more intact because the wave action hasn't destroyed them. One of the wrecks I really like is the *Alaunia*, south of Sovereign Harbour, a massive liner almost the size of the *Titanic*, which sticks up 20 metres from the sea bed. You can go alongside with torches, but personally I don't go inside them.' The largest wreck in Sussex waters, the *Alaunia* hit a German mine in October 1916 and sank, but all except two of the 166 passengers survived.

Also operating from Sovereign Harbour, Bob at Harwell Charters (*07979 508877, 07713 639066; www.harwellcharters.co.uk, www.seatrainingsussex.co.uk*) offers self-drive hire (experience essential), summer mackerel fishing trips (no experience needed; £18.50 per trip for around two hours; fishing gear can be hired; you obviously keep what you fish) and half-day taster sessions on driving powerboats for absolute beginners or improvers.

Activities in Eastbourne

Swimming is pretty good here, with a large, safe shingle beach which extends into a substantial expanse of sand at low tide. If you want a swim but it's too nasty outside, beat a retreat to the Sovereign Centre (*Royal Parade; 01323 738822*), which has an indoor slide, bubble pool and wave machine. There's also an outdoor paddling pool at Treasure Island, a play centre and adventure park near the Sovereign Centre.

For **frivolous pursuits**, Princes Park takes some beating, with a lake for sailing model boats, and opportunities for mini golf, petanque, putting and bowls. There's also Go Karts in Royal Parade.

Eastbourne is prized territory for **windsurfing**. The Spray Watersports Centre (*01323 417023*) in Royal Parade run taster sessions and weekly courses for all ages; Princes Park Lake is the beginners' spot. They also do courses in canoeing, sailing, body-boarding and power boating. Or armchair windsurfers can watch Britain's top windsurfers in action at Eastbourne during the July sports festival known as Eastbourne Extreme.

If you are in the Eastbourne area in mid-August and like aviation, you might want to coincide your visit with **Airbourne** (*www.eastbourneairshow.com*), a four-day air fest of historic craft, military planes, Red Arrow displays and parachuting displays; you can see it from miles around, but the seafront between the pier and the Wish Tower and Beachy Head are particularly fine vantage points, or you can splash out on a helicopter ride from Beachy Head.

Tennis enthusiasts should beat a path to Eastbourne in June for the tennis tournament held at Devonshire Park that precedes Wimbledon fortnight and features many of the big guns. Some tickets may be available on the day, but booking is strongly recommended; see www.eastbournetennis.com.

Food and drink

There's not a huge amount of places for eating and drinking along the seafront itself, apart from hotels such as the **Waterside** (☏ *01323 646566; famously good for seafood*) and one or two notables like **Fusciardi's**; the best-endowed areas are around Terminus Road, on the sea side of the railway station, and at Sovereign Harbour. Feastbourne is a week-long food festival held around town during October, and includes the Eastbourne Beer Festival, with some 150 brews from Britain and overseas. The **Towner Gallery** has an attractive minimalist café on the top floor, with a balcony looking out towards the Downs.

Fusciardi's 30 Marine Parade ☏ 01323 722128. A classic and reassuringly retro family-run Italian ice-cream outlet and cappuccino bar on the seafront; Italian food and café fare too.

Lamb 36 High St ☏ 01323 720545. In the old town; cosily traditional pub, with a log fire, Harveys beer, bar food and occasional live music.

② Pevensey

It was at Pevensey Bay that William the Conqueror landed in 1066 in what was the last successful invasion of mainland Britain. He erected a wooden fort within the outer walls of a Roman fortification and made it a strategic base. Remarkably **Pevensey Castle** (*English Heritage; 01323 762604*) was still an important stronghold in World War II, on this long, vulnerable shoreline, and not many Norman castles sport a 1940s gun emplacement as does this. It originated as the last of the late-Roman period chain of fortifications known as the Saxon shore forts, begun in the mid 290s, when the marshes and the sea were adjacent enough to be the defences; the Norman fort was rebuilt in the 13th century, then as the harbour silted up it became less strategically important and was abandoned by around 1500.

The outer walls of the castle force a sharp road detour in the village of Pevensey. Most unusually these are substantial portions of standing Roman walls – though the turrets are medieval. Inside you enter a huge enclosed grass oval, where in places you can see where the outer wall has been excavated, and it's easier to spot the Roman parts – look for the pinkish cement and flat red bricks around the West Gate for instance; most of the original facing has been removed to reveal rubble beneath.

A reedy moat surrounds the medieval castle, with its rounded towers, arrow slits and massive walls that are ten feet thick in places. Little is known of what happened between 310 and 1066 here. It was apparently abandoned after a massacre, but is thought to have been inhabited again by the 7th century. The informative audio tour takes you round what is an intriguing mixture: a Tudor gun, a spiral staircase down to a dark, vaulted dank-floored dungeon cell, piles of excavated stone balls used for trebuchets (medieval stone-throwing catapults), and concrete and brick rooms used by British and Canadians as pillboxes in World War II.

Among Pevensey village's other historic buildings, **Old Mint House Antiques** dates from 1342 – there was indeed a coin mint here in early medieval times. The **Court House Museum** (open Easter, May–October) occupies what was the smallest courthouse and jail in England, in use from 1540 till 1883. The Victorian beadle's uniform is displayed in a glass case, and in the judge's changing room are scales used for weighing imported goods. They have a few Roman bits and pieces, and the volunteer on the desk told me she has unearthed Roman coins in her garden. Pevensey's former method of dealing with criminals wasn't too lenient: regular felons were hanged, while murderers were marched down the high street, had their hands tied and were chucked in the river. Downstairs, the whitewashed prison cell looks suitably spartan.

Just north of Pevensey are the fen-like **Pevensey Levels**, with a quiet beauty of their own. The Sussex Wildlife Trust (*01273 492630*) runs guided walks into the National Nature Reserve owned jointly with Natural England (access otherwise by permit only) in summer – it is an important site for flowering water plants, dragonflies, damselflies and aquatic beetles, and the rare fen raft spider is the largest arachnid to be found in Britain. This is rewarding cycling country: a very quiet unfenced road wiggles its way around this reed-fringed expanse of drained marshes, past the hamlet of Rickney. East Sussex County Council produce a free leaflet (downloadable from www.eastsussex.gov.uk/cycling) entitled *Pevensey Levels & Castles Circular* detailing a ride from Pevensey, up the forementioned road, around the Herstmonceux estate to Wartling (an excellent pub stop; see below) and to Bexhill, returning partly along the coast to Normans Bay.

Food and drink

Castle Cottage Tearoom Pevensey Castle ☎01323 460970. Open daily, this café built on to the castle's perimeter walls has a very pretty garden and serves locally sourced hot and cold snacks.

Lamb Wartling BN27 1RY ☎01323 832116 ⌂ www.lambinnwartling.co.uk. A few miles north of Pevensey on the Pevensey Levels, this cosy place has beamed rooms and roaring fires, as well as tasty bar food (not Mon). Closed Sun evening.

Sharnfold Stone Cross, Hailsham Rd, Stone Cross, BN24 5BU ☎01323 768490 ⌂ www.sharfoldfarm.co.uk. West of Pevensey on the B2104 and next to Coopers pub, this farm shop has own-made and local produce, pick-your-own (including apples, blackcurrants, gooseberries, redcurrants and strawberries), a café with terrace, fishing, plenty of farm animals to encounter along the farm walk and tractor rides. Open all day, all year round.

③ Normans Bay

Taking its name as the supposed arrival point of the Normans in 1066, this village is a seaside curio. It's almost entirely a product of modern times, apart from a Martello tower converted into a private house. Seen from the reed-fringed unfenced lane that wends its way through the Pevensey Levels from Pevensey itself, it looks quite surreal: a long line of detached seaside houses, all pointy-roofed and standing close together, side by side, on the shingle ridge. At Normans Bay station, a private level-crossing keeper is employed on a private road – the crossing gates are kept shut for up to ten or so minutes at a time, so there's not much incentive to rat-run around this stretch of coast. It's an amiable enough cycle ride though, whichever way you approach the village. Virtually every house has been adapted in its own way, and on the beach side many sport their own flagpole and pebble garden. Here and there the odd 1930s villa survives unaltered, its piles dug straight into the shingle bank. One area, known as **Beachlands**, extends inland in the form of an estate of flat-topped bungalows of seemingly unique appearance; some are 'oyster bungalows', so called because of their oval shape. Marine Avenue, a dual carriageway with virtually no traffic, pierces into this strangely quasi-American 1950s utopia.

④ Bexhill

The seventh Earl De La Warr was the local landowner who got Bexhill started back in the 1880s by naming it Bexhill-on-Sea, just in case anyone had any doubts as to its status. It's hardly a pulsating resort – but very pleasingly unhurried, benign and cared for, looking along the coast towards its more raucous neighbour, Hastings. The **beach** here is pleasantly divided up and sheltered – good for families.

In the 1930s lucky Bexhill gained Britain's first building in International Modern style, the airy, light **De La Warr Pavilion**. It was built in 1933–35 when Bexhill gained its first socialist mayor, the ninth Earl De La Warr, who decided the town needed a palace to the people. He turned to the designs of Erich Mendelsohn, a highly regarded Jewish architect who'd fled the Nazis, and architect and designer Serge Chermayeff; together they created a masterpiece. The Pavilion looks younger than its years: the sleek curves and ship's-deck railings have been much imitated in far more recent buildings. It is a centre for contemporary arts, with events and exhibitions, but you can just step inside to visit the café, take in the sea views from the sun terraces and admire the supremely elegant staircase encircling a vertical chandelier of chrome disks and neon tubes which runs the full height of the building. For the latest on what's on, visit www.dlwp.com or phone 01424 229111. On two Sundays a month you can join architectural tours of the building. Note the supremely inappropriate brown-and-white signs as you enter town, signposting the De La Warr Pavilion with the standard classical mansion symbol.

There's a lively cultural war among the architectural styles on the seafront, with white Victorian stucco frontages contrasting with the Pavilion, and the extraordinary houses of **Marina Court Avenue** and **Marina Parade**, built 1903–07, where Moghul details such as onion domes and flamboyant chimneys are more reminiscent of India than of the Sussex coast.

Most of the buildings in the town centre went up between 1895 and 1905; in 1911 the **Colonnade** was erected in honour of George V's coronation – its playful cupolas and balustrades an engaging contrast to the De La Warr Pavilion that appeared later.

A scale model of the Pavilion, along with costume displays, is on show at the nearby **Bexhill Museum**; a gallery here of vintage motor-racing cars pays a nod to Bexhill's early links with the sport – around the turn of the 20th century the town hosted the first motor races in Britain. It also was ahead of every other seaside resort in the country by allowing mixed bathing in 1901.

⑤ Hastings

It's always an event arriving here, particularly by train: Hastings has terrific atmosphere thanks in part to the extremely strong physical presence of its towering cliffs and its beguiling, precipitous Old Town – the original and remarkably unspoilt fishermen's quarter – exuding plenty of fishy charm of the thankfully untidied-up sort. It feels further from London than it actually is, and there's something intangibly West Country about the whole place: the higgledy-piggledy nature of the Old Town has a Cornish charm, and the cliffs lying to the east are strongly reminiscent of the Dorset or Devon coast. The newer, and far less distinctive, part of the resort lies further west and metamorphoses into St Leonards. The TV series *Foyle's War* is set in Hastings, to the lasting gratitude of the town's tourism industry.

Hastings has Saxon origins, and boasted its own mint in 984. It is most famous for a battle that actually took place elsewhere, seven miles inland, but from Norman times was of military importance as William the Conqueror set up a castle on a headland – possibly on the site of an already existing Saxon fort, impregnable on three sides – and made the town the premier Cinque Port. In the 13th century storms ripped the town apart, destroying the harbour and causing large chunks of the castle to be undermined and to collapse seawards. The town lost its military role, but lived on as a fishing village in a quarter known as the Old Town. From the 19th century it spread beyond, with the seafront developing westwards towards St Leonards: there are the usual trappings associated with a resort along here, but the town's real distinction lies on its east side.

The seaside resort fun extends to the likes of go-karts, a boating lake with swan pedalos, a miniature railway and mini golf. Close by is the sad site of **Hastings Pier** which was burnt down in 2010 just as plans were coming together for a possible restoration.

Above the town in Bohemia Road and a bit of a way from the centre of things, the free **Hastings Museum and Art Gallery** has permanent displays covering some of its most celebrated former residents – the socialist and author of *The Ragged Trousered Philanthropists* Robert Tressell, the TV pioneer John Logie Baird, the 'concrete king' Sidney Little and the intriguing Grey Owl (the Hastings boy who adopted the persona of a Native American and became an early campaigner for conservation causes). Other exhibits feature bathing in Hastings, natural history and dinosaurs, temporary exhibitions and the splendidly ornate Durbar Hall, created for the Colonial and Indian Exhibition held in South Kensington in 1886, and carved from teak, Himalayan cedar and shisham by Indian craftsmen.

The Old Town

For unstructured wandering, this area snuggled into and around the mouth of the valley between West Hill and East Hill – with **cliff railways** making the ascent to the top of each – is a joy. The West Hill Lift climbs up through a tunnel, while the East Hill Lift, opened in 1903 and the steepest in the country, rises up from the fishing area on to the clifftop heights of Hastings Country Park.

Free **walking tours** (donations appreciated) are led by members of the Old Hastings Preservation Society on Tuesdays from the first Tuesday in May to mid September, and during Hastings Week around the anniversary of the Battle of Hastings on 14 October, starting from the top of the West Hill Lift at 14.30 (*01424 420555*); they also offer tailored walks all year for any size of party (donations required). The Society's archive in the Hastings History House, 21 Courthouse Street (open Thursday to Sunday), has a comprehensive range of photos of the town stretching back over the decades. It is largely thanks to the efforts of the Society that Hastings Old Town has survived so well. The council began demolition to make way for the new road in the 1930s and carried on until the 1950s. Further 'improvements' might have taken place were it not for the campaigning efforts of the group.

One of the great pleasures of Hastings is that fishing and boats are still so much part of the scene. **The Stade** is Hastings' joyously un-tidied up and very much working fishing area, home to the largest beach-launched fishing fleet in Europe: a photogenic mishmash of lobster pots, tattered flags, winching equipment, boat skeletons and crab shells. Fresh, smoked and cured fish is sold by the beach and from an assortment of stalls around the **net shops**, a cluster of tall wooden sheds erected to store fishing equipment, and now preserved as historic structures. At the time of writing opinion was acutely divided as to the effect of the Jerwood Foundation's building of the **Jerwood Gallery** (*www.jerwoodgallery.org*) and community space scheduled for completion during 2011 on a former coach park by the Stade – though visually it does seem very much a change for the better, filling as it does an ugly void on the sea front. This will be a permanent home to the Jerwood Foundation's notable collection of 20th and 21st century British art, on public display for the first time: let's hope it will indeed win over its sceptics.

Looking over the whole scene from just above street level, **Pelham Crescent** is Hastings's most elegant piece of Georgian streetscape. Its centrepiece is St Mary in the Castle, a crisply proportioned church with a striking circular auditorium, designed by Joseph Kaye in 1823 and now an arts venue.

Just beyond the net shops lie an absorbing trio of maritime attractions. The **Shipwreck and Coastal Heritage Centre**, amply justifying the modest £1 entrance charge, displays items from the *Thomas Lawrence*, a Danish ship sunk in 1863, including rusting muskets, gin and brandy bottles, a chunk of what is thought to be the original London Bridge built in Roman times, and part of an iguanodon skeleton that was the best-preserved dinosaur fossil ever found when discovered in 1834. It also tells the story of the *Amsterdam*, the shell of which can still be seen from the beach off Bulverhythe at low tide. On its maiden voyage to Java in 1749 she became marooned on a sandbank, and there was plague on board – and when the crew was quarantined while this happened, mutiny broke out, with drunkenness, violence and death; some finds were recovered and are exhibited, including clay pipes, brass guns and fortified wine. Just opposite, the **Blue Reef Aquarium** has native and tropical species and features a walk-through viewing tunnel and large, child-friendly tanks, all well elucidated by hourly talks. They breed seahorses here – the females produce the eggs, then the males carry them and give birth from a special pouch. Housed in the old Fishermen's Church (which still does baptisms), the appealingly unchanged **Fishermen's Museum** (free entry, donation requested), has the *Enterprise* (1912), the last sailing lugger in Hastings, as its main exhibit – you can climb on board. The museum is stuffed with well-loved mementoes, including a model of the Stade and paintings and sepia photos of smocked, whiskery fishermen. Also commemorated is Biddy the Tubman, who performed a surfing act in a half barrel on the beach, was awarded a medal for his feats of bravery in saving people from a watery grave, and took his boat to rescue troops stranded at Dunkirk.

Just inland, **George Street** and the **High Street** contain an appealing mix of eateries, junk shops (particularly in Courthouse Street), boutiques and jewellers. Narrow, private-looking passages rise from the High Street and All Saints Street, making up a maze characterised by stepped alleys, tiny gardens, snoozing cats and unexpected vistas over the rooftops. Seek out 10 Starr Cottages (next to 60a All Saints Street), known as the Piece of Cheese Cottage – painted bright yellow and thinly wedge-shaped as its name suggests; triangular furniture must be very useful inside. At 58a High Street is a unique little factory and shop, the **Shirley Leaf and Petal Company**, which manufactures cloth flowers and leaves that are supplied to theatres, opera houses and movie-makers worldwide. Carrying out a trade traditionally taught to disabled women, including those missing an arm, it is now the last-surviving establishment of its kind in Europe. Sometimes it receives vast orders – for example 100,000 vine leaves to recreate a vineyard, but individual items are on sale too. They have some 10,000 tools of the trade, and stock antique velvets dating back to the 1930s. The workshop is a working museum, using cutting-tools made with blacksmith's skills. All the dyeing is done by hand. The free **Hastings Old Town Hall Museum**, also in the High Street, chronicles life in the community since the days of Stone-Age rock shelters through to the history of its fishing heyday. The A259 slightly spoils things as it runs along The Bourne, created in the 1950s when a lot of the old town was demolished for the purpose; up to 1835 this was the course of the Bourne watercourse, now buried.

The **West Hill Lift**, completed in 1891 and the older of the town's two funiculars, ascends through a tunnel to the open, sloping lawns of West Hill. On a crumbly-looking headland stands the **castle**, dating from just after the arrival of the Normans. Much of it has fallen into the sea following an almighty battering by storms in the 13th century and subsequent erosion – and King John ordered it to be dismantled in 1216 for fear of it falling into French hands – but the setting is still terrific. The most substantial part to survive is the Collegiate Church of St Mary in the Castle, founded around 1069, which became the King's Free Chapel of Hastings in 1272; its chapel was an important place of pilgrimage, only to be dissolved by Henry VIII. The castle site declined into use as farmland, then started attracting tourists in Victorian times. During World War II it housed an anti-aircraft gun and was used by commandos as a training ground. Today, within a recreated siege tent an audiovisual show, the 1066 Story, presents a rollercoaster of English history from the Norman invasion to World War II.

Just beneath the castle, **St Clement's Caves** are partly natural and partly manmade and have served a variety of purposes – smugglers' caves (of course), a Victorian tourist attraction carved out with arches and pillars (hence the niches for sockets for candles to go in), a ballroom, and air-raid shelters in World War II. They're now run as Smugglers' Adventure – with lashings of mock-Gothic spookiness. The commentary doesn't take itself too seriously, with Hairy Jack the Smuggler introducing it, and there are sundry low-tech games, ghost effects and the like; small children might find it either entertaining or scary.

St Leonards

The western part of Hastings merges into St Leonards, named after a medieval church but entirely 19th century in origin. James Burton bought land in 1828 and saw the development potential, which he and his son Decimus realised over the ensuing decades. The hinterland has some rewarding strolling grounds with handsome hilly streets of opulent Regency villas and grandiose turreted, stepped-gabled Scottish baronial Victorian mansions. For a sample, wander along Highland Gardens, Maze Hill and Upper Maze Hill, around the deep quarried ravine of St Leonards Gardens.

In the 1930s, St Leonards had a futuristic phase. The borough engineer, 'concrete king' Sidney Little – later to be involved in construcing the Mulberry floating harbours used in the 1944 D-Day landings – transformed Hastings and St Leonards into a veritable symphony of concrete and chrome, and ripped up tramlines to make a promenade. The tram rails he recycled as reinforcements for Britain's very first underground car park in 1931. He created a double-decker prom between the two resorts; the lower portion gives surreal, concrete perspectives embellished with wall decoration made of broken glass set into concrete and known as Bottle Alley. His curvaceous concrete wind shelters look as if they would admirably withstand nuclear fallout. Above this rises the sleek, high-rise Marine Court (1937), inspired by the *Queen Mary* ocean liner and dominating the view entire this entire stretch of coast.

Also along the prom is an engagingly old-fashioned weather station set up in 1875 and sporting cartoon Normans, gilded lettering, and a mechanical thermometer with gull and yacht pointers showing the land and sea temperatures respectively. In 1926 change-resistant residents petitioned for a 10mph speed limit along the sea front. I don't believe they succeeded.

Watching seawards

During the months from March to September, **bottlenose dolphins** come close to the shore and to boats along the coast from Bexhill to Rye Harbour. When the water is calm, you have a good chance of spotting them from land early in the morning and later in the evening at high tide. They have a tall hooked-shape dorsal fin and grow up to 13 feet long. During winter and early spring you might glimpse harbour porpoises, which grow up to six feet long, or seals.

Food and drink

No shortage of possibilities in the Old Town: the key places are along George Street, the High Street and near the net shops on The Stade. Not surprisingly there are plenty of places for **fish and chips** along the sea front, most of them very good indeed. **Maggie's** (*Rock A Nore* ✆ *01424 430205*) is Hastings's most celebrated fish-and-chip eaterie (not open in the evenings, and often booked out; opens extremely early in the morning to serve mostly fishermen), tucked away up steps by the net sheds, opposite the East Hill Lift; a spokesman for the local Fishermen's Mission rated this the best place for fish and chips on the south coast, so who can argue with that? If you can't get in, there are plenty of other excellent options such as the **Mermaid Restaurant**.

For **snacks**, there's a similar huge choice. **Land of Green Ginger** (*45 High St* ✆ *01424 434191; closed Mon*) is a nice veggie daytime café using local and seasonal produce, free-range eggs and fairtrade coffee; courtyard garden out at the back. A few doors along at 51 High Street, **Judges Bakery** has tasty cakes, buns and bread and has been baking since 1828; **Penbuckles Cheesemongers and Vintners** are next door at number 50. For takeaway organic burgers and filled rolls, the wooden **Pelican Kiosk** at the sea end of the High Street is good value; at weekends, catch **Tush & Pat's**, which sells delicious fisherman's rolls from in front of the net sheds (weather allowing).

If you just want a drink, the **First in Last Out** (*High St, at the far end from the sea*) has a good selection of real ales.

There's a **farmers' market** in Robertson St (beside Debenhams) on the second and fourth Thursday of the month. A WI-style **country market** at All Saints Church Hall in All Saints Street takes place on Friday morning 10.30–11.30, with preserves, plants, chutneys, knitware and the like.

Entertainment and events

In the High Street, the **Electric Palace Cinema** (🖰 *www.electricpalacecinema.com*) is an enchantingly quirky 50-seater arthouse cinema, with an excellent selection of films – including world cinema, classic films and works by local directors. As intimate a movie house as one could find; you can watch with a glass of organic wine in hand. Hastings has two **theatres** – the White Rock opposite the pier stages commercial productions, while the Stables Theatre and Arts Centre is a small venue for quality amateur theatre.

Major **events** include the Jack in the Green Festival of Morris Dancing on the bank holiday weekend in early May, the extremely lively Old Town Carnival in early August (with wellie throwing, a pram race and a terrific procession), the Seafood and Wine Festival in September and the Bonfire Celebrations in October.

⑥ Fairlight Glen and Hastings Country Park

The oldest rocks in Sussex jut out of the cliffs on the eastern side of Hastings: an area partly covered by the Hastings Country Park, and designated a Site of Special Scientific Interest. This is the only place in the southeast where visible sandstone reaches the sea to this extent. For the newcomer it can be an unexpected scenic transformation into a landscape you might more readily find in the West Country. Paths lace through gorse-clad, heathy tracts above the East Hill Lift from Hastings Old Town. It's top-drawer coastal scenery all the way to Fairlight Cove and the wildlife is richly varied, with breeding birds such as Dartford warblers and stonechats, wooded coombes such as Firehills (at its best when carpeted with bluebells) supporting sizeable numbers of dormice, stoats and weasels, and rare ant-eating spiders, bee-devouring wasps and an outsize weevil known as *lixus algirus*. A very secretive naturist beach awaits at Fairlight Glen, a point where the coastal path dips, though I've only once managed to scramble down to it and access is not officially encouraged.

You return to normality in the form of the suburban roads of Fairlight Cove; east of that, it's undeveloped for a half mile as you drop to shore level at Cliff End, on the edge of the flat farmland of Romney Marsh. The Saxon Shore Way long-distance path has perhaps its finest moment as it follows this coastline.

The great coastal walk: Rye to Hastings

It's quite an effort to do this stupendous full-day 11$\frac{1}{2}$ -mile walk (8$\frac{1}{2}$ miles if starting from Winchelsea), but it is amply rewarding, reflecting this corner of East Sussex in all its dramatic changes of mood. The strange thing is that a walk of this calibre isn't conspicuously waymarked throughout its length; part of it is the Saxon Shore Way, but even those sections are poorly signed in places. It starts through Rye (don't be put off by the first few minutes on the footway alongside the main road; things very soon get much better); on the way you walk round the brooding ruin of Camber Castle, up into historic Winchelsea and beneath the sea cliffs of the Saxon shore – now a long way from the sea. The two-mile stretch along the swan-patrolled Royal Military Canal has an East Anglian-like beauty, reaching the beach at Cliff End before rising on to the sandstone cliffs that continue to Hastings. After you are diverted inland at Fairlight Glen the finest part of the route begins – an energetic three miles of up and down through the lushly vegetated cliffs around Covehurst Bay and through the Hastings Country Park. Only at the last possible moment does Hastings Old Town suddenly appear as you emerge by the East Hill Lift.

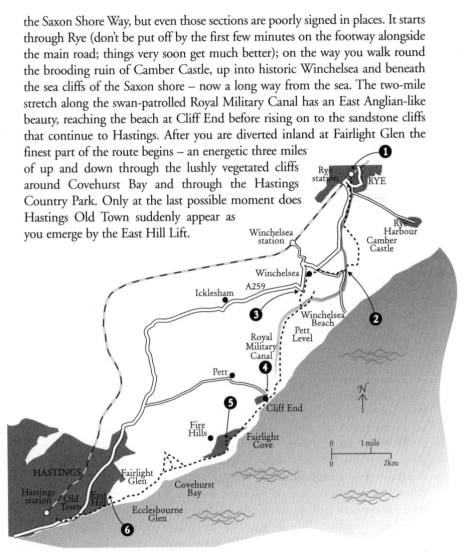

Frequent **trains** get you back from from Hastings to Rye. There are several ways of **shortening** this walk: you could get the bus from Rye to Winchelsea and start from the village centre, or use Winchelsea station and turn right outside it (a good half mile from the edge of the village); or take a taxi from Hastings to Fairlight village or Fairlight Cove and walk the most scenic part of the route (about three miles) into Hastings; or start and finish from the East Cliff lift and walk towards Fire Hills and back. There's inexpensive all-day **parking** at Rye station; more at Gibbet Marsh on the west side of town. For **refreshments**, Rye and Hastings obviously have plenty, Winchelsea has two pubs, and a café within a very good food shop; at Cliff End the Smuggler has Harveys and does fish and chips (there's also a snack kiosk just behind it, by the entrance to the beach). **Public loos** en route at Winchelsea and Cliff End. **OS Explorer maps** 124 and 125 cover the route.

❶ From Rye station, walk along the station approach into town. Cross the main road and go ahead, signposted Ypres Tower and Cobbled Streets. Turn right along the main street, and follow it to the very end (where Mermaid Street comes down from the left). Keep right, between the black-weatherboarded buildings, towards the brick wall near the quay, emerging by the Rye Heritage and Tourist Information Centre (you can see the windmill ahead). Turn right and then left on the A259 signposted to Hastings, using the footway along the left side of the road (this is the least attractive part of the walk, but fortunately only lasts a few minutes). Turn left on Harbour Road (signposted Rye Harbour), and immediately cross the River Brede and turn right on the track on the other side. This follows the river, and just before Castle Mill B&B fork left through a gate into open ground: **Camber Castle** (which you soon pass) comes into view. The route follows a prominent raised grassy causeway: the path does split a few times, but all the variants end up at Castle Farm eventually. It rejoins and then leaves the river – at the next junction it is most rewarding to keep left (yellow arrow waymarker) directly towards Camber Castle, where you continue round to the right on a pronounced track leading through Castle Farm, along a farm road and on to the public road.

❷ Turn right on the road to Winchelsea, later over the canal and along the A259. You are forced on to the right-hand footway, after which turn left up the road signposted Winchelsea. This passes under the **Strand Gate** and bends right. Turn left just after the church, by the New Inn. (If you are starting from here, orientate yourself with the New Inn on your right and the churchyard on your left.) Follow the road out of Winchelsea, past the public loos.

❸ Where the main road bends right (ahead is Wickham Rock Lane), keep right alongside it for a few yards, then just after the jagged ruin of the west wall of medieval **St John's Hospital**, take a stile on the left. Go diagonally right down to another stile, and do not cross the stile immediately beyond this but turn left between field boundaries. Grass lumps on the left mark abandoned buildings of medieval Winchelsea, when the village was larger than it is today. Turn right on the lane, under the **New Gate** (another of the village's entrance gates). 300 yards later (where woods are about to start on the left) turn left on a signposted public footpath. The wooded bank up on the right is **Wickham Cliff**, marking the former shoreline. Very soon leave the woodland edge as it veers away right and continue forward to a prominent wooden enclosure around an electric sub-station by the **Royal Military Canal**. Cross the bridge and turn right to follow the canal towpath two miles to **Cliff End**. At a bridge, when the road is reached close by to the left, cross the road and continue along the concrete promenade; there's also a way up from the canal to the beach a bit further on from the prominent Smuggler pub (or you can just follow the canal to its very end, opposite the public loos). If you're walking along the promenade, carry on past a mobile home park on the right, then take steps on the right signed 'footpath from beach only', turn right on the access road and turn left on the public road, past the end of the canal and public loos.

4 Keep left at the road junction (the right turn goes to Pett), then just after it go left into a lane and immediately keep right up wooden steps on a path that rises behind back gardens. Where a break in the trees allows, you get a **view** along the coast to Dungeness power station in Kent. Further on it opens out by a National Trust sign for Fairlight. The path then shortly bends right inland around a field; carry on for 100 yards until the next field corner, where you turn left (immediately forking left again) through a barrier, and on to a residential road junction (Sea Road goes off to the left; you keep forward on Lower Waites Lane, not labelled as such). Carry on forward along the road, ignoring side turnings (such as Primrose Hill, Clinton Way and Rockmead Road).

5 After ½ mile this road briefly becomes unmade by house number 10 and bends left, then continues as a surfaced road, rising steeply up a road of brick bungalows. At the top, turn right. Turn left at the T-junction to reach the cliff-top, and turn right – just opposite here a bizarre **no through road sign** peeping out of the undergrowth indicates one of the roads that have disappeared over the cliff; near the last house keep left along a fenced path avoiding the parallel driveway on the right. By an information board with a map, you are now in the **Fire Hills** area. The path leads ahead into the most dramatic part of the walk. It is simplest to keep always to the path closest to the sea at any junctions, and to follow any signs for Hastings. It descends three times into deeply wooded glens – for each of these there are more level but longer alternatives that skirt the glens inland.

6 Reach the top of the **East Hill Lift**, where **Hastings Old Town** suddenly appears below you. Drop down the steep path to a street, and wend your way to the very bottom. The station is about ten minutes on and is well signposted from the town centre.

Royal Military Canal

Although this waterway is no longer navigable for craft, you can walk its entire 28-mile length, from Hythe in Kent to Cliff End. It is a haven for wildlife: you have a good chance of spotting kingfishers here in summer. During the Napoleonic Wars this canal was built between 1804 and 1809 as a third line of defence, with the Royal Navy patrolling the English Channel and a string of 74 Martello Towers erected along the coast. Cannons were placed every 500 yards along the canal, and there were station houses manned by guards to control smuggling. It was a construction project riddled with problems, and was completed four years late. To speed things up they built the final sections half as wide and deep as the earlier ones, and it was much criticised as a waste of public money. Nevertheless, it survives as the third longest defensive structure ever built in the British Isles – after Hadrian's Wall and Offa's Dyke.

⑦ Winchelsea

Spaciously ranged on a neat crisscross of streets, Winchelsea has an incongruous sense of grandeur, and although an ancient town it has a village-like calm. Three town gateways and substantial remains of town defences hint that events were once much headier here. In medieval times it flourished as an industrious port planned by Royal command and became one of the Cinque Ports; only King's Lynn was a more important centre for shipbuilding. In its heyday it imported wine at the rate of up to four million bottles a year, and it could have become a great maritime city like Southampton or Portsmouth. Then seemingly everything conspired against it.

There's no trace of **Old Winchelsea**, the earlier sea-level settlement beneath the present hilltop site: it was washed away in a series of storms after 1250. In 1283 Edward I ordered the **new settlement** to be rebuilt on its present hilltop site, with a wall and gateways, and streets laid out on a **grid plan** with 39 rectangular areas of buildings between. He appointed Commissioners to lay out a new town of Winchelsea, which became one of England's top ten ports. If Old Winchelsea had been in this league its loss must have been a strategic disaster. This – and perhaps the fact that subsequent rents went to the Crown – might explain why the King was so generous in his support for his new royal town.

But further disaster followed: in the early 14th century Winchelsea seamen were prone to thuggish behaviour, raiding and burning boats in English ports as well as in France. The French had their revenge in 1360 with a massive attack, which compounded the effects of the Black Death and caused Winchelsea's decline. Then the sea began to recede, and by the early 16th century the harbour had become completely silted up. This was the final blow. By 1565, of the 800 plots there in the 1300s, only 109 houses were left standing; by the mid 17th century the number had dropped to 40. Writing in around 1725, Daniel Defoe described the place as 'rather the skeleton of an ancient city, than a real town'.

Today an influx of retired people and commuters has brought a modest amount of redevelopment to Winchelsea, and in contrast to some unfortunate experiences in the 1960s and 1970s every building site is closely watched by the archaeologists. The subsoil is dense with reminders of the great past of this once Royal port.

In the very centre, the early 14th-century **church of St Thomas the Martyr** fills one of the squares of the grid: its incompleteness stands as a poignant reminder of the village's past torments. All that survives are the chancel and ruined transepts of a much larger church, the tower of which survived into the 18th century, but the tracery and canopied tombs indicate massive wealth in centuries past. As an example of the Decorated style it has few rivals in Sussex: judging from the wealth of stone carving, elaborate canopied tombs and tracery, there was plenty of money to employ stonemasons and builders, and to import Caen stone from Normandy. Just opposite the church, the **Winchelsea Court Hall Museum** incorporates the former gaol, and has a model of Winchelsea as it was.

Winchelsea's **defences** were under construction by 1322 and re-planned on a smaller scale around 1415. The most obvious relics are Pipewell Gate (by the main road) and Strand Gate (on the edge of a cliff, with a terrific view of the coast); the New Gate crosses a country lane outside the village (reached by following the waymarked 1066 Country Walk). During his research, historic buildings archaeologist David Martin stumbled across the remains of an 85-foot length of town wall and two D-shaped turrets on the cliff side of Winchelsea, which incredibly had remained unnoticed.

Winchelsea had a thorough makeover in the 17th and 18th centuries, but many of the houses reveal far older origins. Beneath many buildings, garages and even under a cricket pitch are 32 medieval **vaulted cellars** that originally served to store wine from Gascony at a time when the wine trade was thriving here. These cellars were built to be seen, presumably by buyers visiting to try the wares. Only Southampton has a comparable number of vaulted cellars (Chester and Norwich have stone cellars but they are less grandly built, without vaulting).

><><><

Food and drink

Bridge Inn The Strand ☎ 01797 224302. By the A259 at the foot of Winchelsea's hill; useful pub serving inexpensive, basic pub grub.

Queen's Head Parsonage Lane, Icklesham TN36 4BL ☎ 01424 814552 ⏏ www.queenshead.com. Deservedly popular pub on the edge of the next village west from Winchelsea, with a terrific view at the back garden over the Brede Level, and lots of rustic nicknacks and old bikes hanging from the ceiling and elsewhere. Good selection of real ales, a local cider and food all day at weekends. This is a handy objective for walks west from Winchelsea – along the waymarked 1066 Country Walk, past Icklesham windmill and Icklesham's striking Norman church; you can return by a path descending from the back of the pub to the Brede Level, cross and recross the railway line and walk through arable fields to Winchelsea.

Sutton's Game Dealer Sea Rd, Winchelsea Beach TN36 4LA ☎ 01797 226261. Local seasonal fish, very good-value game, poultry, free-range eggs; closed Tue.

Winchelsea Farm Kitchen and Wickham Organic Meats 11-12 High St ☎ 01797 226287. Interesting selection of breads, cheeses, pies and organic meat; excellent café inside too, with a courtyard at the back, serving deli products and homemade cakes. A much-admired establishment that is very much a Winchelsea institution.

⑧ Rye

A more perfect small medieval hilltop town would be hard to find: indeed Rye is thought have retained a higher proportion of historic buildings than any other town in Britain. It only takes minutes to walk across the centre, but it is certainly not a place to rush. Every house differs from its neighbours, yet the blend of Tudor, Georgian and other architecture could hardly be more harmonious, most famously along the ankle-threatening cobbles of Mermaid Street with its venerable old inn, but there's more of the same standard in West Street, Church Square, Watchbell Street and elsewhere. Rye scores highly as a place for **shopping**, with a surprisingly comprehensive choice of independent retailers for such a small town. Thankfully it's too small for chain stores but it serves a large, prosperous hinterland, and browsing here is part of the pleasure of the place – with the pleasingly unchanged High Street frontages of Ashbee & Son Butchers and Britcher and Rivers' retro sweet shop alongside a range of shops selling crafts, pottery, clothes, books and antiques.

From its hilltop site, all seems a very different world to the surroundings. You can see a long way across flat expanses that were once under the sea which formerly lapped three sides of the town; a Cinque Port in medieval times, Rye lost much of its former importance as the coast receded. However the tidal River Tillingham still accounts for a hub of modern industry along its opposite bank towards the sea; a century or so ago the river would have been much busier, with boats exporting Wealden timber and bringing in coal for the town's gasworks. It's still the focus of seasonal celebrations, with a Maritime Festival and raft race in August.

Rye's fortifications survive in part, with an extant chunk of town wall parallel to Cinque Ports Street and more spectacularly in the form of the **Landgate**, one of three gates built under Edward III. The 13th-century **Ypres Tower** (pronounced 'Wipers') served as the town gaol for 400 years, and its claustrophobia-inducing interior reveals the prisoners' appallingly cramped conditions. In the 20th century it served as a mortuary for 60 years, and in World War II corpses of RAF and Luftwaffe officers washed ashore were brought here, sometimes poignantly laid out side by side. In front, cannons stand outside on a terrace known as the Gun Garden, with a view stretching downriver to Rye Harbour.

Within the picture perfection that is Church Square, **St Mary's Church** crowns the town's highest point. A mixture of Norman and Early English, it is on a grand scale, and you can climb the top of the tower for the best view in town. As you enter, the pendulum of what is England's oldest church town clock swings above, over 450 years old and still working well, with its Quarter Boys chiming on the quarter hour. The bells were stolen when the French ransacked and destroyed the town in 1377, but were recaptured in a later raid on Normandy. Abutting the churchyard is a curious oval brick water tank, where water used to be stored after being pumped up Conduit Hill.

Rye Heritage Centre doubles as the Tourist Information Centre, near the bottom of Mermaid Street and near the Strand Quay. Its **Town Model** is a painstakingly researched depiction of how the town looked in 1872, made on a budget in the 1970s by retired local history teacher Joy Harland and her husband over four years. It was done very much on the cheap, with polystyrene for building blocks and tapioca for road surfaces, but looks astonishingly good; the show every half hour is really worth catching (proceeds go to the town), with commentary and lighting. From here you can also rent a **self-guided audio tour** or join a historical **Ghost Tour** in winter (no dressing up or gimmicks, but a look at some sites where paranormal activity has been recorded). Upstairs is an entertaining collection of antique penny-in-the-slot machines, where a pound gets you a stack of old pennies to try out shooting cats, activate a scene of Charlie and Mabel in the Park (his hat self-tilts politely as he hitches her skirt ever so slightly) or view Davy Jones's Locker, with a shipwreck revealing mermaids watching TV.

In East Street, the **Rye Castle Museum** has among its local history items maps showing how the coastline has changed over the ages; one wonders how similar to present-day Chichester Harbour it must have once looked. Also on display are the town's hand-pumped fire engine that was in service from 1745 to 1865, E F Benson's recipe for poison pancakes supplied as a joke for a recipe book being compiled locally, and examples of a very striking local wood mosaic known as Tunbridge Ware, using a technique revived by one Tom Green of Rye – but the secret reputedly died with him in 1959.

In West Street, **Lamb House** (*01580 762334; open mid Mar to mid Oct, Thu and Sat afternoon only*) was home to the American writer Henry James. Built in 1723 and now owned by the National Trust, it plainly suited James down to the ground. He lived here from 1898 to 1916 like an 18th-century man of letters, far away from the social pressures of London, and entertained many other literati, including Rupert Brooke, Joseph Conrad and H G Wells – who proclaimed it 'one of the most perfect pieces of suitably furnished Georgian architecture imaginable'. Inside are James's walking sticks, photos and manuscripts, and in the walled garden are memorials to his dogs. He wrote such late works as *The Ambassadors* and *The Golden Bowl* in a garden house, one of Rye's few buildings to be destroyed by bombing in World War II. His friend E F Benson later rented the house with his brother, and wrote his Mapp and Lucia stories – set in Rye (called Tilling in the stories).

South of town, it's not a pretty journey along Harbour Road (frequent buses from the town) through the industrial estates along by the river, the legacy of Rye's own version of oil refining: an industry developed here from the 1860s to distil tar from gasworks into products such as creosote and paint thinners. However, at the sea end, **Rye Harbour Nature Reserve** is appealingly wild and remote, a rare shingle habitat, where little terns, curlews and oystercatchers coexist alongside plants such as yellow-horned poppy. Access to the site and bird hides is free, and a nature reserve centre supplies information; wheelchair-accessible paths lead out through saltmarsh and past pools created by gravel extraction towards the beach (shingle, with low-tide sand). The reserve extends towards the impressive hulk of **Camber Castle**, built by Henry VIII around an earlier circular tower, which apart from its gentle decay is totally unchanged since then. It didn't have a long service: within a hundred years of its erection the coast had silted up, stranding it far inland. The sheep graze right up to the walls, and though it's not manned you can walk right up to it peep through the windows and doorways; it is passed on the Rye-to-Hastings walk featured on page 240. Monthly tours are given (*01797 223962*).

Food and drink

In and around the High Street, **cafés** are plentiful enough, from ultra-traditional to more contemporary like **Hayden's Coffee Shop and Restaurant** which offers local, organic and fairtrade produce, with a good choice for vegetarians and vegans, in two airy rooms and on a plant-filled terrace behind (they also do bed and breakfast).

For picnic ingredients, **Rye Delicatessen** has tasty quiches, salads, soups and homity pies, and a small-scale farmers' market operates on Wednesday mornings at Strand Quay. Two special **food events** are the Scallop Festival in the last week of February and the Taste of Rye event in October, when themed events take place across town. The **Ypres Castle** (℡ *01797 223248*), beneath the Ypres Tower, is my favourite Rye pub, with an informal garden and chatty bar. For a drink or meal in really historic surroundings the obvious choice is the **Mermaid Inn** (℡ *01797 223065*), a stupendous medieval timber-framed building full of comfortable corners and antiques.

⑨ Camber Sands

The best beach for miles around, and the only place in Sussex apart from West Wittering (near Chichester; see page 43) with extensive, ever-present sand. It's a huge seven-mile expanse backed by dunes, but does get very crowded in high summer, when the nose-to-tail stop-start traffic jams aren't much fun; a much better way to arrive is to start from Rye and either get bus 100 from Rye rail station (which runs from Hastings to Lydd) or cycle an easy three miles along the signposted off-road cycle path. Swimming is good and family-friendly. Dog owners should be aware that some parts of the beach are not dog-accessible in summer.

If you want to combine a beach trip with some unconventional sightseeing, **Dungeness** – over the Kent border – is as surreal a place as you could find on these shores. A vast spit of shingle dominated by a nuclear power station and built up with a random series of shacks, it may sound bleak, but the place has a beauty of its own, and on a crisp winter's day is a photographer's dream. The film director Derek Jarman appreciated the desolation of the area, and lived out his days here in a fisherman's shack when diagnosed as HIV positive. He created a garden out of driftwood, bits of twisted metal, broken tools and shells; this has become a focal point of pilgrimage for many of his fans, and featured in his films *War Requiem* and *The Garden*.

Into the Weald

⑩ Kent & East Sussex Railway

An ideal way to arrive at Bodiam Castle (see page 250), this preserved railway gives a 10 ¹/₂-mile trip through the Rother countryside from Tenterden station to Bodiam, via Northiam (*01580 765155; www.kesr.org.uk*). A mixture of steam and diesel locos run here; the oldest steam engines date from the 19th century. Note that you can park only at Tenterden and Northiam, and that Tenterden station is some way outside Tenterden itself. The films that have been shot on this line range from *Nineteen-Eighty Four* and *Cold Comfort Farm* right down to an all-dog cast for a TV commercial for 'New Bakers' Gravy Bites – don't miss the gravy train!'.

Over the border into Kent, **Tenterden** is well worth a wander round. With its broad leafy street of grass verges and white weatherboarded houses this little town reminds me strongly of some of the villages in New England, though its amiably wonky architecture lacks the regularity of its American counterparts.

⑪ Great Dixter

Even among the world-class gardens of Sussex, Great Dixter stands out as one of the very finest (*Northiam TN31 6PH; 01797 252878; www.greatdixter.co.uk; closed Mon except bank holidays, and all winter except for special weekends when the crocuses and snowdrops are out*). It's not large or grand, but laid out in an intimate, almost disorienting series of outdoor 'rooms' that change in mood from one surprise vista to the next. Wealden barns and oast houses overlook an octagonal pond in the middle of the sunken garden, and there is a wildflower meadow speckled with ox-eye daisies and orchids. Shapely yew hedges, neatly clipped, enclose gardens that shift level and are punctuated by spectacles of blooms and foliage. It was the creation of the late, great Christopher Lloyd (1921–2006), whose parents moved here in 1910; a few fruit trees survive from the early days, but his remodelling was dramatic. The buildings form an important backdrop, with a weatherboarded barn wall and oast houses. Colour and contrast were keynotes of his densely planted garden design.

It all surrounds a half-timbered house of the medieval 'Wealden hall' design, restored and extended by Edwin Lutyens for the Lloyd family in 1910: Lutyens opened up the main room to reinstate its medieval form, with a ceiling the full height of the building, by removing the first floor inserted in Tudor times – with its huge bay windows and central heating it feels much more light and comfortable than it would have done originally. The parlour beyond, where Lloyd wrote, has a cosier feel with books and piano. Upstairs the solar, originally a private room for the ladies, with its medieval squint window for looking down at the goings on in the Great Hall, also has a very personal atmosphere. The furniture includes examples of Lloyd's collection of modern wooden furniture – sculptural and somewhat incongruous in this setting, but he believed they would blend in within a hundred years.

The nursery Lloyd began in 1954 is an excellent place to stock up for your own garden, and you can order by post. Throughout the year (usually on Mondays) they hold study days here – into such subjects as meadow gardening, exotic gardening, propagation and preparing borders for spring and summer.

⑫ Bodiam Castle

Swans paddle around the lilies in the water-filled moat surrounding this most perfect-looking of medieval castles, situated in the Rother valley. Although a ruin, Bodiam Castle (*Bodiam TN32 5UA; 01580 830436; www.nationaltrust.org.uk*) is a substantial one, and has retained much of its original appearance from outside. A knight of Edward III, Sir Edward Dalyngrigge, began it in 1385, justifying it by fears of a French invasion – though it seems to have been built more for display than defence, at the centre of an early 'designed landscape' featuring sheets of water: the car park was once the 'flote' or harbour, and the low-lying area between the car park and the castle was a mill pond fed by a leat. Dalyngrigge created its quadrangular plan with massive drum towers at each corner, two gate towers and the top robustly crenellated, using heavy military symbolism. It wasn't exactly top-notch as a fortification when built though, as the concentric forms favoured elsewhere were much better at dealing with an attack.

Fortunately for posterity the castle did not see any serious military action, surviving the Wars of the Roses and then serving as a Royalist stronghold in the Civil War until being partly dismantled. It then languished as in a state of picturesque decay until careful restoration in the 19th century and again in 1916 by Lord Curzon who left it to the National Trust in 1925.

Though it's roofless inside, this is a most evocative structure, and spiral staircases take you up to a higher level for a different perspective among the battlements. I have yet to see a child there who hasn't been transfixed by it. On a warm day the lawns surrounding the site make ideal picnicking terrain.

The Kent & East Sussex Railway has steam and diesel services that most conveniently end at Bodiam station (see page 249).

Food and drink
The **Wharf Tea-room** is inside the entrance gate, and the **shop** has local wine and honey.

Wilderness skills

Roger Harrington has made a life-long passion for the outdoor life into a business where he teaches a range of skills to do with living in the wilderness. For those who'd like to know how to build a shelter in the wilds or start a fire without matches, **Bison Bushcraft**, his business based near Heathfield, offers weekend and week-long courses in various aspects of bushcraft, axecraft and foraging, as well as one-day one-to-one sessions. In learning about axecraft you would be taught about green woodwork and acquire the skills to make hurdles and stools. A foraging course gives a grounding in knowing how to identify wild fungi, how to kill and butcher rabbits or venison, and preserving and cooking what foods you acquire in the wild.

Bison Bushcraft PO Box 157, Battle TN33 3DD ☏ 0845 8387062 ⌨ www.bisonbushcraft.co.uk. Weekend courses typically cost around £225–£250 with food and accommodation; participants can be picked up from Stonegate station by arrangement.

⑬ Battle: 1066 and all that

Battle is a typical Wealden town – with an attractive if traffic-spoilt High Street sporting plenty of the tile-hanging and timber-frame buildings one expects to find in the area, and its own railway station, bonfire society, choral society and bowls club. But the name of the place makes it unique: where else do you find a town that is there solely because of an abbey that was the first thing to be built there, and it was only built there because of a battle?

The key point of interest here is obviously Battle Abbey (see below). Elsewhere in town, the medieval **Almonry** has a small local history museum, containing a model of the parish church and prints depicting 18 panels of the Bayeux tapestry in as near as possible the original colours. The Guy Fawkes effigy is the very one used in the town's ebullient Bonfire Procession each year; Battle, as elsewhere in Sussex, has a flourishing bonfire society which joins others for the grand procession in Lewes on 5 November. To get an idea of the cumbersome clutter that folks had to lug around in battle, you could try on replica chain mail or armour: the staff will give you much-needed assistance to put it on. The garden outside, at the back, is a wonderfully semi-secret place for a picnic.

Opposite the Abbey, **Yesterday's World** provides a comprehensive immersion into nostalgia, with recreated period shops and rooms such as a wartime kitchen and a Victorian laundry, a royalty exhibition, and a back garden containing a children's play village and miniature golf.

Harold's downfall

The Battle of Hastings (at what was then called Senlac) on 14 October, 1066, the most famous date in English history, was decisive in the last successful invasion of the British mainland. The full story behind the conquest is mighty complex: the succession to the throne was not at all a simple matter. But the key points are that Harold II was Edward the Confessor's brother-in-law rather than his son (as one might assume), while William of Normandy was Edward's cousin and claimed Harold had sworn to uphold his right to the throne – though this oath, if it existed, may have been extracted under duress when Harold was rescued from a shipwreck in France. When Harold took the English throne on Edward's death, William of Normandy claimed he had reneged on a promise, and decided to enforce his side of the bargain. Harold's men had already defeated an invasion by another would-be successor, King Harald Hardrada of Norway, at the Battle of Stamford Bridge in Yorkshire on 25 September, and then had to march rapidly south to deal with William, who had landed at Pevensey Bay on 28 September. It was not the ideal prelude for the second battle as far as the English were concerned.

All the same, this was a battle that Harold probably should have won, though it is the subject of endless conjecture. The shield wall of the English was doing its job on top of the hill – the Norman horses could not muster enough speed to get up the slope and breach it, and the slope was slowing down the rate of their arrows (also, the English weren't firing a lot of arrows, so there were very few to return). However when William's Normans retreated, some English made the mistake of descending in pursuit – they were then surrounded by mounted Normans and hacked to bits. The Normans saw how this retreat had worked to their advantage and so feigned to do it again – and the hapless English pursued only to be systematically annihilated.

All the English really needed to have done was to hold out till nightfall, and wait for reinforcements. Or they could have waited a little longer to regroup for battle in the first place. But it was not to happen, and at the end of that fateful day when some 7,000 perished, William had won. William's army of under 10,000 had thus invaded a country of 1.5 million.

As an act of contrition, William decided to build an abbey on the very spot where Harold fell. At first monks started building the abbey elsewhere, on a more practical site (with decidedly useful things like level land and a water supply), but this did not please the new king, who ordered the whole project be moved here.

It is not known if Harold really died by an arrow in the eye. The Bayeux Tapestry, which can be viewed as a contemporary strip cartoon informed by an eye witness (if you forgive the pun), does indeed have the word 'Harold' above a man killed by an arrow apparently in the eye; but there is another adjacent man, who might be Harold, being killed by swords. Either way, he had been so hacked about that only Edith, his mistress, was able to identify him.

It all leaves you wondering what might have been. Had the Saxons won, our laws, language, politics and architecture would have been very different; the feudal system the Normans set up would not have happened as it did. Harold was an experienced soldier, and a popular monarch. He had the reputation for being rash; so perhaps William goaded him into battle when it might well have been more prudent, for him to have bided his time and rallied new troops.

Battle Abbey and battlefield: the site today

Entering at the **abbey gatehouse** (*01424 775705; www.english-heritage.org.uk*), you pick up an **audio tour** – one type for adults, and one for families with children. You can choose between a short walk along a paved terrace, or a longer (one mile) route which winds on a well-drained path.

Ironically, the setting for such a horrific event is very beautiful today. Through the impressive gatehouse, you see the stately home (now **Battle Abbey School**) that was created out of the site after Henry VIII's Dissolution. The lie of the land is much as it was, though the top part has been levelled off for the building of the abbey, so the hill would have been even more formidable an obstacle for the Norman invaders. From there you have the choice of the full **battlefield tour**, or making a short cut along the terrace above the battlefield, close to where Harold's men stood. The battlefield tour drops into a typically lush, green, hilly Wealden landscape; ahead you can see a lake where gunpowder mills once operated.

The tour of the site goes anti-clockwise as you emerge from the gatehouse, and Battle Abbey School appears in view immediately. A reverse time line, starting from the present and ending at 1066, gets you into period as you enter the **exhibition area**. An excellent film narrated by David Starkey and featuring bits of animated Bayeux Tapestry keeps children interested and entertained, and sets the scene extremely well.

Of the **abbey**, you can pick out the gravel outlines of the church. The former abbot's residence now forms part of Battle Abbey School, and one side of the cloister now constitutes one of its walls. Of the abbey buildings, just the sleeping quarters and latrines remain, but these are impressive for their size and state of preservation. The monks' common room and novices' room are both intact, with vaulted ceilings and columns of Sussex marble; headbangingly low doorways lead into the guesthouse range undercroft, with one room leading off another. A 19th-century thatched dairy and ice house close by is a fetching late addition. The Battle Abbey Museum, up steep steps on the right side of the gatehouse as you leave, shows stone, tile and window glass fragments as well as a scale model of the abbey in its heyday and intriguing archaeological finds like a piece of slate ruled with the lines of a music stave.

I once visited on the day after the battle anniversary: the slab marking the site of Harold's death was adorned with flowers and cards. One tribute was from the 'English Mercians', who seemed to think we were fighting the Normans at the Normandy landings ('To Harold II – good on ya mate – we got them back in 1944…'): a most unexpected link to contemporary nationalistic culture.

The shop has a good selection of Saxon and Norman-themed products for adults and children, and also houses Battle's Tourist Information Centre.

Food and drink

A very decent minimalist café in Battle Abbey makes an obvious lunch place, with good soup, hot sandwiches and the like. Several places along the High Street too; for picnic items, **Battle Deli** at number 58 has pork pies, home-made cakes and local cheeses like Sussex Charmer.

Carr Taylor Wines Wheel Lane, Westfield TN35 4SG ☎ 01424 752501 ⏏ www.carr-taylor.co.uk. Just east of Battle outside the village of Westfield is the vineyard of Carr Taylor Wines; their range includes sparkling, white and rosé as well as eight types of fruit wine. The vineyard is open to visitors daily, and there are guided tours and wine tastings, as well as a shop and small café.

Sussex marble

Italian-style marble is one rock not extant in Britain's uniquely diverse geology, and although Sussex marble isn't the real thing, it has filled a useful gap for many centuries of building. Also known as winkle stone or Petworth marble, it is found only in Sussex and southern Kent, and is formed from fossilised winkle shells in shallow salt water – hence the spiral shapes. When cut and polished it makes a very fine building material not that dissimilar to its more prestigious namesake. It has been used for many high-status buildings in Sussex, including as chimneypieces in Petworth House, interior columns in Battle Abbey and pillars in Chichester Cathedral.

⑭ Herstmonceux Castle

Not at all a conventional country-house visit, although it looks astonishing from outside: the castle now houses the International Study Centre for Queen's University, Ontario, and has a wholly collegiate atmosphere (*near Herstmonceux BN27 1RN; 01323 834444; www.herstmonceux-castle.com; open early Apr–end Oct*). In its previous incarnation the estate was home to the Royal Observatory from 1946, and the BBC pips were broadcast here for 40 years until the scientific establishment moved out because of light pollution and went to La Palma in the Canary Islands. Happily, plans for a leisure centre with golf course were thwarted by the early 1990s property crash, and Queens University took over the castle in 1993.

Inspired by French châteaux of the period, the castle was the very first brick building on such a large scale anywhere in England, with Flemish bricklayers brought in for their expertise. It was completed in 1446 after Sir Roger Fiennes, Henry VI's treasurer was granted licence to improve his manor. It is quite a sight, with its brick turrets high above a lily-filled moat.

At first sight it's hard to fathom how such a complete brick building should have survived in near pristine state. It was abandoned in the 18th century when it was thoroughly stripped out for the building of a new mansion called Herstmonceux Place and remained ruinous until 1910. Then Lt Colonel Claude Lowther began restoration, while his tame ram – a mascot of his territorial battalion – was given the run of the castle. The **tour** is not quite what you might expect from outside – you're taken round classrooms, chapel and a panelled Elizabethan room, and there's a brief glimpse down into a dungeon; an ensuite stone toilet was positioned to empty into the moat, and there's an alleged siege tunnel.

The whole place comes to life very entertainingly each August bank holiday weekend with a huge **medieval fair** featuring cannon-firing, knights in armour, archery, falconry, a traders' market and medieval food and ales.

The **grounds** have an exquisitely restful atmosphere – with a folly by the lake studded with water lilies and frequented by kingfishers and dragonflies, a large walled garden, and little arches leading into a wilder area. An Elizabethan walled garden features rhododendrons and azaleas enclosed into large 'rooms' by yew hedges, while a tiny Japanese garden and knot garden sports Shakespearean quotations posted around the beds. A great mulberry bush grows by a sundial erected in 1975 to mark the Royal Observatory's 300th birthday.

A short way east of the castle, the former Royal Observatory itself now houses the **Observatory Science Centre** (*near Herstmonceux BN27 1RN; 01323 832731; www.the-observatory.org; closed most of Jan and Dec*). The great green telescope domes, which have been collectively likened to the poor man's Taj Mahal, are a feature of the East Sussex skyline and are Grade II* listed. Carefully laid out and exuding a strange sort of 1950s period charm, they evoke a mini university campus – the design may not have been appreciated by some astronomers, who tended to find it somewhat hazardous at night and kept stumbling over edges and falling into the lily pond. Science exhibits bring in the school parties – with microscopes to look into, a clock to assemble and any number of experiments to try. The star-gazing ceased in 1979, and the lab left in 1990, but the 1896 telescope here is still one of the largest in the world. One area chronicles the story of the Royal Greenwich Observatory. See their website for details of open evenings and astronomy courses; to come here at night and scan the skies through the telescopes makes the ultimate Slow experience.

Index